THROUGH ORTHODOX EYES

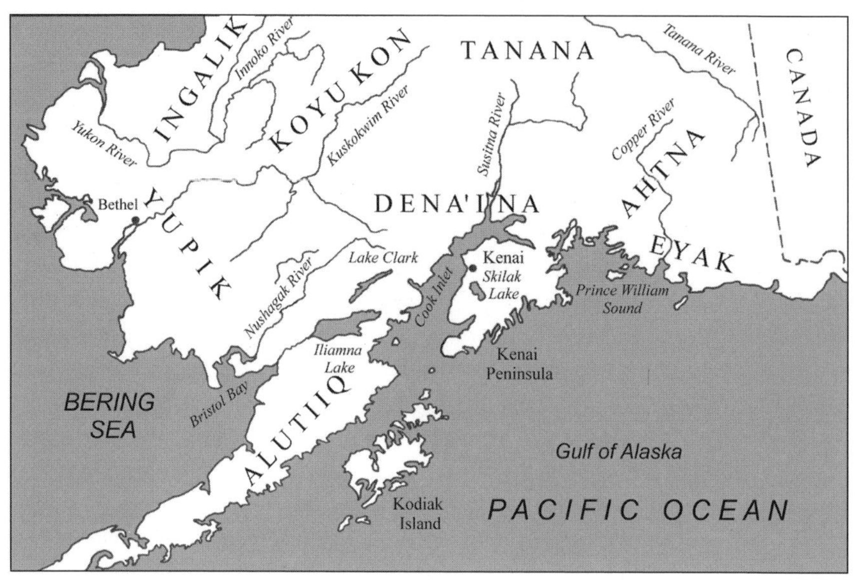

Indigenous groups of south-central Alaska

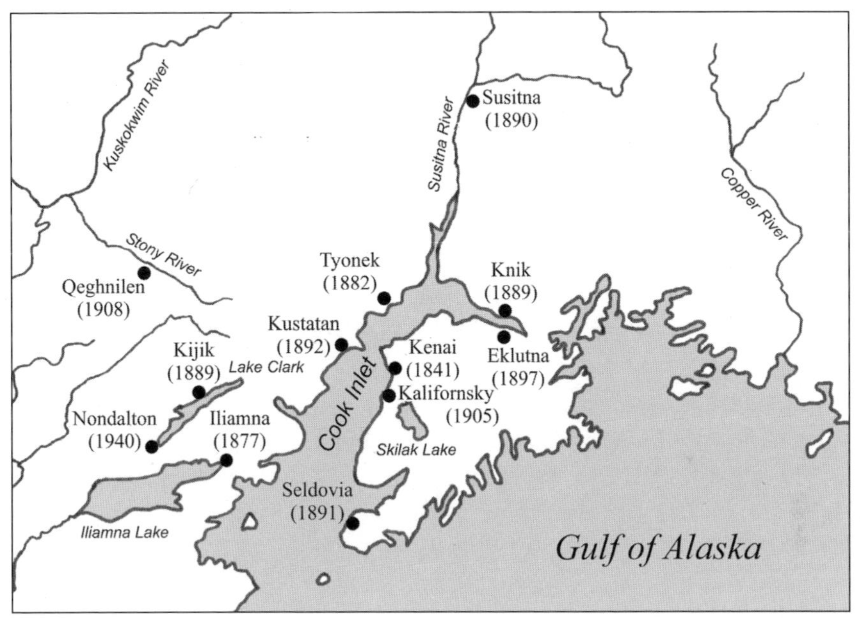

Orthodox chapels in Dena'ina historical villages and the years of their establishment

Marvin W. Falk, Editor

1. *Holmberg's Ethnographic Sketches* by Heinrich Johan Holmberg. Edited by Marvin W. Falk, translated from the original German of 1855–1863 by Fritz Jaensch. 1985.

2. *Tlingit Indians of Alaska* by Anatolii Kamenskii. Translated, with an introduction and supplementary material, by Sergei Kan. 1985.

3. *Bering's Voyages: The Reports from Russia* by Gerhard Friedrich Müller. Translated, with commentary, by Carol Urness. 1986.

4. *Russian Exploration in Southwest Alaska: The Travel Journals of Petr Korsakovskiy (1818) and Ivan Ya. Vasilev (1829)*. Edited, with an introduction by James VanStone, translated by David H. Kraus. 1988.

5. *The Khlebnikov Archive: Unpublished Journal (1800–1837) and Travel Notes (1820, 1822, and 1824)*. Edited by Leonid Shur, translated by John Bisk. 1990.

6. *The Great Russian Navigator, A. I. Chirikov* by Vasilii A. Divin. Translated and annotated by Raymond H. Fisher. 1993.

7. *Journals of the Priest Ioann Veniaminov in Alaska, 1823 to 1836*. Introduction and commentary by S. A. Mousalimas, translated by Jerome Kisslinger. 1993.

8. *To the Chukchi Peninsula and the Tlingit Indians 1881–1882: Journals and Letters* by Aurel and Arthur Krause. Translated by Margot Krause McCaffrey. 1993.

9. *Essays on the Ethnography of the Aleuts* by R. G. Liapunova. Translated by Jerry Shelest with W. B. Workman and Lydia Black. 1996.

10. *Fedor Petrovich Litke* by A. I. Alekseev. Edited by Katherine L. Arndt, translated by Serge LeComte. 1996.

11. *Grewingk's Geology of Alaska and the Northwest Coast of America: Contributions Toward Knowledge of the Orographic and Geognostic Condition of the Northwest Coast of America, with the Adjacent Islands* by Constantine Grewingk. Edited by Marvin W. Falk, translated by Fritz Jaensch. 2003.

12. *Steller's History of Kamchatka: Collected Information Concerning the History of Kamchatka, Its Peoples, Their Manners, Names, Lifestyle, and Various Customary Practices* by Georg Wilhelm Steller. Translated by Margritt Engel and Karen Willmore. 2003.

13. *Through Orthodox Eyes: Russian Missionary Narratives of Travels to the Dena'ina and Ahtna, 1850s–1930s*. Translated with an introduction by Andrei A. Znamenski. 2003.

Through Orthodox Eyes

Russian Missionary Narratives of Travels to the Dena'ina and Ahtna, 1850s–1930s

TRANSLATED
WITH AN INTRODUCTION BY

ANDREI A. ZNAMENSKI

UNIVERSITY OF ALASKA PRESS
Fairbanks, Alaska

Printed in the United States of America.
This publication was printed on acid-free paper that meets the minimum requirements for American National Standards for Information Sciences—Permanence of Paper for Printed Library Materials, ANSI Z39.48-1984.

LIBRARY OF CONGRESS CATALOGUING-IN-PUBLICATION DATA

Znamenski, Andrei A., 1960–
Through orthodox eyes : Russian missionary narratives of travels to the Dena'ina and Ahtna, 1850s–1930s / Andrei A. Znamenski.
p. cm. — (The Rasmuson Library historical translation series ; v. 13)
Includes bibliographical references.
ISBN 1-889963-50-X (pbk. : alk. paper)
1. Dena'ina Indians—Missions. 2. Ahtena Indians—Missions. 3. Russkaia pravoslavnaia tserkov'—Missions—Alaska. I. Title. II. Series.
E99.T185 Z53 2002
266′.19798—dc21 2002008017

Publications of the Russian Imperial Mineralogical Society at St. Petersburg.
Volumes for 1848 and 1849
St. Petersburg: Carl Kray, 1850

Publication coordination by Jennifer Robin Collier
Text design by Rachel Fudge
Cover design by Mike Kirk

Contents

List of Illustrations

To little Andrei, Susan, and my parents.

Acknowledgements

Working on this book for the past four years I was blessed with generous financial help from various sources, which allowed me to do research wherever I wanted: in Alaskan archives and native villages, continental states and in Russia. First of all I would like to acknowledge the help of the Alaska Humanities Forum, which twice provided me with two large grants in 1998 and 2000. This money was topped by a 2000 Phillips Fund grant from the American Philosophical Society. I also want to thank the Extending the Reach program of the National Endowment for the Humanities and the John W. Kluge Center of the Library of Congress, whose awards came just in time, when I exhausted the first two sources. These funds were used not only for the retrieval of primary documents, but also for financing my Alaskan field trips to historical Dena'ina and Ahtna villages such as Kenai, Tyonek, Eklutna, Nondalton, and Copper Center. Such trips allowed me to get a better knowledge of landscapes and localities described in the present publication. Although unlike nineteenth-century Orthodox missionaries, who had to rely on dogs, *baidarkas,* or even on their own feet, my trips were sped up by enjoyable airplane flights and car drives, I was able to grasp at least partially the spaces they had to traverse.

By their constant help and advice, my Alaska colleagues, Professor Steve Haycox and Mrs. Barbara Smith, contributed very much to this project. Jim Ducker, the editor of *Alaska History,* by publishing a few of my translations from Bortnovskii's records, paved the way to the present publication. The person who should be credited for a direct contribution to the present collection of primary sources is another Alaskan colleague, Professor Lydia Black, who located missionary records on the Stony River Dena'ina and invited me to work with them in St. Herman's Theological Seminary Archive. She allowed me to "dig" and copy in this partially sorted archive whatever I wanted and whenever I wanted.

Moreover, my research brought me as far as to St. Petersburg, Russia, where in Russian State Historical Archive (RGIA) I was able to search through the documents of the Holy Synod for all necessary missionary materials related to the Athabaskans. Here in RGIA help received from Serafima I. Vakhareva made my work productive and efficient and I extend her my gratitude. I especially appreciate helpful feedback from Professor Sergei Kan, who did so much in the field of indigenous Orthodoxy and whose works always served for me as an inspiration. Sergei took time to read the lengthy introduction to the present publication and also provided moral encouragement and support for the past two years. I wish we had met each other earlier. I also want to thank Professor Andrei V. Grinev, a Russian colleague from St. Petersburg, for provocative debates we had about the status of Athabaskans in Russian America. Although these debates hardly resulted in an agreement, I want to thank this diligent researcher for drawing my attention to some specifics of native status in Russian America I might have missed.

I extend a deep gratitude to my Dena'ina informants, who introduced me to native Orthodoxy: Karen Standifer from Tyonek; Sharlene Rooker, a reader from the St. Nicholas Kenai Church; and Sava Stephan, a native elder from Tyonek. My special thanks go to my Nondalton hosts, Michael "Jimmy" Balluta, a sub-deacon in the local St. Nicholas Church, his wife Olga Balluta, Rev. David Askoak, and Rev. Michael Trefon. All of them made my short stay in Nondalton not only productive, but also pleasant. I am grateful to Rev. Macarius Torgonsky, who helped me to get access to missionary records in the attic of the Kenai church, and to Lydia Taradonova, who pulled out from under her bed a box with personal papers and journals of Father Paul Shadura and let me copy them. Without her help the section devoted to this missionary, her father-in-law, would not be complete. Two other persons to whom I extend my gratitude are Alan Boraas and James Kari. Professor Boraas came just in time to help me speed up my access to some primary documents, while Professor Kari personally and through his works provided me with many useful details about various localities and place-names in Dena'ina country. The reader will notice that I tried to color this publication with as many visual materials as possible. The person who was of special help here is John Branson, a historian ranger from Lake Clark National Park. John not only retrieved valuable photographs from family collections related to the inland Dena'ina, but contacted each family and secured rights to publish these pictures.

I want to extend deep gratitude to my colleagues at Alabama State University, first of all to Dr. T. Clifford Bibb, dean of the University College; Professor Michael Howley; Dr. Virginia Jones, my departmental chair; and Dr. Karl Westhauser. Their warm response to my research gave me a necessary inspiration to attempt the present work. My special thanks go to Dr. Jones, who, since my coming to Alabama State University, gave me a nice retreat in my office "on the hill," where I had and still have an excellent opportunity to practice my "writing vigils." Finally, I would like to acknowledge the help from the Summer Research Laboratory of the Russian and Eastern European Center of the University of

Illinois, which provided me for two weeks with a conveniently secluded environment and excellent library resources that allowed me to put the whole manuscript in a good shape. Jennifer Horne, a poet and an editor, generously responded to my arrogant please-do-it-right-now request and promptly polished this text, for which I want to thank her so much.

INTRODUCTION

Orthodoxy Among Dena'ina and Ahtna

IN THE SUMMER OF 1998 I interviewed Sava Stephan, a native elder from the Tyonek village, who lived in the Mary Conrad Elderly Center in Anchorage because of his weak health. During our talk I questioned Sava about his Dena'ina[1] heritage and the Orthodox Church, the topic I have been interested in for the past six years. He seemed to be glad to share with me his memories about old native life in Susitna and Tyonek villages, and we talked for three hours. I was afraid of exhausting the old man with my questions and was about to leave. At the end of the interview, among other things, the elder lamented that now fewer young Dena'ina visit an Orthodox Church: "All turn into white people." Then Sava just in passing made another remark. Mentioning one of the nurses who took care of him and who by mistake threw away a paper icon he kept on his desk, Sava added, "These people here don't know what's icon, they're white people. They can take the icon and throw it away. That is the kind of people they are. If you can throw the icon away, you can throw the money away. That is what I told them. And they laughed at me."[2] Sava's words came to my mind when I reread the memoirs of Hannah Breece, *A School Teacher in Old Alaska*, in which an American teacher who worked among Dena'ina Indians in 1910 mentioned that these Indians believed that they had Bible stories before Russians came to Alaska.[3] What does this tell us? Such attitudes toward Christianity suggest that Orthodoxy became part of a native spiritual legacy. Integrated into indigenous tradition, Orthodoxy turned into popular Christianity. No wonder Cornelius Osgood, the first anthropologist to conduct a comprehensive study of Dena'ina culture, complained that when in the early 1930s he tried to retrieve some "traditional" native cosmogonic or creation stories, to his frustration he found that many of his Dena'ina informants gave him "as pure Indian" slightly altered Mosaic tradition.[4] Indeed, Christianity came to occupy a significant place in the life of this native group. By the turn of the twentieth century all Dena'ina were considered Christians and eventually started to view Orthodoxy as their native religion. It also seems that despite a general secularization the Orthodox Church plays an important role for present day Dena'ina as the marker of their ethnicity. Even those of them who do not go to church traditionally call themselves Russian Orthodox.[5]

This collection of selected missionary documents provides snapshots of the dissemination of Orthodoxy among Athabaskan Indians: the Dena'ina and their neighbors, the Ahtna, native peoples who reside in southcentral Alaska. These records, written by clerics, naturally represent the missionary side of the story. As with many similar narratives, they reflect the life of indigenous peoples through "missionary mirrors" with their biases and misconceptions. The reader will find here many stereotypical pictures of native life common to the writings of Christian clergy in the nineteenth century. Incidentally, as such these materials might be a good source to explore the perceptions of native societies by Russian missionaries. However, I do not want to reduce the meaning of these records to a text that tells us about clerics' images of natives and nothing about native society itself. To those who are ready to look beyond the clerical vocabulary abundant in these records, their documents provide plenty of information on Dena'ina seasonal hunting and fishing cycles, settlement patterns, migrations, demography, shamanism, marriage practices, relations between natives and miners, and alcohol abuse. In addition, missionary reports allow us to determine more or less exactly the years when chapels were first established in various Dena'ina villages, which might be important, considering the vague data we currently have on the beginning of chapel construction in Dena'ina country.

Dena'ina Society and Beliefs in Early Contact Period

The Athabaskan-speaking Native American group, the Dena'ina, occupied Cook Inlet, Iliamna, and Lake Clark areas in southcentral Alaska. As did other groups who belong to the same language family, in the eighteenth and the first half of the nineteenth century Dena'ina developed seminomadic hunting and fishing economies. However, they differed from the Athabaskans of interior Alaska, who had more of a hunting culture, whereas the Dena'ina displayed elements of both hunting and fishing economies. Dena'ina southern groups hunted large animals, but depended more on river and sea fishing. Regular seasonal salmon fishing was the most important food resource for the Dena'ina, especially when the caribou population decreased on the Kenai Peninsula in the nineteenth century. The salmon fishing economy allowed the Dena'ina to develop a semisedentary lifestyle. Northern bands, though also fishers, relied more on hunting. Generally, all Dena'ina devoted the spring and fall seasons to extensive tribal hunts of large game, when they would make collective drives and set up fences to capture caribou. During these long hunting expeditions, the Indians left their sedentary villages and moved to small mobile hemispherical structures. During the summer season whole villages moved to the fishing sites to harvest salmon and prepare for winter. By the second half of the nineteenth century the fur trade introduced nomadic patterns for all of the semisedentary Dena'ina population.[6]

It is difficult to estimate the Dena'ina population during the early contact period, the second half of the eighteenth century. At the end of the eighteenth century they lived in semipermanent settlements with an estimated population of 200 people per village. However, more definite data exist, provided by Russian missionaries for later years. Parish accounts indicated that by the end of the nineteenth century the population of six major Dena'ina villages after being reduced by epidemics varied from 48 to 197 people in each settlement. Missionary accounts of 1895–1896 show Dena'ina numbers at 2,507,[7] and Joan Townsend estimates that the Dena'ina population was approximately 3,000 at the end of the nineteenth century.[8] The Indians maintained relationships with neighboring Yupik and with Athabaskan groups through trade, war, and intermarriage. Incidentally, it was from the Yupik that the Dena'ina, originally forest hunters, later adopted maritime living techniques that helped them survive in new surroundings.[9] In referring to the Athabaskans scholars emphasize an extreme flexibility to adapt to new ecological conditions. James VanStone writes that the Athabaskans "moving into different environments in most cases readily borrowed techniques and technologies from the people already present and accommodated these techniques within Athabaskan culture." Moreover, as the newcomers to the maritime areas populated by Yupik and Sugpiaq communities, Dena'ina apparently had to enhance these adaptive qualities. Townsend, for instance, maintained that one of the most outstanding characteristics of the Dena'ina was their extreme adaptability. She emphasized the respect for individual initiative and the lack of excessive social sanctions, which gave them much freedom for experimenting with alien values.[10]

Like the Tanaina used in earlier ethnographies, the name Dena'ina is superficial and is a later anthropological construction. The Dena'ina bands spoke closely related dialects and lived in small communities, independent of each other. Later, as a result of Russian and American colonization, epidemics, and subsistence changes, they consolidated their villages, after which they apparently began thinking about themselves as "the Dena'ina" and accepted this classification into a single entity. Dena'ina society had changed so much by the middle of the nineteenth century that it is difficult to speculate further about social organization during the precontact period. Still, it appears that in the early nineteenth century, consisting of ten to fifteen matrilineal clans, Dena'ina kin relations followed a matrilineal system of succession. Consequently, women occupied an important place, controlling the distribution of food and the marriage of their daughters. Even chiefs and headmen moved to the houses of their wives after marrying. During the nineteenth century, an extended family occupying a large semisubterranean house was the major social unit.[11] Anthropological works point to the existence of an elite (*qeshqa*) and commoners (*os'qala*), although later contacts with the Russians enhanced this division. The *qeshqa* status and prestige depended on accumulating riches and regularly distributing them among other members of the community through the potlatch ceremonies frequently described in anthropological literature. However, it was not wealth itself or its distribution that fully defined *qeshqa* power and status, but the ability to organize supporters for productive purposes that elevated one's position and prestige. *Qeshqa* were enterprising individuals who introduced technological innovations into Dena'ina society and were mindful of the well-being of their community. This group of people provided the candidates for headmen positions, along with the village shamans.[12] Like other Native Americans, in their belief system the Dena'ina generally did not separate the natural from the supernatural world, but integrated them with other elements such as polity, economy and social order. Furthermore, dependence of native lifeways and economies and spiritual activity on the unpredictable forces of nature did not allow creation of dogmatic structure or rigid religious institutions. Rather, in their major approach to supernatural indigenous beliefs they emphasized fluid individual religious experiences. In addition, native worldviews did not picture a battle between sinister and good forces for a final victory, something that Euroamericans, who had been raised in the spirit of Judeo-Christian tradition, could not grasp. It was hardly surprising that many missionaries concluded that natives practiced no religion. Clerics who worked among the Indians believed that instead of genuine religion they found a few superstitions. Because of this false perception, missionaries seriously maintained that they had come to fill a spiritual vacuum. Christianity views the earth as transitory, a preparation for the new order that will tell the ultimate meaning of history. In contrast, the Dena'ina believed overall that the meaning of existence was already given and the purpose of religious practice was to sustain or restore the equilibrium inherent in nature. For this worldview, the most feared thing was the fragmentation of the existing order, which disturbed the existing balance.

Animated spirits of animals, mountains, plants, and insects populated the native universe, and people were to maintain constant contact with these "other human beings." This idea made people act as an inseparable part of the natural system. The Dena'ina believed that spirits controlled all living things, the land, and all natural objects. Each river, hill, and lake was endowed with its master-spirits. Osgood stressed that Dena'ina animated the entire animal world and all natural objects, which were endowed with less or more power. They were also expected to speak like human beings. It was believed that stones, mountains, trees, and grass were able to talk with people, and animals were viewed as simply a different kind of people.[13]

The person who maintained a dialogue with all these spirits on behalf of a community was a shaman. Like among many other peoples belonging to so-called "shamanistic complex," among the Dena'ina an individual turned to shamanism after receiving a vision or a revelation or any other communication with spirits during a dream or sickness or, for instance, from a voice heard during the hunt. The Dena'ina designated shamans by a specific word, *el'egen*, meaning "like a dream," pointing to the way people acquired shamanistic power. Among the Dena'ina the personal gift of shamanic art was a choice made by the spirits. Chosen persons who wanted to avoid being shamans battled the spirits, but if they failed to resist or relinquished the battle, then they had to live with this "assignment" until death. Therefore a Dena'ina could become a shaman even against his or her personal wishes.[14]

After stressing their "great importance" for the community, Osgood noted the multipurpose function of a Dena'ina shaman, who, as in other indigenous societies, was a "doctor, prophet and high priest."[15] The Dena'ina also drew a distinction between little and big medicine men and women, "bad" and "good" ones. In addition, spiritual practitioners belonged to the wealthy *qeshqa* rank. If they gained enough power, they could even occupy the position of chief.[16] During their sessions Dena'ina shamans used a special outfit, a caribou skin parka and an apron decorated with bird claws, and used hand rattles and masks. Osgood found that drums were rarely used and that the Dena'ina shamans used instead simple wooden planks, which had been painted according to the dreams received by their owners. One of the major parts of the shamanistic session was, as missionaries called it, a "devil" or "bewitched" doll, which represented a miniature human figure and served as a healing tool absorbing sickness from a human body.[17] On the whole, Galina Dzeniskevich notes that generally the performances of Athabaskan and Dena'ina shamans in the nineteenth century differed little from those of their Siberian counterparts.[18]

In their belief system Dena'ina, like other Native Americans, constantly filtered their religious views through personal, tribal, and other spiritual experiences. Ake Hultkrantz observed that American Indian traditions emphasized the direct experience of spiritual power through dreams and visions. He added that the sacredness and prestige of these striking revelations often resulted in the modification or replacement of previous traditional elements.[19] For instance, Dena'ina sought help and medicine power from neighboring Yupik shamans. Moreover, the fluid nature of Dena'ina religion manifested itself in regular public performances and competition among Dena'ina shamans to maintain prestige among the people and to compete with rivals within a group or from other communities.[20] It is possible that later the religious stance that encouraged a constant search for medicine power led them to active experimenting with Russian Christianity.

Dena'ina and Euroamericans

There were two major outposts from which newcomers penetrated Dena'ina and Ahtna countries. The first was the Kenai Peninsula, where Russians established

Nikolaevskii (St. Nicholas) Redoubt (Kenai) around 1786-1787,[21] which later became the center of the Russian-American Company's (RAC) operations in this region. The area where the fort was located was blessed with a nice climate. It was one of a few areas in Russian America where people were able to collect considerable amount of potato, turnips, and other vegetables that were even shipped to Sitka.[22] The second center built in 1793 was Nuchek or Konstantinovsky (St. Constantine) Redoubt in Prince William Sound.[23] During the period of Russian presence in Alaska, the number of newcomers in each settlement never exceeded sixteen people, who were represented by a few Russians, but mostly by mixed-bloods from Kodiak or the Aleutian islands and also by Siberian natives. Therefore, speaking about Russian-native relations in this and, incidentally, in other areas of Alaska, we should use the definition of "Russian" with large reservations. In addition to the two major outposts there were a few small trade stations and posts (*odinochkas*) in Cook Inlet and inland areas (Knik, Tyonek, Iliamna). Some of them reached the size of "a small fortress," as the Iliamna *odinochka* was described in 1797. This trading post had few houses fenced by a wooden stockade and was populated by fifteen Russians and the Itelmens, Siberian natives from the Kamchatka peninsula, who constantly kept a guard armed with a saber at the gates.[24] Others were tiny trading posts such as the Mednovskaia *odinochka* in Ahtna country, which represented a fortified house staffed by only one Russian worker.

Despite occasional hostilities it is wrong to depict relations of the Dena'ina with Eurasians, including their early stage, as a state of total war. The Russians, Siberian natives, and Siberian and Alaskan residents of mixed origin traded with the Dena'ina for the pelts of sea otters, beavers, river otters, and martens. By 1800 many "Russians" married into Dena'ina society and remained with their native wives after the fur animals diminished in the Kenai area.[25] Interestingly, indigenous oral histories more often mention conflicts with neighboring Yupik and Sugpiaq groups than wars with the "Russians," suggesting that, despite earlier hostilities, the newcomers were more interested in establishing trade relations with the Indians than in fighting them.[26] It is better to say that from the second half of the eighteenth century, the beginning of the active interactions of the natives with newcomers, Dena'ina country represented a common frontier situation with its "lines of uncertainty"[27] and a kaleidoscope of interactions that included trade and clashes, peace and occasional military conflicts, cooperation and intermarriage, abuses and reciprocity.

One recent work on the early Russian activities in the Cook Inlet area directly confirms such conclusion. As members of the Vancouver expedition, which visited the Cook Inlet area, found out in 1794, at St. Nicholas Redoubt and Tyonek newcomers and natives lived in the mixed settlements side by side. This suggests that at the end of the eighteenth century it was not only animosity that colored relations between Russian and Dena'ina. On the other hand, there was enough evidence that points that unfair treatment of the Indians by individual fur trappers and their foremen resulted in armed conflicts such as massacres of fur trappers' bands by the Indians in Tyonek and Iliamna in 1798.[28] There was nothing strange in such undefined relationships. Frontier situations at an early stage in other areas of the American West demonstrate the same type of interactions with different levels of conflict and cooperation. Yet with the establishment of the Russian-American Company monopoly in Alaska in 1799 and the decline of a competition among rival fur trappers' groups, life in Dena'ina country became more peaceful and predictable.

From the beginning of the nineteenth century there were no more violent clashes between Dena'ina and Russians except occasional incidents. The first one happened when a native who had been cursed and beaten by a Russian killed his tormentor with an axe. The killer admitted the murder and was sent to an Okhotsk prison in Siberia. In 1854 a chief administrator of Russian colonies was worried about unspecified "unruly behavior and disobedience" among the "Kenaitze" and had to instruct one of the regional managers to visit St. Nicholas Redoubt and to establish there "a proper order."[29] Moreover, Maksim Chutaki, one of the "disobedient" "Kenaitze" was exiled to Kodiak. Yet within a year he was already allowed to return in reward for his "good behavior." The low prices paid by the company for Indian furs and occasional abuses practiced by some managers of St. Nicholas Redoubt remained the major sources of the "Kenaitze" discontent.[30] It appears that the Dena'ina preferred using established RAC channels to settle their complaints. Thus, in 1847, in response to their complaint about the mistreatment from Ivan Komkov, the manager of the St. Nicholas Redoubt, M. D. Teben'kov, the chief administrator of Russian America, personally visited Dena'ina country trying to settle the argument. Incidentally, two years earlier similar complaints about abuses from a manager of the Konstantinovsky Redoubt resulted in his dismissal.[31] The Dena'ina "disobedience" never reached such proportions as to provoke armed confrontation with the newcomers. Ironically, for some strange reason Efim Borisov, who succeeded Komkov, was more worried not about the Dena'ina, but about "hostile plans" of the Kolchans [the Tanana], who were expected to attack the fort.[32] The rumor certainly never materialized, for this native group resided hundred of miles from the redoubt.

In the early 1860s arrogant attitudes of P. Zazubovich, the new redoubt manager who came from Poland, threatened to break a well-established reciprocity between the "Kenaitze" and the newcomers. Clearly lacking any knowledge of local conditions and RAC's relations with natives, he not only antagonized the local Dena'ina with his rude behavior, but also excessively cheated them during the trade deals. In 1863 some "Kenaitze" who lived in the vicinity of the redoubt even attempted to murder Zazubovich. It was only because of the mediation of local mixed-blood residents and their Dena'ina wives that his life was saved and the conflict was settled. As it turned out, Zazubovich tried to solve his personal financial problems not only at the expense of the Indians but also the company. While Indians complained that he underpaid them, the company documents in 1862 showed that the manager overpaid natives 1,265 rubles.[33] The RAC chief administrator Ivan Furugel'm ordered an investigation of the matter, which apparently led nowhere because Zazubovich suddenly died. Because of the chronic lack of manpower, for a long time the RAC was not able to find any replacement for him until in 1864 Furugel'm sent Vladimir Stafeev to take the position of the manager.[34] Although the new manager, a "greenhorn" Russian from Estonia with aristocratic inclinations, was equally unfamiliar with local conditions, he adopted a different approach to the locals. Trying not to change anything in the St. Nicholas Redoubt, Stafeev let things run their natural course and apparently relied on local mixed-bloods. Moreover, the manager married a local Dena'ina girl, which eventually helped him entrench himself in the native society.

On balance, RAC leadership understood very well the weak presence of their company in Alaska and persistently asked local managers to appease "savages" or at least not to irritate them. In his instructions to Zazubovich and later to Stafeev, Furugel'm repeated that the managers were to learn more about the "ways and habits of the savages" and their seasonal activities "in order not to interfere with their life ways." Specifically, Furugel'm instructed Zazubovich not to send the "Kenaitze" into trade expeditions in winter, the time "when the savages move to mountain ranges to hunt the deer." Both managers were also ordered not to distract natives from their occupations by employing them at a local brick workshop and other company works. They were forbidden "to disturb them during red fish runs" and were also instructed to make sure that the natives stored enough dried fish to feed their families in winter. Furugel'm concluded his guidelines by stressing that "observing these rules will strengthen our friendly relations with the savages."[35]

By the 1860s the overall situation in the Kenai area was so stable that prince Dmitrii Maksutov, a new chief administrator of Russian colonies, stressed that maintaining a fortified structure of St. Nicholas Redoubt in Kenai did not make any sense "because neighboring tribes of the Kenaitze and others are peaceloving people, and nothing suggests that they might ever attack us or cause any kind of harm."[36] Moreover, during these years the total Russian presence in the Cook Inlet area diminished. St. Nicholas Redoubt gradually started to lose its significance as the fur-trading center. A small brick-making workshop that was to supply the colonies with building materials produced bricks of poor quality and did not bring any profit, so the company officials made a decision to terminate the works, redirecting all activities to salting fish. In 1866 RAC decided to reduce the number of its workers in the redoubt.[37]

The rigid bureaucratic structure of Russian America, which cloned the semifeudal system of the mother country, and lack of aggressive commercial incentive in RAC activities, harmed interests of the company and made it impossible to practice colonial hegemony in relations with such groups as the Dena'ina and especially the Ahtna. Trading posts were not permitted to trade guns and ammunition to natives, especially to those who resided outside of the direct RAC jurisdiction. As a matter of fact, the company itself experienced shortages of these items. In short, one cannot avoid making analogies with colonial experiences of France and Spain in North America, where similar bureaucratic colonization peppered with feudal patriarchal tradition left native people a significant leverage in maintaining their sovereignty and identity.

Despite the meager Russian presence in southcentral Alaska, those "Kenaitze" who resided in coastal areas, especially around St. Nikolas Redoubt, were already connected to and employed by the RAC on a regular basis. Some of them were sent with trade goods to buy furs from their northern fellow-tribesmen in the Knik, Susitna, and Iliamna areas and from the Ahtna Indians. Thus, in the 1830s "trusted" Indians with a supply of goods were regularly sent to trade with the inland Dena'ina.[38] Later Ivan Furugel'm, the chief administrator of Russian colonies, even advertised this experience of employing loyal natives as a model for other trading posts.[39] The RAC leadership went further, trying to employ Dena'ina as trade agents not only among the Ahtna, but also among other inland Athabaskans. Thus, Furugel'm instructed the manager of St. Nicholas Redoubt "to arouse in the Kenaitze a desire to visit the distant Kolchans [Tanana] to purchase furs of sables, muskrats and foxes." Specifically, the chief administrator recommended to recruit for this role of inland traders the "Kenaitze" headmen, who were to be provided with goods on credit and after a successful completion of their missions were to receive bonuses for their ventures.[40]

By the 1860s some Dena'ina communities, at least in the Kenai Peninsula, were to some degree incorporated in the colonial administrative, social and economic system. Dena'ina chiefs were required to send one man and one woman from each village to perform summer jobs for RAC such as catching fish, cutting wood and storing hay, for which they were paid in trade goods at the amount of seven rubles. Although this obligation most probably concerned Chkituk [*Shk'i-tuk't*], a Dena'ina village in the vicinity of the St. Nicholas Redoubt, Grinev draws a conclusion that this fact illustrates overall dependency of the Dena'ina on RAC.[41] Furthermore, chief managers of Russian colonies regularly confirmed the headmen [*toions*][42] of the native villages in their positions. For instance, in 1864 Furugel'm in his official order, which was to be forwarded to the manager of St. Nicholas Redoubt, noted, "Stepan Unikulshin and Stepan Ataduchin, who are elected *toions* in the settlement of Knik and Chkituk are hereby confirmed in their positions."[43]

At the same time, the integration of the Dena'ina into the colonial administrative structure and their participation of the economy of Russian America should not be exaggerated. Although not so obsessively protective of their sovereignty as the Tlingit Indians in the Sitka area, the "Kenaitze" were nonetheless far from subjects of the colonial administration like the Aleuts. Dena'ina status in Russian America could be better described as semi-independent. Correspondence of RAC chief administrators directly or indirectly points to this fact. The chief administrator Nikolai Rozenberg in his letter to Petr Doroshin, an engineer who explored the valley of the Kenai River for deposits of gold, referred to the Dena'ina of the Skilak village inside the Kenai peninsula as "free Kenaitze, residents of the mountain Skilak settlement."[44] On the basis of this casual remark we may assume there were other "Kenaitze," who were more dependent on the RAC. Most certainly this second group of the Dena'ina resided in the vicinity of St. Nicholas fort.

Moreover, RAC managers could not simply require that the "Kenaitze" perform company works. In order to do this, even in such localities as the St. Nicholas Redoubt area, it was necessary to secure an agreement of native leadership. The engineer Feodor Furugel'm, who was sent to the Kenai area to start coal mining works, tried to recruit about forty "Kenaitze" as carriers, fishermen and auxiliary workers, but faced reluctance of natives to meet his demands,[45] which might have interfered with their seasonal activities. Pointing out to Furugel'm that he had broken the accepted procedure, a RAC chief administrator reminded him that usually "hiring of the Kenaitze is always conducted through their *toions,* who should be invited for negotiations" and who, according to the "established order," were to receive gifts and food from a special fund for "savage treats."[46]

Despite the practice of confirmation of native leaders in their positions by chief administrators, it was villagers themselves who selected their headmen. Thus, in 1856 the chief administrator specified that, "according to their [Kenaitze] request," certain Roman Al'kal'jukin had been appointed as *zakazchik*[47] and acting *toion* of the "first Knik settlement." In 1862 a Dena'ina *toion* from a Kondazlit village was confirmed in his office after the native leader had been selected [*izbran*] by the residents of his settlement. In 1865 RAC confirmed Stepan L'tatuchik, another "Kenaitze" *toion* and even assigned him an annual salary of 180 rubles and an award in the sum of 30 rubles.[48] On the surface, the latter decision certainly might be viewed as an example of the Dena'ina integration into the colonial system. Yet most probably the allocated money pointed to an attempt to appease native leadership and draw it closer to the Russian administration. This especially concerned the "free Kenaitze." In 1851 Rozenberg sent a few unidentified items as gifts to the *toion* of the Skilak Lake village, whose inhabitants provided a general support to the Doroshin survey party. On top of this, the chief administrator presented to "all native residents of the Skilak settlement" a box of carpentry tools as a reward for "their benevolence toward Russian people in general."[49] This gesture clearly indicated that they were independent from the Russian administration. Finally, Hegumen Nikolai, who was closely familiar with the Dena'ina life and whose observations the reader will find in this collection, clearly pointed that the "Kenaitze" enjoyed a considerable sovereignty in their affairs: "with the exception of trade, Russians do not exercise any control over administration of the Kenaitze whatsoever." On the whole, RAC control never extended beyond Lower Cook Inlet. As late as 1860 the chief administrator Furugel'm still referred to the Dena'ina residing in the Knik and Susitna areas as "tribes independent from the company."[50] The notes of Hegumen Nikolai on the geography and population of the Kenai area, which are published in the present collection, point in the same direction. Such characteristic was even more relevant to the "Kenaitze's" neighbors, the Ahtna, whom RAC never included in the sphere of its formal jurisdiction. Ahtna contacts with Russians were episodic and the company's modest attempts to penetrate their habitats failed.[51]

The majority of Dena'ina not only maintained basic hunting and fishing economies, but with the intensification of the fur trade in the nineteenth century, even enhanced them. Lacking manpower, RAC pursued the cautious policy of encouragement of natives in their traditional pursuits, at first in hunting fur animals and then before the Alaska purchase in fishing. Until the middle of the 1860s the "Kenaitze" in coastal areas left the permanent villages, taking entire families in search of "soft gold." Because of the depleted fur supply, the search for new trade routes in inland Alaska became a priority under Baron Ferdinand P. Wrangell's administration (1830–1835). The Russians in Cook Inlet pressed the Dena'ina to journey across the mountains in search of furs. Until the very end, before St. Nicholas Redoubt activities were reoriented to fishing, RAC leadership continued to issue bonuses and awards to encourage "Kenaitze" to bring their furs to the redoubt. For instance, in 1860 Furugel'm ordered the allocation of 625 rubles to reward Dena'ina *toions* and *zakazchiks* "to encourage the procurement of furs [*pooshrenii k pushnomu promyslu*]." Those native leaders who agreed to pursue the RAC interests were allowed to select goods of their own choice in the company store in Kenai.[52] By the 1860s, losing a trade battle in inland areas populated by the Athabaskan tribes to the advancing Hudson Bay's Company, RAC ordered its local agents to pay Athabaskans and other natives higher prices for their furs than the English traders from Hudson's Bay Company paid in Fort Yukon.[53]

The increasing role of nomadism in the life of Dena'ina throughout the nineteenth century under the influence of the fur trade established the semipermanent settlement patterns that became characteristic of the Dena'ina social and economic life, which was described as "traditional" in the classical ethnography of the Dena'ina written by Osgood. At the end of the nineteenth century the residents of only one Dena'ina village, Seldovia, still lived a relatively sedentary life, while all other communities regularly embarked on long hunting and fishing trips a few miles from their villages or even journeyed into the interior territories of another Athabaskan tribe, the Ahtna. By the nineteenth century many Dena'ina villages could hardly be called permanent settlements. For example, between the 1850s and 1880s Knik, located in Upper Inlet, was always described not as a single settlement, but as Kniks, a group of villages or camps. In his confessional and communion registers the missionary Hegumen Nikolai [Militov] (1850s–1860s) constantly made references to five Knik villages and provided services in each village separately. As late as 1893 Old Knik (future Knik town) had only three permanent residential houses and one trading post. The greater part of the population normally was scattered two, three, six, and more miles from the village. In the 1880s, in another village, Tyonek, people stayed at home only about four months a year. The rest of the time they spent in forest hunting and fishing.[54] A Russian missionary to the Dena'ina, Ioann Bortnovskii [Bortnovsky], noted that only in May and August did the Indians stay in their permanent settlements; all other months "residents of all Kenai villages primarily live as nomads, especially in the northern part of the parish."[55]

The weak Russian presence and inefficiency of RAC trade activities never made the Indians overly dependent on Russian staple foods and trade goods. Stafeev, an RAC chief manager in Kenai, stressed that in the 1860s each "Kenaitze" *toion* received from the RAC an annual allowance consisting of one pound of tea, twenty pounds of flour, and one drink of vodka. The others did not receive anything and apparently had to rely on traditional sources of subsistence. It was only after Americans arrived in Kenai that the natives start drinking tea and eating bread on a regular basis. He also added that the "Kenaitze" started brewing alcohol and drink "even more than Russians" as late as the 1880s.[56]

After the Alaska Purchase, competition between several American fur companies replaced the RAC monopoly. These companies included the Alaska Commercial Company (ACC) and the Western Fur and Trading Company (WFTC). In order to win native markets, trade companies paid inflated prices for furs and provided unlimited credit. As a result, the Indians occupied a favorable position, since the prices paid for furs constantly increased. The most favored items of trade were usually sugar, flour, hard bread, lead, percussion caps, rifles, tobacco, and calico. Overall, the time from 1867 to 1895, when natives and newcomers maintained balanced relationships based on trade, proved a stable period for the Dena'ina.[57] However, by the end of the 1890s the reorientation of the Alaskan economy toward commercial fishing caused the fur trade to decrease. In the 1880s and the 1890s a few canneries were built in Cook Inlet. Although these canneries endangered traditional fishing resources and even caused a severe famine in some of the Dena'ina villages,[58] by hiring natives for seasonal jobs they became a significant source of income for Dena'ina families. Then, in 1903, a railroad project cut through Dena'ina country, reshaping the traditional economic and ecological landscapes, and also employing many Indians on railroad construction. By 1900 incomes from hired jobs came to occupy as much of a place as the traditional subsistence activities. Thus, wage labor supplemented hunting and fishing and gradually integrated the Dena'ina into a market economy.

After the 1895 discoveries of gold at Bear and Palmer creeks, thousands of miners flooded the northern Kenai Peninsula. Gold seekers ventured to Dena'ina country as early as 1876, and even during the Klondike gold rush mining never stopped in this area. Prospectors who moved to Kenai in great numbers broke the equilibrium established between the natives and newcomers. The Dena'ina villages of Tyonek and Knik became major supply and disembarkation points for prospectors. In 1906, 150 Indians and forty whites lived in the village of Knik. A decade later, in 1915, the number of Europeans in Knik had increased to 500.[59]

This influx of newcomers and their intermarriages with native women changed the ethnic composition of Dena'ina society. In fact, this process started with the establishment of "Russian" settlements in the Cook Inlet area and intensified further at the turn of the twentieth century. After settling in Kenai some Russian, Siberian native and mixed-blood people of the Aleut and Sugpiaq origin married into Dena'ina families and became entrenched in the "Kenaitze" society, learning their language and customs. Later this small segment of people of Russian-Aleut/Sugpiaq-Dena'ina origin served as trade agents, *toions* and *zakazchiks*, churchwardens, and lay readers. Confessional registers for 1847 and 1850 composed by Hegumen Nikolai show us that among eleven newcomers residing in Kenai, a number of Russians and mixed-bloods took Dena'ina women as their wives. Such Russian employees of RAC as Petr Kalashnikov, "an expert brick maker" (*kirpichnii master*), Nikolai Eliseevskii and Evgraf Iakovlev were married to Indian women. Among RAC workers of so-called Creole category,[60] Ivan Balashov and Zinovii Berestov were also married to Dena'ina. Of five St. Nicholas Redoubt residents who belonged to the category of "free settlers," two, Savva Kiselev, a peasant from the Tobolsk district in European Russia, and Petr Osipov, a Sakha native from eastern Siberia, were married to Dena'ina women.[61]

By the end of the nineteenth century such Dena'ina settlements as Seldovia, Kenai, and Iliamna were not "pure" Indian villages anymore. Here Creoles mixed with the Dena'ina people. To this ethnic mosaic there should be added American and Scandinavian merchants, professional hunters, sailors, cannery workers, and especially miners who started to come to Dena'ina villages at the turn of the century. Even such remote inland Dena'ina villages as Kijik, which was very much cut off from Cook Inlet area, had a population of seventy-six Dena'ina and seventeen Euroamerican prospectors by the beginning of the twentieth century.[62] Some of these miners married native women and joined Dena'ina society, and even after the boom ended they remained in Dena'ina country working as trappers and hunters, and as freighter and sawmill operators. Ellanna and Balluta stress that by the turn of the twentieth century these newcomers acted as cultural brokers who brought to Dena'ina society the values of middle-class American culture.[63] The fact that many present-day Dena'ina are descendants of white miners and Indian women demonstrates the profound influence of mining development on Dena'ina ethnicity.[64]

In the beginning of the twentieth century missionaries issued a large number of marriage certificates to ethnically mixed couples, which reflected the rising number of newcomers in Dena'ina country and the growth of the mixed-origin segment. Here are a few examples of this "ethnic cocktail" for 1908–1909: William MacKeon, a Presbyterian American who resided in Seldovia, married a widowed Dena'ina woman, Anna Nanitak. Malcolm McNeil, temporarily residing in Knik, married Anna Chshidalusion, a Dena'ina woman from the same village. William Hughes, a Roman Catholic, also from Knik, married Maria Stepanova, a Dena'ina from the Susitna village. In addition, Dena'ina continued to intermarry with representatives of ethnic groups that had earlier arrived at Cook Inlet. Andrei Tolchok, a Dena'ina from Seldovia, married Marfa Tapani, a resident of Aleksandrovsk, an Sugpiaq village. Moreover, among the marriages consecrated by the Orthodox Church we may find such "exotic" couples as Posto Lavrenze, a Roman Catholic Filipino from Manila, who married Olga Nikanoroff, a Dena'ina woman from Kenai.[65]

Even remote Dena'ina from the Iliamna and Lake Clark areas actively intermarried with white prospectors and merchants. Some of the latter came to occupy important positions in Dena'ina social life. This could be said about Hans Siversen (1870–1939), an immigrant from Minnesota and a prominent prospector and a merchant, who was married to a Dena'ina woman, Yenlu Nudlash Brooks from Old Nondalton, and who played a crucial role in an establishment of a new Iliamna village. It could also be said of John M. Hobson, a prospector who deeply grounded himself in Dena'ina life style, or Jack Kinney (1868–1933), who prospected for gold in the Mulchatna district in 1909 and subsequently married a native, Elena Balluta, from Qeghnilen.[66] On the whole, by the turn of the twentieth century Dena'ina country became cultural and ethnic "middle ground," where "Kenaitze," Aleut, Sugpiaq, Russian, American and Scandinavian elements merged with each other.

Russian Missionaries in Dena'ina Country

Not much is known about missionary activities in Kenai and surrounding areas prior to 1845, except half-mythologized deeds of the monk Iuvenalii.[67] Proselytizing at the end of the eighteenth century somewhere north of the Iliamna area, Iuvenalii aroused the animosity of inland natives (Dena'ina or Yupik), and he paid with his life for his overzealous activities. Stories of Iuvenalii's life and death were so impressive and information about him so scarce that Ivan Petroff, one of the members of Hubert Bancroft's famous "history team," apparently could not resist the temptation to fill the gap and forged a "Iuvenalii's diary."[68] Vladimir Donskoi, Dean of Alaska Clergy, trying in 1893 to compose a summary of the Kenai mission's activities, also admitted that he was not able to locate any information on missionary activities among the "Kenaitze" prior to 1845–1846.[69] However, one thing can be stated with certainty. Given the semi-sovereign status of the Dena'ina and the weak presence of the "Russians" in the Cook Inlet area, adoption of Orthodoxy could be considered not an imposition, but rather the Dena'ina's own choice.

Hegumen Nikolai (c. 1806–1867) became the first priest to conduct regular work (1845–1867) among the Dena'ina. As early as 1845, assigned by Bishop Innokentii [Ivan Veniaminov] to the Kenai area, he came to Dena'ina country and baptized local Indians who had been previously converted by a layman. He also made efforts to train local natives for missionary work and for church services. Two orphans, Makarii Ivanov (Russian-Sugpiaq) and Ivan Orlov (Russian-Dena'ina) served as good candidates, and Nikolai gladly accepted them, providing them with schooling and accommodation. In 1852 Orlov and Makarii were admitted to the ranks of clergymen.[70] Formally, the missionary was put in charge of a huge area that covered not only Cook Inlet, populated by the Dena'ina and Sugpiaq people, but also Prince William Sound as well as the territories of the Ahtna and Eyak Indians. In addition, because of the illness of the priest Il'ia Petelin, in 1846 Nikolai was temporarily put in charge of the large Nushagak mission that encompassed the Nushagak, Kuskokwim, and Stony River basins. In this parish Nikolai was expected to serve the needs of the Yupik people and inland Dena'ina (Iliamna, Mulchatna, Kijik, and Qeghnilen). Nikolai usually had to conduct his missionary travels accompanied only by an interpreter and *baidarka* paddlers or in the company of his songleader, Makarii Ivanov, who was the son of a Russian peasant from the Tiumen province (*guberniia*) and an Sugpiaq woman. The second person who was temporarily attached to the Kenai mission to help its missionary was another student, Ivan Orlov, a songleader, who was a son of the aforementioned Iakovlev, a peasant from Iaroslavl', and a Dena'ina woman.[71]

Needless to say, it was hard for Nikolai to make regular visits to all these remote areas, many of which still were not sufficiently explored by the RAC. Sometimes in planning his trips Nikolai had to choose between visiting natives of his mission and Nushagak. As a result some Dena'ina villages of Cook Inlet remained unvisited for one or two years. For instance, in 1847 the missionary went inland to perform services for the Dena'ina of the Iliamna and Lake Clark areas. Most certainly Nikolai visited the Iliamna village, where he heard confession and gave communion to Savva Riktorov [Rickteroff], a Creole foreman [*baidarshchik*], Lukeriia, his Dena'ina wife, their children, and thirty-two

Dena'ina. According to the missionary, the total number of Iliamna residents was forty-six (forty Dena'ina and six members of the Creole Riktorov family). Furthermore, Nikolai's confessional registers also indicate that the Indians from three other Dena'ina inland villages such as Kijik (nineteen people), Mulchatna (forty-seven) and the Stony River area (thirty-one) also partook in sacraments.[72] It may be doubted that the missionary visited each of these three localities because of the hardships of such travels. Yet, with a high degree of certainty it can be said that it was the Iliamna village where Nikolai stayed, providing sacraments both to the local Dena'ina and to their fellow tribesmen, who apparently had been notified in advance about his arrival and came from the other localities to meet the missionary. Iliamna was the locality where in 1821 the RAC rebuilt an *odinochka* supervised by Riktorov. It might be suggested that Savva, who was fluent in Dena'ina, acted in this area as the major cultural and language broker mediating between the missionary and the Dena'ina. Nikolai's correspondence with the chief administrator of St. Nicholas Redoubt [Borisov] suggests that the priest did use Savva as an interpreter from time to time.[73]

It was obvious that Nikolai and his songleader had a hard time attending to the needs of native populations of both the Kenai and Nushagak missions. Eventually, in 1854 this situation prompted church authorities to send to Nushagak its own missionary, Hieromonk Feofil Uspenskii. In the same year the Dena'ina of the Stony River and Iliamna areas were also attached to the Nushagak mission. Yet despite the establishment of a special mission Feofil primarily worked among the Yupik natives and hardly visited his "Kenaitze" parishioners. For example, he was never able to reach them between 1862 and 1864.[74] As for Hegumen Nikolai, since the middle of the 1850s he received an opportunity to conduct more regular work in Cook Inlet.

Nikolai originated from the family of a songleader and received religious training in the Tambov Theological Seminary. It is known that he did not finish his studies, but it is unclear how many years of theological education he completed. As Nikolai indicated in his short autobiographical note, he was discharged from this school because of poor health. However, after leaving the school the future missionary accumulated a significant monastic experience. From 1830 to 1841 Nikolai lived in three different monasteries and also took monastic vows. In 1841, responding to a call from church authorities, who were interested in recruiting missionaries to the newly organized diocese of Kamchatka, the Kuriles, and the Aleutian Islands, Nikolai asked the church to send him to Russian America. After staying in Sitka for a few years, he was consecrated Hieromonk and was appointed as a missionary to Kenai in 1845. In 1845 and 1846, for his zealous activities in baptizing respectively ninety and 200 natives, Nikolai received a special gratitude and blessing from the Holy Synod; he later was awarded an imperial order of St. Anna of the Third Rank, and in 1852 he was granted the title of Hegumen.[75] When Nikolai arrived at the Kenai mission there were hardly any facilities available to conduct missionary work. Two small chapels built by the RAC in Kenai in 1841 and in Konstantinovsky Redoubt in 1846, furnished with a few church items, were all he had.[76] In September of 1849, after converting the greater part of the Dena'ina people, Nikolai rebuilt the Kenai chapel into a permanent church and stayed in this area for the next twenty-five years.[77]

To make his Orthodox message more effective, Hegumen Nikolai organized a small parochial school. Moreover, along with his songleader Ivanov, Nikolai vaccinated hundreds of natives for smallpox in the 1860s, and treated injuries and wounds. These medical activities deeply affected the local Dena'ina. In his 1860s diaries and reports Nikolai referred to himself and Ivanov as "healers of the natives." In fact, later on, after the first successful results of the vaccination, when they heard about a coming smallpox epidemic, the Dena'ina themselves started to approach the missionary asking for treatment and evidently connecting healing with the power of Orthodoxy. By the time of Nikolai's death in 1867, the majority of Dena'ina had formally adopted Orthodoxy and become familiar with its basic rituals, and many of them, especially in the Kenai area, took part in Orthodox services on a regular basis. Available documents do not say anything about the active resistance of the native population to Christianity. Yet, we may assume that the effects of the Dena'ina conversions remained dubious. On the one hand, Nikolai's missionary journals provide examples of the Dena'ina's pious behavior such as reverence for crosses, and regular and mass participation in Orthodox feasts. On the other, the missionary recorded the coexistence of elements of shamanism and Christianity.

Reading Nikolai's reports and browsing his confessional registers, one is amazed at the piety, diligence, and tremendous zeal shown by this missionary. Even more surprising is that Nikolai persisted in advancing Orthodoxy despite the poor state of his health and his regular requests that he be relieved of missionary duties and allowed to return to Russia.[78] Inland his conversion activities extended up to the Dena'ina of the Stony River area, whereas in the south he regularly visited the Sugpiaq natives of Prince William Sound. Moreover, about 1850 he was even able to convert fourteen Ahtna Indians, who were considered independent natives.[79] The Kenai area, however, the residence of the missionary, remained the center of his proselytizing activities. In 1864 Nikolai was formally discharged from his position as the Kenai missionary.[80]

Yet in April of 1865, instead of permitting the ailing cleric to return to Russia, the ecclesiastical consistory ordered Nikolai to transfer all church property to the Kenai songleader Ivanov and journey to Sitka, where he was assigned to work among the Tlingit.[81] It appears that by transferring him to the capital of the Russian America church authorities, who experienced a constant shortage of missionaries, hoped at least partially to meet Nikolai's complaints about the Kenai climate. In the meantime, the consistory apparently was going to consider his request about a return to Russia. Suddenly in 1866 church authorities, who could not find a replacement, changed their mind and convinced the Hegumen to stay in Kenai "for a while."[82] On top of everything, the RAC, which paid salaries of Russian missionaries in Alaska, hoped to use Hegumen's experience in salting fish to teach Stafeev and other redoubt workers, who were instructed to turn St. Nicholas Redoubt into a supply base that was to provide Sitka with fish.[83] Yet by this time Nikolai was already too seriously ill to perform not only this but his direct duties. Feeling that he might soon die Nikolai wrote a testament where he instructed that all his money be distributed among three monasteries in Russia, the poor Alaska clergy, and the Kenai Church to support a school or some other "benevolent institution."[84]

After the Alaska Purchase the Russian government reduced funding for the Orthodox Church in the region, and missionary activities temporarily subsided. No one replaced Nikolai after he died in 1867, and until 1880 the position of the Kenai missionary remained vacant. All services were performed by the song-leader Ivanov and other Creole readers educated by the Hegumen. During the 1880s, when the Russian government renewed its funding of Orthodoxy in Alaska, a Valaam monk, Hieromonk Nikita [Marchenkov], was sent to Kenai, where he stayed until 1887. This choice was not entirely successful because Nikita did not plan to devote himself to missionary work in the first place. It appears that this Russian nobleman and a former first lieutenant officer [*poruchik*], a graduate of the Polotsk Military Cadet School, at a certain point became disillusioned with his military career. Marchenkov became more interested in Orthodoxy and the monastic life. As a result, in 1866, at his own request Nikita was discharged from the army and came to live in the Valaam monastery, where he was tonsured as a monk in 1874. At this monastery he became fascinated with the life and deeds of St. Herman, one of the Valaam monks, who came to Alaska in 1794 with the first Orthodox mission and ended his life in retreat on the Spruce Island. Following the example of his role model, Nikita wanted to move to the same island and live there in solitude near the grave of the famous hermit.[85] To his regret, when Nikita arrived in Alaska he found out that the Alaska see needed missionaries rather than hermits. Instead of Spruce Island Nikita was assigned to fill the position of a missionary in Kenai, whose residents had approached church authorities in 1878 asking for a priest.

Hieromonk Nikita was not zealous in fulfilling his involuntary assignment. Although he did visit the Dena'ina on a regular basis, Donskoi, the Dean of Alaska Clergy, did not give him much credit and stressed that Nikita's missionary work did not bring any significant results. Neither did another church hierarch in Alaska, V. Vechtomov, who even added that it would be better for everybody if Nikita quit his missionary work. Although Nikita promised to start proselytizing work among the Ahtna Indians in 1882–1883 and even received from the ecclesiastical authorities $100 for his trip, nothing was done because instead going to the Ahtna the missionary spent much of this time on Kodiak away from his parish.[86] During Hieromonk Nikita's entire stay, only two Ahtna Indians were converted.[87] In all fairness, it was not solely the missionary's fault. Nikita's conversion report indicated that the natives whom he baptized could be better described as returned to Orthodoxy rather than newly acquired souls. As a result, according to Nikita, the entire work of his mission was devoted in that time to "correction of native manners and their erratic customs."[88] Nikita's reports and letters create a picture of a troubled person who was deeply disappointed with his involuntary assignment. He did renew a parochial school in Kenai for native and Creole children. Moreover, he paid from his own pocket for the room and board of a few native orphans. At the same time, Nikita disliked teaching and did not feel comfortable working with children. Unlike his zealous predecessor, Nikita did not feel at home with the Indians and Creoles he visited. He never missed a chance to release his frustration by castigating the Indians, Creoles, and even Russians for shamanism and superstitions. From the very beginning Nikita started petitioning church officials asking them to relieve him from the burden of missionary work and permit him to move to Spruce Island.[89] It appears that the frustrations of his work turned him to heavy drinking. Stafeev, who was an ACC trade agent in Tyonek and who was familiar with Nikita, made an ironic remark about Nikita's "weakness" during the priest's visit to the village: "Father was in the same mood as always: he drained a glass of beer to the bottom, and then kept on drinking without stopping until late at night."[90] Church officials and a Russian consul in San Francisco, who apparently knew about his drinking, ordered him to come back to Russia. I was not able to find any official document that met Nikita's original request. With or without such permission, it is known that the Hieromonk would not go to Russia, but left for Spruce Island, where in 1887 he died a tragic death in a fire.[91]

Although Hieromonk Nikita's successor, priest Nikolai Mitropol'skii (1888–1892), similarly arrived at Kenai not exactly of his own will, he was a very zealous and energetic cleric, who radically increased the number of converts, which brought him praise from the Dean of Clergy. For Mitropol'skii the appointment to Kenai as an acting missionary was a move downward on the church ladder and from the active social life he enjoyed in Sitka and later in San Francisco. A son of a songleader [*ponomar*] from the town of Kaluga, Mitropol'skii successfully graduated from theological seminary with the certificate of the first merit in 1868. He belonged to the group of clerics whom Bishop Ioann Mitropol'skii, his brother, brought to Alaska in 1870 to upgrade the work of the Orthodox mission. By moving up from songleader to priest through the church ranks, he eventually became a member of the ecclesiastical consistory, the chief administrative power of the Orthodox Church in North America. But in 1886 his career temporarily declined. During his work in Sitka Mitropol'skii sold some church lands to reduce his big debts and on behalf of the church issued to an American merchant bills of exchange that had not been authorized by the ecclesiastical consistory. This prompted church authorities to dismiss Mitropol'skii from his position for misuse of church property.[92] His subsequent transfer to Kenai to the position of acting missionary became an escape, which helped him to reestablish his priestly reputation.[93] Mitropol'skii took his new responsibilities very seriously and expanded the work of the mission. Moreover, he became the first Russian missionary to break a tradition of short visits to Dena'ina villages. Mitropol'skii spent the winter of 1888–1889 in the northern Dena'ina village of Knik, which he considered a potential outpost of Orthodoxy among the local "Kenaitze" and especially the Ahtna Indians. In Old Knik the priest along with his songleader completed building a chapel and made advances to convert the Ahtna Indians, who came there for trade.[94]

In 1893 Mitropol'skii was replaced by the deacon Aleksandr Iaroshevich, for whom the appointment to Kenai and simultaneous ordination as a priest was a step up in his career. The new assignment was conditioned by an obligation to stay in Kenai for five years.[95] Iaroshevich, the son of a noncommissioned officer in Warsaw [*unter-ofitser*] received his religious training at the Warsaw Theological School, from which he graduated in 1886. At first he apparently wanted to continue his religious education and entered the Kholm Theological Seminary. Although characterized as a student of good behavior, Iaroshevich's performance was poor, especially in mathematics and languages. Twice he tried to pass the annual exams on these subjects and twice he failed them.[96] These failures may have convinced him to terminate his studies and try his luck as an Alaskan missionary. In 1888, having fulfilled mandatory military service, Iaroshevich came to Sitka, where he worked as a songleader at the St. Michael the Archangel Cathedral, as a teacher of Russian in the local Indian school, and also as a teacher of church singing for Russian children.[97] Iaroshevich was an active proselytizer. Bishop Nikolai, his superior, giving him high praise, noted that this young cleric stood out among all other Alaska missionaries because of his "love of and zeal to his work."[98] Iaroshevich renewed a school for native and Creole children, established Orthodox brotherhoods, and also began building the new church in Kenai to replace the old one that had started to fall apart. The missionary was very outspoken about alcohol abuse in the region and harassment of local natives by Alaska Commercial Company (ACC) agents. It seems that such a stance involved him in disputes and violent quarrels with Alex [Alec] Ryan and A. Krisson, ACC representatives in Kenai and Knik.[99] Eventually, these conflicts complicated the life of Iaroshevich in Kenai, and apparently became one of the reasons why Iaroshevich arranged, in 1896, to exchange places with Ioann Bortnovskii, his colleague and friend.

Like Iaroshevich, Bortnovskii studied at the same theological school and at the same seminary. Having failed his course work too, he left the seminary and volunteered to work as a missionary in Alaska. By the time the two colleagues came to a decision to exchange places, Bortnovskii was working as a missionary among the Tlingit Indians in the Juneau area. Church authorities did permit the two clerics to switch places, and in 1896 Bortnovskii arrived in Kenai, where he stayed until 1907. This missionary not only expanded the work started by his predecessor, but also founded the St. Nicholas Temperance Society, and renewed proselytizing among the Ahtna. In 1907 Bortnovskii, who was returning to Russia, was replaced by the deacon Pavel Shadura.[100]

Unlike the previous Kenai missionaries, Pavel [Paul] Shadura, had both a religious and secular background. Born to the family of a cleric in the Minsk Region, which is in present-day Belarus, Shadura graduated from the Kholm Teachers Seminary in 1897 and then worked in a parochial school. Later on he sent a petition to Bishop Tikhon of Alaska and North America, asking for an appointment in Alaska. From 1900 Shadura worked as a songleader and then as a deacon at Unga and on Kodiak. In 1907 he was ordained as a priest and simultaneously appointed to the position of missionary in the Kenai church.[101] However, ten years later Shadura's career was shattered by the Bolshevik Revolution, which destroyed the power and finances of the Russian Church. Shadura's records after 1917 show that missionary trips, regular church services, and other religious activities in the Kenai area were disrupted. At first, ecclesiastical authorities stopped paying a salary to his songleader. Then it was Shadura himself who lost his salary. As late as 1929 the missionary existed on an annual church allowance of $300 and on an income Shadura received by performing various manual jobs.[102] To make ends meet, the missionary started fishing on a regular basis and cutting wood for canneries. Under these circumstances Shadura was unable to make any regular rounds to the Dena'ina villages. Nonetheless, like Hegumen Nikolai, the first Kenai missionary, Shadura had a resilient character and showed a remarkable commitment to his priestly duties. Despite numerous frustrations with the unfavorable circumstances and with his Creole parishioners, some of whom left the church, Shadura continued to perform services in Kenai and in surrounding areas. After his financial situation slightly improved in the late 1920s, he renewed his trips through the parish and continued to serve his parishioners without a salary.

Now a few words about Nushagak missionaries who worked among inland Dena'ina of the Lake Clark, Iliamna, and Mulchatna areas. As was mentioned, at first the inland Dena'ina country was the domain of the Kenai missionary. Yet in 1854 it became part of a separate Nushagak Mission. Still, for missionaries these areas remained hard to get to. Therefore, proselytizing activities in the inland country were very irregular. For many years the local Dena'ina did not have a chance to partake of the sacraments. After Hieromonk Feofil left Nushagak for Russia in

1868, Vasilii Shishkin became the first cleric to work with the inland Dena'ina more or less closely in the 1870s and 1880s by visiting Iliamna and Kijik villages once in two or three years.[103] Shishkin, the son of a deacon, grew up in Alaska, and received his religious training in the Sitka Theological Seminary. In 1856, after three years of studies, he was sent to Siberia as a songleader [*ponomar*] and served under Archbishop Innokentii [Veniaminov] at the Yakutsk Mother of God church in eastern Siberia. After his petition to permit him to come back to Alaska was granted, in 1859 he was transferred to Sitka to the position of songleader at the Sitka Cathedral. Here Shishkin simultaneously worked as a teacher at the local Orthodox orphanage from 1863 to 1868. In 1872 he was ordained as a deacon and four years later became a missionary priest at St. Peter and St. Paul Nushagak Church.[104]

It appears that Shishkin, being of mixed origin, native to Alaska, found a common language with local Creole and native people, and was even frowned upon for his allegedly loose approach to Orthodox rituals. In 1880 Shishkin completed the job of Dena'ina conversion by bringing to Orthodoxy "twenty-eight souls" of the Mulchatna people, who were the last "Kenaitze" to accept baptism.[105] In Nushagak Shishkin worked closely with his Creole deacon, Vasilii E. Orlov. Orlov was the son of a Russian peasant and an Aleut woman and lacked formal religious training, so it is hardly surprising that his journals are written in the manner of a person of a limited education.[106] Orlov belonged to the above-mentioned group of Creole students who were raised and educated by Hegumen Nikolai in his Kenai parochial school. Despite his rudimentary education, Orlov was appointed as a songleader and in 1880 was even ordained as a deacon.[107] In 1893, when Shishkin retired, and the position of the Nushagak missionary remained vacant for a short time, Orlov was the person who performed missionary duties.[108] He apparently hoped that he would eventually become a missionary priest in this region. In other circumstances, Orlov would have been a perfect choice as Shishkin's successor. However, the lack of a formal Orthodox education apparently kept him from this work.

The next year, priest Vladimir Modestov, a missionary from Russia, came to fill the vacancy and stayed in the Nushagak mission until 1899. Modestov, the son of a priest from the town of Tula, after studying at the Tula Theological Seminary for four years, interrupted his studies in 1889, and joined the military in 1890. One year later he became a teacher at the Pustinsk parish school at the Pustinsk Holy Trinity Monastery of the Poltava province. In 1893 Modestov petitioned the Holy Synod asking to be sent to Alaska for missionary work. The Synod granted his request, and in 1894 Modestov received the appointment to Nushagak.[109] Despite his desire to work as a missionary, Modestov had little knowledge of the region and the people he would be serving. Coming directly from Russia and being very ignorant about local conditions, this cleric also had an explosive temper, which hindered his missionary work. Modestov soon became the object of various intrigues and quickly aroused the animosity of the

Nushagak Creoles, specifically members of the so-called Clark-Shishkin-Orlov clan that expected to see Orlov rather than the newcomer as the Nushagak missionary.[110] In 1895 church authorities, who apparently had learned about these problems, gave Orlov a new appointment at the remote Yukon [*Kvihkpakh*] mission. Orlov had to take care of his severely ill wife and refused to comply with this order, which resulted in his being removed from the ranks of clergy "for failure to come to the place of his appointment and for not paying debts to certain individuals."[111] This incident certainly did not add to the popularity of Modestov.

To make things worse, Modestov quarreled with a second Creole clan, the influential Riktorov family of Russian-Sugpiaq-Dena'ina origin that controlled the Iliamna village.[112] As a result, Modestov had to spend the better part of his tenure responding to various accusations and was not able to do much for his mission. Modestov also faced a constant dilemma. Having no knowledge of Yupik and Dena'ina languages, the priest had to recruit the same Creole people with whom he quarreled as interpreters and cultural mediators. For example, Modestov was helpless in the Iliamna and Kijik area without the Riktorovs, who were fluent in Dena'ina, Russian, and English. Despite his conflicts with Creoles, it appears that the missionary had fewer problems with the native Dena'ina and Yupik people. Occasionally he tried to bypass the Creoles by hiring native guides and interpreters, but the cultural gap was apparently too wide, which again frustrated Modestov. Exhausted by his quarrels with the Creoles, whom Modestov called "the poison that spoils all my health,"[113] he started petitioning ecclesiastical authorities to allow him to return to Russia, using as an excuse his own health problems and the poor health of his wife. On the whole, Modestov was not able to expand the work of his mission, especially among the Dena'ina, which is reflected in the records included in the present collection. Modestov did visit inland Dena'ina, but these were random trips. Moreover, we may find frequent references in his travel journals that he could not reach Iliamna or Kijik because of weather conditions. Yet Christian life in these communities did not stop, primarily because local native lay leaders took the supervision of and control over chapel services into their own hands.

Vasilii P. Kashevarov, who succeeded Modestov in 1899, was the son of a Kodiak priest and belonged to a new generation of North American Orthodox clerics. He was educated in an American public school, and received his religious training in the San Francisco Theological Seminary.[114] Unfortunately, available records on this priest are very sparse, not well organized, and do not contain even the limited Dena'ina-related information that we may find in the Shishkin and Modestov journals.

It remains to be added that geographically about fifty Dena'ina who resided in the Queghnilen village (spelled as Kangallen in missionary narratives) in the Stony River area belonged to a third Russian mission, Yukon-Kuskokwim, that operated both among the Yupik people and Athabaskans of the lower Yukon and Kuskokwim. This mission was established in 1892 as a result of a transformation of the Kvikhapakh Mission, whose center was removed from St. Michael Redoubt to the Chuathbaluk village in the vicinity of the Kolmakovskii Redoubt on the Kuskokwim River. Visiting missionaries, in describing residents of Queghnilen, called them "Kanaitze," a slightly different version of "Kenaitze." By 1914 there were forty-five Stony River Dena'ina registered as members of the Orthodox Church.[115] In addition to the Dena'ina, in this region a few dozen other Athabaskans (Ingaliks, Kolchans and Koyukons) also belonged to the Orthodox Church.[116] Descriptions of Orthodox activities among the Dena'ina of Stony River are very few and sketchy,[117] which could be explained both by the remote location of this area and a confusion among clerics about the mission affiliation of these natives. Formally Stony River Dena'ina belonged to the Nushagak parish, but because of the hardships of traveling priests hardly visited them. For this reason, in 1898 Modestov recommended them to turn to the newly opened Kuskokwim mission. Because of the close connections between Queghnilen residents and their fellow tribesmen in Kijik, Iliamna, and Mulchatna, inhabitants of the Stony River "Kanaitze" simultaneously used the services of both the Nushagak and Yukon-Kuskokwim missionaries. The career of Konstantin Pavlov, a Yukon-Kuskokwim missionary who began to work directly with the Stony River natives, in some respect resembles those of some other Russian missionaries to the Dena'ina. Although he originated from a family of a priest and studied at the Vologda Theological School, like Bortnovskii and Iaroshevich, Pavlov did not graduate from a seminary. We do not know the reason, but after being admitted in 1885 to the Vologda Theological Seminary, either failure in classes or simply disillusionment with his studies drove him to petition in the same year to discharge him. During next four years he lived as a novice in the Pavlo-Obnorsk monastery, and later in 1893 sent a petition to Bishop Nikolai to accept him to serve in Alaska. After working in different religious positions in Unalaska, San Francisco and Prince William Sound area, he was ordained as a priest in 1898 and in 1901 asked to be sent as a missionary to the Kuskokwim area.[118]

His 1904 visit to the Stony River Dena'ina, their inclination to follow the Orthodox path, and gifts they endowed on him pleasantly surprised and even stunned the priest. From this year the Stony River people started to appear on a regular basis in the formal registers of the Kuskokwim mission. The most complete records about proselytizing among the "Kanaitze" of Stony River belong to the priest Nikifor Amkan (1906–1909), a Yupik native, who diligently tried to attend to the needs of his flock on the Stony River. Amkan was raised in the orphanage at the Unalaska two-year parish school. From 1897 to 1905 he worked as a songleader at the Kvikhpakh Mission and in 1905 in a span of a few months was ordained as a deacon and then as a priest. Another priest, who succeeded him, was Matvei Berezkin, an Aleut, who graduated from the same school. Unlike the first two clerics, Berezkin produces an impression of a semiliterate person, whom Hieromonk Amphilokhii, the Dean of Alaska Clergy, characterized as a person of "unreliable behavior" and lacking any proselytizing skills. Moreover, in 1908 Berezkin was under arrest for beating a woman while intoxicated. Strange as it may sound, in the same year Berezkin was ordained as a priest.[119] The most obvious explanation is lack of manpower resources in the Orthodox mission. Berezkin's journal of his journey to the Stony River Dena'ina suggests that he simply copied relevant entries from Amkan's notes.

Although clerics' visits to inland Dena'ina were not frequent, in the Cook Inlet area, and especially in the vicinity of Kenai, Orthodox activities were more or less regular. In this area missionaries usually visited settlements within their parish twice a year: one trip was scheduled for summer (before the beginning of a fish run) and targeted northern villages such as Tyonek, Kustatan, five Knik and two Susitna settlements. The second one took place in March and included a southern Dena'ina settlement, Seldovia, along with the Sugpiaq village of Aleksandrovsk and the Creole settlement Ninilchik. In wintertime the Cook Inlet was usually full of floating pieces of ice and thus almost impassable to missionaries, who usually traveled by *baidarkas*. During the Russian period, an RAC manager was obliged to provide a missionary with transportation, paddlers, and an interpreter. Later on clerics either hired native guides and workers using travel funds provided by the church or were transported for free by the Dena'ina themselves. At least, we have evidence from a Dean of Alaska Clergy, priest Donskoi, who reported that in the 1880s–1890s Dena'ina transported priests free of charge, and the only reimbursements they received were daily rations of bread, tea, and sugar, which clerics shared with natives en route.[120]

Transmitters of Orthodoxy: Russian, Creole and Dena'ina Cultural Brokers

In discussing the role of missionaries in spreading Orthodoxy among the Dena'ina and surrounding Athabaskan communities we should keep in mind the following things. Except for the Kenai area, the center of permanent Orthodox activities, all other native communities had random contacts with missionaries. The hardships of a missionary journey in southcentral Alaska were so abundant that clerics devoted as much attention to a struggle against the elements as they did to their work of eradicating "native ignorance." For this reason, the missionary journals are not the stories about missionary-native relationships and nuances of conversion politics, but also narratives of attempts to carry gospel through Arctic landscape to native villages located in the middle of nowhere. It was hardly surprising that missionaries in southcentral Alaska usually spent more time en route than in native villages.

Unavoidably, clerics devoted a lot of attention to conditions of their routes, surrounding landscapes and struggle against the elements. In such cases natives stepped aside and their place was taken by the pictures that might stir in one's mind scenes from the writings of Orthodox desert dwellers.

Falling under lake and river ice, traveling in blizzards, pulling out sleds drowned in snow, dropping from mountain slopes, suffering from throngs of mosquitoes, and facing hunger are described not as extraordinary incidents, but as routine events. For instance, describing unsuccessful attempts of Shishkin and Orlov to reach the Kijik Dena'ina in the winter of 1882, one of the church hierarchs casually mentioned that Shishkin fell in an ice-cold river, while his songleader "could not use his legs due to their freezing [*vsledstvie oznoba ikh*]."[121] Missionary narratives clearly indicate that many Athabaskan villages were hard to reach and therefore priests' visits there were rare. Even if clerics were able make it to their long-distance parishioners, staying in each village for a few days, missionaries had few chances to supervise local Dena'ina religious life. Priests usually visited Cook Inlet settlements once a year, in inland areas even once in two or three years, which was certainly not enough for the intensive indoctrination of people in Orthodoxy. When one reads their narratives the first image that comes to one's mind is not the one of a "missionary anthropologist" from Jesuit Relations, who stayed among natives for a long time and whose life was threatened by romantic and "ferocious" Iroquois. Orthodox journals from south-central Alaska rather bring to mind a portrait of a "missionary traveler" from Nikolai Leskov's *On the Edge of the World*, whose most stubborn enemy was not so much native "ignorance," but arctic elements.

Second thing, which some missionary records manifest directly or indirectly, is a communication gap between clerics and the Athabaskans. Driven by high expectations about their parishioners as true believers, some priests threw on the Indians sermons and religious talks loaded with a complete set of gospel truths and Biblical metaphors, which was hard to grasp not only for native hunters and fishermen, but even for their compatriots exposed to Orthodoxy for hundreds of years. A few clerics, like Hegumen Nikolai, did partially succeed in finding a common ground. For others working with native population was a total frustration. The most vivid example is Hieromonk Nikita, who tried to enlighten the "Kenaitze" about the "limitless nature" of God, the concept of Holy Trinity, and even about the great schism. To be true, Nikita honestly added that "only God knows if they understood me or not." In another case explaining the meaning of church rituals Nikita admitted that it was not easy for him to find appropriate words to make himself understandable to the Dena'ina. Moreover, he gave a hard time to his interpreter, who lowered his head, standing in silence and being unable to render Nikita's high truths.[122]

Unfortunately, none of the Russian clerics who worked among the Dena'ina and other Athabaskan groups knew their languages. As far as I know, with the exception of a few occasional attempts of Seldovia lay leaders to put down on paper some Orthodox prayers in Dena'ina, no Orthodox texts were ever translated into the Athabaskan in the nineteenth and early twentieth centuries. Although the nature of the Orthodoxy with its stress on ceremonialism frequently saved missionaries in cases when they did not have interpreters, it could not serve as a permanent remedy. Hence, an interpreter always stood between a missionary and natives. Even Hegumen Nikolai, who stayed among the "Kenaitze" more than twenty years, never mastered Dena'ina and had to work with an interpreter. Although some Dena'ina, for example, the entire population of the Seldovia village and a few natives from Tyonek and Kustatan,[123] spoke Russian and therefore could comprehend what clerics tried to convey, in Knik, Susitna, and even in Kenai, the center of the mission, missionaries always worked through interpreters. The last missionary to the Dena'ina, Shadura, who liked to organize regular Sunday evening talks with the Indians on religious topics, stressed that the "Kenaitze" like to listen to them "especially if it is done in their native language," with regret had to admit there that there was nobody except one person to interpret such talk. His explanation was simple: "this is very difficult aborigine tongue to interpret."[124]

The troubles that Fr. Shadura experienced during his missionary trips to northern Dena'ina villages illustrate the extent missionaries depended on their translators. When from 1910 to 1912 Pamfilov, an ever-present and never reimbursed interpreter for Kenai priests since the end of the nineteenth century, for some reason became busy and could not accompany Shadura, it became a disaster for the missionary. The person whom he recruited as a substitute hardly understood northern Dena'ina, and Shadura had to rely only on the ceremonial part of his services. Fortunately, Pamfilov, who was still unavailable for long distant visits, was able to continue to help the missionary with his services in Kenai. Only much later, in 1932, Shadura was able to recruit a Dena'ina Indian, Mikhail Tolchok, a "good interpreter from the Kenaitze language," who despite some elementary training in Church Slavonic and Orthodoxy he received at the Seldovia parochial school was essentially a self-taught person.[125]

Thus, to conduct their work successfully missionaries had to rely on people who interacted with Dena'ina communities on a daily basis and were able to mediate among the Orthodox, Russian/American, and Dena'ina worlds and languages. Although missionary travel journals and letters do not always emphasize this, the major promoters of Orthodoxy among the Dena'ina were mixed-bloods of Russian-Aleut, Russian-Sugpiaq and Russian-Dena'ina origin and Dena'ina lay leaders. There were also examples in which Russians and Americans who lived in Dena'ina communities acted as lay church leaders. An interesting example was Vladimir V. Stafeev, a Russian from Estonia, who at first worked as an RAC manager of the St. Nicholas Redoubt in the 1860s. Married to a Dena'ina woman, a daughter of a *toion*, in addition to Kenai Stafeev lived and worked in the Tyonek village as a manager of an ACC trading post from 1884 to 1888. Simultaneously, he was deeply involved in local chapel life as a lay leader and occasionally even took on the role of a missionary. Along with local Dena'ina Stafeev maintained and decorated the Tyonek chapel. He also was responsible for baptizing native children, and performing services on major Orthodox feasts.[126] Stafeev definitely knew more about native customs than visiting missionaries. His entrenchment in the "Kenaitze" society resulted in his attempting to learn the Dena'ina language, which eventually led him to compose a Dena'ina dictionary for the Bureau of American Ethnology. Stafeev's is the only well-recorded example of the dissemination of Orthodoxy among the Dena'ina by a European lay newcomer. Another one and less recorded was John Hobson, an American fur trapper and miner who lived among the Stony River "Kenaitze" and who, like Stafeev, married a Dena'ina woman. Hobson was rather fluent in Russian and Dena'ina, and after his conversion to Orthodoxy he acted as lay leader. It will not be a mistake to conclude that the decision of this American, who wanted to ground himself in the "Kenaitze" ways, to convert to the Russian Church suggests that by the early twentieth century Orthodoxy became native Dena'ina church.

Very important as regular transmitters of Orthodoxy were offspring of the Aleut and Sugpiaq families who grew up in Kenai. Their fathers and grandfathers had been brought by the RAC to the Cook Inlet area or came as "free settlers." Living close to the "Kenaitze," learning their language, or marrying Dena'ina women these people and especially their children represented good candidates for interpreters, church assistants, and cultural mediators in general. For example, Ivan Balashov, a Creole RAC worker, after having married a Dena'ina woman, mastered the "Kenaitze" language and in 1857 was even appointed an official interpreter for the St. Nicholas Redoubt.[127] Ivan Kvasnikov [Kvasnikoff], the son of Grigorii G. Kvasnikov, a townsman from the Kaluga province, and the Creole woman Mavra, was raised in Kenai, learned the Dena'ina language, and later became a lay Orthodox leader who frequently helped clerics during their missionary trips. Moreover, Bortnovskii recommended Ivan Kvasnikoff for the position of parochial school teacher among the Dena'ina because he had received elementary Orthodox training at Hegumen Nikolai's parochial school and was also fluent in the "Kenaitze's" language.[128] At the end of the nineteenth and in the beginning of the twentieth centuries in Kenai, a Creole, Aleksei F. Pamfilov (of Russian-Sugpiaq or Russian-Aleut origin), acted as a permanent interpreter of all missionaries' addresses, sermons, and prayers into the Dena'ina language. Like Kvasnikoff, Pamfilov was fluent in Dena'ina.[129] Two Seldovian Creoles, Ivan Aleksandrov (Russian-Sugpiaq) and Zakhar Balashov (Russian-Sugpiaq-Dena'ina), similarly did readings and interpreting, and in addition supervised the building of a new chapel in 1891.[130] In 1902 Bortnovskii referred to another Creole (Russian-Sugpiaq) Ivan Soloviev, a graduate of the Sitka School who was later appointed as a songleader and a teacher to the Susitna village, as a "good find." Soloviev accompanied the priest on his trips to the Dena'ina as an interpreter for three years, earning one dollar per day. In addition to his work as an interpreter, Soloviev acted as a songleader.

Savva Riktorov (1808–1884), an RAC Creole employee who resided in Iliamna, provides an even more vivid example of how a newcomer became entrenched in Dena'ina society and later took on the role of cultural and spiritual mediator. In the 1840s Savva frequently commuted between Kenai and Nushagak, being responsible for transporting RAC merchandise and various goods. Eventually, in the 1850s, he settled permanently in the Iliamna area, where he was in charge of the RAC *odinochka* working as a foreman. When Hegumen Nikolai visited the Iliamna village, he served as the major mediator between the Indians and the missionary. Since the latter was absent in Iliamna most of the year Riktorov took responsibility for performing some services that did not require a necessary presence of a priest. For instance, in 1849 the foreman read funeral prayers over two Indians, Feodor Kil'kantal'iun from the Kijik village and Vasilii Tuntal'tal' from Iliamna.[131] Later on in this village, Savva laid the foundation for the St. Nicholas chapel, where he continued serving as a lay leader by baptizing children and performing simple services. Having taken a Dena'ina woman, Lukeriia, as his legal wife and another Iliamna native as his concubine and having ten children with both of them, Riktorov gave rise to the clan of Iliamna Creole people, who became influential cultural brokers in inland Dena'ina country, working as guides, lay chapel leaders, and interpreters.[132] In an 1895 travel report Modestov mentioned that Mikhail Riktorov, one of Savva's sons who worked as a local ACC agent, also served as a lay chapel reader and accompanied the missionary on his trips to the Dena'ina villages as an interpreter. Mikhail Riktorov proved fluent in Dena'ina, Yupik, Russian, and English.[133] Hannah Breece, who worked in Iliamna as a teacher in the beginning of this century, points to another Riktorov named "Old William" [Vasilii?], who similarly served as a lay reader. Breece noted that "he stood in place of a priest" because the missionary "was supposed to come once every three years, but at this time had not turned up for the past five."[134] Among the Lake Clark Dena'ina, in Kijik and later in so-called Old Nondalton, the similar role of a village *toion* and lay reader was played by Zakhar Ivanov [Zackar Evanoff] (1860?–1935), whose father was a Russian Jew and mother was Dena'ina, and who was fluent in Dena'ina, Russian, English and Aleut.[135]

Interpreters, lay readers, or low-rank songleaders of mixed origins accompanied missionaries on their trips or disseminated Orthodoxy when missionaries were not around. Unfortunately, we rarely hear their voices on the pages of clerics' travel journals. In missionary narratives such assistants often act as faceless travel companions, although their role as transmitters of Orthodoxy was tremendous. Occasionally clerics did admit their contribution. Hieromonk Nikita, for instance, credited Nikolai Sorokovikov, his Creole songleader, regular assistant, and interpreter. Nikita stressed that without Sorokovikov he would have hardly been able to work in "Kenaitze" country at all. This songleader not only helped him make inroads into native society, but collected statistical information for church registers and even kept a travel journal of Nikita's trips! Nikolai Sorokovikov grew up in the Creole family (Russian-Sugpiaq) of a deacon, and received his Orthodox training at the Yakutsk and Blagoveshchensk Theological Seminary in Eastern Siberia. After working for a time in Kodiak in 1875, Sorokovikov was transferred to Kenai where he began to work as a songleader [*prichetnik*].[136]

More than a modest fee that they sometimes received for their services, such middlemen apparently enjoyed more their status of experts that gave them power and influence over the two sides of the cultural encounter. Pamfilov did not receive any reimbursement for his interpreter services from the church officials and continued to fulfill his duties despite the large burden religious services and long-distance travel placed on his hunting and fishing activities. Shadura noted that Pamfilov was elected to this position by the natives themselves.[137] It became natural that the Kenai Dena'ina and mixed-bloods later elected him to the formal position of *toion*.

Kvasnikov, sent by Bortnovskii in 1897 to winter in Tyonek to repair the chapel building and revitalize the chapel life in the village, in his letter was proud to report to the missionary that the "Kenaitze" treated him as "a brother" and that they listened to him "in everything and feed with what they have because they are glad to see a songleader in their village." The songleader understandably tried to ascribe all initiative and authority in chapel affairs to himself. Although he did admit that the Dena'ina worked willingly on the improvement of the chapel he drew to the attention of the missionary that "I told them if they do not listen to me, I would live on the ship *Jenny*. The Kenaitze were afraid of this, and now they even do not dare to hammer in a nail without my permission."[138] Moreover, after staying in this village Kvasnikov acquired an influential status of a middleman versed in Church Slavonic and Orthodoxy, which allowed him to claim, "I now live very well and all Kenaitze listen to me as if I were their father."[139] Bortnovskii was very pleased with the accomplishments of his songleader. Unfortunately, after his return from Tyonek Kvasnikov was caught with a fox fur he had stolen from a native hunter's trap and became the object of a church investigation. The missionary, who earlier had been always sympathetic with his songleader, now had to state, "Kvasnikov was noticed doing this a few times and now I would like to expose his misdeed."[140]

In addition to Creole go-betweens, who successfully moved between Orthodox and native worlds, clerics tried to find and promote lay Orthodox leadership among the "Kenaitze" themselves. We cannot say with certainty if there were any Indian students in Hegumen Nikolai's parochial school. Yet, there is evidence that in 1882 Nikita, who temporarily revived the Orthodox school in Kenai, brought from Tyonek an orphan boy, who received religious training. However, two other boys, children of a *toion* in the Chkituk village, became homesick and were taken home.[141] Sometimes, missionaries assigned as readers adult Dena'ina Indians who knew elementary Russian and basic prayers in Old Church Slavonic. In 1893 in Tyonek, Iaroshevich entrusted Aleksandr Shichkatakhin, a Dena'ina fluent in Russian, to conduct baptism of infants.[142] Later, during his 1893–1894 winter stay in Old Knik, Iaroshevich trained two other Dena'ina, Ruf Stepanov and Nikolai Kuliktukta. Kuliktukta later moved to Susitna, where he regularly read psalms, and even asked permission to lead Sunday and chapel services on feast days. Although Bortnovskii mentioned that Kuliktukta was still an "imperfect songleader," he nevertheless granted such permission.[143] Moreover, Kuliktukta was also recommended for the position of teacher at an elementary parochial school.[144] We may assume that such lay leaders instructed other members of their communities. It appears that these transmitters of Orthodoxy became especially important in the 1920s and 1930s, when the work of the Russian church in Alaska decreased. For example, Sava Stephan related the way Orthodox instruction was transmitted in Tyonek between the 1920s and the 1940s: "Old chief Chickalusion used to be working in church, he knew how to read Russian. He was trying to learn from Father Paul Shadura. He was trying to learn Russian to hold service. Chickalusion learned how to read in church and he was teaching a Tyonek boy, Nickefor Alexan. He was teaching him how to read in church. Nickefor held services then after Chickalusion died."[145]

From the available information, it can be concluded that missionaries and brotherhoods recommended specific candidates for the position of churchwarden and reader. A system of regular church awards to distinguished individuals was an additional tool the Orthodox Church used to promote native lay leadership. At the turn of the century, Kenai missionaries in their letters to the Ecclesiastical Consistory in Sitka asked church officials to reward specific people, not only for religious zeal, but for the general improvement of native living conditions. In his 1896 report, Bortnovskii nominated Petr Chickalusion, then a *toion* at the Kustatan village, and Stepan Tuchketelketan, *zakazchik*, as possible recipients of awards for both their religious and secular work. Bortnovskii also campaigned for another Dena'ina, Aleksei Kalifornskii [Kalifornsky], who combined positions of *zakazchik* and churchwarden in the Kalifornskoe village. The missionary identified him as a person who "absolutely alone built the local chapel" and contributed much to the general improvement in the village, which then "enjoyed order and good life."[146]

Creole and Dena'ina interpreters and lay readers with only a rudimentary Orthodox education unavoidably gave their own creative spin to Russian Christianity. Mikhail Riktorov provides a good example. According to a missionary report, although Riktorov knew "rather well" how to read Old Church Slavonic and taught local children, he performed chapel service and baptism "in his own way" (the priest does not specify how) and the missionary had to correct him.[147] Breece provides a description of a sermon performed by Ivanov [Evanoff], a village chief in Nondalton:

> On the important Russian religious holiday we all went to church in the village,[...] even though the rain was pouring torrentially as we made the three-mile trip up the lake in open boats. This time the service was not silent. Zackar stepped out in front of the standing congregation and in Kenai preached a sermon. If his words were as eloquent as his expression and gestures, it was an excellent sermon. Afterwards I asked him about it. He said that [...] he had been speaking this way in church, drawing upon truths from Bible, stories from the Sunday school lessons and from the discussions and stories told among us in his tent.[148]

Students of the Dena'ina have commented on this rereading of Orthodoxy by the Indians. For instance, Ellanna and Balluta write, "The delegation of liturgical responsibilities to lay readers promoted free personal interpretations of Russian Orthodoxy which corresponded to the needs of the Dena'ina Indians."[149]

Orthodox Mission in Dena'ina Social Life

Missionary reports from Kenai show that in addition to recording the progress of their religious work, clerics frequently addressed social problems such as regular starvation among the Dena'ina, alcohol abuse, and epidemic diseases. Moreover, they attempted to connect these social issues with the general goals of proselytizing. Missionaries not only tried to "heal" emotional and social devastation produced by epidemics with rich Orthodox ceremonies, but also became involved in social work. The establishment of Orthodox brotherhoods (mutual-aid societies) in Dena'ina villages from the 1890s on is one example of such activities.

Missionaries regularly reported that by spring the Dena'ina people were suffering from starvation. By this time the Indians had usually exhausted their winter supplies of fish, and entire villages were starving. Like their counterparts working among other indigenous peoples, Orthodox clerics sometimes blamed the natives themselves for this situation, arguing that the "Kenaitze" lacked the ability to plan ahead and lived careless lives by attending only to their daily needs. Yet, at the same time, missionaries admitted that there were other reasons responsible for this situation, such as the building of fish canneries at the end of the nineteenth century, which disrupted annual fish runs. Clerics also stressed that hunting had become poor especially in the coastal areas. Some missionaries, beginning with Hegumen Nikolai, tried to introduce gardening among the Dena'ina and later, indeed, some of the natives started to plant potatoes and turnips on a regular basis. Moreover, Nikolai provided collective meals to the Indians during major Orthodox feasts as, for example, in 1859, when on St. Nicholas day and Christmas he treated all common "Kenaitze" to fish soup and their headmen to tea and pies.[150] It was also apparently a tribute to the Dena'ina tradition of sharing, of which Nikolai repeatedly wrote in his reports. Despite Bishop Innokentii's dismissal of any missionary gifts and treats to natives, Hegumen Nikolai in 1849 reported to his superior, "Without giving too much credit to myself, I still feel obliged to mention that I dressed many of the local poor in clean white clothing to insure that Our Lord gives me strength to conduct services in this temple. As a matter of fact, I practice this good Russian tradition of generosity during all major feasts right before or on the eve of the liturgy. Though modestly, I nevertheless dress and feed natives several times a year."[151]

Later Orthodox mutual-aid societies became the major tool used by missionaries and accepted by the Dena'ina to balance the material hardships of the native population. Again capitalizing on the native traditions of sharing (although clerics did not always admit this), Orthodox brotherhoods were designed not only to indoctrinate the Indians and Creoles in the basics of Orthodoxy, but also to provide material and financial help to the poor and sick. The concept of Orthodox brotherhoods in North America had appeared since the second half of the nineteenth century and was directed to increasing the prestige and social role of Orthodoxy among Slavic immigrants. With regard to native groups in Alaska, these mutual aid societies pursued not only economic and social goals, but also missionary purposes.[152] The first brotherhood among the Dena'ina, with 132 members, was established in Kenai by Iaroshevich in 1893 and consecrated after the feast of Protection by the Most Holy Mother of God.[153] The missionary tried to advance the influence of this society as representing the interests of all "Kenaitze" villages. Yet native people came to the conclusion that separate brotherhoods on a village level would better address their needs and instead of just one; missionaries and natives organized several mutual-aid societies: Seldovia St. Theodosius Brotherhood (1896), Knik St. Sergius Brotherhood (1896), Susitna St. Metrophanes Brotherhood (1896), Tyonek St. Innocent Brotherhood (1897), and Iliamna Meeting of the Lord Brotherhood (1904). The last one to be organized was the St. Nicholas mutual-aid society, established in 1908 in the Queghnilen village. It is interesting to note that by the middle of the 1920s, while in other Dena'ina villages, including Kenai, Orthodox brotherhoods disintegrated, in Queghnilen it continued to function and included forty-eight members.[154] No detailed records that reflect the work of Knik, Tyonek, Susitna, Seldovia, Iliamna, and Queghnilen brotherhoods exist except a few references to their activities in clerics' travel journals related to the turn of the twentieth century. It is only the activities of the Kenai Holy Protection Brotherhood that are well documented, most certainly because of the permanent presence of the missionary in Kenai.

It appears that brotherhoods did not confine their activities only to mutual help. These societies, which were usually headed by local Orthodox native leaders, apparently played the role of an informal vehicle of self-government. In the second half of the nineteenth century the native people of Cook Inlet found themselves in a state of legal limbo, a common frontier situation, which was enhanced by the decline of Russian social and political structures in Alaska and by the lack of attention of the territorial government to the establishment of the new structures. For several decades Alaska remained without legitimate governmental representatives and localized law and order. Incidentally, this legal and administrative void could partially explain the desire of some ACC agents to subordinate the Dena'ina to their own control in the 1890s. Obviously, activities of the native Orthodox leadership, brotherhoods, and missionaries sometimes hindered this monopoly. It could be the administrative role of Orthodoxy that Lieutenant J. C. Castner referred to when, visiting the Cook Inlet Dena'ina in 1898, he wrote that "the affairs of each small hamlet are influenced greatly by the power of missionaries."[155] That the Russian Church tried to fill the vacuum of power created as a result of the American negligence we can clearly see in the words of V. Vechtomov, one of the church hierarchs in Alaska. Thus, in 1879 the metropolitan Isidor complained that the United States did not maintain in Alaska any legal representative. As a result, "brutal despotism reigns" in some settlements. In addition to his suggestion to increase missionary activities to maintain the shrinking number of parishioners, Vechtomov recommended to adopt urgent measures to protect the Alaskan Orthodox "from a negligent attitude of the local [American] government." Among these measures was organization of mutual-aid Orthodox societies.[156] It appears that the Orthodox Church temporarily filled the administrative void that existed during this time in some areas of Alaska.

Missionary documents related to the Dena'ina at the end of the nineteenth century indicate that Orthodox Indians and visiting missionaries actively participated in village administration. Not only churchwarden positions, but village leadership, *toion* and his assistant (*zakazchik*), were concentrated in the hands of Orthodox natives, who were sworn by a missionary in their offices. The practice of electing Dena'ina village leaders from the Orthodox leaders and a ceremony of taking an Orthodox oath continued as late as the first decade of the twentieth century. Missionary journals contain plenty of information on such elections and their procedure. In summer of 1906 during his annual visit to Susitna after performing a religious service, Bortnovskii supervised elections of a new *toion*, "Big Ivan," to replace the old one, who became sick. After the election the missionary swore him in the new office.[157] Even in such remote settlement as Queghnilen, which was hardly visited by priests, in 1904 natives scheduled election of their *toion*, *zakazchik* and churchwarden for time when a missionary visited them and sworn the newly elected in their offices.[158] Shadura described the similar election of *toion* in Kenai. In August 1908 local Dena'ina gathered in a parochial school building to elect a *toion* to replace the old one, "who did not meet expectations people connected with him." As a result of debates, natives unanimously decided to elect Creole Aleksei Pamfilov, who served as the long-time interpreter from Dena'ina for a few missionaries. A few days later during the Kenai church feast of Assumption, after a religious service Pamfilov was sworn in his new position. In addition, during the same day a new Dena'ina native, Stepan Knuguudul', was elected and sworn in as a new churchwarden.[159] Three years later "residents of the Kenai settlement" elected Petr Bakhov, a Dena'ina, to the posotion of the churchwarden. Shadura, who supervised these elections, added that "he was elected by the will of the people for a three year term."[160]

In addition to native administration, missionaries and their lay leaders attempted to launch a sobriety movement. Widespread alcohol consumption among the Dena'ina as well as among mixed-blood, Russian, and later American residents represented, according to clerics, the major threat to the well-being of the area.[161] Far from being an "Indian problem," alcohol served a favorite "stress relief" for all segments of population. In 1898 Hieromonk Anatolii indicated that "the major vice raging in the Kenai Peninsula is drunkenness."[162] Thus, local mixed-bloods and miner populations were prone to drinking. Some mixed-blood families in Kenai distilled homemade liquor, drank and sold it to their neighbors. Bortnovskii vividly described a drinking spree that took place in the Kenai village in 1898. Sailors and traders from *Pery* rolled down a large keg of whisky of ten gallons and invited everybody to help themselves. From his account it is obvious that in this case it was not the Indians, but local Creoles, including a churchwarden, Ivan Ivanov, who joined the "feast." Incidentally, the missionary used this episode as an excuse to speculate about the "miserable" nature of the Kenai mixed-blood people, who, in the words of Bortnovskii, acted in a subservient manner in relations with Americans unlike the other groups of population.[163] The most notorious drinkers were miners represented by single males, who not only stayed in Dena'ina villages with short visits, but frequently wintered there, and whose drinking especially during the winter months reached epidemic proportions. In his metaphorical manner Shadura even called these people "zealous carriers of the culture of evil."[164] It appears that miners and traders were the major providers of alcohol to remote Dena'ina villages. By 1908, for instance, in the Susitna village traders opened two saloons and two restaurants specially to serve the needs of the visiting miners, but involved all local Indians.[165] It is hardly surprising that heavy drinking accompanied all major Orthodox feasts, native dances, potlatches, and was generally practiced whenever people received a chance to obtain alcohol. Stafeev in his 1880s Tyonek diary vividly captured scenes of frequent drinking sprees of the Dena'ina, Creoles, and Russians.

In 1886, on New Year's Day, Stafeev, for example, wrote, "Served the Hours. Almost the entire village was drunk, especially the *toion*." He also mentioned that visiting Ahtna Indians became so scared of the whole scene that they did not know how to react. Another entry made five days later on the feast of the Nativity of Christ read: "I served the Hours, there were many people. Then we went to sing carols to the *toion* and *zakazchik*'s places. Almost the whole village became drunk. Some people hardly could walk. They kept on dropping on the ground, some were carried on, while others circled around trying to keep themselves steady." Ten days later, "during the night again there was a drinking spree at the *toion*'s." In 1887 during Christmastime villagers bought five large barrels of sugar to brew them into alcohol. Stafeev, who noted that natives "had quite a drinking this time," complained that he almost ran out of sugar.[166] Missionary Iaroshevich, who visited Tyonek in 1893, stressed that in this village natives were also accustomed to a shot of vodka on the day of communion. Trying to replace this shot of vodka with a cup of tea, he had to devote a greater part of his tenure in 1893–1894 to fighting alcohol abuse among those in his parish. Iaroshevich complained that "vodka is the curse of this people" and also acknowledged that his campaign brought little success.[167] Yet, according to the missionaries, it was not Tyonek but Seldovia that was the most notorious in its addiction to alcohol, which earned the settlement the nickname of the "drunk village." Bortnovskii wrote that "here everybody drinks, not only men but also women and even children." He mentioned particularly that American miners and traders contributed much to the spread of this habit.[168] To these groups of people we should add Chinese cannery workers, who also brought alcohol to the Kenai Peninsula.

It appears that clerics were fighting a losing battle. Moreover, some missionaries, their songleaders, and readers, who were expected to manifest model Christian behavior, sometimes could not avoid this "stress relief." Bortnovskii had to get rid of his Kenai churchwarden, who preferred to spend all major holidays in drinking sprees, which damaged the missionary's reputation and prestige of Orthodoxy in the eyes of Dena'ina.[169] Hieromonk Nikita, who like other missionaries constantly reported to his superiors that vodka was the major vice of the natives in the Kenai area, was himself addicted to this "evil." Moreover, Stafeev complained that the missionary during his visits, Tyonek constantly demanded from him alcohol treats.[170] In another case, a Dena'ina *zakazchik* from the Iliamna village who visited Tyonek complained about the missionary Shishkin, who replaced communion wine with water.[171] These snapshots of alcohol abuse I have provided here serve to explain why missionaries repeatedly highlighted this "evil" and eventually decided to target it as a separate problem. At first, newly established brotherhoods had attempted to handle alcoholism-related problems. Later, in the beginning of the twentieth century, with the social drive for general temperance, both in Russia[172] and in the United States, the Orthodox Church decided to treat this social problem separately from other ones. To relieve brotherhoods from temperance activities the church founded special temperance societies. One of them, St. Nicholas Temperance Society, was established in Kenai in 1906. The new organization copied the structure of existing brotherhoods.[173] It is also interesting that in contrast to the brotherhoods, which were established in each village separately, the temperance society formally included all Cook Inlet villages under its umbrella. The major requirement for members of the society was to take an oath to abstain from drinking for a certain time, usually for a year. Some Indians and Creoles took such an oath for life. In Seldovia, which was reported as the most addicted to alcohol, forty-three Dena'ina and Creoles eventually joined the St. Nicholas Society, and eleven members took the oath never to drink again.[174]

In addition to the regular meetings filled with prayers and hymns, the society's members were involved in various "decent" forms of amusement such as various "decent games" [*nevinnie igry*], for instance, chess-playing, tea parties, dancing, collective meals on the occasion of various Christian feasts. The major form of intellectual activities of the society was group readings of Orthodox temperance literature in translation from Russian to Dena'ina.[175] Members of the Kenai Brotherhood and the St. Nicholas Society had their own insignia, banners, and "brotherhood badges" as well as separate sections in village cemeteries. Missionaries insistently cultivated a corporate spirit among members by stipulating a system of various penalties and rewards. It is clear that the brotherhoods and the temperance society wielded significant influence over native members. Many Dena'ina who were excluded for various violations of the Kenai Brotherhood's by-laws (drinking, polygyny, not paying dues, etc.) often asked to be readmitted. Russian priests publicized the most active members as village leaders, "model" residents, and Christians, and regularly recommended them for various religious and even secular positions.

Like brotherhoods, the temperance society accepted people irrespective of their ethnic affiliation. This practice was stipulated in the regulations of the society. As a result, its composition was multilingual and multiethnic. Yet the majority of members were Dena'ina, who also acted as marshals of the society. Leadership positions were occupied by a priest and a mixed-blood, who served as secretary of the society. Despite their initial success, the authority of the temperance society was increasingly challenged by increasing easiness with which alcohol became obtained by the beginning of the twentieth century. Shadura pessimistically assessed the perspectives of this society in Dena'ina life. He had to admit that by 1910 the temperance movement was essentially undermined, and those natives who took an oath of abstinence from drinking did not fulfill their promises. In 1908 while accepting an oath of new temperance society members in the Susitna village, the missionary was worried that the natives might slip down again.[176] Moreover, the addiction to alcohol became so entrenched among some native communities that two years after in response to his suggestion to join St. Nicholas Society, all Dena'ina of the Knik area rejected this idea except their *toion* Nikolai, who did join the society and took an oath not to drink for twelve years.[177]

As in some other native societies, epidemics that struck the Dena'ina served to enhance the role of missionaries, who were able to offer consolation and "sacred medicine" against unfamiliar diseases. The first major known wave of epidemics (in this case smallpox) visited the Kenai area in the 1830s. Although a direct correlation between the epidemics and the growth of missionary work is hard to establish, successful inroads that Hegumen Nikolai made into Dena'ina society at the turn of the 1850s might be partially explained by the impact of this devastating disease, which apparently weakened the role of native shamans. In the 1860s, anticipating another wave of smallpox, the missionary ordered his deacon, Makarii Ivanov, to vaccinate a large number of the Dena'ina in Kenai and neighboring villages. Registers of the Dena'ina vaccinated show that Ivanov's activities reached a large number of natives, for which the songleader was awarded by the officials of Russian-American Company.[178] At first hesitant to use "Orthodox medicine," the natives themselves later came and asked Nikolai to inoculate them against smallpox. It seems that by this time the Dena'ina had begun to view the missionary as a person in possession of strong medicine. In 1863 Nikolai made the following entry in his journal: "According to Kenaitze's notion, I stand much higher than an ordinary man."[179] Referring to the correlation between his successful medical performances and the spread of Orthodoxy among the native population Nikolai underscored that "their vivid results had instructive influence on the Kenaitze."[180] The program of mass vaccination was not a personal initiative of the Hegumen. Although practiced on a random basis in earlier times, it became part of a general project established in 1856 by special decree of the Holy Synod that obliged all missionaries in eastern Siberia and Alaska to introduce inoculation.[181]

In the second half of the nineteenth century, the Dena'ina were frequently visited by other epidemics. During his 1880 visit to the Dena'ina of the Mulchatna area, priest Vasilii Shishkin drew a grim picture of the devastation produced by an epidemic of scarlet fever, which wiped out 117 of 144 residents of this locality.[182] Modestov described the overall consequences of epidemics in the same area. Reportedly, of 600–800 people who populated Kijik, Iliamna and Mulchatna areas in the 1870s, by 1895 only 138 "Kenaitze" remained alive.[183] Later, in 1921, Shadura, writing about four major Cook Inlet Dena'ina villages, noted that the Indians "die like flies" from influenza and measles.[184]

Dena'ina of the Kijik village who suffered through several epidemics eventually came to the conclusion that the ground where their village stood had been poisoned and apparently on both a missionary's and their elders' advice they abandoned the old site in 1901 and founded a new settlement, Nondalton, close to the trading post on Iliamna Lake and the canneries of Bristol Bay.[185] Similarly, Kustatan, another village that was abandoned, had been devastated by epidemics, which was interpreted as the curse of an unfriendly shaman from the Susitna village.[186] Yet natives of the latter village suffered the same fate. At first reduced in number by epidemics, the Susitna Dena'ina eventually left the village site and scattered around the country after a fire completely destroyed their chapel sometime in the 1920s.[187] In the beginning of the twentieth century a number of other small depopulated villages such as Laida, Kalifornskoe, Skilak, and a few others were in the process of disintegration. About Chkituk, one of the depopulated villages struck by influenza and haunted by famine, Hieromonk Anatolii wrote in 1896 that its inhabitants were planning to "move to Kenai, closer to the church itself."[188] In 1904 a conversation with a Kuskokwim priest Pavlov, residents of the Queghnilen village stressed that fifteen Dena'ina who lived fifty miles up the Stony River and more people from the declining Kijik village promised to settle in Queghnilen when a chapel was constructed.[189] Along with trade stations, Orthodox chapels seem to have been attractive as communal, social and spiritual centers for those Dena'ina who were scattered around or abandoned their depopulated villages in the wake of epidemic diseases and economic changes.

Chapels and Chapel Life in Dena'ina Country

Before first chapels and prayer houses were established in Dena'ina country, visiting missionaries performed their services in mobile tents, with the exception of Kenai, where a permanent church existed. In addition to various services such as confession and communion, consecration of marriages, extreme unction, baptisms, anointment with holy myrrh, and customary prayer services, priests held religious processions with holy water and a cross to protect a village from danger, sprinkled houses and food caches and gear with holy water to guarantee well-being of households and to bring hunting and fishing luck. Priests were also occasionally involved in the social life of communities they served. When chapels were established, in addition to the above-mentioned duties, clerics were to report on the status of chapel finances, items, and maintenance of the buildings. The documented construction of prayer houses in Dena'ina villages took place from the 1870s to the 1890s and was not totally a missionary initiative. In many cases native communities themselves started such projects, asking the priest to help them with general advice or with obtaining unavailable building materials. On some occasions natives acted without consulting clerics. For example, the first Seldovia chapel, which, according to Hieromonk Nikita, was built between 1880 and 1881, was erected at the initiative of the inhabitants themselves [*po proizvolnomu pochinu poselian*] in an "incorrect manner" without securing the permission of the church authorities. As a result, the missionary refused to consecrate the prayer house as a chapel and blessed it only as a regular house.[190] Later the priest Mitropol'skii insisted that the Seldovians demolish this "incorrect" structure and build a new one, which the residents of the village did in 1891.[191] In Iliamna, an inland Dena'ina village rarely visited by missionaries, the first prayer house consecrated after St. Nicholas was built in 1877 by Savva Riktorov, and six years later was rebuilt anew "by residents themselves," who maintained the building and in 1907 renovated it.[192] In the village of Tyonek, where the St. Nicholas chapel was built in 1882, natives decided in 1891 to rebuild it completely at their own expense and finished the work by 1894.[193] In one of his letters Iaroshevich reported that the Kustatan village chapel, built in 1892 and consecrated after St. Olga Equal to Apostles, was started as a totally native initiative, and that "residents of the village conducted all work upon their own inspiration."[194] Dena'ina of the Kijik village built their chapel, which was named after the Precious and Life-giving Cross, in 1889,[195] while at the end of the same year a missionary along with local natives completed construction of the Knik St. Nicholas chapel. The next year residents of the neighboring Susitna village erected their prayer house, later consecrated after the Holy Martyress Barbara.[196] The last chapel built by Dena'ina in that period was St. Nicholas chapel, erected in the Queghnilen village on Stony River during 1907–1908 and consecrated on January 5, 1908.[197] Again, it is worthy of note that the latter project was initiated by the Queghnilen Dena'ina themselves. Although located very far from missionary centers and rarely visited by clerics, the "Kanaitze" of Stony River had to conduct prayer gatherings in a residential cabin. As early as 1902 they started to plan construction of a chapel, and even made a special long-distance visit to the Yukon-Kuskokwim mission to secure help and a word of advice from the missionary priest Pavlov regarding their project.[198]

Sometimes chapel construction enjoyed the financial and in-kind support of local trade agents interested in keeping a good rapport with the native population. Reading excerpts from Kenai missionary journals published earlier[199] one might receive the mistaken impression that all ACC trade agents in Dena'ina villages treated chapels and Orthodoxy in general with animosity. Records reproduced in this work show that such was not always the case. Some of these traders provided significant help and support in building and maintaining prayer houses and did not necessarily view Orthodoxy as a challenge to their power. In 1897 in Tyonek a local trade agent provided the Indians with tools and building materials. In 1901 Bortnovskii credited one Adam Bloch, an ACC agent from Seldovia, who "contributed much effort to put the interior of the chapel in a proper order," and also "donated half of the paint used for painting the whole building, and himself took part in the work."[200] In addition to altruistic motives, there were certainly practical considerations for such a positive attitude. Encouraging chapel construction and chapel life was a good way for local agents to entrench themselves in Dena'ina communities. In 1902 the same missionary praised another trade agent, Arthur McConahay, who was stationed in Susitna and "who contributed a great deal to the successful completion of the new chapel" in this village by helping with building materials and providing free food to Dena'ina working on the construction. Incidentally, McConahay, who was a Protestant, later married Stefanida Istutulianishin, a Dena'ina woman from Tyonek, and even expressed a desire that their children to be brought up in the Orthodox tradition.[201] Some of these people went even further. Thus, John M. Hobson (1868–1949), a prospector-trapper and then a trader, in his desire to ground himself in Dena'ina society not only married a Dena'ina woman and adopted a native lifestyle but also converted to Orthodoxy, which by this time became Dena'ina native church. At first he settled in Kijik in 1902 and then moved to the Queghnilen village, where in 1904 he was elected a churchwarden and regularly appeared in church registers as "American citizen Grigorii Mikhailovich Hobson." Along with his Dena'ina assistant Pavel Konstantinovich [Constantine?], "Grigorii Mikhailovich" supervised a construction of a local chapel.[202]

In the beginning some of the first chapels were fairly crude structures built of logs, frequently without floors, and with roofs covered with birch bark. Later in the 1890s the Dena'ina, missionaries, and songleaders working together improved the appearance of these buildings. The styles of the chapels combined ancient Orthodox elements and the forms brought from eastern Siberia. Thus, the Kijik chapel represented a six-sided structure with the east side of the sanctuary having three sides. The latter form goes back to ancient Christian baptismal chapels of the pre-Byzantine era. The altar faced east, which symbolized the true faith that comes from the rising sun.[203] It was expected that after the construction was complete, natives would maintain and improve these prayer houses by themselves. And indeed, by the turn of the century Dena'ina were in the process of taking control of chapels and chapel maintenance. By this time a prayer house had become an inseparable part of the village landscape. It should be mentioned that historically the Russian Church, while trying to control chapel life itself, at the same time encouraged the growth of chapel autonomy by placing much responsibility for local religious services on Orthodox lay leadership. According to Vera Shevzov, in Russia itself, especially in remote northern areas, the religious life of many Orthodox communities in the nineteenth century often revolved around these chapels and was little connected with the local parish. In those areas where people did not have access to a church, a prayer house became the only outlet for religious activities. In the Russian north laymen frequently decorated and enlarged the chapels without consulting priests and church officials. Moreover, people normally elected an elder to supervise services and maintain the church building. Hence, the status of chapels and their autonomy were not clearly defined. Interestingly, in Russia many such prayer houses were unlisted and the official church did not know of their existence. There were also numerous misunderstandings between local people and church authorities about how to interpret the activities of these chapels.[204] Dena'ina materials essentially support the observations made by Shevzov.

In "Kenaitze" country we may also observe similar chapel autonomy, where for example in the remote Iliamna village all religious leadership was concentrated in the hands of local Creoles and Dena'ina readers. There were some misunderstandings when natives moved or rebuilt prayer houses without consulting a missionary. Thus, in 1897 when the Dena'ina moved their village from Old Knik to New Knik (Eklutna) they disassembled their St. Nicholas chapel and brought it to the new place where it was put together. Bortnovskii, when visiting the Knik Dena'ina, was quite surprised with this arbitrary decision of the natives, because the Russian Orthodox Church, though giving great autonomy to local lay leaders, still tried to convince them to secure permission from ecclesiastical authorities before making any changes to chapels or churches. Similarly, Dena'ina from Susitna, who abandoned their old village, rebuilt their chapel in 1900–1901, when they moved to a new site. Bortnovskii, who did not control the construction, visited the new village, when the major work was already completed. Although he regretted that the structure looked like a "regular house," the missionary nevertheless noted that "the new chapel produced a favorable impression" on him.[205]

Although once a year natives were to report to a missionary about their chapel life and finances, a chapel was completely in the hands of local headmen and churchwardens. Normally a chief (*toion*) and his assistant (*zakazchik*) along with a churchwarden took care of a prayer house together. Usually people collectively selected a churchwarden, who was later sworn in his position by a missionary. Yet occasionally, as for instance in Tyonek in the 1930s, a chief could put a person (Sava Stephan) in charge of maintaining a chapel building and simply inform a missionary about this decision, and the priest would approve it.[206] Ideally village leadership and a churchwarden were to supervise chapel life in the following way: the chief acted as the treasurer, and kept all chapel money, while the *zakazchik*, as a headman responsible for village economic well-being, was obliged to collect donations, and to turn them over to the *toion* for safekeeping. The churchwarden was in charge of selling candles and cleaning the chapel, and was also to encourage people to bring donations. Money acquired from the sale of candles and other church items, a churchwarden turned over to the chief in the presence of *zakazchik*.[207] Involvement of secular leadership in chapel supervision and maintenance reflected another important role prayer houses started to play in Dena'ina villages. Chapels became places where villagers came not only to pray and perform basic sacraments, but also to elect their local leadership, hold meetings of their mutual-aid societies, and conduct general gatherings to discuss various social issues that ranged from alcohol abuse to schooling. The Dena'ina apparently began to view these chapels as both the spiritual and social centers of their villages.

Missionary travel journals show that some of these structures were well taken care of, while others were neglected. In 1899 Bortnovskii compared a clumsily built old prayer house in the Susitna village to a cattle barn.[208] On the other hand, Modestov, who worked among inland natives, who rarely saw the missionary, as a characteristic feature of the "Kenaitze" religious life noted the "special love" of the Dena'ina for their chapels, particularly for their maintaining and decorating.[209] For another priest, Amkan, to work among the inland Dena'ina was a real pleasure compared to the difficulties he had to encounter proselytizing among the neighboring Ingalik.[210] Priest Paul Shadura, who assailed the Dena'ina for poor religiosity, and even stamped them as "miserable people," at the same time admitted that "if the church or chapels need some repairing, residents readily donate from their meager salaries as much as they can."[211] Maintenance and decoration of prayer houses depended on the well-being of village residents and the diligence of particular churchwardens, who were also often in charge of the chapel finances. The temptation was great and on some occasions churchwardens embezzled chapel money to buy food or alcohol. Yet the village population usually exposed them in front of a missionary.

In many other cases, however, missionaries praised churchwardens and readers for their caring attitudes toward Orthodox chapels.[212] In 1906 about a Tyonek churchwarden Bortnovskii wrote, "We can say that a local churchwarden is a model person. I wish with all my heart that not only chapels, but also churches had such churchwardens. Like me, this person is finishing his ten-year service."[213] There were also incidents when churchwardens had to take away or lend all money from a chapel fund in order to support traditional potlatch circuit, when those native who gave potlatch gifts ran out of money and goods and had to borrow them from neighbors. Shadura, who discovered that in Tyonek all chapel money had been wasted for a potlatch, with indignation assailed this ceremony, which he called either festivals (*igrushki*) or "national dances" and believed that these customs would soon ruin them like "card-playing." When the missionary found out that the natives had done the same thing with the money of the local brotherhood, he became so angry that in desperation he shut off entirely the local brotherhood.[214]

Dena'ina Orthodoxy

Compared to surrounding native groups, missionaries graded highly the Dena'ina commitment to the Orthodoxy. By the 1870s and 1880s there apparently existed a large group of Dena'ina and Creoles in the coastal areas who had already begun to treat Orthodoxy as part of their native religion. An 1878 petition by the "residents of all Kenai Gulf" proves that the Indians played an important role in the church life of Cook Inlet. In this petition Kenai area people complained that they had not had a priest since 1867 and asked Orthodox ecclesiastical authorities to send them one. More important, the petition indicated that 105 Creoles and 746 "Kenaitze" had signed the document, including chiefs of Tyonek and two Knik villages, although a number of the neighboring Sugpiaq most probably also signed the document.[215] In his diary Stafeev repeatedly indicated that faithful Dena'ina from Susitna and some other neighboring villages that did not have prayer houses regularly visited the Tyonek chapel to pray and partook in Orthodox rituals. On one occasion natives stayed for seven days in order to participate in the feast day of the Nativity of Jesus Christ.[216] Moreover, Stafeev complained that many Indians came to the chapel even after the feast ended: "These savages have worn me out. They still keep on going to the church and absolutely exhausted me with their feast day greetings."[217]

The most interesting example of the "Kenaitze" initiative in bringing Orthodoxy to their communities are the Stony River Dena'ina, who were frequently neglected by missionaries because of their remote location. Thus, people of the Queghnilen village, as well as the neighboring Kolchans of the Venissari village, not only expressed an interest in the Orthodox religion and made persistent efforts to draw Orthodox missionaries to their villages. Thus, headmen of the Stony River natives traveled hundreds of miles in order to bring priests to Queghnilen and even developed a certain ritual of welcoming a coming priest, who was usually greeted by a large American flag that fluttered over the village and by a continual salute from rifles, after which the entire village population approached a priest to receive blessing. Missionaries also stressed that unlike the Yupik villages, where prayers were recited in their native language, the Dena'ina and Kolchan population of the Stony River area sang them in Slavonic.

Still, despite the attempts of the Stony River people to establish an organized religion in Queghnilen, as late as 1902 Pavlov, a priest who served in the Kuskokwim mission, did not know what to do with a group of zealous "Kenaitze." He could not make up his mind if he should serve this Dena'ina community or send them to Nushagak where they formally belonged.[218] This year the Stony River people themselves crossed hundred of miles and descended the Kuskokwim River in order to help bring the missionary to their village. Unfortunately, they missed Pavlov, who was busy at his missionary trip to the Yupik people. In 1904 the Queghnilen Dena'ina repeated their route, and now secured Pavlov's agreement to go with them up to the Stony River. By the beginning of the twentieth century Orthodoxy and its rituals became part of Dena'ina culture both in the Cook Inlet and inland areas.

Despite missionaries' formal success in bringing the Dena'ina to Orthodoxy, shamanism survived, especially in the northern part of Cook Inlet, and more importantly, it seems to have blended with Orthodoxy, creating a Dena'ina version of popular Christianity. Thus, Hegumen Nikolai, who gladly reported the success of his conversion efforts, still referred to his encounters with medicine men and of having to reprimand them. Stafeev, while living in Tyonek in the 1880s, met a Knik shaman, Konstantin Knikov, whom the trade agent called "sorcerer" and "devil" worshipper. Stafeev added that this "sorcerer" was such a "beast" that he did not allow his wife and daughter to visit the chapel to pray.[219] Hieromonk Nikita, who made trips to this village during the same years, similarly pointed to the survival of shamanism. Although we cannot accept his evidence at face value, for this missionary assailed both the Indians and Creoles, and even Russian peasants, for "shamanistic inclinations," we cannot entirely dismiss it. In 1881 and 1882 Hieromonk Nikita wrote that among the Dena'ina "superstitions and crude heathen customs characteristic of the semi-savage people still exist everywhere." In 1883 he complained that in most Dena'ina villages people "switched from the Christian religion to their former customs," and that he had to reconvert them.[220] Nikita reported to his superiors:

> In each village, especially in the distant ones, where there were no Russian Creoles, I found one, two or even three shamans, who keep people so firmly in their grip and who are trusted so much that one cannot even imagine the extent of it. One should see it.[221]

Even in Kenai, where the Dena'ina were in frequent contact with Orthodoxy, during his church services Nikita had to threaten "natives with punishments at the Judgment Day for secretly observing their ancient beliefs."[222] Yet other of Nikita's remarks indicate that at this time there were few direct manifestations of shamanism. Thus, on another occasion the missionary again stressed that "shamanism, which was about to spread around villages, has now subsided and does not exist openly."[223]

Nevertheless, evidence provided by Dena'ina elder Sava Stephan suggests that shamanism still existed as late as the 1920s, although his stories indicate that it was a dying vocation. Thus, Stephan, referring to the activities of a certain Semeon, a medicine man in Tyonek at the end of the 1920s, stressed that this shaman refused to go to church and continued to practice his healing skills. Sava provided an interesting example of a clash of shamanistic and Orthodox "medicine":

> Once he came [from Tyonek] to fix us at the Susitna Station. He put us in the middle of the floor, covered us with a blanket, and then he started dancing around us singing his song. And then, Billy Pete [Sava's cousin] and me prayed, we prayed. "No," he said, "I can't help them because they pray." He-he-he-he. He told our fathers tell us not to pray: "I can't fix them." He find out that we praying under the blanket, inside. He told our fathers it's no good, they're praying, and he say he can't fix us like that when we're praying. And how he

> fixed us, I don't know, I was too young, seven years old. He come up and they [Dena'ina] pay him to work on them. I told my father we don't need to pay him. You see him dancing all around us, he's crazy, and then we pray, that is our habit, ours, our own craft.[224]

Yet examples of open clashes between Dena'ina shamans and Orthodox believers were few. We might assume that shamanism more often blended with Christianity rather than openly challenged it. Moreover, we have an earlier example of a reassessment of shamanism through the prism of the more powerful Christianity. In 1887 Stafeev encountered a young Indian, a son of the Susitna shaman. The youth, according to the trade agent, went "insane" by coming to Tyonek and praying in front of the chapel on his knees. The shaman's son also imitated an Orthodox priest's hand and body movements. The Indian claimed that he saw God and that now God was inside him. When the young Indian regained his senses, he admitted that this spiritual pressure had haunted him for three days.[225] As described, this incident stands as a classical example of a shamanistic call wrapped in the symbolism of Orthodoxy. We do not have information about the eventual vocation of this native. Yet this person could later could well have fit the role of churchwarden or chapel reader. A few records suggest that some natives did not see any contradiction in following both shamanistic and Orthodox traditions, which apparently merged in their minds. In the 1880s the Tyonek Dena'ina partook with equal enthusiasm in both potlatch ceremonies and Orthodox feasts such as the Nativity of Jesus Christ along with Christmas carols.[226]

For the priests, who measured even their own Russian compatriots by high standards of formal Orthodoxy, such a practice was certainly unacceptable. On a popular level it apparently caused few discrepancies, as among peasants in Russia, who digested formal Christianity through the glasses of popular beliefs and local tradition. What could be found in Dena'ina settlements visited by missionaries by about 1900 was the apparent interpenetration of native rituals and Christianity, which gradually evolved into the popular or village Christian tradition. The basis of this developing spiritual system was certainly Christian, but it was a popular version of Orthodoxy, which might not always have lived up to the expectations of priests with their formal theological training. In 1893 Iaroshevich indicated that he had had to reprimand two Dena'ina medicine men. At the same time, from his journal we indirectly learn that both were practicing Orthodox.[227] It was probably this type of people that anthropologist Townsend meant when she pointed out that many Dena'ina shamans practicing their craft were nevertheless "devout Christians."[228] As late as 1910, Shadura wrote that although natives of the Knik area did participate in Orthodox ceremonies, he noticed that for them Orthodoxy served only as an outward expression of their religiosity without any inner feelings. With regret he also stated that "among the local people there are irreconcilable enemies [of Christianity], who are involved into sorcery." Six years later, during his visit to the same area, again mentioning regular participation of the Dena'ina in Orthodox ceremonies, he at the same time felt it necessary "to draw attention of local people to shamanism" because their faith was weak.[229] Even in Kenai, where Russian missionaries resided on a permanent basis for many years, Shadura had to confront the Orthodox Dena'ina who tried to integrate native memorial potlatch in the Orthodox funeral rites. Thus, in 1910 during his trip to the Dena'ina of the northern Cook Inlet area, Kenai natives took advantage of his absence and held their "national funeral festival [*igrushka*]." Having returned home, in his sermon Shadura explained to the Indians that "the festival by itself is not a bad thing at all," yet he stressed that was against its adaptation "to the celebrating the deceased," which automatically turned "into a some sort of a memorial rite, which is not appropriate for a Christian to take part in." The missionary had to admit that "it is very difficult to fight against this custom, especially in remote settlements."[230]

As a result of the penetration of Orthodoxy into the Dena'ina tradition a number of Russian religious terms were incorporated into their language. These terms are still used by those few individuals who speak Dena'ina. Some of these words mean exactly what they mean in Russian. Yet others, in the process of linguistic mutation, partially lost their original meaning and acquired additional connotations. For example, "dichuk" (from Russian *diachok*) now means not only the "the reader," but also the "bishop." Still, a churchwarden is known as "sdarisda" (from Russian *starosta*). Other Orthodox words which describe church services, the Bible, and religious artifacts were all incorporated into the Dena'ina language: icon ("buzhi" from *bozhii* which literally means "related to God"), "malitva" (prayer), which means the same in Russian, "gris" (cross) from Russian *krest*, "aldar" (altar) from Russian *altar*, "sadana" (devil) from Russian *satana*, "sergu" (church) from *tserkov*, and "gelih" from Russian *grekh* (sin).[231]

In the first quarter of the twentieth century, it was not so much occasional manifestations of shamanism that disturbed missionaries, but the weakening position of formal Orthodox institutions, which faced a strong challenge from the advancing American Protestant culture. The inroads made by this advance were not so noticeable in remote Dena'ina villages, but they directly affected Kenai, the center of the mission. Shadura's reports show that the Creole segment of his parish, which was earlier viewed as a transmitter of Orthodoxy, increasingly cooled toward the Russian Church. Eager to be assimilated into American society, Creole families of Kenai not only wanted to dissociate themselves from the "Indian" church, but considered offensive missionary requirements that they participate regularly in Orthodox feasts. In the 1910s and 1920s many Creole and Dena'ina women who resided in Kenai and who married new arrivals from the continental United States began to ignore local Orthodox institutions such as the parochial school and the brotherhoods. Some Creoles treated activities of the Orthodox Church as a symbol of the old passing age that did not fit the modern American reality. It appears that such animosity found its expression in a growing disapproval of marriages between Dena'ina and mixed-bloods, who considered themselves superior to the natives and strove to resemble Euroamericans in their manners and behavior.[232] The Dena'ina's continuing loyalty to Orthodoxy and the drift of Creoles toward Protestant culture created a large social gap between the two groups in Kenai. Shadura wrote with alarm that the center of parish had become divided into so-called "black" (Indian) and "white" (Creole) camps. It appears that here we observe a trend similar to the one described by Sergei Kan in his studies on the Tlingit attitudes to Orthodoxy. Kan specifically stresses that Orthodoxy became a spiritual and cultural outlet for a conservative and traditionally oriented element of Tlingit society, whereas the more assimilated group drifted toward Protestantism and American culture.[233] During these years of mass intrusion of American Protestant tradition, which stigmatized Native American culture and language as backward and inappropriate, in Kenai we may observe the cases of shifting identity, when some assimilated Dena'ina also attempted to get rid of the label of "Indians" and in their status at least to reach the level of local Creoles. For instance, in the registers of the Kenai St. Nicholas Church for 1927–1929 we find the name of the churchwarden, "American citizen, Kenai Creole, Nikolai Alekseevich Kalifornskii," who was elected to this position by the "will of the people" for three years.[234] It is interesting to note that the same person, Nikolai Kalifornskii, who was incidentally the father of the famous Dena'ina storyteller Peter Kalifornsky, in earlier church rosters by the turn of the twentieth century, reported himself as "the Kenaitze native." The same could be said about the Dena'ina interpreter Mikhail Tolchok, who was similarly registered at first as "the Kenaitze native" in the Bortnovskii's registers and twenty years later as "Creole and American citizen" in the Shadura records.[235] Such examples when mixed-blood and even native Dena'ina in Kenai increasingly downplayed their nativity and underlined that they were "Creoles" and "American citizens" vividly show how changing attitude of the surrounding society toward Native Americans shaped their ethnicity.

The reader will notice that Shadura's reports for the 1910s and 1920s are colored with pessimism. However, we should keep in mind that Shadura tended to extend his frustrations with the desertion of the Kenai Creoles and with the general lack of support for his activities from formal church institutions to the status of Orthodoxy among Dena'ina in general. Thus, he viewed the long absences of some Dena'ina people from their villages in search of jobs as a symptom of the deep crisis of parish life. Furthermore, he was afraid that, far from their villages, the natives might become an easy target for various "alien" denominations. For example, Shadura was very upset that many Indians who temporarily or permanently migrated from Knik-Eklutna (the place name Shadura used in some reports dated in the 1920s) to Anchorage did not see an Orthodox missionary for long periods of time. He was very worried about the local Dena'ina's "negligence to the faith and to the temple" and reported that residents of Eklutna also used the local Episcopal Church to perform services, while the half-rotten structure of the chapel built in 1897 stayed neglected.[236] Incidentally, because of lack of an Orthodox church in Anchorage, Shadura himself used the Episcopal facilities for services when he visited Anchorage.

Shadura's pessimism about the status of Orthodoxy among the Dena'ina seems to have been exaggerated. New Knik-Eklutna natives, whose migrations to Anchorage so concerned the missionary, were far from being apostates. Moreover, Shadura himself stressed in his 1930s notes that some Eklutna people gradually started moving back from Anchorage to the old village site, building new houses and repairing the old ones. It is notable also that they also asked Shadura to begin performing services in the Eklutna chapel rather than in the Anchorage Episcopal Church. Later the missionary had to admit that the Dena'ina were steadfast in their Orthodox beliefs. In a 1947 letter to his colleague priest, Hieromonk Feofan, complaining about the shrinking ranks of his parishioners, Shadura nevertheless noted:

> There are still people who are strong in their spirit. These are Indians who live far from the whites and stand firm in their Orthodox faith. As for the Creole offspring from mixed marriages, I do not rely on them. Moreover, they do not view themselves as Creoles and become very upset with our clergy that use this name. Creoles switch to alien denominations and immediately try to act as whites, which raises their spirits. After this they view themselves as "real people," and their faith, in which they had been baptized by their Orthodox parents, is already of little interest to them.[237]

In addition, the above-mentioned gap, which grew between Creoles and Dena'ina, existed only in Kenai; available sources do not say anything about such a deep division in other Dena'ina villages. Moreover, in such remote villages as Iliamna both the Creoles and Dena'ina segments continued to live together and to practice the Orthodox faith. It also might be suggested that during the temporary decline of the formal institutions of the Russian Church after 1917, when they had to take more control over their chapels and religious life in general, the Dena'ina came to view Orthodoxy as their own native church.

Kenai Missionaries Among the Ahtna Indians

Although this documentary collection primarily deals with the clerics' activities among the Dena'ina, we cannot separate this work from attempts to proselytize among the "Mednovtsy" (Ahtna) Indians,[238] the "Kenaitze's" neighbors. Beginning with Hegumen Nikolai, almost all missionaries stationed in Kenai were interested in spreading their activities to the "Mednovtsy," this Native American group. Yet the results of the clerics' work among the Ahtna were hardly noticeable despite the "Mednovtsy's" desire to establish a dialogue with Orthodoxy. Below I will briefly outline a few possible motives that drove the Ahtna to seek baptism.

Unlike the Dena'ina, until the 1890s the Ahtna had little direct access to trading posts. For this reason, they had either to use the services of Dena'ina middlemen traders or to descend from their mountains to exchange furs for Russian and later for American merchandise. Prior to 1867 Russians did make random attempts to penetrate "Mednovtsy" country. Between the 1820s and 1850 there even existed a tiny trading post called Mednovskaia *odinochka*, which worked on an irregular basis and became the only evidence of Russian presence in Ahtna country. In 1850 the post was populated with one Russian (Andreian Ponomarev, a townsman from Tver city), eleven Creoles, one Dena'ina woman along with fourteen Ahtna living in its vicinity.[239] The meager Russian presence made the fate of the entire trade with the Ahtna entirely depended on their benevolence and disposition. Unfortunately, activities of some of the RAC employees did not help to establish mutually peaceful relations between the Ahtna and Russians. Especially harmful was Serebrennikov's expedition. While exploring the Ahtna country, Serebrennikov provoked a conflict with the Ahtna and became its victim.[240]

In all fairness, the Ahtna themselves were not eager to let the Russians establish direct trade relations with inland Athabaskan groups. In this case, their role as trade mediators would have been reduced. This might partially explain why the "Mednovsty" kept on preventing newcomers from establishing a permanent settlement in their country. At the same time, the Ahtna eagerly traded with the Russians by descending to Knik or southward to the mouth of the Copper River to Konstantinovsky redoubt. Such attitude made the status of the Mednovskaia *odinochka* very shaky. When in 1850 the starving northern Ahtna raided the *odinochka* and took all food provisions from its manager, the post was abandoned and trade relations with the Ahtna were infrequent. Still, RAC tried to revive its presence in the Copper River area. In 1860 and 1862 the chief manager of the Russian colonies a few times pointed to the manager of the Konstantinovsky Redoubt to renew this trading. The renewal of the Mednovskaia *odinochka* became especially acute when the Knik trading post, where the "Mednovtsy" regularly traded with the RAC, was ordered to be abandoned in 1862.[241] In 1860 Furugel'm wrote to Grigoriev, the chief of the Konstantinovsky Redoubt, "I order that you immediately renew the Mednovskaia *odinochka* as soon as you receive confirmation from Mednovsky's *toions* that this *odinochka* will be safe from any attack of hostile savages."[242]

Because of the Ahtna sovereign status, RAC leadership sought to cultivate their partnership through regular presents, which were assigned to the Ahtna headmen each time, when a trade deal was successfully completed. It appears that there was a group of the natives in the vicinity of the *odinochka* that were interested in Russian goods and welcomed their advance. In 1861 eight Ahtna headmen, who helped RAC to rebuild the *odinochka*, to procure pelts for the RAC and to provide useful information about the Copper River area, were awarded by the goods at the expense of 500 rubles.[243] Moreover, some of them were employed by RAC on a regular basis from three to four months and received a salary of about thirty rubles.[244] Yet, on the whole, the Copper River residents were not exposed to intensive contact with Euroamericans until the end of the 1880s. The geography of Ahtna country including hardships of traveling by the Copper River partially might explain their weak contacts with the Russians and later with the Americans. It was hardly surprising that many Ahtna found it easier to trade in the Knik area. During these frequent trade trips to Knik the Ahtna depended on the hospitality of the Dena'ina in whose homes they stayed and whose meals they shared. Moreover, for some Russians, who lacked a detailed knowledge of the ethnic mosaic of the area, such contacts appeared as a blood link. For instance, the engineer Doroshin stressed that the Copper River natives maintained on a regular basis connections with "the Kenaitze, their fellow-tribesmen."[245] For missionaries such winter visits represented an excellent opportunity to expand evangelization to Ahtna country, which could not penetrate. It also might be assumed that Dena'ina, whose homes the Ahtna used for accommodations, acted as informal carriers of popular Orthodoxy.

Although the Ahtna could not insulate themselves from epidemic diseases, which devastated their villages, until the 1890s they were able to avoid the demoralizing effects of alcohol. It was hardly surprising that Russian stereotypes of the Ahtna were a mixture of praise of the "unspoiled" "Mednovtsy" nature and condemnation of their "savage" and "brutal" character. Stafeev, who frequently interacted with the Ahtna in Tyonek, said of them: "They are very tall and healthy people and very smart. It seems they do not have any special diseases. They like trading and never drink liquor. There are no beggars among them."[246]

Descending to Knik, Konstantinovsky Redoubt or sometimes to Tyonek and even St. Nicholas Redoubt the Ahtna interacted with Orthodox mixed-bloods and Dena'ina. Although the first recorded instance of the Ahtna's contact with Christianity took place in 1797, when Russian officer Dmitrii Tarkhanov tried to preach Orthodoxy to them,[247] available sources suggest that missionary work among the Copper Indians did not start until the 1850s. It seems that those Ahtna who were interested in the Russian trade adopted Orthodoxy to strengthen the relationships with the trading posts and Christian Dena'ina. It was obvious, for instance, in the behavior of Vasilii Tinal'tet, one of the Ahtna headmen. RAC wanted to make him a company's middleman in the Copper River country, the role he evidently adopted and successfully performed. In 1858 he and his fellow tribesmen sold a large number of furs to the company, for which RAC awarded him goods in the amount of twenty rubles. In the same year Tinal'tet adopted Orthodoxy, which was specially noted in the RAC documents.[248]

In 1851 the register of parishioners of the Kenai area prepared by Hegumen Nikolai for the first time mentioned forty-six Orthodox Ahtna men and thirty-six women.[249] However, Nikolai, as he explicitly stated himself, never visited Ahtna country, and the names that he listed in his confessional registers were most probably those Ahtna who visited the Knik area or St. Nicholas Redoubt, which, according to some Ahtna, was easier to reach than the Konstantinovsky Redoubt.[250] Throughout the 1850s and in the early 1860s the missionary constantly stressed in his confessional registers that he did not attempt not reach the Ahtna country because of the hardships of such a journey. Thus, in 1851 Nikolai wrote that he "did not visit the place yet, but they themselves descended in *baidarkas*." Moreover, in 1865 and 1867 Nikolai wrote that even the Mednovskaia *odinochka*, the closest locality where Russians occasionally traded with the Ahtna was inaccessible for him. "Those who know say that communication [with the *odinochka*] is almost impossible."[251] We also might suggest that those "Mednovtsy" whom the Hegumen baptized practiced few Orthodox rites by the 1880s. Stafeev indirectly pointed to this when he wrote, "It seems that there are baptized people among the Mednovtsy, but they apparently forgot Christianity. At least I did not see any Mednovtsy to make the sign of the cross while entering a house."[252]

Thus, we might explain the initial drive to accept Orthodoxy by the Ahtna's desire to strengthen reciprocal relationships both with the Dena'ina population and Russian/mixed-blood trade agents who worked at first for the RAC and then for the ACC. By the 1880s the Copper Indians had established close connections with trading posts in the Old Knik area and Tyonek. By the end of the nineteenth century "Mednovtsy" developed a taste for American merchandise. Thus, after an Ahtna Indian killed an ACC agent in Knik in 1886, his fellow-tribesmen approached Stafeev wishing to pay redemption money. The natives especially stressed that they were so used to tea, gunpowder, and other "white men's" merchandise that they did not want the Knik trading post to be closed.[253]

We also have evidence of how the Ahtna initiated requests for baptism during trade meetings. For example, in 1887 in Tyonek, Stafeev traded with three "Mednovtsy" natives,[254] two of whom, an old Indian, Bychanishta, and his young fellow tribesman, Kechigiugunuglin, asked the trader about the opportunity to accept baptism. Then in the evening of the same day the Ahtna again reminded Stafeev that "they want to accept baptism very much."[255] As a result, the next day, on December 15, 1887, Stafeev baptized these two natives and gave them new names, Pavel and Karp. Two Dena'ina from the Tyonek village, Pavel Shitachka and Karp [Nukhdichugin], acted as their godparents.[256]

Stafeev described in detail how he introduced these two Ahtna to Orthodoxy: "I baptized them at my home. After the baptism I took them to the chapel, showed them icons with images of major feasts, and explained to them the meaning of baptism, the Nativity and other feasts. I also spoke about and showed them the icon depicting martyr Nestor. The old man liked icons so much that he did not want to leave the chapel for a long time. He especially enjoyed looking at the images of the Savior and Kazan Mother of God. After this I treated them with tea and cakes [*prianiki*]. Then the Mednovtsy passionately thanked me for everything, first for the baptism, then for my talk in the chapel and finally for the tea and cakes. Yet, these two savages somehow had already learned quite enough earlier, specifically how to make the sign of the cross and even knew how to recite the prayer 'Glory to the Father, and to the Son, and to the Holy Spirit.'"[257]

Yet to reduce the Ahtna's interest in conversion to their trade goals might be too narrow an explanation. It seems that there were internal developments in their society that intensified the "Mednovtsy's" desire to start a dialogue with Orthodoxy at the end of the nineteenth century. By this time the Ahtna had entered a period of dramatic changes. Epidemic diseases and the beginning of American advances into Copper River country forced them to reassess their ideology and status in the changing social and economic environment. In 1886, a story spread about an Ahtna who died and, while his friends were making a coffin, was miraculously resurrected for only six days before "falling back asleep" again. During these six days this Ahtna Indian shared with his fellow-tribesmen a vision, in which an old man, a messenger from God, instructed the Ahtna to denounce shamanism and accept Orthodoxy. Moreover, the resurrected Indian assailed a shaman who happened to be nearby. The messenger of God supposedly asked the resurrected man to convey the following words to all shamans: "I would have said to you how you will be punished for your vocation, but you will not hear it from me. I will only say that you will face big trouble in the other world" and also "in the other world you will feel worse than others because you spoil people with your devil tools, force us to live and act in a bad manner."[258] The resurrected Indian then added that he "was raised just to tell people how they should live and that they should abandon all old things." Having delivered this message, the native instructed his friends to finish making his coffin.

We should also single out two other important elements of this vision. The old man who allegedly visited the above-mentioned Ahtna in his dream said that Ahtna country would soon shrink in size and expressed regret that people still did not accept baptism, which apparently could have prepared them for this calamity. Moreover, the messenger of God supposedly showed the old man a tiny piece left of Copper River country. Second, the old man stressed that all surrounding native peoples had already accepted Christianity, and in order to be saved the Ahtna also should follow the pattern. It appears that the vision and the events that followed demonstrate a response quite common among indigenous groups having to cope with expanding Euroamerican society. This spiritual encounter stirred a wide movement among the Ahtna, and in 1886 many of them were ready to go to Knik and Susitna in order to accept baptism.[259] More important, two years later the Ahtna, through Knik Dena'ina, sent a message to Mitropol'skii, an acting Kenai missionary, asking him to come and enlighten them about Orthodoxy.[260]

It appears that far from being a sudden revelation the "dead man's" prophesy fell on the ground that was already planted with the seeds of Orthodoxy. A year before, the above-mentioned miracle lieutenant Henry Allen, who visited the Ahtna, had already indicated that among the Ahtna there existed natives who were ready to bolster their traditional powers with new "spiritual medicine." According to Allen, an Ahtna "influential chief" named Nicolai [Nikolai] did not tolerate shamans and successfully competed with them by using new Orthodox spiritual medicine: "His power is supposed to come from the church (Greek), of which he is an apostle. He wears on a hat a Greek cross as talisman, and has a small quantity of paper and a pencil, with which he pretends to keep a record of all matters of importance to his people."[261] We also learn that natives in the lower part of Ahtna country believed in Nicolai's spiritual remedies: "Some have such confidence in his healing power as to send the garment of a sick child many miles to him in order that he may sleep on it."[262] This evidence suggests that Nicolai reinterpreted his role as a shaman, and in order to boost his healing skills he seems to have added Orthodox "medicine power" to the old one.

It is evident that the Russian Church decided to capitalize on this favorable situation. Yet navigation on the Copper River was dangerous and in general access to Ahtna country was difficult. Additionally, missionaries who usually visited northern Dena'ina villages in summer were not able to visit the Ahtna, who descended from mountains only in winter. This convinced clerics to extend their stays and to change the season for their visits. The Knik area, which the Ahtna visited more frequently, was selected as the major proselytizing center. Mitropol'skii became the cleric who for the first time since the 1850s encountered and baptized the Mednovtsy, which earned him praise from ecclesiastical authorities. Mitropol'skii had bought a house for $70 in Old Knik. It became a church property, and he stayed in this village during the winter of 1888–1889. In September of 1888, the missionary along with his reader, Creole Nikolai Sorokovikov, completed building the Knik chapel, started by local Indians, who earlier had erected the chapel walls. By the beginning of October Mitropol'skii was able to offer the Divine Liturgy at the new building.[263] The missionary reported that in that winter he baptized about eighty Ahtna.

Encouraged by this success, Vladimir Donskoi, Dean of Alaska Clergy, even considered moving the center of the mission from Kenai to Tyonek, Susitna, or

Knik,[264] but his project remained unfulfilled. Iaroshevich, who succeeded Mitropol'skii, similarly went to Old Knik, where he stayed for seven months during the winter of 1894–1895, but to his frustration the "catch" was only eighteen Ahtna. As the documents represented in this collection show, Iaroshevich reported that unexpectedly that winter fewer Ahtna visited Knik, which the missionary explained by the opening of new trading centers competing with Knik. His general prognosis of missionary work among this native group was pessimistic. At the same time, we should remember that the life of Iaroshevich in Old Knik was complicated by violent clashes with the local ACC agent A. Krisson, who harassed the priest and prevented him from expanding his missionary work.

Bortnovskii, who came to replace Iaroshevich, was more successful. Like both of his predecessors, this missionary decided to winter in the Knik area and again to introduce the "Mednovtsy" to Orthodoxy. So during the winter of 1897–1898 Bortnovskii stayed in so-called New Knik (Eklutna), to which the Dena'ina had removed their village and St. Nicholas chapel from Old Knik in 1897. Unlike Iaroshevich's account about attempts to proselytize among the Ahtna, Bortnovskii's narrative of his Eklutna experiences sounds very optimistic. Moreover, Bortnovskii tailored his notes not as a dull register of what he did on a daily basis, but as a travel sketch, which provides some information, although stereotyped, about the Ahtna culture, life, and customs and their first contacts with Americans.[265] Unfortunately, his missionary work and the Ahtna's own attempts to start a dialogue with Orthodoxy did not receive further support. Unlike Bortnovskii, who praised the new Knik chapel as the spearhead of the Ahtna Christianization, Shadura, his successor, assailed his predecessor for letting Indians maintain the Knik chapel in such, in his view, an inconvenient locality. In the summer of 1908 having landed in the Eklutna vicinity, he and his Dena'ina companions for three hours had to go through deep forest infected with mosquitoes, "which relentlessly beat us." This experience and a few natives he met in the vicinity of the chapel colored his impressions of the Knik area. He sounded like Iaroshevich and stressed that Eklutna was the most inconvenient locality not only for missionary activities, but even for regular church services. He mentioned that the Ahtna came here very rarely and that even Dena'ina visited the Eklutna area only in winter when hunting, insisting that the rest of the time the natives lived in the Knik town (Old Knik), which was conveniently located close to water and where they could get access to paid work and the store. In his view, the "chapel located deep in the woods" could not perform the designated goals. Shadura gathered local Indians and tried to convince them to move the chapel back to the Knik town. Although natives agreed with his suggestion and a local American judge also promised to help, the project never materialized. In the Knik town, where Shadura performed services for seventy natives residing in the town, he had to use a house of local American Episcopal priest as a temporary chapel.[266]

Although during this visit he did meet a few Ahtna in the Knik town, who came for a trade and even helped him to correct confessional registers, Shadura stressed that it was extremely hard to track them and some of them did not see a priest for ten or fifteen years. For instance, he mentioned a very old woman who came to Knik with her children to partake in sacraments twenty years after being baptized and receiving communion.[267] He continued to serve Ahtna during his next summer visit to the Knik area, where in addition to regular services, he consecrated a marriage between Maria Shiko, an Ahtna woman permanently residing in the Knik town, and Eric Larsen, a Scandinavian.[268] Shadura continued to mention Ahtna in his confessional rosters until 1919. After this, he wrapped up all missionary work among this native group and his registers for 1922 did not contain any names of the "Mednovsty."[269] A chronic lack of resources prevented clerics from establishing a permanent mission among the Ahtna. For the next twenty years all proselytizing work among the "Mednovtsy" became frozen and the names of the baptized Ahtna disappeared from the conversion rosters.[270]

We have little information about the status of Orthodoxy among the Ahtna in the first quarter of the twentieth century. Letters of Hieromonk Antonii, Dean of Alaska Clergy, do show that the Copper River natives continued to approach Russian clerics with requests to build chapels in their country, but again for financial reasons such requests did not receive a response. Later, in the 1930s, the Russian Church regenerated for a while its missionary work in Copper River country. Sketchy travel notes by the priest Povarnitsyn, who visited the Ahtna in the late 1930s, suggest that renewal of Orthodox work among the Ahtna was quite successful, and the initiative for contact again came from the "Mednovtsy" themselves. Moreover, by the 1930s the Ahtna had already built several Orthodox chapels in their country. The remains of one of them (in Copper Center) could be seen until the present day. Still, it appears that the Russian Church failed to provide adequate support for its own mission. Although the history of the Ahtna's contacts with the Russian church needs further research, to my knowledge, Orthodoxy, especially after all Ahtna chapels were destroyed in fires in the 1950s,[271] gradually lost its significance for their spiritual life being replaced by other Christian denominations. Middle-aged and young people do not know anything about this page in the Ahtna history. Moreover, many Ahtna who belong to the older generation and who had erected Russian Orthodox crosses on the graves of their deceased relatives could not explain the origin of this tradition. During my field trip to Ahtna country in summer of 2000 I saw native cemeteries where neglected and ruined old Ahtna Orthodox graves stood side by side with Protestant ones, which were well taken care of. This is a visible proof that, unlike the Dena'ina, Orthodox tradition did not take root in the Ahtna culture.

Missionary Records and Notes on the Translation

To make the records selected for this publication more accessible to readers who are unfamiliar with Orthodox terminology and the practices of the Russian Orthodox Church, at the end of this collection I have included a glossary. In working on the translation of the documents, whenever possible I have tried to provide a descriptive interpretation of some Orthodox terms, rites, and ceremonies. Thus, in Orthodoxy the faithful are to receive confession and communion at least once a year. Before they partake in this sacrament, the Orthodox have to perform the rites of contrition, penance, and fast, which are defined by the single word *govenie*. I translated the latter expression either using these three words or by the phrase, the "rites of preparation for communion." The Russian Orthodox Church also widely practices so-called *molebens*, which means short customary prayer services performed by a priest on various occasions, for instance before people undertake or complete some project or plan a long-distance trip. During a *moleben* a priest attempts to secure help of a saint. The present work describes this rite as a "customary prayer service." I do not think that understanding the other definitions will cause serious problems for the reader. For this reason I have avoided a detailed description of Orthodox Church services and doctrine. For those who are interested in learning the general history of the Russian Church, Nicolas Zernov's *The Russians and Their Church* will provide useful information.[272] Furthermore, an anonymous handbook prepared by a monk from St. Tikhon's Monastery provides a good description of Orthodox Church ceremonialism, feasts, and artifacts. For those desiring a short review of the Orthodox ritual cycle, the best reference is a sketch prepared by Lydia Black as a part of her translations of Iakov Netsvetov's journals.[273] A manual of Orthodox services prepared by Isabel F. Hapgood would give the English-speaking reader a good introduction to Russian church services and terminology as they existed at the turn of this century.[274]

The vocabulary Russian missionaries in Alaska used to define native people shows that Russian clerics made little distinction between the ways of "American savages" and Siberian "savage" culture. A number of definitions, such as *toion*, used by missionaries as the name for both Native American and native Siberian chiefs; *barabora*, the name for a native dwelling that originated in Kamchatka; or *inorodtsy*, a generic definition for native peoples in Russian borderlands; and many other terms suggest that the early Orthodox missionaries generalized about Alaskan natives, drawing on the earlier missionary legacy of encounters with Siberian natives. Incidentally, the expression *inorodtsy* I translated as "natives," which unfortunately does not exactly convey its meaning, "of a different kin." Occasionally, in the late nineteenth century missionaries also used the expression *tuzemtsy*, which in Russian literally means "natives." Clerics rarely applied to the Dena'ina and Ahtna the term "Indians," so characteristic of Anglo-American usage, which indiscriminately attached it to both Native American Indians and the Sugpiaq and Yupik people and even to the Chukchi natives, residents of northeastern Siberia. To be exact, in his travel journals Hieromonk Nikita once did define the Dena'ina as "half-Indians." Yet, it was only Shadura who increasingly started using the expression "Indians" in the 1920s and 1930 under the influence of his long-time residency in the United States. However, he still widely used the old *inorodtsy*.

Reading these records, we should also remember that the greater part of them were designated as formal reports and letters composed by persons for whom such writing was simply one of their formal duties. In their journals missionaries recorded the daily life of their parishioners and reported on the progress of their proselytizing activities and about chapel and brotherhood financial activities. Ecclesiastical authorities accumulated such records and later used them for compiling general reports for the Holy Synod in St. Petersburg, then the supreme authority in the Russian church. It is not surprising that the authors of these documents attempt to present a picture of the missionaries' success among the natives.

Another thing that strikes a scholar about the clerics' travel journals is the impersonal character of the narratives, along with their monotony and repetition.[275] Not only do these narratives frequently omit the names of church assistants and native headmen who helped missionaries, but they also refer to priests themselves in the third person: "the missionary pointed to them" or "they do not listen to the missionary," or "the priest instructed the Kenaitze." These documents are also overburdened with the wordy metaphors Russian missionaries often used in addressing their superiors. These phrases evidently reflect a strict church hierarchy along with Orthodox concern with humility. In addition to the common "Your Grace," the Russian Orthodox code of address perpetuated such elaborate forms of address as "The Most Honorable Father," "Your Most Reverence," "Humbly kneeling in front of Your Grace, our merciful Father and Archpriest," or at the end of letters and reports: "Your most humble servant," "I have an honor to be Your humble servant (novice)," or "we, unworthy people." The hierarchy of the church is especially evident in missionary requests and petitions, which were routinely wrapped in such elaborate phraseology.

Missionaries usually prepared their records (travel journals and formal reports) in several versions, sometimes different from one another. Moreover, the text of some of these narratives was revised for full or partial publication in missionary periodicals. In addition to travel journals, clerics were obliged to keep separate records of their church services. The latter are very repetitive and served to demonstrate that a cleric followed the requisite sequence of the Orthodox cycle and services. Unlike travel journals, the church service records do not provide much material for a historian or an anthropologist. Yet, some missionaries did not distinguish between travel and church service journals and mixed both formats, especially when they stayed away from Kenai for a long time. For instance, Iaroshevich wrote the notes about his winter stay in Old Knik in the form of a church service journal. In a similar manner, his travel journals that describe his trips to other "Kenaitze's" settlements were not separated from church service records.

The hardest part of preparation of this publication was retrieval of records belonging to the first Kenai missionary, Hegumen Nikolai. Although I have all his confessional rosters, I was not able to locate his journals for the years between 1844 and 1857. My only hope is that some future researcher will have more luck in this search. Yet, we can chronicle relatively well his activities from 1858 to 1864. I found out that his journals for 1858–1862 had been published in Russia as part of a compendium of other priestly writings, *Tvoreniia sviatikh ottsov v russkom perevode*, and later had been even reproduced as a separate print out in 1863. In this edition the traditional sequence characteristic of missionary journals, where events are recorded day by day, is partially broken and the attempt was made to turn the journals into a more consistent narrative. The Alaska Church Collection (Library of Congress), however, contains manuscripts of Nikolai's journals for the same years, and these maintain the daily sequence. Moreover, in the Russian Historical Archive in St. Petersburg (RGIA) we find Nikolai's journals for 1863 and 1864,[276] where again the daily sequence of events was broken. It appears that these two records represent digests prepared by church authorities in Sitka to be sent to the Holy Synod. Comparison of these two journals with the daily journals for the same years written in the Hegumen's own hands shows that both versions omitted some events. My approach in preparing this publication was to merge two versions in one narrative to present Nikolai's activities as fully as possible.

A few excerpts from travel journals of some Kenai missionaries (Hegumen Nikolai, Bortnovskii, Hieromonk Nikita) were translated into English between 1936 and 1938 as part of the Alaska Historical Research Project, which was left uncompleted with the death of its editor and translator, T. I. Lavrischeff.[277] In 1974 anthropologist Joan Townsend edited and published these translated materials. Recently, another anthropologist, Galina Dzeniskevich, a student of Athabaskan ethnohistory, reproduced RGIA versions of Nikolai's records for a Russian publication. Moreover, a few other researchers have translated excerpts from Bortnovskii's travel notes related to Seldovia and Eklutna, historical Dena'ina villages.[278] The present publication continues the work started by all these scholars. It represents the first attempt to bring together all major Orthodox records related to the Dena'ina and Ahtna, which have not yet been published and translated.

Notes

1. About the definition of Dena'ina: Dena'ina means "people." Until recently ethnohistorical literature used the name "Tanaina," which is the anglicized version of "Dena'ina." As James Kari stresses, Dena'ina themselves, especially those who read and write this language, prefer the latter term. James Kari, "Preface," in *Dena'ina Noun Dictionary*, Comp. by James Kari (Fairbanks, AK: Alaska Native Language Center, University of Alaska, 1977), 1. Yet in the Lower Inlet area, especially in the Kenai area, where Dena'ina were more exposed to European influences from the very beginning, some Dena'ina call themselves "Kenaitze," the definition that Russians gave to this tribal group. The latter is an interesting example of how an ethnic group tries to distinguish itself from outsiders and develops self-awareness by using alien definitions.

2. Sava Stephan, a Tyonek elder and church warden, Mary Conrad Center, Anchorage, AK, interview by author, July 12, 1998.

3. Hannah Breece, *A School Teacher in Old Alaska*, ed. with commentary by Jane Jacobs (New York: Random House, 1995), 131.

4. Cornelius Osgood, *Ethnography of the Tanaina* (New Haven: Human Relations Area Files Press, 1976), 173.

5. Karen Standifer, a Tyonek resident, Tyonek, AK, interview by author, July 15, 1998.

6. For more on the Dena'ina culture, see Cornelius Osgood, *Ethnography of the Tanaina* (New Haven, CT: Human Relations Area Files Press, 1976); Robert E. Ackerman, *The Kenaitze People* (Phoenix, AZ: Indian Tribal Series, 1975); James Arthur Fall, "Patterns of Upper Tanaina Leadership, 1741–1918" (Ph.D. diss., University of Wisconsin, Madison, 1981); Joan B. Townsend, "Ethnohistory and Culture Change of the Iliamna Tanaina" (Ph.D. diss., University of California, Los Angeles, 1965); idem, "The Tanaina of Southwestern Alaska: A Historical Synopsis," *Western Canadian Journal of Anthropology*, no. 2 (1970): 2–16; Linda J. Ellanna and Andrew Balluta, *Nuvendaltin Quhttana: The People of Nondalton* (Washington, DC: Smithsonian Institution Press, 1992).

7. Ioann Bortnovskii, "Kenaiskaia missiia (istoriko-statisticheskoe opisanie)," *Russian-American Orthodox Messenger* 2, no. 18 (1898): 531.

8. Townsend, "Ethnohistory and Culture Change of the Iliamna Tanaina," 99.

9. Idem, "Tanaina of Southwestern Alaska," 7–8; Osgood, *Ethnography of the Tanaina*, 73–75.

10. James W. VanStone, *Athapaskan Adaptations: Hunters and Fishermen of the Subarctic Forests* (Chicago: Aldine Publishing Company, 1974), 125; Townsend, "Tanaina of Southwestern Alaska," 8, 15.

11. VanStone, *Athapaskan Adaptations*, 8; Townsend, "Tanaina of Southwestern Alaska," 8; Ackerman, *Kenaitze People*, 27; Ellanna and Balluta, *Nuvendaltin Quhttana*, 58.

12. Ellanna and Balluta, *Nuvendaltin Quhttana*, 268–271.

13. Osgood, *Ethnography of the Tanaina*, 169.

14. Galina I. Dzeniskevich, *Atapaski Aliaski: ocherki materialnoi i dukhovnoi kultury: konets XVIII–nachalo XX v.* (Leningrad: Nauka, 1987), 82; Ackerman, *Kenaitze People*, 48; Osgood, *Ethnography of the Tanaina*, 181.

15. Osgood, *Ethnography of the Tanaina*, 177.

16. Townsend, "Ethnohistory and Culture Change of the Iliamna Tanaina," 305, 308; Ackerman, *Kenaitze People*, 48.

17. Osgood, *Ethnography of the Tanaina*, 177–179; Townsend, "Ethnohistory and Culture Change of the Iliamna Tanaina," 302, 303.

18. Dzeniskevich, *Atapaski Aliaski*, 81.
19. Ake Hultkrantz, *Native Religions of North America: The Power of Visions and Fertility* (San Francisco: Harper & Row, 1987), 21.
20. Osgood, *Ethnography of the Tanaina*, 180.
21. Andrei V. Grinev, *Indeitsy Tlinkity v period Russkoi Ameriki (1741–1867)* (Novosibirsk: Nauka, 1991), 101; Katerina Solovjova and Aleksandra Vovnyanko, "The Rise and Decline of the Lebedev-Lastochkin Company: Russian Colonization of South Central Alaska, 1787–1798," *Pacific Northwest Quarterly* 90, no. 4 (1999): 195.
22. Dmitrii Maksutov, "Ob obozrenii otdelov kolonii, November 5, 1865," Records of the Russian-American Company, 1802–1867 (hereafter cited as RRAC) (Washington, D.C.: National Archives, 1942), microfilm (77 reels), roll 65, vol. 47, l. 115.
23. Grinev, *Indeitsy Tlinkity v period Russkoi Ameriki*, 101; Solovjova and Vovnyanko, "The Rise and Decline of the Lebedev-Lastochkin Company," 199.
24. L. A. Sitnikov, "Materialy dlia istorii Russkoi Ameriki ("Otvety" Filippa Kashevarova)," in *Novie materialy po istorii Sibiri dosovetskogo perioda*, ed. N. N. Pokrovskii (Novosibirsk: Nauka Sibirskoe otdelenie, 1986), 101.
25. Petr Tikhmenev, *A History of the Russian-American Company* (Seattle: University of Washington Press, 1978), 96.
26. Alice J. Lynch, *Qizhjeh: The Historic Tanaina Village of Kijik and the Archeological District* (Fairbanks: Anthropology and Historic Preservation Cooperative Park Studies Unit, University of Alaska, 1982), 7.
27. I borrowed this neat metaphor from Thomas M. Barrett, "Lines of Uncertainty: The Frontiers of the Northern Caucasus," in *Imperial Russia: New Histories for the Empire*, ed. Jane Burbank and David L. Ransel (Bloomington and Indianapolis: Indiana University Press, 1998), 148–173.
28. Solovjova and Vovnyanko, "The Rise and Decline of the Lebedev-Lastochkin Company," 195–196, 198, 202.
29. Stepan Voevodskii "Gospodinu praviteliu Kadi'akskoi kontory, October 30, 1854," RRAC, roll 60, vol. 35, l. 143.
30. Vladimir Stafeev, "Ubienie russkikh v Tuinoke," Vladimir Vasiliev Stafeev Papers, 1869–1895, Alaska State Historical Library, Juneau, l.1-4; Voevodskii "Gospodinu pravitelu Kadi'akskoi kontory," l. 141.
31. Andrei V. Grinev, "Torgovo-promyslovaia deiatelnost Rossiisko-Amerikanskoi kompanii v 1825–1849 g.g.," in *Istoriia Russkoi Ameriki, 1732–1867: Russkaia Amerika: ot zenita k zakatu, 1825–1867* (Moskva: Mezhdunarodnie otnosheniia, 1999), vol. 3: 55, 81.
32. Stepan Voevodskii, "Kadi'akskoi kontore otnositel'no namereniia kolchan napast' na Nikolaevskii redut, November 11, 1859," RRAC, roll 62, vol. 41, l. 55ob.–56.
33. Ivan Furugel'm, "Kadi'akskoi Kontore, November 1, 1862," RRAC, roll 64, vol. 44, l. 105.
34. Idem, May 14, 1864, RRAC, roll 64, vol. 46, l. 30.
35. Ivan Furugel'm, "Ispolni'aushchemu dolzhnost' upravl'aushchego Nikolaevskim redutom Zazubovichu, September 27, 1860," RRAC, roll 63, vol. 42, l. 159ob; idem, "Naznachennomu upravl'iaushchim Nikolaevskago reduta Stafeevu, June 2, 1864," roll 64, vol. 46, l.42.
36. Dmitrii Maksutov, "V glavnoe pravlenie ob obozrenii otdelov kolonii, November 5, 1865," RRAC, roll 65, vol. 47, l.116
37. Idem, "Pravitel'u Kadi'akskoi kontory, June 23, 1866," RRAC, roll 65, vol. 48, l. 131ob, 132; idem, "V glavnoe pravlenie, September 23, 1866," RRAC, roll 65, vol. 48, l.77.

38. Grinev, "Torgovo-promyslovaia deiatelnost Rossiisko-Amerikanskoi Kompanii," 41–42.

39. Ivan Furugel'm, "Upravl'aushchemu Mikhailovskim redutom Vakhrameevu, May 2, 1860," RRAC, roll 63, vol. 42, l. 54.

40. Idem, "Ispolni'aushchemu dolzhnost' upravli'aushchego Nikolaevskim redutom Zazubovichu," l. 159ob.

41. Grinev, "Torgovo-promyslovaia deiatelnost Rossiisko-Amerikanskoi Kompanii," 41–42.

42. A definition for native leaders introduced by the Russian in Siberia and Alaska. In a dialect of a Siberian native group Sakha (Yakut) this word means "leader."

43. Ivan Furugel'm, "Kadi'akskoi kontore, October 14, 1864," RRAC, roll 64, vol. 46, l. 60ob.

44. Nikolai Rozenberg, "Korpusa gornikh inzhenerov poruchiku P. Doroshinu, April 20, 1851," RRAC, roll 57, vol. 32, 145ob. This was a Dena'ina band known as Tsaht'ana, which means "rock/cliff people." James Kari and Priscilla Russel Kari, *Dena'ina Elnena/Tanaina Country* (Fairbanks, AK: Alaska Native Language Center University of Alaska, 1982), 27.

45. Stepan Voevodskii, "Gospodinu pomoshniku glavnago pravitel'ia kolonii kapitanu pervogo ranga i kavaleru A. I. Rudakovu, May 16, 1856," RRAC, roll 61, vol. 37, l. 110.

46. Idem, "Grazhdanskamu inzheneru Furugel'mu, May 27,1855," RRAC, roll 60, vol. 36, l. 67. Incidentally, in the 1850s at the St. Nicholas Redoubt a similar fund reached fifty rubles each year. Idem, "Upravl'iaushchemu Nikolaevskim redutom Borisovu, July 26, 1857," RRAC, roll 61, vol. 38, l. 188.

47. *Zakazchik* was a definition introduced by the Russians in Alaska to describe assistants to indigenous chiefs (*toions*). *Zakazchiks* were responsible for hunting and fishing and for the economic well-being of their communities in general.

48. Stepan Voevodskii, "Praviteli'u Kadi'akskoi kontory, October 29, 1856," RRAC, roll 61, vol. 37, l. 192ob; Ivan Furugel'm, "Kadi'akskoi kontore, May 8, 1862," RRAC, roll 64, vol. 44, l. 70ob; Dmitrii Maksutov, "Upravl'iaushchemu Nikolaevskim redutom Stafeevu, June 6, 1865," RRAC, roll 65, vol. 47, l. 164ob.

49. Rozenberg, "Korpusa gornikh inzhenerov poruchiku P. Doroshinu," 145ob.

50. Ivan Furugel'm, "V glavnoe pravlenie, November 30, 1860," RRAC, roll 63, vol. 42, l.195ob.

51. For more about the Ahtna-Russian relations during the period of Russian presence, see Andrei V. Grinev, "On the Banks of the Copper River: The Ahtna Indians and the Russians, 1783–1867," *Arctic Anthropology* 30, no. 1 (1993): 54–66.

52. Ivan Furugel'm, "Byvshemu upravl'iaushchemu Nikolaevskago reduta Borisovu o nagrade toionam i zakazchikam, July 5, 1860," RRAC, roll 63, vol. 42, l.125ob.

53. Idem, "Upravl'iaushchemu Mikhailovskim redutom Stepanovu, May 5, 1864," RRAC, roll 64, vol. 46, l. 25ob.

54. Aleksandr Iaroshevich, "Putevoi Zhurnal Kenaiskago Missionera Sviashchennika Aleksandra Iaroshevicha," *Pravoslavnyi blagoviestnik*, no. 20 (1894): 186; Stafeev, "Diary, Tyonek, February 13/25, 1885."

55. Ioann Bortnovskii, "Iz putevogo zhurnala sviashchennika Kenaiskoi missii I. Bortnovskago za 1898-ii god," *Russian-American Orthodox Messenger* 3, no. 19 (1899): 513; Ioann Bortnovskii to Hieromonk Anatolii, "Pochtitel'neishii raport, September 19, 1896," Alaska Russian Church Archives Records, 1733–1938 (hereafter cited as ARCA) (Washington, DC: Library of Congress), microfilm (376 reels), roll 181, box D263.

56. Vladimir Stafeev, "Korabl'-chelovek: Kenaiskii rasskaz, Tyonek, February 23, 1886," Vladimir Vasiliev Stafeev Papers.

57. Fall, "Patterns of Upper Tanaina Leadership, 1741–1918," 82.

58. Ioann Bortnovskii, "Zimovka pravoslavnago missionera v Kenaiskom selenii Knik," *Russian-American Orthodox Messenger* 2, no. 20 (1898): 583.

59. Louise Potter, *A Study of a Frontier Town in Alaska, Wasilla to 1959* (Vt.: Thetford Center, 1963), 7, 10; Fall, "Patterns of Upper Tanaina Leadership, 1741–1918," 98.

60. Although scholars have frequently used this definition to describe people of mixed-blood origion, it is not correct. This group indeed was composed predominantly of the offspring of the mixed-blood marriages. Yet the Creole category hardly said anything about the ethnic origin of a person. For example, Russian-Dena'ina, Dena'ina-Aluet/Sugpiaq or Russian-Aleut/Sugpiaq equally could be defined as Creoles. In certain cases, when the situation demanded, a native could be defined as a Creole. The Creole status defined the degree of integration of native Alaskans into the RAC system and was equal to that of a burgher, townsman, in metropolitan Russia. The level of education to which Creoles were entitled under the Russian regime often determined their position in the administrative sector, with Russians sometimes serving in subordinate positions. Lydia Black, "Creoles in Russian America," *Pacifica* 2, no. 2 (1990): 142–155.

61. "Ispovedal'naia rospis' Kenaiskoi missii za 1847," and "Reestr nalichnykh dush prinadlezhashchikh k Kenaiskoi tserkvi k 1851-mu godu," ARCA, roll 196, box D291; "Spisok o privivanii koroviei ospennoi materii po Nikolaevskomu redutu Kenaiskoi missii d'iachkom Makariem Ivanovim c iunia 4 dnia 1862 goda," ARCA, roll 201, box D299.

62. John Branson, ed. *Lake Clark-Iliamna, Alaska, 1921: The Travel Diary of Colonel A. J. Macnab* (Anchorage: Alaska Natural History Association, 1996), 101.

63. Ellanna and Balluta, *Nuvendaltin Quhtana*, 233–234.

64. Fall, "Patterns of Upper Tanaina Leadership, 1741–1918," 97.

65. "Register-obyski, 1904-1909," ARCA, roll 192, box D284.

66. Branson, *Lake Clark-Iliamna, Alaska, 1921*, 91, 94–95.

67. For more about the early history of Orthodoxy in Alaska, see Lydia Black, *Orthodoxy in Alaska* (Berkeley, CA: Patriarch Athenagoras Orthodox Institute, 1999), 3–55.

68. See more about this story: Lydia Black, "The Daily Journal of Reverend Father Juvenal," *Ethnohistory* 28, no. 1 (1981): 33–58; Michael Oleksa, "The Death of Hieromonk Juvenal," *St. Vladimir's Theological Quarterly* 30, no. 3 (1986): 231–268.

69. Vladimir Donskoi, "Otchet o sosto'ianii tserkvei i chasoven Kenaiskoi, Kadi'akskoi i Bel'kovskoi za 1893-ii god," ARCA, roll 201, box D299.

70. "Svidetel'stvo no. 719 and 720, November 1852," RRAC, roll 58, vol. 33, l. 485–485ob.

71. "Klirovaia viedomost' o tserkviakh, sviashchennosluzhitel'iakh i prikhozhanakh Kenaiskoi missii za 1854-ii god," ARCA, roll 192, box D284.

72. "Ispovedal'naia rospis' Kenaiskoi missii za 1847," ARCA, roll 196, box D291.

73. It should be remembered, however, that Savva who lived in Iliamna had a younger brother. For some reason, the latter, who resided most of the time in St. Nicholas Redoubt, carried the same name. In confessional rosters they were registered as Savva 1 and Savva 2. Therefore, sometimes it is hard to say which Savva provided Nikolai his services in each specific case.

74. "Zhurnal, vypiski iz zhurnalov i otchet o deistviakh missionerov v seleniakh Rossiisko-Amerikanskoi kompanii v 1862-1865," Russian State Historical Archive, St. Petersburg (Rossiiskii gosudarstvennii istoricheskii arkhiv) (hereafter cited as RGIA), f. 796, ed. khr. 445, d. 58, l. 1–6, 27–28ob.

75. "Klirovaia viedomost' o tserkviakh, sviashchennosluzhitel'iakh i prikhozhanakh Kenaiskoi missii za 1854-ii god," ARCA, roll 192, box D284.

76. "Klirovaia viedomost' o tserkviakh, sviashchennosluzhitel'iakh i prikhozhanakh Kenaiskoi missii za 1849-ii god," ARCA, roll 192, box D284.

77. "Report of Bishop Innokenty to the Holy Ruling Synod, no. 153, January 31, 1845" and "Report of Bishop Innokenty to the Holy Ruling Synod, Novo-Arkhangelsk, November 28, 1852," Documents Relative to the History of Alaska (hereafter cited as DRHA) (Fairbanks, AK: University of Alaska, Alaska History Research Project, 1936–1938), microfilm (11 reels), roll 1, vol. 1, 354–356.

78. Hegumen Nikolai, "Kenaiskoi missii raport, July 22, 1857," ARCA, roll 20, box B19.

79. "Kopiia ispovedal'noi rospisi Kenaiskoi missii za 1847-ii god," ibid., roll 196, box D291; "Viedomost' skolko kakova zvaniia prikhozhan Kenaiskoi missii nalichnikh v 1851-om godu," ibid., roll 196, box D292.

80. Ivan Furugel'm, "Kadi'akskoi kontore, March 30, 1864," RRAC, roll 64, vol. 45, l. 5.

81. For more about this short and very frustrating interlude in his missionary career, see Sergei Kan, *Memory Eternal: Tlingit Culture and Russian Orthodox Christianity Through Two Centuries* (Seattle and London: University of Washington Press, 1999), 160–163.

82. "Ukaz Novoarkhangel'skoi dukhovnoi konsistorii no. 13, March 16, 1866," ARCA, roll 20, box B19.

83. Dmitrii Maksutov, "Upravl'iaushchim Nikolaevskim redutom Stafeevu, March 16, 1866," RRAC, roll 65, vol. 48, l. 21ob.

84. "Dukhovnoe zaveshchanie igumena Nikolaia, 13 February, 1867," Michael Z. Vinokouroff Papers, Alaska State Historical Library, Juneau, box 23, folder 33.

85. Donskoi, "Otchet o sosto'ianii tserkvei i chasoven."

86. V. Vechtomov to Metropolitan Isidor, October 10/22, 1883, RGIA, f. 796, op. 205, 1878-1883, ed. khr. 467, l. 32ob.

87 . Donskoi, "Otchet o sosto'ianii tserkvei i chasoven."

88. [Untitled], Kenai Peninsula, Conversion Reports, Shamanism, Nikita Marchenkov, 1883, ARCA, roll 182, box D264.

89. Hieromonk Nikita, "Pokorneishee proshenie, August 28/September 9, 1885," ARCA, roll 19, box B18.

90. Stafeev, "Diary, Tyonek, July 10/22, 1885,"

91. Petr Dobrovol'skii, "Raport v Aliaskinskoe dukhovnoe pravlenie," January 4/16, 1887," ARCA, roll 19, box B18.

92. Archbishop of Warsaw Nikolai, *Iz moego dnevnika: putevyia zamietki i vpechatlieniia po Aliaski i Aleutskim ostrovam* (St. Petersburg: Synodalnaia Tip., 1893), 75; for more details on the biography of Mitropol'skii and his activities in Sitka, see Kan, *Memory Eternal*, 196–201, 239–242, 581.

93. "Posluzhnoi spisok sviashchennika Nikolaiia Mitropol'skago," Michael Z. Vinokouroff Papers, box 23, folder 18; Nikolai Mitropol'skii, "Vipiska iz klirovoi viedomosti Aleksandra Nevskago kafedral'nago sobora v San Franscisco za 1885-ii god," ARCA, roll 20, box B19; Nikolai Mitropol'skii to Bishop Vladimir, February 26, 1891, Ibid.

94. Nikolai Mitropol'skii, "Kniga dlia zapisi prisoedinivshiksiia k pravoslaviiu iz inovercheskikh khristianskikh ispovedanii i prosveshchennikh sv. khreshcheniem nekhristian, dannaia iz Amerikanskago dukhvonago pravleniia pritchu Kenaiskoi Uspenskoi tserkvi na 1888-oi god," ARCA, roll 182, box D265; Donskoi however indicates that Mitropol'skii converted eighty-eight Ahtna. Donskoi, "Otchet o sosto'ianii tserkvei i chasoven."

95. Aleksandr Iaroshevich to Vladimir Donskoi, January 29, 1893, ARCA, roll 13, box B9.

96. "Svidetelstvo no. 107, Kholmskaia dukhovnaia seminariia, February 6, 1888," ARCA, roll 13, box B9.

97. "Formuli'arnii spisok sviashchennika Kenaiskoi Uspenskoi missionerskoi tserkvi otsta Aleksandra Iaroshevicha," Michael Z. Vinokouroff Papers, box 23, folder 15; Hieromonk Nikolai to Vladimir Donskoi, Dean of Clergy of Sitka District, January 12/24, 1893 and Bishop Vladimir to Alaska Ecclesiastical Consistory, October 22, 1890, ARCA, roll 13, box B9.

98. Nikolai, *Iz moego dnevnika*, 72.

99. Hieromonk Anatolii to Bishop Nikolai, August 11/23, 1896, ARCA, roll 13, box B9.

100. I do not expand here on Bortnovskii's biography and his activities. For more details, see: Andrei A. Znamenski, "Native Culture Through Orthodox Eyes: Russian Missionary Ioann Bortnovskii on the Dena'ina and Ahtna, 1896–1907," *Alaska History* 13, no. 1–2 (1998): 1–26.

101. "Kenai, o pritche oznachennoi tserkvi," Michael Z. Vinokouroff Papers, box 23, folder 9.

102. Pavel Shadura, "Klirovaia viedomost' Kenaiskoi sviato-Uspenskoi tserkvi za 1927, 1928 i 1929 godi," ARCA, roll 193, box D286.

103. Vladimir Modestov to Bishop Nikolai, July 4, 1897, ARCA, roll 21, box B20.

104. "Klirovaia viedomost' o sviashchenno-tserkovnosluzhitel'iakh Nushagakskoi missii Petropavlovskoi tserkvi za 1878-ii god," ARCA, roll 144, box D203; Nikolai, *Iz moego dnevnika*, 48.

105. "Viedomost' Nushagakskoi missionerskoi Petropavlovskoi tserkvi s pokazaniem prinadlezhashchikh k onoi molitvennikh domov, selenii, razstoianie selenii i molitvennikh domov ot tserkvi pri kakom ozere ili reke i skol'ko zhitelei po natsionalnostiam za 1878-ii god," ARCA, roll 144, box D204; Vasilii Shishkin to Bishop Nestor, April 24, 1882," ARCA, roll 149, box D216.

106. Antoinette Shalkop, "The Travel Journal of Vasilii Orlov," *Pacific Northwest Quarterly* 68, no. 3 (1977): 134

107. "Klirovaia viedomost' o sviashchenno-tserkovnosluzhitel'iakh Nushagakskoi missii Petropavlovskoi tserkvi za 1878-ii god," ARCA, roll 144, box D203.

108. Nikolai, *Iz moego dnevnika*, 48.

109. "Viedomost' Petropavlovskoi tserkvi nakhodiashcheisia v Nushagakskoi missii za 1895-ii god," ARCA, roll 144, box D204; "Vladimir Modestov, stavlennicheskii dopros," ibid., roll 21, box B20.

110. Vladimir Modestov to Bishop Nikolai, July 4, 1897, ibid., roll 21, box B20.

111. "Viedomost' Petropavlovskoi tserkvi nakhodiashcheisia v Nushagakskoi missii za 1895-ii god," and "Viedomost' Petropavlovskoi tserkvi nakhodiashcheisia v Nushagakskoi missii za 1896-ii god," ibid., roll 144, box D204.

112. Vladimir Modestov to Bishop Nikolai, July 4, 1897, ibid., roll 21, box B20.

113. Ibid.

114. "Viedomost' o tserkvi sviatikh apostolov Petra i Pavla, Nushagakskoi missii pri reke Nushagak v Aleksandrovskom redute na materike poluostrova Aliaske Aleutskoi eparkhii za 1910-ii god," ibid., roll 144, box D205.

115. "Viedomost' o prikhozhanakh po plemenam Kuskokvimskoi missii za 1914," ibid., roll 171, box D246.

116. Some of the descendants of these people still consider Orthodoxy their own faith and have Orthodox Churches like, for example, a modern-day Athabaskan (Kolchan) Orthodox community in the Nikolai village. For more about this community, see: Mira Bergelson, "V kraiu pravoslavnikh indeitsev," *http://www.prof.msu.ru/book/articles2.htm*.

117. Incidentally, the journals of priest Iakov Netsvetov, published by Lydia Black, provide an extensive coverage of the first period of activities of the Orthodox among these

Athabaskan groups. Lydia Black, ed. and transl., *The Journals of Iakov Netsvetov: The Yukon Years, 1845–1863* (Kingston, Ontario: The Limestone Press, 1984).
118. "Klirovaia viedomost' Kuskokvimskoi missii na 1902 god," St. Herman's Theological Seminary Archive, Kvikhpakh Mission, Church Registers (Viedomost' o tserkvi), box 4, folder 5, l. 12, 14.
119. "Viedomost' o tserkvi za 1910 god," "Viedomost' o tserkvi za 1917 god pri Kuskokwimskoi missii," and "Tserkovnaia viedomost' za 1914 god pri Kuskokwimskoi missii," ARCA, roll 170, box D246.
120. Donskoi, "Otchet o sosto'ianii tserkvei i chasoven."
121. V. Vechtomov, "Missionerskaia deiatel'nost v Aleutskoi eparkhii za 1881 god and pervuiu polovinu 1882 goda," RGIA, f. 796, op. 205, 1878–1883, ed. khr. 467, l. 39.
122. Ibid., l. 51ob–53.
123. "Pogreshnosti amerikanskoi statistiki: chislennost pravoslavnago naseleniia Aliaski," *Russian-American Orthodox Messenger* 2, no. 9 (1898): 290.
124. Pavel Shadura, "Bogosluzhebnii zhurnal Kenaiskoi sviato-uspenskoi tserkvi na 1908-ii god," ARCA, roll 194, D289, l. 96.
125. Idem, "Bogosluzhebnii zhurnal vidannii iz Severo-Amerikanskago dukhovnago pravleniia pritchu Kenaiskoi tserkvi na 1910-ii god, no. 16," roll 194, box D290, l. 55, 57; "Viedomost' o tserkvi za 1932-ii god," ibid., roll 193, box D286.
126. For more about Stafeev and his Tyonek diary, see Richard Pierce, "Tyonek in the 1880s: from the Diary of V.V. Stafeev," in *Adventures Through Time: Readings in the Anthropology of Cook Inlet, Alaska*, ed. Nancy Yaw Davis and William E. Davis (Anchorage, AK: Cook Inlet Historical Society, 1996), 175-179.
127. Stepan Voevodskii, "Upravli'aushchemu Nikolaevskim redutom Borisovu, July 26, 1857," RRAC, roll 61, vol. 38, l. 187ob.
128. Bortnovskii, "Iz putevogo zhurnala sviashchennika Ioanna Bortnovskago za 1901-ii god," 263; idem: "Putevoi Zhurnal Sviashchennika Ioanna Bortnovskago za 1902 God," 224; idem: "Putevoi zhurnal sviashchennika Ioanna Bortnovskago za 1900-ii god, Kenai, Aliaska," 321; Ioann Bortnovskii to Arkhimandrite Anatolii, "Pochtitel'neishii raport, August 20, 1897," ARCA, roll 181, box D263.
129. "O pritche oznachennoi tserkvi, Pavel Shadura," Michael Z. Vinokouroff Papers, box 23, folder 9.
130. Nikolai Mitropol'skii to Bishop Nikolai, September 7, 1892, ARCA, roll 201, box D299.
131. "Metrichskoi knigi na 1849 god chasti pervoi ob umershikh, otdelenie vtoroe o pogrebennikh bez sviashchennika," ibid., roll 349, box F52.
132. "Reestr nalichnikh dush prinadlezhashchikh k Kenaiskoi tserkvi k 1851-mu godu"; Vladimir Modestov to Bishop Nikolai, July 4, 1897, ibid., roll 21, box B20.
133. Vladimir Modestov, "Bogosluzhebnii zhurnal, from July 17, 1894 to June 30, 1895," ibid., roll 149, box D216.
134. Breece, *A School Teacher in Old Alaska*, 99.
135. Branson, *Lake Clark-Iliamna*, 104.
136. A. Olarovskii to Nikolai Sorokovikov, July 16, 1886, ARCA, roll 30, box B34.
137. "Viedomost' o tservi za 1911" ibid., roll 193, box D286, l. 13.
138. Ioann Bortnovskii, "Bogosluzhebinii zhurnal no. 984, January 1, 1897–December 31, 1897," ibid., roll 193, box D288, l. 37, 38.
139. Idem, "Bogosluzhebinii zhurnal no. 752, January 1, 1898–December 31, 1898," ibid., roll 194, box D288, l. 38.

140. Idem, "Bogosluzhebinii zhurnal no. 367, January 1, 1900–December 31, 1900," ibid., roll 194, box D288, l. 16–17.
141. Hieromonk Nikita to Bishop Nestor, April 15/27, 1882, ibid., roll 182, box D268.
142. Aleksandr Iaroshevich to Vladimir Donskoi, August 2, 1893, ibid., roll 201, box D299.
143. Bortnovskii, "Kenaiskaia missiia," 531.
144. Aleksei Ivanov to Ioann Bortnovskii, "Nizhaishee proshenie, July 28, 1896," ARCA, roll 203, box D302.
145. Sava Stephan, a Tyonek elder and churchwarden, Mary Conrad Center, Anchorage, AK, interview by author, July 12, 1998.
146. Ioann Bortnovskii to Hieromonk Anatolii, September 27, 1896 and Ioann Bortnovskii to Bishop Innokentii, May 20, 1907, ARCA, roll 182, box D264.
147. Modestov, "Bogosluzhebnii zhurnal, from July 17, 1894 to June 30, 1895."
148. Breece, *A School Teacher in Old Alaska*, 126, 151–152.
149. Ellanna and Balluta, *Nuvendaltin Quhtana*, 299.
150. Hegumen Nikolai [Militov], *Vipiska iz zhurnala Kenaiskago missionera igumena Nikolaia s 1858 po 1862 god* [Reprint from *Pribavlenie k tvoreniiam sviatikh ottsov* 22, no. 4 (1863): 463–492] (Moskva, n.p., 1863), 11.
151. Ivan Barsukov, ed., *Pisma Innokentiia, mitropolita Moskovskago i Kolomenskago. 1828–1878* (St. Petersburg: Sinodalnaia tipografiia, 1897), vol. 1, 371.
152. More about origin of these brotherhoods see in Constantance J. Tarasar and John H. Erickson, eds., *Orthodox America, 1794–1976: Development of the Orthodox Church in America* (Syosset, NY: Department of History and Archives, Orthodox Church in America, 1975), 113–117.
153. Missionary sources usually shorten the name of this society as Kenai Holy Protection Brotherhood (Kenaiskoe sviato-pokrovskoe bratstvo).
154. "Oprosnii list o sostoaianii tserkvi i prikhoda Aliaskinskoi territorii za 1925 god, Kuskokwimskaia missiia," St. Herman's Theological Seminary Archive, Kuskokwim Mission, Church Registers, box 4, folder 9, l. 2.
155. J. C. Castner "A Story of Hardship and Suffering in Alaska," *Compilation of Narratives of Explorations in Alaska*, 56th Congress, 1st Session, Senate, Report no. 1023 (Washington, DC: Government Printing Office, 1900), 703.
156. V. Vechtomov to Mitropolit Isidor, 30 October 1879, RGIA, f. 796, op. 205, 1878-1883, ed. khr. 467, l. 15ob.
157. Bortnovskii, "Bogosluzhebnii zhurnal na 1906 god," ARCA, roll 194, box D288.
158. Konstantin Pavlov, "Bogosluzhebnii zhurnal za 1904 god," St. Herman Theological Seminary Archives, Kuskokwim Mission, Journal of Worship Service, 1898–1907, box 5, folder 5, l. 20, 22.
159. Shadura, "Bogosluzhebnii zhurnal Kenaiskoi sviato-uspenskoi tserkvi na 1908-ii god," l. 80, 82.
160. "Viedomost' o tservi za 1911," ARCA, roll 193, box D286, l. 11.
161. The Indians learned moonshining from the Russians, which they started to define by a Russian word, "makula." Yet, vodka was described by a native word "tahna'ina milna." Kari, *Dena'ina Noun Dictionary*, 222.
162. Hieromonk Anatolii, "Iz otcheta o poezdke dlia blagochinnoi revizii prikhodov Kenaiskago, Kadi'akskago, Afognakskago i Nuchekskago letom tekushchago goda 1898," *Russian-American Orthodox Messenger* 3, no. 3 (1899): 94.
163. Ioann Bortnovskii, "Bogosluzhebinii zhurnal no. 752, January 1, 1898–December 31, 1898," ARCA, roll 194, D288, l. 55.

164. Shadura, "Bogosluzhebnii zhurnal vidannii iz Severo-Amerikanskgo dukhovnago pravleniia pritchu Kenaiskoi tserkvi na 1910-ii god, no. 16," l. 58–59.
165. Shadura, "Bogosluzhebnii zhurnal Kenaiskoi sviato-uspenskoi tserkvi na 1908-ii god," l. 70.
166. Stafeev, "Tyonek, January 1/13, 25/6, 16/28 1886, January 31/12, 1887."
167. Aleksandr Iaroshevich, "Putevoi zhurnal Kenaiskago missionera sviashchennika Aleksandra Iaroshevicha," *Pravoslavnyi blagoviestnik*, no. 19 (1894): 123.
168. Ioann Bortnovskii to Antonii, March 12, 1901, ARCA, roll 201, box D302, l. 1–3.
169. Ioann Bortnovskii, "Bogosluzhebnii zhurnal na 1901-ii god," ibid., roll 194, box D288, l. 9.
170. Ironically, Stafeev's record did not look spotless either. As Hegumen Nikolai journals show he was far from a social drinker.
171. Stafeev, "Tyonek, April 27/8, 1887."
172. Patricia Herlihy, *Strategies of Sobriety: Temperance Movement in Russia, 1880–1914*, Kennan Institute for Advanced Russian Studies, Occasional Paper no. 238 (Washington, DC: Woodrow Wilson International Center for Scholars, 1990), 7–8.
173. "Pravila Kenaiskago Sviato-nikolaevskago obshchestva trezvosti, February 22, 1906," ARCA, roll 181, box D263.
174. "Spisok Sv. Nikolaevskago obshchestva trezvosti v Seldevskom selenenii," ARCA, roll 202, box D300.
175. "Protokoly zasedanii Sviato-nikolaevskago obshchestva trezvosti," ibid., roll 181, box D263.
176. Shadura, "Bogosluzhebnii zhurnal Kenaiskoi sviato-uspenskoi tserkvi na 1908-ii god," l. 70.
177. Shadura, "Bogosluzhebnii zhurnal vidannii iz Severo-Amerikanskago dukhovnago pravleniia pritchu Kenaiskoi tserkvi na 1910-ii god, no. 16," l. 56
178. Ivan Furugel'm, "Kadi'akskoi kontore, May 11, 1862," roll 64, vol. 44, 75ob.
179. Iegumen Nikolai [Militov], "Iz zhurnala Kenaiskogo missionera igumena Nikolaia, Nikolaevskii redut, 1863 god," in *Russkaia Amerika: po lichnym vpechatleniiam messionerov, zemleprokhodtsev, moriakov, issledovatelei i drugikh ochevidtsev* (Moskva: Mysl, 1994), 236.
180. Idem, "Iz zhurnala Kenaiskogo missionera igumena Nikolaia, Nikolaevskii redut, 1862 god," ibid., 232.
181. Ivan Barsukov, ed., *Tvoreniia Innokentiia, mitropolita Moskovskago i Kolomenshago* (Moskva: Synodalnaia tipografiia, 1887), vol. 2, 488
182. Vasilii Shishkin to Bishop Nestor, "Nizhaishii raport, April 24, 1882," ARCA, roll 149, box D216.
183. Vladimir Modestov to Aleksandr Kedrovskii, June 29, 1895, ibid.
184. Pavel Shadura to Bishop Aleksandr, "Kratkii otchet o sostoianii prikhoda Kenaiskoi missii za 1920 god," February 7, 1921, ibid., roll 201, box D299.
185. Lynch, *Qizhjeh*, 10, 76; Andrew Balluta, "The Dena'ina of Kijik and Lake Clark National Park and Preserve," in *Russia in North America*, ed. Richard P. Pierce (Kingston, Ontario: The Limestone Press, 1990), 41.
186. Frederica De Laguna, *The Archaeology of Cook Inlet, Alaska* (Philadelphia: University of Pennsylvania Press, 1934), 138.
187. Pavel Shadura, "Klirovaia viedomost' Kenaiskoi Sviato-uspenskoi tserkvi za 1927, 1928 i 1929 godi," ARCA, roll 193, box D286.

188. Hieromonk Anatolii, "Iz puteshestviia po Aliaske v 1896 g. blagochinnago missionera ieromonakha Anatoliia," *Russian-American Orthodox Messenger* 1, no. 11 (1897): 208.
189. Pavlov, "Bogosluzhebnii zhurnal za 1904 god," l. 21.
190. "Viedomost' ob Uspenskoi tserkvi Aleutsko-aliaskinskoi eparkhii Kenaiskoi missii chto v selenii sv. Nikolaevskom za 1881-ii god," ARCA, roll 192, box D284.
191. "Viedomost' o Kenaiskoi missionerskoi tserkvi vo imia Uspeniia Bozhei materi chto v Kenaiskom zalive za 1893-ii god," ibid., roll 192, box D285.
192. "Viedomost' o tserkvi sviatikh apostolov Petra i Pavla Nushagakskoi missii, chto pri reke Nushagak v Aleksandrovskom redute, na materike poluostrova Aliaska Aleutskoi eparkhii za 1910-ii god," ibid., roll 144, box D205; "Viedomost' Nushagakskoi missionerskoi Petropavlovskoi tserkvi s pokazaniem prinadlezhashchikh k onoi molitvennikh domov, selenii, razstoianie selenii i molitvennikh domov ot tserkvi pri kakom ozere ili reke i skol'ko zhitelei po natsionalnostiam za 1878-ii god," ibid., roll 144, box D204. At the same time, in one of his journals Modestov indicated that Riktorov laid down the chapel as early as 1871 (Vladimir Modestov, "Bogosluzhebnii zhurnal za 1895-ii god, no. 181, July 1894 to June 1895," ibid., roll 149, box D216); yet, it also might be a slip of a pen because all other mission registers point to 1877.
193. "Viedomost' o Kenaiskoi missionerskoi tserkvi vo imia uspeniia Bozhei materi, chto v Kenaiskom zalive za 1893-ii god," and for 1894, ibid., roll 192, box D285.
194. Aleksandr Iaroshevich to Vladimir Donskoi, August 2, 1893, ibid., roll 201, box D299. Yet, in his church register for 1893 Iaroshevich reported that the chapel was built in 1891. "Viedomost' o Kenaiskoi missionerskoi tserkvi vo imia uspeniia Bozhei materi, chto v Kenaiskom zalive za 1893-ii god." It appears that later the residents of this small village, numbering only twelve Dena'ina, moved the village site to another place and in 1905 built a new chapel. Bortnovskii, "Bogosluzhebnii zhurnal na 1905 god," ibid., roll 194, box D288, l. 33.
195. "Viedomost' o tserkvi sviatikh apostolov Petra i Pavla v Aleksandrovskom redute na materike Aliaske za 1894-ii god," ibid., roll 144, box D204. This information contradicts earlier suggestions that the Kijik Church was built between 1877 and 1881 or in 1884. Lynch, *Qizhjeh*, 60.
196. "Viedomost' o Kenaiskoi missionerskoi tserkvi vo imia uspeniia Bozhei materi, chto v Kenaiskom zalive za 1893-ii god," ARCA, roll 192, box D285.
197. "Kuskokwim, Viedomost' o tserkvi za 1910-ii god," ibid. , roll 170, box D246.
198. Pavlov, "Bogosluzhebnii zhurnal za 1904 god," l. 20; Konstantin Pavlov to Aleksandr Kedrovskii, the Dean of Clergy, March 30, 1902, ibid., roll 171, box D246.
199. Joan Townsend, "Journals of Nineteenth Century Russian Priests to the Tanaina: Cook Inlet, Alaska," *Arctic Anthropology* 11, no. 1 (1974): 15–17, 23.
200. Ioann Bortnovskii, "Bogosluzhebinii zhurnal no. 984, January 1, 1897–December 31, 1897," ARCA, roll 193, box D288, l. 44; Ioann Bortnovskii, "Putevoi zhurnal sviashchennika Ioanna Bortnovskago za 1900-ii god, Kenai, Aliaska," *Russian-American Orthodox Messenger* 5, no. 17 (1901): 366. For more on Bloch and his role as a philanthropist, see Susan Woodward Springer, *Seldovia, Alaska: An Historical Portrait of Life in Zaliv Seldevoe/Herring Bay* (Littleton, CO: Blue Willow, 1997), 75–76, 78, 80, 86, 100–101.
201. Ioann Bortnovskii, "Putevoi zhurnal sviashchennika Ioanna Bortnovskago za 1902-ii god," *Russian-American Orthodox Messenger* 7, no. 13 (1903): 224; "Register-obyski, 1904–1909," ARCA, roll 192, box D284.
202. Pavlov, "Bogosluzhebnii zhurnal za 1904 god," l. 22.
203. Lynch, *Qizhjeh*, 80.

204. Vera Shevzov, "Chapels and the Ecclesial World of Prerevolutionary Russian Peasants," *Slavic Review* 55, no. 3 (1997): 607, 588, 609, 612.
205. Ioann Bortnovskii, "Iz Putevogo zhurnala sviashchennika Ioanna Bortnovskago za 1901-ii god," *Russian-American Orthodox Messenger* 6, no. 12 (1902): 265.
206. Sava Stephan, a Tyonek elder and churchwarden, Mary Conrad Center, Anchorage, AK, interview by author, July 12, 1998.
207. Aleksandr Iaroshevich to Vladimir Donskoi, Dean of Clergy, August 2, 1893, ARCA, roll 201, box D299.
208. Ioann Bortnovskii "Putevoi zhurnal sviashchennika Ioanna Bortnovskago za 1899-ii god, Kenai, Aliaska," *Russian-American Orthodox Messenger* 4, no. 9 (1900): 182.
209. Vladimir Modestov, "Tserkovno-istoricheskoe opisanie Nushagakskoi missii Aleutskoi eparkhii," *Russian-American Orthodox Messenger* 1, no. 15 (1897): 304.
210. Nikifor Amkan, "Bogosluzhebnii zhurnal za 1916 god," St. Herman's Theological Seminary Archive, Kvikhpakh Mission, Parish Records, l. 60-61.
211. Pavel Shadura to Mikhail Andreadi, Dean of Clergy, April 25, 1913, ARCA, roll 201, box D299.
212. Ioann Bortnovskii, "Putevoi zhurnal sviashchennika Ioanna Bortnovskago za 1900-ii god, Kenai, Aliaska," *Russian-American Orthodox Messenger* 5, no. 16 (1901): 339.
213. Bortnovskii, "Bogosluzhebnii zhurnal na 1906 god," l. 35.
214. Pavel Shadura, "Bogosluzhebnii zhurnal Kenaiskoi sviato-uspenskoi tserkvi za 1912-ii god," ibid., roll 194, box D290, l. 43.
215. "V Aliaskinskoe dukhovnoe pravlenie zhitelei vsego Kenaiskago zaliva proshenie," May 20, 1878," ibid., roll 182, box D266.
216. Stafeev, "Tyonek, January 5/17, 1888."
217. Idem, "Tyonek, January 12/24, 1888."
218. Konstantin Pavlov to Aleksandr Kedrovskii, the Dean of Clergy, March 30, 1902, ARCA, roll 171, box D246.
219. Stafeev, "Tyonek, July 3/15, 1886."
220. Hieromonk Nikita to Bishop Nestor, April 15, 1882, ARCA, roll 201, box D300; Hieromonk Nikita , "Iz putevikh zapisok Kenaiskago missionera ieromonakha Nikiti za 1881 g.," ibid.; [Untitled] Kenai Peninsula, Conversion Reports, Shamanism, Nikita Marchenkov, 1883, ibid., roll 182, box D265.
221. [Untitled], Kenai Peninsula, Conversion Reports, Shamanism, Nikita Marchenkov, 1883; Townsend, "Journals of Nineteenth Century Russian Priests to the Tanaina," 12.
222. "Bogosluzhebnii zhurnal, vidannii pritchu Nikolaevskoi tserkvi, chto v Kenaiskoi missii na 1879-ii god, no. 22, September 14, 1883," ARCA, roll 193, box D287.
223. Hieromonk Nikita to Bishop Nestor, April 15, 1882; "Report of Hieromonk Nikita of Kenai to the Alaska Ecclesiastical Consistory," May 28, 1884, DRHA, roll 1, vol. 1, 357.
224. Sava Stephan, a Tyonek elder and churchwarden, Mary Conrad Center, Anchorage, AK, interview by author, July 12, 1998.
225. Stafeev, "Tyonek, March 14/26 and 15/27, 1887."
226. Idem, "Tyonek, December 1884–January 1885."
227. Aleksandr Iaroshevich, "Putevoi zhurnal Kenaiskago missionera sviashchennika Aleksandra Iaroshevicha," *Pravoslavnyi blagoviestnik*, no. 19 (1894): 120–121.
228. Townsend, "Ethnohistory and Culture Change of the Iliamna Tanaina," 308.
229. Shadura, "Bogosluzhebnii zhurnal vidannii iz Severo-Amerikanskago dukhovnago pravleniia pritchu Kenaiskoi tserkvi na 1910-ii god, no. 16," l. 56; idem, "Pokhodnii zhurnal,1915–1916," Lydia Taradonova, Personal Collection, Kenai, AK, l. 191.

230. Idem, "Bogosluzhebnii zhurnal vidannii iz Severo-Amerikanskago dukhovnago pravleniia pritchu Kenaiskoi tserkvi na 1910-ii god, no. 16," l. 63.
231. Kari, *Dena'ina Noun Dictionary*, 187, 234–235, 251
232. A. J. McClanahan, ed., *Our Stories, Our Lives: A Collection of Twenty-Three Transcribed Interviews with Elders of the Cook Inlet Region* (Anchorage, AK: CIRI Foundation, 1986), 68.
233. Kan, *Memory Eternal*, 237, 549.
234. "Klitovaia viedomost' za 1927–1929," ARCA, roll 193, box D286.
235. "Viedomost' o tserkvi, za 1932," ibid., roll 193, box D286.
236. Pavel Shadura, "Klirovaia Viedomost' Kenaiskoi Sviato-Uspenskoi Tserkvi za 1927, 1928 i 1929 Godi," ARCA, roll 193, box D286 and idem: "Pokhodnii zhurnal po missii, April 6, 1915-August 4, 1916," Lydia Taradonova, Personal Collection, l. 192-193.
237. *Russian-American Orthodox Messenger* 43, no. 10 (1947): 157.
238. The Ahtna Indians received their Russian nickname "Mednovsty" (literal translation is "Copper People") from the copper deposits, rumors of which reached the Russians.
239. "Reestr nalichnykh dush prinadlezhashchikh k Kenaiskoi tserkvi k 1851-mu godu"; "Klirovaia viedomost' o sviashchenno-tserkovnosluzhiteliakh Kenaiskoi Missii za 1851-ii god," ARCA, roll 192, box D284.
240. For more about this episode, see: P. P. Doroshin, "Iz zapisok, vedennikh v Russkoi Amerike," *Gornii zhurnal* 1, no. 3 (1866): 378–381.
241. Ivan Furugel'm, "Kadi'akskoi kontore, November 1, 1862," roll 64, vol 44, l. 105–105ob.
242 Idem, "Upravl'iaushchemu Konstantinovskim redutom Grigorievu, July 14, 1860," RRAC, roll 63, vol. 42, l. 129.
243. Ibid., 143ob–144.
244. Doroshin, "Iz zapisok, vedennikh v Russkoi Amerike," 384–385.
245. Ibid., 383, 389.
246. Vladimir Stafeev, "Mednovtsy," Vladimir Stafeev Papers, l.1.
247. A.V. Grinev, "The Forgotten Expedition of Dmitrii Tarkhanov on the Copper River," *Alaska History* 12, no. 1 (1997): 8.
248. Nikolai Rozenberg, "Upravli'aushchemu Konstantinovskim redutom otnositel'no rastorzhki s Mednovtsami, December 4, 1852," RRAC, roll 58, vol. 33, 563; Ivan Furugel'm, "Kadi'akskoi kontore, November 12, 1858," ibid., roll 62, vol. 39, l. 147ob.; Grinev, "On the Banks of the Copper River," 62.
249. "Ekstrakt o chisle prikhozhan Kenaiskoi missii," ARCA, roll 196, D292.
250. Stepan Voevodskii, "Kadi'akskoi kontore o rastorzhke v Mednoi odinochke, November 18, 1857," RRAC, roll 61, vol. 38, l. 144.
251. See "Klirovaia viedomst' o sviashchenno-tserkovnosluzhitel'iakh Kenaiskoi missii za 1851," and also for 1865 and 1867, ARCA, roll 192, box D284.
252. Vladimir Stafeev, "Mednovtsy," Vladimir Vasiliev Stafeev Papers, l. 2.
253. Idem, "Tyonek, January 13/25, 1886."
254. The trade agent called them "mountain range people" (*khrebtovskie*).
255. Stafeev, "Tyonek, December 14/26, 1887."
256. "Kniga dlia zapisi prisoedinivshiksiia k pravoslaviiu iz inovercheskikh khristianskikh ispovedanii i prosveshchennikh sv. khreshcheniem nekhristian, dannaia iz Amerikanskago dukhvonago pravleniia pritchu Kenaiskoi Uspenskoi tserkvi, 1887–1889," ARCA, roll 182, D265, l. 3.
257. Stafeev, "Tyonek, December 15/27, 1887."
258. Idem, "Tyonek, March 16/23, April 3/15, 1886."

259. Idem, "Tyonek, April 16/23, 1886."
260. Nikolai Mitropol'skii, "V Aliaskinskoe dukhovnoe pravlenie ispolniaushchego dolzhnost Kenaiskago missionera sviashchennika Nikolaiia Mitropol'skago raport, July 22/August 3, 1888" and also for March 1889, ARCA, roll 201, D299.
261. Henry T. Allen, *Report of an Expedition to the Copper, Tanana, and Koyukuk Rivers in the Territory of Alaska, in the Year 1885* (Washington, DC: GPO, 1887), 135.
262. Ibid., 136.
263. Nikolai Mitropol'skii, "V Aliaskinskoe dukhovnoe pravlenie ispolniaushchego dolzhnost Kenaiskago missionera sviashchennika Nikolaiia Mitropol'skago raport, March 1889."
264. Vladimir Donskoi to Aleksandr Iaroshevich, July 29, 1893, ARCA, roll 182, D268.
265. See the translation of this sketch in Znamenski, "Native Culture Through Orthodox Eyes," 9–14.
266. Pavel Shadura, "Bogosluzhebnii zhurnal Kenaiskoi sviato-uspenskoi tserkvi na 1908-ii god," l. 60, 55, 57, 61.
267. Ibid., 59, 62–63.
268. Pavel Shadura, "Bogosluzhebnii zhurnal Kenaiskoi sviato-uspenskoi tserkvi za 1911-ii god," ARCA roll 194, D290, l. 33. "Register-Obyski, 1904–1909," ARCA, roll 192, box D284.
269. "Klirovaia viedomost' Kenaiskoi Sviato-uspenskoi tserkvi za 1922-ii god," ibid., roll 193, box D286.
270. Pavel Shadura, "O prikhozhanakh oznachennoi tserkvi, 1927–1929," ARCA, roll 193, box D286.
271. From the information provided to the author by Dr. Lydia Black, July 8, 1999, and Dr. James Kari, July 11, 1999.
272. Nicholas Zernov, *The Russians and Their Church* (Crestwood, NY: St. Vladimir's Seminary Press, 1994).
273. Lydia Black, "Introduction," in Iakov Netsvetov, *The Journals of Iakov Netsvetov: The Atkha Years, 1824–1844*, trans. Lydia Black (Kingston, Ontario: The Limestone Press, 1980), xxviii–xxxiii.
274. Isabel F. Hapgood, *Service Book of the Holy Orthodox-Catholic Apostolic Church* (Englewood, NJ: Antiochian Orthodox Christian Archdiocese of North America, 1996).
275. Shalkop, "The Travel Journal of Vasilii Orlov," 132.
276. "Zhurnal, vipiski iz zhurnalov i otchet o deistviakh missionerov v seleniakh Rossiisko-amerikanskoi kompanii v 1862–1865 g.g.," RGIA, f. 796, op. 445, ed. Khr. 58, l. 6ob–11ob, 29–32ob.
277. Those documents that have been translated are available on microfilm: *DRHA*, 7 reels.
278. Townsend, "Journals of Nineteenth Century Russian Priests to the Tanaina," 17–23; Andrei A. Znamenski, "Through Orthodox Eyes." The translations prepared by Katherine Arndt, Sergei Chulaki, and Mina Jacobs were incorporated by Susan Springer in her book on the history of the Seldovia community from ancient times to the present. Springer, *Seldovia, Alaska*, 71–98.

CHAPTER ONE

Hegumen Nikolai (Nikolai Militov)

Report of Hegumen Nikolai to His Grace, the Most Reverend Innocent, Bishop of Kamchatka, the Kuriles and the Aleutians, Cavalier, September 13, 1850[1]

CONCERNING ORDER 132 issued by the Ecclesiastical Consistory on December 1849, I have the honor to inform You that since my arrival at Kenai the church has successfully established itself among the local people. The number of its parishioners grew due to the number of newly baptized people. On the whole, natives here became more enlightened. The piety of the people increases as word of the gospel reaches them. Before the missionary came to the Kenaitze, these people were wild, rude, treacherous, vengeful, superstitious, and devoted to shamanic customs. Nowadays, thank God, all these things, which earlier were so dear to the Kenaitze, are almost eradicated from their memory. Moreover, they have almost abandoned their native dances, which should make ashamed those enlightened peoples who still view dancing as an acceptable amusement.

The Kenaitze are very diligent in church services and regularly attend them. When the missionary visits distant villages, their residents with zeal and piety hurry to attend each service. Moreover, many Kenaitze complain that I rarely visit them, and even become upset. They join in the holy mysteries with reverence and fear so characteristic of Christian true believers. This attitude is widespread among all parishioners except distant tribes. Because the missionary rarely visits them, the latter still have not reached the necessary stage of piety as have their other fellow tribesmen. On the whole, nearby Kenaitze zealously fulfill their Christian duties of fast and penance each year. When the missionary visits them, distant Kenaitze also readily fulfill their Christian duties. I did not see anybody who rejected or opposed partaking in holy sacraments.

One certainly cannot expect from these natives a deep knowledge of the basics of holy truth, although many of them already know enough. The Kenaitze know many prayers, and learn them from each other. To their credit, many Kenaitze express a desire to sing in church and like to chant hymns. I encourage them to do this by praising this desire. When the missionary has free time, he himself teaches them prayers. The rest of the time they teach each other. If priests approach them gently and kindly, the Kenaitze treat clergy with respect and show their reverence. But if one is only strict and demanding with them, they soon become cold and unfriendly. There is nothing strange here. All people will express the same attitude in such situations.

Charity has not yet developed here very much. It might be my own mistake. I taught them little principles of Christian charity, because I was afraid to overburden these adolescents in faith and make it difficult for them to follow their Christian duties. Incidentally, the Kenaitze themselves praise mutual charity. If a Kenaitze native has something to share and you ask him about it, he will never refuse you. Moreover, a Kenaitze tries to make sure to help you before you even ask about it. Without any invitation he supplies a needy person with everything, from a piece of meat to decent clothing. Among them, to have a reputation as a stingy person is a great shame. A native will rather remain himself half-naked than be stingy.

Humble novice of Your merciful archpastoral Grace, Kenai missionary, Hieromonk Nikolai.

A Note About Some Activities of the Kenai Missionary Nikolai (from 1853 to the Half of 1857) and Incidents That Happened with Him[2]

The place of missionary work of Hegumen Nikolai is the Kenai Peninsula[3] with surrounding islands, with the headquarters at the St. Nicholas Redoubt, which is located at Kenai Bay. The peoples who populate the Kenai Peninsula partially belong to the Aleutian tribe and partially to the American tribe and reside mostly at the seacoast because fish is their major source of food, and sea hunting and fishing are their major occupations. It is only for a time that some of them leave for the mountains of the peninsula to hunt so-called *iamans* (wild goats) whose meat supplements in winter their major food—fish.

In order to visit his parishioners to propagate the word of God, each year the missionary sails by *baidarkas* along the peninsula seacoast and through the currents that separate surrounding islands. He stops in major settlements scattered along the seacoast and islands and gathers together residents from other neighboring villages for the performance of church ministrations and instruction. The communication of the missionary with his parishioners scattered around this wide area is difficult. For this reason, the missionary sometimes cannot visit all members of his flock even once a year. Under these circumstances, it is hard for the missionary to strengthen among Christian natives the appropriate principles of Christian life. To succeed in this, he would have to supervise them constantly, to watch and instruct them when they show their ignorance and expose it if he noticed resistance. And besides, all missionary instructions are frequently weakened by the inappropriate activities of the Russians who work for the company. In one entry for 1853 the missionary noted that since the time the Russians settled in Kenai the morality of the Kenaitze has apparently declined. In 1856 having visited the Coal Mining [Mountain] Expedition, he made the following remark: "I would not like to have this expedition in my parish. Since I am not in a position to change the situation, I would like at least to see the church and the missionary headquarters removed to this locality. Provided a good example and active work, the shepherd shall be able to some extent to keep this noisy crowd from moving to the abyss [*gibelnogo puti*]. Yet, this work will be better performed not by myself, but by some educated shepherd who is a teacher in his mindset. Maybe in this case the Kenaitze and Chugach will retain their modesty and good behavior. Otherwise, all good new sprouts might perish from bad examples."

Sometimes, not only by their behavior, but also by issued orders some of the company's employees might unintentionally harm missionary efforts. Thus, on December 30, 1856, the missionary writes in his journal, "I performed a service, but not many Kenaitze faithful participated simply because the visiting faithful have no place to stay. Earlier they could be accommodated in a large barrack, but to my deep regret the present manager[4] turned this barrack into a storage area. Those company employees who lived here have recently been removed to a different place, which is so small that it hardly can accommodate the company workers themselves. For this reason the Kenaitze from distant villages stopped coming to pray to God. I trust the Lord will excuse them because it is not their fault or laziness. Kenai's severe weather is hard to survive, not only for women with small children, but even for adult men.

Yet, missionary instructions sometimes produce a favorable effect. Thus, during his visit to the Coal Mining Expedition in 1855, he made the following remark: "Reluctantly I had to stay in the Coal Mining Expedition. I did not want to stay there because the expedition employees live in lust and sin. Their head told me that they have to bring women by necessity for there is nobody to do sewing and cleaning. Yet, I refused to perform ministrations for them before they agree to send away all women. Thank God, the head of the expedition followed my advice and all women were moved to the Aleksandrovsk settlement. Although the expedition workers grumble at me [*zlosloviat menia*] in protest, I do not care what they say, for I serve God's cause."

Here is another example, even more remarkable. The same manager who denied the Kenaitze who came to church services accommodation in the redoubt and harassed the missionary for the priestly reminding [*uveshchevania*] concerning the manager's inappropriate behavior, finally showed sincere repentance. The missionary relates this episode: "The dream of the manager. He dreamed of the church and a certain old man approaching him. Together they went to church. It is hard to imagine how wonderful it was. The manager wanted to come in, but the old man pushed him aside: 'You are not allowed to come here because you offend your priest. Go and ask him to forgive you, for you have not many years to live.' In his dream the manager visited me, bowed to the ground and asked for forgiveness, but I supposedly pushed him aside with irritation. Yet he started pleading even more persistently and I forgave and blessed him. After this the manager went to his coffin and lay there, after which he woke up. The next day he had another dream. In this dream some people were cutting his neck and sides with knives and repeated, 'Look how stubborn he is, he does not want to ask for forgiveness.' He promised to ask for forgiveness immediately and again woke up. In the morning, not in his dream, but in real life he came to me, knelt down, related his dreams and asked for forgiveness. According to him, it was I who showed him the true way and he promised that he would respect and thank me for this. On my part, with all my heart I thanked the Lord for bringing to reason this unreasonable man and sincerely forgave him. I also ask the Lord to send me some instructions too." In his letter to his Grace, the missionary indicates that the manager now lives in a good manner and the others, observing him, have also improved their behavior. I am very glad of this change in his character and wish that he retains this change."

Because of the lack of opportunity to keep all native Christians under appropriate supervision and the unfavorable influence of Russians on native morality, it is not surprising that some native Christians sometimes violate the rules of Christian behavior. Thus, in his journal the missionary recorded three incidents of illicit connections, which he attempted to stop, once unsuccessfully and two times successfully: "October 27, 1857. A Kenaitze native took a sister of his brother and asked me to marry them. I tried to talk him out of this for a long time, but all my arguments failed. This Kenaitze said, 'I shall live with her all the same,' and, indeed, he continues to live with although I forbade it.

October 27, 1856. I called on a Kenaitze from the Titukil[5] village, who carried away another Kenaitze's wife. I started my persuasions by praising him. This is the only way to talk a Kenaitze into doing something. Stern language and reprimands do not work with them. Talking with him in this nice manner I convinced him to marry another woman. November 3. Today a Kenaitze, one of my parishioners, who left his wife two years ago, changed his mind and took her back. Several times did I try to persuade him, but he did not listen to me. Yet now he himself came to me, knelt down and said (he speaks Russian very well), 'Please, forgive me, father, for not listening to you! Now I have taken my wife back and I shall live with her as required.' With all my heart I thank God when He makes the lost sheep change their minds."

There are no other incidents of this kind in the missionary journals. On the other hand, we may find many examples that produce a favorable impression. The Kenaitze respect the missionary very much. When the natives from neighboring settlements go on their hunting trips they always come to secure his blessings. They also always welcome the missionary, when he visits them. They listen to his advice even in situations when we are usually used to pay little attention to our shepherds. Once the missionary found out that natives, under the influence of the Russians, planned to hold a party [*vecherinka*] with dances and *balalaikas* on the third day of the feast of the Nativity of Christ. Having finished the Divine Liturgy, the missionary addressed those who wanted to amuse themselves in this non-Christian manner, reprimanded them, and also explained the meaning of the Nativity and how they were to observe this feast. The missionary's words proved convincing and the party was canceled. The *balalaika*[6] was given to small children for a toy and later was thrown into a fireplace.

Travel Journal from September 1858 to 1862[7]

September 1858. Since it is impossible to travel to remote corners of the parish in fall, winter, and spring, the missionary usually spends this time at home being occupied with his regular work such as church services during major feasts, performing different ministrations for local residents, various daily chores and so forth. During the religious feasts many Kenaitze from nearby settlements frequently come to services. In addition to Sunday services, they are familiar with other feasts, especially with the major ones. To remember them, natives make marks on small wooden boards or sticks. Many natives, even those from remote villages, come to church. Especially a large number of the Kenaitze gather in the mission on St. Nicholas Day (when the missionary celebrates his name day), on the feast of Nativity of Christ, and on Easter. They come both because of their zeal for church services and, partially, maybe because the missionary provides all the faithful with food treats at his own expense.

The Kenaitze fulfill all sacraments: they baptize their children and accept ceremonies of holy matrimony. To celebrate their name days many natives request the missionary to perform prayer services in honor of their specific patron saints. They also invite the priest to the neighboring village [the Dena'ina village in the vicinity of St. Nicholas Redoubt] to provide confessions and communion to those natives who are ready to pass away, and also to perform funeral rites. Earlier, when they were heathens, the Kenaitze, like many other savages, burned the deceased people, then put their bones in boxes and buried them in cemeteries. Close relatives from time to time visited the cemetery and hysterically wept. Others who were also grieving came to a cemetery too and exchanged various gifts. At the anniversary of the funerals relatives of the deceased usually gave a feast, during which they treated all expected and unexpected guests with dried fish, berries mixed with grease and divided everything that could be found at the host's place. Guests danced and afterwards the host was to bestow a present on each of them. Honored guests received more, the poor ones received less. Thus, the host gave away almost all his meager possessions. Nowadays the Kenaitze have gradually abandoned this custom. Instead, nearby Kenaitze now come to church and ask the priest to perform a requiem service to commemorate the anniversary of a relative's death.

Using any available opportunity, the missionary tries to encourage them to pray and ask for God's blessing before they begin doing something. The priest also instructs them to thank God for His help upon completing their work. As a matter of fact, nearby Kenaitze, before going to hunt river beavers or mountain sheep, often come to church and ask the missionary to perform a customary prayer service in order to secure divine help in their enterprise. Upon returning from their hunting trips the natives again request a customary prayer service to thank a saint or the Savior. During each major fast, many Kenaitze, who live in neighboring villages, come themselves to the mission to pray, to confess, or to receive communion.

Although hearing the Kenaitze's confessions is exhausting work, and the whole confession proceeds too slowly, the priest does not feel comfortable rushing them and tries to be patient. During the confession they do not respond immediately to a question from the priest, but only after contemplating it for a while. When questions and responses are exhausted, the missionary usually asks: "Do you have anything else to confess?" A native again might go through all his work, words, and plans and might admit that he, for instance, wanted to pull out a nail from some barn. He might also expand endlessly on his expectations of becoming a rich and prestigious person and so forth.

In 1859 during the first week of the Great Lent there were more than 100 Kenaitze communicants. It happens that the missionary has imposed an *epitimia* on some of the natives for major sins. For instance, as a punishment, they might have to make a series of low bows down to the ground both in church and at home. Thus, during the first week of the Great Lent the missionary made two stubborn shamans keep bowing down during each service, and they promised not to shamanize anymore.

It is only in summertime that the missionary usually visits remote villages to perform spiritual ministration and propagate the word of the Gospel. Since the settlements of savages are scattered around the huge area, it is impossible to visit all of them during one summer. Therefore, one summer the missionary visits the western and southern parts of the parish. The next year he usually goes to the eastern and northern parts. About his journey, which he made in summer of 1859, the missionary writes the following:

May 12. Having served a customary prayer service, my reader, interpreter, and myself sailed in *baidarkas* to the southwestern part of the Kenai parish. First, we arrived at the Ninilchik village, populated by free Russian and Creole settlers. On May 15 we reached the Mountain Expedition place, where they mine coal. In the Expedition I restricted myself only to performing the most urgent ministrations because I found it necessary to sail to the south, to the Nuchek village, trying to take advantage of good weather. I promised the company's workers to come by on my way back...

Thank God, I finished all my business in Nuchek. Now I have to sail further southward to the Ugalentsy.[8] The Ugalentsy are related to the fierce tribe of the Kolosh.[9] The Ugalentsy's language, manners, clothing, customs, and way of life are the same as among the Kolosh. Yet, we get along well. During our journey the weather was quiet, but quite rainy. On June 22 we reached the Ugalentsy village. They welcomed us with gun shooting as the sign of hospitality. My Kenaitze paddlers were afraid of the Ugalentsy, but we know them very well and calmed the Kenaitze. That same day I baptized forty people including the infants. It was very hard to write down the names of the baptized in the open air: hosts of mosquitoes constantly disturbed us. Besides, I had to converse with local natives through two interpreters: one from the Ugalentsy and another from the Chugach. My conversation with the Ugalentsy dragged on until midnight. By this time I had exhausted all my patience, and was very tired especially from the mosquito attacks, but did not dare to rush the Ugalentsy. On June 23 after the service I baptized twenty-three more natives.

On June 24 and June 25 after the services and the sermon I heard the Ugalentsy's confessions, and the next day gave them communion (117 people except children). Some Ugalentsy asked me to perform a marriage ceremony for them, but knowing that they often switch their wives I decided not to satisfy this request. After dinner I sang requiem services for their deceased people, and explained to them what this ceremony means. Like the Kenaitze, the Ugalentsy burn the deceased, as they say, to prevent worms from eating away the dead bodies, which might upset the relatives of the deceased. I told them to abandon this custom, but did not persist in order not to upset them, since they are still shaky in their faith. On June 27 I worked to strengthen their Christian faith and instructed them on how the baptized should live and so forth. Having blessed them and left their souls to the God's protection, I set out back to Nuchek.

On June 29 we arrived at Nuchek. The next day I let my Kenaitze paddlers go home. They had been asking me about it for a long time. To do otherwise means that next time the natives would never agree to sail with me. After the Kenaitze left, I alone with my songleader stayed in Nuchek waiting for a *baidarka*, which was expected to come from the Copper River country to Nuchek and to bring me to the Mednovtsy[10] for propagation of the word of the Gospel. A few days later the Ugalentsy *toion* with his people visited Nuchek, and informed us that in the mouth of the Copper River they found two *baidarka* paddles carved in the Mednovtsy style.

This makes us assume that something happened with the Mednovtsy. Maybe they were turned over while going downriver? Several years ago while descending the river their boat turned over and several natives drowned. The same incident might have happened now, and they might have drowned. Or the Mednovtsy whom we awaited might have died from winter starvation, which frequently visits their country, or maybe some other misfortune happened. And besides, we had already missed the most convenient time to ascend the river. Now streams of water have begun to flow down from the mountain ranges, and the water current is very fast. Before water starts melting up on the mountain ranges, it usually takes twenty days to reach the Mednovtsy villages. Now it might take all forty days to get there. Moreover, from the middle of September drift ice fills the Copper River. Therefore, one faces a risk of getting stuck there without a chance of returning. At the same time, wintering there is impossible.

I concluded that God had decided not to grant me an opportunity to baptize the inhabitants of the Copper River. Although I am certainly upset about this, I find a consolation in telling myself that it was Providence that might have showed me that it was too early to baptize the Mednovtsy. Let their determination to accept the true faith and salvation be inflamed with a large fire of desire. Therefore, I decided to return to my Kenai. On July 25, having prayed to God, I parted with Nuchek and set out for Kenai.

1860. I am always pleased with the zeal, with which the Kenaitze from two neighboring villages express their faith. If bad weather does not keep them at home, they almost always come to the church on all feasts. In like manner, on St. Nicholas Day and on the feast of the Nativity of Christ many Kenaitze visited the church. As always, during these days I treated them with food. I cooked fish soup in several pots for common Kenaitze, while for honored natives and for the company workers I made tea and baked a pie. In Kenai people usually spent the Christmastide quite peacefully and quietly. We usually do not practice any noisy Christmastide games. I have had them gradually stopped since my arrival at Kenai. At first, some of the company's workers grumbled about discontinuing these games, but now they do not complain anymore. Russians sometimes set bad examples, which encourages the Kenaitze to continue native dances. Yet I always remind people from the redoubt that the Christians should be ashamed to jump and hop like the possessed, and that God does not like all this.

In 1860 many Kenaitze came to celebrate the feast of Epiphany. They revere this feast and understand the significance of the holy water, which they keep and store in their houses for the whole year. On important occasions they drink this water with considerable reverence. They treat communion bread, which I also give to them, with the same attitude. On January 23 of 1860 an extraordinary event happened. Before Sunday, I was performing the vigil service during which I read *akathist* in honor of the Mother of God. After the service ended I put out all the candles, which I always do myself. After this I, along with the songleader, left the church. As soon as we reached the door of my house, the songleader by chance turned his head back and saw light inside the church. Returning to the church, the reader noticed that right in front of the icon depicting the Mother of God a candle was still burning and he put it out. Yet as he was about to leave the building the candle was again aflame. The songleader was scared. With great fear he approached the candle and put out the flame. Then he came back and told me what he had seen. I was so confused that I could not find any explanation except telling him that probably somebody might have prayed zealously and that the Mother of God shows us that the pious prayer, as the undying candle, is aflame before Our Lord God.

During the first week of the Great Lent few Kenaitze came to partake in the rites of fast and penance preparing themselves for communion. So I served primarily for the residents of the redoubt. Because of a shortage of food and despite severe frost the Kenaitze now have to wander in forests and tundra hunting for wild animals. They asked me to excuse them and promised to partake in these rites during the Assumption fast. The word has spread around that everywhere the Kenaitze starve badly, and many of them have already died from hunger. From nearby villages they often come and ask for food. I gave away to them almost everything that I had with me: dried fish, bones, salted fish, and potato. I also brought to my house a sick Kenaitze native. I give him shelter, food, and consolation. This native worked for the company and ruined his health by carrying heavy cargo. B. [Efim Borisov], the redoubt manager, became angry with him for being ill so long, and moved him from the company house to the Kenaitze village. This native worker was so weak that he even was not able to walk there. And besides, even healthy natives in this village have nothing to eat. So I took him to live with me, for God's sake.

In the meantime, the head of the Mountain Expedition of the company sent me a letter asking me to visit them before Easter to give them sacraments of confession and communion. I set out for this place on March 16th. In the straits and on the shore there was still much ice left, and we had to maneuver through large icy blocks. Stopped for a night at the village of Kasimov. Here I gave last rites to ailing Kenaitze, a man and a woman. On March 18th en route we came by Kachemak Bay, where we stayed for a night at some open empty spot. It was very cold to sleep here. No matter how hard we tried to start the fire, the strong penetrating wind put it out , and we could not warm ourselves.

On March 19th, having crossed the harbor, we landed on a small island. Here we found many natives who were looking for food. Yet there was no food here except shellfish. The strong and nasty wind held us back and we continued our route only because there was no place to stop for shelter. On March 20th with great difficulty we reached the Aleksandrovsk *odinochka*, which is in fact the company's house, where its agents from time to time trade with savages. Here in this trade station at least we will warm ourselves and dry our clothing. It was impossible to perform services in a travel tent due to the rainy weather and strong wind. And besides, we could not proceed because of the bad weather. So we had to stay here until March 25th. It was very boring to stay here doing nothing. Moreover, we did not have any food. Thus, we involuntarily had a good fast here.

On March 15 the weather improved slightly, and we were able to cross the bay to get to the Expedition.... We spent the first three days of the Holy Easter here and then returned to the Aleksandrovsk trade station, where the Aleuts had already gathered and were waiting for me to help them perform the rites of fast and penance. The natives asked me to serve for them as fast as possible because they were in hurry to hunt otters. On April 6th we set out a tent for services. Stakes would not go into the frozen soil. So we brought more snow, made it solid and finally stuck the stakes into the snow. Fortunately, the wind stopped. On March 6 and 7 I performed services, taught the natives, and on March 8 I joined in the holy mysteries sixty-three people, baptized three infants, married two couples, conducted funeral services for the deceased, and during the vigil service I performed a customary prayer service for communicants. By nighttime we were again en route. Next day in the afternoon we reached another small island. Here we found many natives. They do not live on this small island permanently, but were driven here by hunger in hope of feeding themselves with shellfish.

On March 19 in the evening I safely returned home to Kenai. A few days after my return, the Kenaitze from distant villages visited the redoubt, and complained about the severe famine. They added that quite a few people had died from hunger during the winter. The whole week I was busy attending to the needs of these Kenaitze, which took much patience. The Kenaitze constantly distracted me, and I did not have a chance to sit and write or to do some other urgent work. Yet I could not tell them to visit me less frequently, which would be in their eyes the greatest offence and might upset the Kenaitze forever. The savages have their own customs, which we have to learn and to which we have to adjust ourselves as far as possible. In this way they will come to love you.

After St. Nicholas Day, for a few days I was occupied with digging soil in gardens and planting vegetables. Having finished this work, I decided to visit the northeastern part of my parish. On May 25, having prayed to God, we sailed out to sea, and on June 6 reached the mouth of the Susitna River,[11] which is located in the upper part of the Inlet. The Kenaitze from a few neighboring villages gather at this place to catch small fish called *telkha*, which are plentiful here at this time of a year. On the same day I began serving for those who were performing rites of fast and penance, and also baptized ten infants. On June 7 after the service and sermon I heard confessions, and on June 8 I gave communion to 121 natives. Then I sang funeral services for the deceased, married six couples, and after giving my blessings to all Kenaitze immediately went on. The reason for such a rush was two-fold. First, the Kenaitze have already finished fishing in this area and have started to scatter around to other places in order to continue gathering their winter supplies. Second, I received a message that his Grace would soon visit our redoubt, and I certainly needed time to return home before his vessel arrived.

We sailed the whole night and on June 9 reached the Tyonek village. On the same day I baptized four infants and began services for those who were performing rites of fast and penance. Soon after my arrival the Susitna *toion* also came to Tyonek and with great fear confessed, "I committed a terrible sin. When I was changing my shirt I did not notice how I dropped on the ground right under my feet a small icon, which his Grace had given to me and which has not yet been blessed. Please, forgive me and bless this icon." Deep in my soul I was very pleased with such reverence of the holy object. I took this small icon, made the sign of the cross, and kissed it. Then with this icon I made the sign of the cross for the *toion*, gave it to him to kiss, and added, "Do not be confused, carry the icon on your neck and pray. The Mother of God will not be angry with you, because you dropped it on the ground by accident." This Susitna *toion* is famous for his piety and charity. During famines he feeds many Kenaitze from his own supplies and reconciles people who quarrel with each other.

On June 10 I performed services, delivered a sermon and heard confessions. Next day I gave communion to seventy-six natives, married two couples, sang funeral services for the deceased, and having blessed the communicants sailed further. At night we reached Kustatan village. Here I baptized two infants, gave services to those who were performing rites of fast and penance, heard confessions, and tried to convince a shaman to quit his vocation, which is so offensive to God. On June 13 I gave communion to forty-eight natives, sang funeral services for the deceased, and after dinner left the village. On June 14 in the village of Titukil I baptized five infants, performed services, and delivered a sermon. During the next day I heard confessions, and on June 16 gave communion to fifty-one people. On June 17 I performed services in Kondazlit[12] village, where during the next day I heard confessions, and on June 19 gave communion to thirty-one natives, and also sang funeral services. With the visit to this village, I completed my trip.

I cannot describe in detail everything that I said to the natives. It would take too much room and there is no time to do this. I would only like to mention that while visiting the aforementioned villages and performing ministrations, I was very much satisfied with the Kenaitze piety. Lord, make them always behave like this.

On June 24 I returned to my redoubt. On June 29 I met his Grace, and welcomed him in our church and at my house. Next day we visited the nearby Kenaitze village [Chkituk] together, where people greeted us by shooting guns, which is a sign of hospitality. His Grace and I visited the *toion*'s house, where we talked for a while with him and drank tea he offered us. The Kenaitze were pleased that we shared their tea. Three other Kenaitze *toions* from remote villages were also here. They informed his Grace that I am not a bad person and do my work well.

On July 9 I baptized five natives from Copper River, who had come to Kenai for trade. On July 10 I performed the liturgy, and joined in the holy mysteries both the newly baptized and those Kenaitze from remote villages who were away when I was visiting their villages. The Mednovtsy invited me to visit their country. I told them, "I would be glad to come to you, but it is hard to get to your country. I am not a bird and do not have wings. Neither will have I energy and resources to cover on foot such a great distance. It will take two or three months to go through forests, tundras, and swamps and I will have to spend the same time in order to come back home. May those who wish to be baptized come to my place themselves."

On July 24 I served the liturgy, and after dinner I set out up the Kaknu River[13] to the Kenaitze village Skilak[14] to perform ministrations. Three days we sailed up river, and all this time my paddlers had to struggle with a rapid current, and finally they wore themselves so much that we had to return. It seems that I will have to visit the Skilak Kenaitze in winter. Although the winter route is also very difficult, I certainly have to visit these natives. Back in Kenai those Kenaitze who did not have a chance to receive communion during the Great Lent began partaking in the rites of fast and penance during the Assumption fast. And I also invited the others who do not have a chance to prepare themselves for communion this time, to do it some other time. During the feast of Transfiguration of Our Lord Jesus Christ I gave communion to these natives and instructed them how to behave upon receiving communion, and at the end I blessed them. These Kenaitze were going for their hunting trips to the mountain ranges. In September I visited the Chkituk village, where I sang a funeral service for a Kenaitze who had become ill and soon died from a fright. He had seen some scary animal-like monster that was coming from the water. Soon this native lost his speech, his mind became cloudy, and within three days he died.

During the feast of Nativity of Our Lord Jesus Christ [Christmas], many Kenaitze from remote villages again gathered in the church despite severe cold. After the service I treated everybody to fish soup. Then the rest of the day Kenaitze kept on coming to my place by groups and singing carols in a long drawling manner [*dlinnim raspevom*]. This time I was prepared to be patient. To those who sing carols I usually give either a piece of pie or bread or some tea. As a treat for small children, in advance I bake patties [*pirozhki*]. I regularly practice such treats since I came here, and this helps teach the natives to celebrate Christmas.

As a result, now all Kenaitze, even five-year-old children, know how to sing carols. Moreover, small children constantly and persistently ask their parents, when does the feast come, and when do they have to go to church to pray. Next day for the most zealous carol singers I served prayer and requiem services. Although in Kenai parishioners never pay the priest for performing these services, I work for these children of nature and infants in the faith with pleasure.

Moreover, to the poor natives I myself donate either a candle or groats with sugar for cereal to make a requiem meal. By providing them with such small things, I accustom them to requesting customary prayer services to celebrate their name days or to asking me to perform requiem services for the deceased and so forth. In due time these customs will become their habit. During Christmas a Kenaitze man came to me asking me to settle a dispute with his wife. Yet after looking into the causes of their disagreement, I found that both of them were wrong, and I talked them into reconciling with each other. The husband and the wife agreed with me and even kissed each other, upon my encouragement. Having blessed and instructed them in how to prevent family quarrels I let them go in peace. I have to settle plenty of cases like that. There is no way to record all of them in detail. The Kenaitze consider me some sort of father in their family. Like small children, they come to me with various trifles, and I patiently listen to them, investigate their complaints, reconcile, calm them and so forth.

1861. There was a need to visit two Kenaitze villages. The most distant one was located ninety miles inland from our church, beyond the mountain ranges. It is impossible to get there in summer because of the vast swampy tundras, lakes, and small rivers. People travel there only in winter on snowshoes. In this country there are no roads, and people, when they have to travel, use various natural landmarks or simply look for the most convenient routes.

In February the weather grew warmer and I decided to start my journey. On the 11th [of February] at daybreak I departed, along with my songleader, interpreter, and six carriers. All of us wore snowshoes, carried loaded backpacks, and held crooks in our hands. At first, we went through a forest, then through wide tundra, which is swampy and impenetrable in summer, but it was covered with deep loose snow, in which our snowshoes drowned. Soon a wind started to blow, then this wind turned into a blizzard, and I felt that I could not move farther. Yet there was no convenient place to stay. By nine o'clock in the evening we were able to make it to a forest. Dug a pit in snow, covered it with branches of trees from inside. Then we made a big fire, melted some snow and made tea. It will be hard for you to imagine how nice it was to drink tea with salty fish and black zwiebacks after the exhausting day journey. I will not exaggerate if I say that at that moment such a humble meal was much more pleasant than a luxurious dinner.

We rested as much as we could in this snow pit, and continued our route early in the morning on February 12. Before dinnertime we were going through a thick forest and constantly had to climb hill after hill. Branches of trees got in our eyes, and our snowshoes constantly got stuck in bushes or windfallen branches. Many times we fell to the ground. Yet my travel companions did not lose heart and cheered each other up with jokes. These Kenaitze are good to travel with, and no hardship makes them upset. After a while we stopped and ate some dried fish and drank tea. Then we descended to the Kakna River [Kenai River], which is notorious for its rapid current, against which one cannot sail in summertime. Even now in winter the river was not frozen in the middle. So we went on staying close to the riverbank. Yet the banks were very slippery. At some spots unfrozen water covered the ice, and small tributaries were filled with deep snow mixed with water. Finally, we realized that to move farther was practically impossible. But what could we do? Like it or not, we had to move on.

By about the middle of the night, directly in front of us we noticed the first Kenaitze winter dwelling. Yet as luck would have it, the cabin stood on the opposite bank of the river in the deep forest, and the river, as I said, was not frozen in the middle. We shouted and fired our guns, but nobody heard us. We were wet and sweaty. Quite soon we were chilled to the bone from sitting too long in the same place. But we could not make a fire because there was no firewood around except wet windfallen branches. After a long time somebody heard us and sent two birch boats [*baki*]. The Kenaitze finally brought us to their camp, where they cordially welcomed and warmed us, and fed us with their food to the extreme. To make natives satisfied, I never look down at their foods, and usually try everything as much as I can. If you reject his food, a host might be offended. A savage might consider what accidentally slipped from your tongue as disrespectful, which may make him into your mortal enemy. In this village we stayed only for a night, and I planned to perform here all necessary ministrations on my way back to Kenai.

On February 13, early in the morning, we were again en route. Crossed a few capes, and having found a convenient ravine in a mountain range stopped for the night. It was very cold at night and only by drinking tea did we keep ourselves warm. During the whole night a teapot was kept on fire. The Kenaitze are ardent tea drinkers, and I try not to be stingy en route knowing how difficult the road is. At least by giving the natives these small treats I might somehow make the journey easier for them. It might be for this reason that my travel companions, with the help of God, do not lose heart. At some spots where the route was especially difficult, they were even ready to carry me on their hands. On February 14 we left very early and reached the heart of the mountain ranges. Then moving through small gullies and a thick forest, we crossed a river and a few hills covered with forests. At the end of the day I was completely exhausted. The Kenaitze suggested that I stay and they would go to the village, take a sledge, and come back for me. I did not agree and said that after a short rest I would somehow walk there on my own feet. And, thank God, at night we did reach the village. Its inhabitants welcomed us with gun shooting. They always do this when they meet a dear guest. They accommodated me in a small house, which, as I understood, they had built specially for me.

On February 15 I started to perform church services along with sermons (during each service I offered the natives words of instruction). Baptized six infants, and in my spare time I again conducted instructive talks with natives. On

February 16 after a service I heard confessions. To provide a place to perform my services and to protect praying people from the wind, the natives built in a thick forest, from branches of pine trees, a structure that reminds one of a native dwelling [*barabora*]. On February 17 I gave communion to seventy-four Kenaitze. During these days the weather grew warmer. Having finished all ministrations and given to the natives a short instruction along with my blessing, I hurried back home because I did not want to miss the warm weather. The route was relatively easy until we reached the lake [Skilak]. As soon as we stepped on the lake, we felt how hard it was for our tired feet to walk on its slippery surface. A wind had blown away all the snow and the ice looked like a mirror. On February 18th we were en route the whole day, and by night I felt that my feet with snow shoes on them were so heavy that at some point I even could not step over a hummock of about seven inches in size, and had to help myself with my hands. By evening we reached the village. On February 19 I served, taught, and also baptized an infant.

On February 20 I heard confessions, and next day I gave communion to thirty natives. I also joined one couple in holy matrimony. My feet were so tired that all these days, when we stayed in the village, it caused me great pain to move around. At the times when I was not performing services I taught the natives their Christian duties, and they listened to me attentively. On February 22 at 5 o'clock in the morning we departed. Although my feet did not get a good rest, we had to go. Until 4 o'clock in the evening we proceeded by the bank of a river. Walking gave me unbearable pain. Warm weather partially melted the snow. At this point we already did not care to look for convenient routes, and went straight through with water reaching our knees and upper legs. Then we took a rest on a small hill we ran across. Later on, our route went through a forest, and we had to put on our snowshoes, which we had had to take off earlier, when we were moving through the melted snow. Here in the forest in deep snow one will not be able to walk even forty feet without snowshoes. Snow stuck to our wet snowshoes. So we felt as if we were dragging at least twenty pounds of weight on our feet. When we finally decided to stop for the night, I sent my travel companions forward and asked them to prepare the place for the night. When they left, I slowly followed them.

In the morning we woke very early. Although we did not get enough rest, we decided not to slow down and continued to move. The same bad route as yesterday, and again the feet feel heavy. Everything around us is wet. Next day the same weather and the same route. To make things worse, a rain started and completely softened the snow. This day we went by tundra, constantly crossing some tiny lakes, and became all wet. We were so exhausted that we could not walk farther. I do not know how, most probably, with God's help, I hobbled to my house. One of my legs was so numb that I could not feel or move it at all. So, for a while, when I walked around the room, I helped myself with a stick. Yet, thank God, we are finally at home!

If somebody asked me why I ventured to go through such unbearable hardships, I would respond, "My duty demands such self-sacrifice." As was mentioned earlier, in summer it is impossible to get to the villages I visited. To ask natives to come to our redoubt in winter would be cruel and inhumane. And besides, how would they come: the old, the young, the blind, and the crippled? How can they walk? Still, one should not forget that they are Christians who feel the need to be instructed and join in the holy mysteries. Although some of these natives, who feel strong enough, do come to the redoubt by themselves in order to partake in the rites of fast and penance, confession and communion.

During the Great Lent I performed a service both for residents of the redoubt and for neighboring Kenaitze who were conducting rites of fast and penance preparing themselves for communion. There were about 160 communicants except children. Many Kenaitze gathered in the redoubt to celebrate the Holy Easter, including natives from remote villages. During the first three days of the feast the Kenaitze diligently visited each service. They love to sing Easter hymns, and usually because of their zeal the Kenaitze like to sing very loudly. Yet I do not restrain them, but allow them to sing as they want and glorify the resurrected Savior. On the first day of Easter I treated them with food, providing as much as I could afford. During their stay in the redoubt, distant Kenaitze constantly visited me simply to talk or to say good-bye, some asked me to give them holy water, communion bread, medicine, turnip seeds and so forth. On the fourth day everybody was gone. Life again returned to a regular routine.

During this year, 1861, at my house I taught Russian reading and writing to four boys and one girl. In spring we worked in our gardens by planting vegetables. Then, when the fish ran from the sea to the rivers, we caught them and stored the catch as our food supply. During winter, spring, and fall, fishing is poor, and one cannot buy fish anywhere. What we can store for ourselves in summer (usually fish or vegetables), we usually eat for the rest of the year. With their carefree nature Kenaitze do not make enough fish supplies even for themselves. Moreover, they do not portion these supplies, but eat fish without any measure. For this reason, in spring they often suffer from hunger. For the same reason, the redoubt residents have to store both vegetables and fish by themselves, for it is difficult to rely on the natives. I myself catch and store a fair amount of fish, so that in case of a famine I am able to share with the Kenaitze a considerable part of my supplies.

For the past year I performed on a regular basis all spiritual ministrations both in the redoubt of the Russian-American Company and in the neighboring Kenaitze settlements. I often had to go to these localities, within eighteen and more miles from Kenai, in snowshoes in winter. The natives in all the villages that I visited have already been baptized. They are familiar with all major feasts, regularly come to church to pray, ask me to sing funeral services for the deceased, request requiems and customary prayer services, when they celebrate their name days on other occasions. In my parish, only the inhabitants of Copper River still remain heathens. Unfortunately, so far I cannot find a convenient opportunity to visit them. The Mednovtsy live far away and the route to their lands is difficult. Without appropriate cooperation from the Russian-American Company, it is impossible to penetrate their country.

1862.[15] On January the 6th having served the Liturgy and a customary prayer service, I delivered a requisite sermon addressed to the Russians. To the Kenaitze I explained through an interpreter the meaning of Epiphany. Many Kenaitze from nearby villages usually came to church to celebrate this feast. This year was not an exception, and a fair number of natives again came to the redoubt. On the occasion of Epiphany I served vespers and matins, and I also wanted to perform the Liturgy, but the frost was so severe that nothing could be done in the cold church. For this reason, I had to restrict myself to the rite of water blessing inside the church. I performed the service with great difficulty, and afterwards became ill from this cold weather. On January 7 I served the Hours and offered a sermon. Then I performed many prayer services at the request of those Kenaitze who celebrated their name days. I have been teaching them for a long time that they should honor their guardian angels with prayers and with good deeds as far as they can, because these angels protect us throughout our whole lives and pray for us. For example, I pointed out to them that to feed at least one poor or sick person for the sake of God, might be a good way to honor names of their respective saints.

At 8 o'clock on the evening of January 7 (this was Sunday) three boys whom I teach left my house at different times and each of them saw the light of a burning candle inside the church. After the third boy mentioned this miracle, I went out myself, but could not see anything. In this regard, it came to my mind that in ancient times in the same manner the voice of the Lord reached an adolescent, Samuel, rather than the High Priest Elijah, which made me upset a little.

On January 9 and 10 I went to Kondazlit, a Kenaitze village, which is located about twenty miles from Kenai, in order to visit a sick *toion* and to give him last rites. I myself felt so sick that I was hardly able to return home. Sitting in a draft in the *toion*'s *barabora* added more to my cold. Many times have I told the Kenaitze to build their winter dwellings tighter and caulk the walls with moss. In this case the wind would not have blown through their *baraboras*, and it would have been warmer and better for their health. But they would respond, "We are used to cool air. It does not disturb us when the wind blows right through. If we become used to the warm air, how will we tolerate cold weather, when hunting in a forest, where we happen to get wet, and besides our clothing does not warm us enough. Present day youngsters are nothing compared to the old timers. Now boys learned how to drink tea and boil the food. In old times people did not eat hot food and did not drink anything hot. At the same time, they easily caught up with the deer, went up the mountain ranges by running, and did not know any shortness of breath. And now when they happen to go outside for a short while to collect the firewood, youngsters already begin complaining that they have caught cold. We know that it is because they got used to Russian tea and food."

On January 23 I went to a neighboring Kenaitze village to visit an ailing Kenaitze who suffered from a very bad abscess on his back. People predicted that he would soon die. I brought a special plaster, and although this Kenaitze had already lost consciousness, I put the plaster on the sick spot. Next day the abscess softened, then the songleader [Makarii Ivanov] cut it, and some pus came out. By the evening the ailing native regained consciousness, and started to speak. For the next few days I sent the songleader to change the plaster. The native started to recover and repeated, "If it was not for the Father's help, I would have died." During the first week of the Great Lent I suggested that the Kenaitze start to perform rites of fast and penance, although it was still cold inside the church. But what could I do? On Wednesday I began hearing Kenaitze's confessions. They tend to confess very slowly, but one cannot rush them in such important business. On Saturday I served the Liturgy and gave communion to 107 people, and also delivered a sermon, where I explained to the natives how they should behave after receiving communion.

On Sunday the Kenaitze began returning to their villages, and before departure each of them approached me asking for blessing. During the fifth week of Lent I served to those who could not come to partake in the rite of fast and penance during the first week. On March 25 I joined in the holy mysteries twenty-seven natives. Two days later I along with my songleader left for the company settlement called the Mountain Expedition, which is located ninety miles to the west of the redoubt. It takes three days of travel by *baidarka* to reach the Expedition. Afterwards, I was planning to go to the other side of the Inlet and perform services in a Chugach village, but bad weather did not allow me to perform services in a movable tent.

For this reason, I invited the Chugach to the Expedition and served for them in a local chapel, baptizing their infants. On April 7 I joined in the holy mysteries fifty-seven people. On April 14 I set out for the Creole village Ninilchik. Sailing against the head wind completely wore out my paddlers. When we were about three miles from Ninilchik, the wind pushed our *baidarka* to the shoreline and a large wave raised and threw us onto the shore. We were completely drenched. It was helpful that the shore was sandy. If it had been rocks, our *baidarkas* would have been damaged, and we ourselves would have been harmed. Free Creole settlers[16] who noticed us came to help and carried out *baidarkas* to a safe place, far from water. The Creoles carried our belongings and gave us shelter in their houses, where we warmed and dried ourselves, and felt better.

Having returned home, I met in the redoubt many Kenaitze, who usually at this time of the year come from different villages to trade with the company. And of course each day and at any time natives came to visit me, some of them on business, but mostly for no reason. They definitely did not want to leave me in peace. Yet one cannot close the door in front of them. Rejection might offend the Kenaitze and they might stray away from you. The most frequent reason for their visits is to complain about each other. I try to reconcile them, and the Kenaitze take my word of advice seriously. Sometimes it is boring to talk with them. An inexperienced person could have lost all his patience a long time ago, but I somehow have become used to their baby talk.

On May 1 an ailing Kenaitze was brought to me from the Kondazlit village, which is located about twelve miles from the redoubt. The native was very weak. I heard his confession and gave him communion, after which this Kenaitze felt better. In a few days he recovered and visited me in order to thank me for the care I provided to him. Since the beginning of May I and the boys I teach have been working in the gardens digging and planting vegetables. In Kenai if one does not plant vegetables for himself, he will never and nowhere be able to get them. In the middle of May the king salmon reached our area. This is the best red fish we have here, and the Kenaitze celebrated the fish run with some sort of festivities, during which they treated each other with food. When about ten months of the year they have to eat dried fish, which is not always enough, one can understand why the natives felt so happy.

Having finished various chores, I started to prepare myself for the trip to the northeastern part of the parish. On May 25, having prayed to God, I along with my songleader and an interpreter departed. On June 4 we reached a village and set up our tents and the church tent, and explained to the Kenaitze that those who wanted to perform rites of fast and penance and also confession should come to the church service. In this village I saw the same Kenaitze who had been brought to me hardly alive on May 1. He said to me, "Since now I am absolutely healthy, it looks like God is powerful." Then I asked him, "Do not you believe that God is all powerful?" The Kenaitze responded, "Until now I somehow believed and did not believe at the same time, but now I do believe." Such simple words from the mouth of a native had a clear instructive impact on the other Kenaitze. During June 5th and June 6th I performed services, taught those who were fasting, baptized infants, heard confessions, and on June 7 gave communion to fifty-two natives. Then I married two couples and having blessed them, left for the Titukilek [Titukil] village. Some Kenaitze, whose villages I was still planning to visit, gathered here in Titukilek. So I served for them as well. On June 8 and 9 I taught all the people, then baptized infants, heard confessions and on June 10 gave communion to fifty-four natives. Then I married one couple. The second couple changed their minds at the last moment for some reason. After dinner I continued my route.

On June 11 I reached the mouth of the Susitna River. To this place each year the Kenaitze from various villages come to catch small fish called *telkha*. On the same day I started my services, and also pointed out to the Kenaitze that they should fast. Local natives, who reside far from the church and do not live a settled life, know little about church rituals and do not understand that one has to fast before receiving holy communion. They fast when they do not have food. Yet, they are very patient when they have to suffer from hunger. On June 12 I again performed services and taught them, baptized nineteen infants, heard confessions, and gave last rites to an ailing native. On June 13 I joined in the holy mysteries 173 natives, and married two couples. In the end I was so tired that I hardly reached my tent. I became exhausted not from fatigue, but more from sweltering heat. It was unbearably hot outside. Besides, it was hard to stand the very bad smell coming from the drying fish and from the Kenaitze, who filled the church tent to capacity and also crowded outside. Upon finishing my business here I hurried to go farther to catch some fresh air.

On June 14 I started performing services in the Tyonek village, where I baptized eleven infants. I also punished the local *toion* with a genuflection for his gross misbehavior. If it had been some other *toion*, I certainly would have not imposed on him such a church punishment. Yet that this one is very loyal to me, and I know that he will not be angry with me. In the meantime, the punishment by genuflection will serve as a good example for the others. On June 15 during the liturgy I joined in the holy mysteries eighty-four natives, then married three couples, served requiem rites and then left for the Kustatan village.

In Kustatan I found some Kenaitze who came from the other two villages. On June 17 and 18 I performed services, taught, baptized six infants, and heard confessions. The next day I joined in the holy mysteries fifty-four natives, married three couples, and served a requiem for all deceased Kenaitze in this area. I explained to them what the requiem means and how this rite might be useful to the deceased. The Kenaitze thanked me for performing these services for their people who passed away. Having finished all business and using the favorable current, we set out back home to the redoubt, where we safely arrived on June 21st. On the whole, we traveled about a month.... By the end of July many Kenaitze had gathered in the redoubt. They wanted to buy various goods in the company's store. After buying gunpowder and lead the natives intended to go to the mountain ranges to hunt the mountain sheep. They requested that I perform a customary prayer service to help their plans.

In September the chief of the Mountain Expedition wrote me that somewhere in the south, among those Kolosh, who reside in English possessions, a smallpox epidemic was spreading. He asked me to vaccinate those local inhabitants who still had not been inoculated. I ordered the songleader to visit the neighboring villages and inoculate natives. He worked almost all October and visited four villages. As a result, both adults and the young natives who needed it were inoculated. In the first days of November a few Kenaitze came from a distant village called Skilak. Having heard about the coming epidemic, they persistently asked me to send somebody to their village to vaccinate them against the smallpox. I knew very well that in the absence of any roads it would be very hard for the songleader to go on foot to such a remote locality ninety miles away. I also realized that paying and feeding guides would induce high expenses, but I had to respect this Kenaitze request.

On November 12, having received my blessing, the songleader [Ivanov] departed. He reached two villages, which together number more than 100 people, vaccinated the natives, and on December 3 returned. While the songleader was en route, inclement weather constantly changed from humidity to severe frost with snowstorm. On the way back he was tired to the point of exhaustion, and hardly could make it home. While the songleader was working with the natives from Skilak, an old ailing Kenaitze woman from this village asked him to tell me to send her a shirt, a small cross and some canvas to cover her in a coffin. She also added, "I will be waiting and will not die before they bring me those." Indeed, everything happed as she predicted. Next day, after the songleader came back, with a Kenaitze guide, who accompanied the songleader, I sent what she asked for. As the guide was approaching his village, the old woman breathed her last.

On November 25, about 9 o'clock in the evening, we witnessed the total eclipse of the moon, which was even more impressive to observe because the sky was crystal clear and cloudless. When the moon was gone, such darkness descended on the earth that even the stars could not be seen. The Kenaitze explained this phenomenon in their own way by saying, "Something bad will happen." In their reasoning, the moon is a person or a thinking creature. As soon as she learns that God is angry with people and wants to punish them, she weeps by covering her face with her hands. That is why, they say, the light disappears for a while.

After I visited the part of my parish that occupies the upper part of the Kenai Bay, I spent the rest of the year doing my regular work: performing services and giving sermons during feasts, serving different ministrations both in the redoubt and in neighboring Kenaitze villages. Sometimes I had to go twelve miles to give last rites to the ailing. In considerable numbers and on a regular basis Kenaitze visited church services, including natives from villages that are located twelve miles away and more. They frequently asked me to perform customary prayer services during their name days or before going on their hunting trips. The natives also asked me to sing requiems to commemorate their deceased relatives. As in former years, St. Nicholas feast on December 6 gathered an especially large number of the Kenaitze. This is when I celebrate my name day. I treat all visiting Kenaitze with food as far as I can afford. During the feast of Nativity of Our Lord Jesus Christ, when both the adult and young Kenaitze come to my house to sing carols and to glorify Christ, I usually give them small patties [*pirozhki*], which pleases them very much. During this year I was not able to join any other adults to the church because there are no heathen people left in my parish. All natives in the villages that I visited or those Kenaitze who visited me in the redoubt have already been baptized. Only the Kolchane[17] and the Mednovtsy remain to be baptized. Yet their habitats are located so far away that I cannot reach them with those resources that are available to me, not to mention all the dangers related to such a trip. I also think that due to their extreme savagery, it might be too early yet to baptize these two tribes, especially the Kolchane. They live so far away, and the route to their country is so difficult that I cannot visit them even in summertime. As for wintering among them, I hardly think about it because this is practically impossible.

1863. January 1. New Year. Due to the Lord's mercy we stepped into the New Year, but it happened so routinely that we did not even notice it. I do not feel at all that we renewed ourselves. Nothing changed. It might be that there are only a few select people who deserve to be renewed. Unfortunately, the rest of us are simply unworthy creatures. The weather is extremely bad, cold and with a blizzard. Hardly saw any Kenaitze at the service today. I served the Hours, requested customary prayer services, and added a few words about the New Year.

January 2. I went to the Kenaitze village of Chkituk to give last rites to an ailing old *toion*. It was snowing, and very cold.

January 5. Performed a service. We are preparing for the feast. A fair number of Kenaitze came for the service. Luckily, it is getting warmer. I should give the Kenaitze credit, they are very attentive to major church feasts. Despite severe frost in winter, frequent snowstorms, deep snow and lack of any roads, natives come in advance to the redoubt from villages which are located twelve and more miles away. Thus, they come in large numbers to celebrate the feast of Epiphany. As always, this year many Kenaitze came to the church during this feast.

January 6. Served the Liturgy without consecration, and spoke about the meaning of this feast through an interpreter. As for the Creoles, they know Russian very well. Then outside of the church I performed a rite of water blessing.

January 7. At the request of the Kenaitze I sang requiem services. Also, quite a few natives today celebrate their name days, and I performed customary prayer services for them too. Later on, to encourage the Kenaitze to do this on a regular basis and to make this day memorable, I invited those who celebrated their name days to my house, where I offered them some food along with a shot of vodka for each. They view the latter as the most precious treat. It is amazing how American natives [*tuzemtsi*], and also Creoles, are susceptible to vodka! Give a drink even to a native child and he will gulp it and will not wince. As far as adults are concerned, they do not know any measure in drinking. Drinking of vodka without measure would have done a great evil for the American peoples. Fortunately, the far-sighted company authorities do not sell vodka freely. Otherwise, it is hard to imagine what could have happened.

January 13. I could not perform a service because of severely cold weather. In my own room, which I warmed twice, it is still so cold that I have to wear a coat. A thermometer outside blew up from the severe frost. So now I even cannot measure the temperature.

January 18. Performed a requiem and a customary prayer service at the request of a company worker, who celebrates today his name day.

January 20. Served the Hours, then delivered a sermon, and later performed a customary prayer service at the request of a person who celebrated his name day. My songleader started to fill out our various church papers. As for me, I still cannot do this work properly, because days are too short in winter, and my eyesight is too poor to write by candlelight. Besides, for a long time I have been suffering from a toothache, which does not allow me to concentrate on anything.

January 27. Served the Hours, delivered a sermon, and sang a requiem at a Kenaitze's request. The Kenaitze who reside in neighboring villages are gradually coming to understand the rites of the Orthodox church much better.

February 2. Feast of the Purification. I served the Liturgy without consecration, then delivered a sermon, in which I told the Kenaitze how and when our Savior was brought to the temple, and stressed that since we are all Christians, each woman who delivered a child should come to church after forty days to cleanse herself.

February 3. Served the Hours, a customary prayer service, and a requiem. My toothache subsided a little.

February 4. Shrove-tide. Here during the Shrove-tide people do indulge themselves in various festivities and amusements. It might be because before or after this time the natives are not burdened too much with work to have additional amusements. It would not be a bad idea for the company's chief authorities to pay more attention to the native American peoples. It seems that the natives deteriorate from idleness and eventually become flabby and decrepit and get old prematurely. I know many Kenaitze who were boys when I came here, but now they call themselves old men. I tried to make them understand how useful active labor might be. Thus, using my personal example, I tried to involve them in gardening, and even gave them seeds. Yet, so far not many of them have turned to gardening. Without a significant inducement from the authorities, it will take a very long time before natives are used to European sedentary housekeeping. The Kenaitze might be induced. I do not see any special danger in this approach, because by now the Kenaitze have become quite mild-mannered. Still, one needs to possess experience in order to know how to approach them. Having these skills, one will be able implant into their minds necessary ideas about civic duties.

February 10. Farewell Day [*Proshchalnii Den*]. I served the Liturgy without consecration, and in my sermon I reminded the Kenaitze of the necessity of mutual forgiveness. I stressed that if people are angry with each other, all of them are guilty in the eyes of God. Therefore we should ask Him to forgive us our sins. In the evening, before their departure, the Kenaitze paid me a farewell visit. They introduced this tradition at the time I arrived in Kenai.

February 11. The first week of the Great Lent. I conducted requisite services. I teach those who perform rites of fast and penance as much as I can. A large number of the Kenaitze from neighboring villages came to perform these rites.

February 15. I heard confessions from 107 natives. If all of them had been Russians, it could have been easier to serve them. But with the Kenaitze everything goes very slowly. It was exhausting to listen to all their trivialities they wanted to report to me. Besides, while hearing their confessions I caught cold, and now feel sick. However, I cannot interrupt the rites and leave people without confession. Although it is very difficult, I will have to continue.

February 16. With great difficulty, I served the Liturgy without consecration, and thank God, I was able to complete this service, and my spiritual children received blessings, and their consciences were cleansed.

February 17. I rested a little, and then served the Hours, and instructed the communicants. After having blessed all natives who were present, I ended the service.

February 18. Today I started to heal myself, and I feel a little better. Yet I cannot go outside into the open air. At the same time, it is so boring to stay inside. It is hard to imagine how hermits can live in solitude all their lives.

February 27. I still cannot perform services, and the songleader had to replace me to sing the Hours. Then I and the songleader started working on reports. I am debating about going to the Mountain Expedition. If I had a choice, I would not go there, but without information from the Expedition chapel I cannot complete my report. During the whole year I did not receive any information from them, and I do not know what they are doing there.

March 1. My health has improved, and we are occupied with writing the report.

March 3. I served the Liturgy without consecration, and instructed those Kenaitze who could not partake in the rites of fast and penance during the first week of Lent to come and to do this.

March 10. I served the Hours, reminded the Kenaitze to come to church on a regular basis, and also to pray and fast. I performed services all this week, and the Kenaitze partook in the rites of fast and penance.

March 15. Baptized two infants.

March 16. We prayed, and then I heard confessions.

March 17. I served the Liturgy without consecration, where thirty-five people received communion. If the weather cleans the Inlet from blocks of ice a little, I will sail this week to the Mountain Expedition, and will visit those villages that are located en route.

March 22. Today we departed. With great difficulty maneuvering among blocks of ice, we neared Ninilchik.

March 24. We reached a river that flows into the Kachemak Bay, where we had to stop, awaiting better weather. We could not cross the harbor because of a strong wind. When we were approaching the shore, a high tide turned over our *baidarkas*, and one of them was seriously damaged. Fortunately, nobody was harmed.

March 27. We reached the Mountain Expedition. A good man named G. Cheusov, who is the chief of this Expedition, insisted that I stay at his house. Cheusov is such a good Christian, and after all, he is a Russian.

March 28. I started to perform services for those who fast and cleanse their consciences, and also baptized three infants.

March 29. Performed serves, heard confession from all people who live at the Expedition along with a few Aleuts.

March 30. I served the Liturgy without consecration, during which fifty-seven people received communion. After dinner I heard confessions from the Aleuts, who had prayed with all the others. In the evening I performed a rite of water blessing, because here they had run out of their supply of holy water.

March 31. Easter. On the occasion of this feast, I performed the service according to prescribed feast rules, and also gave communion to thirty-one people. Here in Expedition they celebrate the Easter rather joyfully, but in a seemly fashion, because Mr. Cheusov is strict with the ill-behaved, but at the same time, he is very responsive to a good behavior.

April 1. I again performed the service in a feast manner on the occasion of Easter, and also served for those who partook in the rites of fast and penance. The Aleuts wanted to complete these rites as soon as possible because the company was rushing them to go hunting for sea otters. After vespers I served requested requiems and customary prayer services. A fair number of such unfulfilled ministrations have accumulated here during this year.

April 2. Performed a service. Joined one couple in holy matrimony. I realize very well that I am not to perform the rite of holy matrimony during this season, but the groom is going on a hunting expedition, and will not be able to see the priest until the next year. In the meantime, I continued to instruct those who want to be married to avoid living in an illicit manner with each other before they are formally married.

April 4. I served the Liturgy without consecration, where I gave communion to thirty-eight people. After the end of the service I performed a customary prayer service, then did some chores by putting everything in the chapel in order. Finally I finished all my business in the Expedition and departed after dinner. My next stop is a small island populated by the Aleuts, which I reached at night.

April 5. This small island is located in Kachemak Bay. We found here only women because all the men were away, occupied with hunting. Performed a service, baptized an infant, and heard confessions.

April 6. Performed a service. There were twenty-seven communicants. Then I sang a requiem service for all the local people who had died during the past year. In the evening we crossed the bay and reached Laida village.[19]

April 7. Performed a service, baptized an infant, and heard confessions. Here I would like to mention one thing. My superiors might reprimand me for staying in villages I visit for only a few days, which does not give natives who partake in the rites of fast and penance much time to fast. Yet long experience has convinced me that one cannot overburden natives who are still infants in their faith with long services and fasts. I have noticed that native savages do zealously pray for a short while, and while listening to divine stories, they express their inner feelings by sighs or some other emotions. Furthermore, they are more persistent than us, Europeans, in abstaining from food during a fast. At the same time, I have noticed that natives get tired quickly. Since the Kenaitze's food is primarily meat, when they fast they simply do not eat anything. During these days they do not give meat even to small children. Only sometimes might they give them a little dried fish. When I happened to extend my services and make them longer, I noticed that those who gladly come to church, at the end grow tired and do not show up for the next services so eagerly or else come late. Some of them, who are older and who are not used to standing for a long time, often sit leaning back on church porticos. For this reason, one has to be lenient toward them.

April 8. I performed a service, where I gave a communion to twenty-six people. Sang a requiem service. In this village lives a rascal, whom the Kenaitze treat as some sort of a shaman of a lower rank [*shamanishka*], according to their silly superstition. Yet, in reality, he is not a shaman at all, but a plain deceiver. As I heard from others, he fools people. I ordered him to stop deceiving the local inhabitants, and also threatened in public to punish him by genuflection. The Kenaitze, who are free people and do not recognize any authorities, view this as a considerable punishment. They are not familiar with any fines and do whatever they want and are not afraid of anybody. And here I am forcing him to make numerous low bows down to the ground. What an unbearable blow for their pride and vanity, which are highly cultivated among almost all savages. Yet they do not dare to oppose me. At least, I have not known a single case of disobedience. According to the Kenaitze's notion, I stand much higher than an ordinary man. I ascribe this success not to my skills in dealing with savages, but to God's assistance.

April 9. Ninilchik, free settlers. Here I baptized infants. I had already suggested that the village residents build a chapel. As good Christians, they certainly agreed. Yet they have not been in a hurry to fulfill their promise for almost ten years. I remind them about it each time, when I visit the village. Still, they do not start work. In my view, it is the poverty of Ninilchik residents that prevents them from building a chapel. They are hardly able to feed themselves, and certainly do not have the resources to begin the work. Two or three persons can do it, but the rest of the inhabitants are not able due to various circumstances. As a result, they keep postponing the whole project.

April 10. I performed a service for the faithful who fasted, and also heard confessions.

April 11. I performed a service, twenty-nine people received communion. Also performed a customary prayer service and requiems. After dinner we left Ninilchik and set out back to the redoubt. All night and all day we were en route.

April 12. Returned to the redoubt. Here everything is all right.

April 13. I baptized two infants. One infant was dead and I sang a funeral service.

April 14. I served the Liturgy without consecration, delivered a sermon, and celebrated Easter. When I left Kenai there was nobody here to perform the Easter service, and people could not hear a solemn "Christ is risen!"

April 21. Served the Liturgy without consecration, delivered a sermon, in which I instructed the Kenaitze about feasts in general and especially about the Holy Easter feast. Afterwards, on the occasion of the feast I treated the natives with food as far as I could afford. Since the Kenaitze found out that I have returned from my trip, quite a few of them came for the church service. I still did not receive any [official] mail, and do not know what I am going to do in future and when to start my next trip.[20] Because of this, I still cannot decide whether to plant a garden or not. What if I have to leave? In that case I would feel sorry about the wasted work.

April 28. Served the Hours and a customary prayer service. I also pointed out to the Kenaitze that they bring many furs to the company trade store, while hardly any of them thinks about donating something to the church. Even candles still remain unsold. I stressed that such an attitude does not do them credit as Christians. Also talked about the necessity of helping the poor. In this regard, the Kenaitze are still not quite perfect. I also added a few words about shamanism. About shamans I said, "They are cunning people, who fool you. Yet you pay them for this deception quite a lot. If a shaman does know something, this knowledge comes from the devil, who never helps people, but only harms human beings and destroys the souls of both shamans themselves and people who seek shamans' help."

May 1. All visiting Kenaitze left the redoubt for their villages. When we were parting, the natives complained about the redoubt manager, who offends them when they go to trade. I responded by reminding them that the faithful have to endure insults, and added that they might happen to be even with the manager. After all, it is known that those who prosper by robbery eventually will not make any good of it.

May 5. Served the Hours and delivered a sermon. Then performed a customary prayer service at the request of a Kenaitze *toion*. Today my mail finally arrived.

May 9. The Ascension of Our Lord Jesus Christ. Served the Liturgy without consecration and explained to the Kenaitze the meaning of the Ascension feast. I also spent some time persuading a Kenaitze widow to marry a native who wants to take her to live in his house. I also calmed a *toion* from Laida village, who became very upset when the manager scolded him for not paying a debt.

May 19. Trinity. Served the Liturgy without consecration along with vespers as required. Explained to the Kenaitze the meaning of the feast of the Trinity and about how Holy Spirit endowed the apostles.

May 20. Served the Hours and a customary prayer service. The manager cannot find paddlers to take me to Nuchek. Those who had been assigned to me before have become sick. The members of the Mountain Expedition brought to us some epidemic, whose symptoms are coughing, headaches, and constriction in the chest.

May 21. Baptized two infants. Today I am occupied with packing my belongings and preparing for the [Nuchek] trip.

May 22. Set out for Nuchek. En route I stopped in the Kondazlit village to bless a new house built by the local *toion* in the wharf area.

May 24. We reached the portage harbor, but unfavorable weather stopped us. My paddlers suffer from cough.

May 26. Arrived at the portage. But here an unpleasant surprise awaited us. The surrounding hills, mountain ranges, and our route were covered with snow. Real winter. What to do? To move on will be difficult, to return would be improper. After a short deliberation, we decided to entrust our fate into God's hands, and moved on.

May 26. It was still dark when we departed, and we went across familiar giant mountains covered with ice. Such an early start allowed us to cover many miles before the noon sun melted the snow, which makes it impossible to move farther. At noontime the snow becomes crumbly, and by its blinking and shining harms the eyesight. Rested a little in the middle of our route, and then again I, along with my songleader and an interpreter, continued to move. The route went up and up a high mountain. Without exaggerating, I can say that while climbing this mountain I was not only sweating, but was literally bleeding. Having reached the top, we started to descend to the sea side of this mountain. Because of the snow, the slope was stiff and slippery. Since I did not carry any backpack, I was moving in front of everybody, cutting stairs for those who followed me. Somehow my feet slipped and I rolled down. I rolled about 140 feet before I thought to use my travel crook. This is a very durable crook with an iron tip. Using all my power I stuck this crook in the snow and, thank God, was able to hold myself on this stick. Later on, the muscles of my hands hurt very much. Probably I twisted them. If I had not been able to keep myself from falling down, I would have surely dropped, crushed all my bones, and broken into pieces. There were large rocks down below. The interpreter, who was standing on the top of the mountain, saw me rolling down and became so scared that he himself almost fell down from the shock.

When I was falling down I felt nothing. It seems that there was no time to think about the fear. Only when I came down and stepped on the plain surface and looked back at the high cliff did I feel fear. I felt for a second as if somebody had doused me with ice cold water and my hair stood on end. My heart was beating so fast that I had to sit down to calm down and wait for the interpreter.

May 28. The paddlers moved back and forth carrying our luggage through the portage. By dinnertime all our belongings were safely on the other side. The legs of one paddler became swollen, probably from hard work. After we rested, I issued to each carrier a shot of vodka and also gave them tea. Soon they forgot all about their troubles, got on the *baidarkas* and sailed on joyfully. During my trips I try not be stingy, whereas back home I am very thrifty.

June 2. In the evening we came to the Nuchek redoubt. Here everything is all right except the news that somewhere in the vicinity of Ugalentsy village the Kolosh had gathered in large numbers. Local Chugach natives are a little afraid of them. The Chugach advised me not to sail to the Ugalentsy, but I do not care. I will willingly accept any fate Our Lord prepares for me. As always, the local manager welcomed us cordially.

June 3. I performed a service for those who fast. Delivered a sermon for those who know Russian. During vespers through an interpreter delivered a word of address to the Chugach about the necessity of believing in the son of God and fulfilling his testaments. And if they can not fulfill these testaments, they should repent in their sins.

June 4. I performed a service for those who are fasting and anointed eighteen infants with myrrh. In the evening a Kolosh came along with two young Ugalentsy women, who wanted to baptize their infants and perform rites of fast and penance. In the evening I started hearing confessions.

June 5. Performed services, baptized six infants. I had to spend the whole day hearing confessions, because a large number of people are partaking in the rites of fast and penance.

June 6. I served the Liturgy without consecration, during which 127 natives received communion, except for the very young. After vespers I delivered a sermon to communicants, performed a thanksgiving customary prayer service and sang funeral services for an infant.

June 7. Early in the morning we set out to visit the Ugalentsy. It was raining heavily.

June 8. By evening we reached the mouth of the Alganak River. An old man with poor eyesight, who was attached to us in Nuchek as a guide and interpreter from the Ugalentsy language, lost the direction and could not find the route to the Ugalentsy *baraboras*. We had to roam around in the rain all night long. In the morning we finally came to the right place. At the Ugalentsy village we found only a few inhabitants. The rest are now visiting with the Kolosh, who recently visited the Ugalentsy and invited them to be their guests and also to participate together in hunting sea otters.

June 9. I started to perform services for those who fasted. Baptized five infants. In answer to my question why people did not wait for my arrival, the remaining Ugalentsy responded that the [Nuchek] manager did not tell them to wait for me. This is true. I did write to the manager last year, "It seems that I will be allowed to leave America and to say good-bye to this land. Since I am not sure if I will see you, please, do not make any arrangements and do not wait for my arrival." Well, as it turned out, I am still here [in America].

June 10. Performed services, heard confessions. In the meantime, I am waiting for those Ugalentsy who might return [from the Kolosh country]. Sometimes I ask myself how people can live in such a place as the Ugalentsy's. All Ugalentsy *baraboras*, which are constantly filled with smoke down to the floor, are dirty, and the stinking smell of dried fish is unbearable. For lack of any better place, we had set our church tent on a wet spot. A puddle of water can be seen right in the middle of the tent. To keep my feet dry during services natives put a small wooden board by the Altar, while others had to stand in water. To add to all these inconveniences, a host of mosquitoes kept on attacking us. Even a person of extraordinary patience would spend no extra time here except in case of urgent need.

June 11. Performed a service, and gave communion to thirty-three Ugalentsy. Delivered a few instructive words, blessed them, and then departed, going to the mouth of the river in hope of finding some dry and clean place.

June 12. By dinnertime we returned to Nuchek. In the evening I married three couples.

June 13. Married one more couple. Sang requiem services for the deceased. Baptized an infant, performed the all-night vigil. Tomorrow I plan to serve the Liturgy without consecration, and then to part with this redoubt. I do not feel well. It might be the result of the humid weather for which Nuchek is notorious.

June 14. Served the Liturgy without consecration, then delivered a short sermon, which I ended with words of farewell.

June 15. The weather improved and we left the redoubt. All the residents went outside to see us off. We had to spend a night at a small island. To our regret, there was no fresh water here. From surrounding puddles we were able to collect some water and made tea. I tried this tea, which looked like ink, and found it so disgusting that I could not drink it. It was hard, and everybody suffered from thirst. Well, I told myself, "Be patient. Patience will be rewarded."

June 16. By sunrise we came to the Tsuklok village. Residents of another village named Chanigat had been asked to come here to meet me. As soon as we unpacked our belongings I started to perform a service for those who fasted.

June 17. Performed services, baptized eight infants, heard confessions.

June 18. Again performed services, and gave communion to sixty-five people, then I married two couples. Sang requiems. After all ministrations were finished, I had a talk with the inhabitants. I always follow this tradition, which I established for myself. While visiting a native village [*tuzemnoe selenie*] I never miss an opportunity to converse with residents on moral topics, although I do not write about what and where I talk because putting all this on paper would take too much time. Besides, it will be even harder to read due to my clumsy style. In the evening we departed, going back to Kenai. Thus, we finished all our business in the Nuchek part of the parish. It was only the Mednovtsy whom we did not have a chance to see.

June 19. Arrived at the same portage harbor that caused us so much trouble. My Kenaitze paddlers persuaded me not to sail around along the seacoast, where weather could delay us. And besides, it is dangerous to travel on the open sea with such bad paddlers as the Kenaitze, although on the ground they make excellent carriers. Ascended to a mountain range and stopped here for the night. What a wonderful view! Clean air, diverse vegetation. At such moments one wants to exclaim, "this is the place to live" and remain here forever. Unfortunately, it is no more than two months in a year that such good weather stays here. The rest of the year life in Kenai is simply unbearable.

June 20. Early in the morning we continued our journey and, thank God, having covered many miles, we reached the Kenai side of the harbor, where we were able to dry our clothes.

June 24. Arrived home to the redoubt, and found that a few Kenaitze from a distant village [Iliamna] along with a *baidarshchik*[21] [Savva Riktorov] from the Iliamna village were already waiting for me. They wished to perform rites of fast and penance and asked me to conduct services for them. Although I am very tired, it would be sinful to refuse their request.

June 26. Performed services for these [Iliamna] people who fast and cleanse their consciences.

June 28. Baptized an adult Kenaitze, who has stayed with the Kolchane since he was a small boy, and who now has returned to live with his parents. Then I heard confessions.

June 29. The Feast of St. Peter and St. Paul. Served the Liturgy without consecration and gave communion to those who fasted, then performed a customary prayer service and also delivered a sermon.

July 1. Baptized an infant.

July 7. Served the Hours, through an interpreter instructed the Kenaitze to visit the church more often and pray.

July 13. In the evening the Nuchek Chugach, returning from a hunting expedition for sea otters, suddenly came in order to perform rites of fast and penance. These are the natives who were away when I was visiting their village. I thanked both their *toion* and *zakazchik* for their desire to come and fulfill their Christian duties.

July 14. Performed services for those who fasted, told them about God and about the mysteries of confession and communion.

July 15. Again performed services and heard confessions.

July 16. I served the Liturgy without consecration and gave communion to forty-nine people. I am very glad that the Chugach came to fast and cleanse their consciences. This helps to draw conclusions about their attitude toward Orthodox religion. Judge for yourself. Upon completing their hunting trip they were allowed to come back home to their families, whom they had not seen for five months. It would have been natural for them to return home, but they did not. Instead, the Chugach decided to fulfill their Christian duty first, and only after this did they return home. Such a decision deserves praise!

July 20. The Day of the Holy Glorious Prophet Elijah. Performed a customary prayer service, and then delivered a sermon. The company gives people a day off during this feast, and therefore many faithful attended the church service.

July 28. Served the Liturgy without consecration, and explained to the Kenaitze what we pray about in the church and also what the first Great Litany means.

August 4. Served the Hours and taught the Kenaitze how they should pray to God, how to make the sign of the cross correctly, and how to worship Him. Also instructed the natives to concentrate their minds on God, for example, to imagine as if they stand if front of God Himself and converse with Him. I stressed that if they do not concentrate their minds on God, He will not accept their prayers.

August 6. Transfiguration of Our Lord Jesus Christ. Served the Liturgy without consecration, delivered a sermon in which I explained to the Kenaitze this feast and added some instructive words of advice. Many Kenaitze came for this service.

August 11. Served the Hours. Instructed the Kenaitze to abandon their bad habits such as dances, wild roaring, wild hopping, carelessness, and slovenliness.

August 15. Assumption Day. Served the Liturgy without consecration. Delivered a sermon. I have come to the conclusion that in this land reading a sermon makes no sense because few know Russian. Besides, even those who know do not completely understand bookish figures of speech. In my opinion, it will be better simply to explain to them everything in conversational words. As simply as I could, I explained to the Kenaitze the meaning of the present feast.

August 18. Served the Hours. Instructed the Kenaitze hunters who were going to the mountains [*khrebty*] not to forget about God and to pray to Him, for God is present everywhere. I pointed out to them that they should thank God, if they have good luck in hunting. Even when luck does not come, I reminded them not to lose heart, but again, ask God to help because everything depends on God. When God does not provide, it means that He waits for people to approach and ask Him. I performed a customary prayer service for these Kenaitze who were going to the mountains, and today they departed.

August 26. Performed royal prayer service [*tsarskii moleben*] to celebrate the coronation of the emperor, but with the exception of the redoubt's residents, who came to this service, the rest of the faithful were out of Kenai.

August 28. A steamship arrived and brought us an unpleasant gift: an epidemic. While this ship was staying in Kenai, many residents of the redoubt fell sick. I myself hardly can raise my limbs, but I have no time to lie down and rest.

August 30. Performed the Liturgy without consecration, visited by few of the faithful. The rest of the people are occupied with various work for the company.

September 1. Served the Hours and delivered a sermon. Then performed a customary prayer service for those who were preparing to depart. Indeed, the epidemic that struck us turned into a serious problem. Almost everybody is ill, suffering from coughing, sneezing, and contracting of the chest and weakness in all limbs. Moreover, some people's bodies shake. It is hard to predict what will happen with all of us. Besides, three days before the ship arrived, a dense fog covered the entire Kenai area, and today it is still not gone.

September 3. The fog lifted a little and the ship sailed off. The fog is still not completely gone, and it is hard to breath because of the humidity. With great difficulty I was able to finish some of my reports and letters. The songleader [Ivanov] and a songleader Pamfilov lie ill in bed and cannot even move.

September 5. Gave last rites to a woman who is also seriously ill.

September 8. The feast of Nativity of the Mother of God. Performed the Hours, a customary prayer service, but could not serve the Liturgy without consecration, since all my assistants are ill, and I myself suffer from a bad cough.

September 12. Gave last rites to an ailing woman who suffers from tuberculosis. For a short while she stopped coughing with blood, and now she can accept the holy mysteries.

September 14. The Feast of the Exaltation of the Cross. Served the Liturgy without consecration and a requiem service. From constant coughing we all lost our voices.

September 16. Gave last rites to two ailing people.

September 22. Sang a funeral service for a deceased person.

October 1. The Feast of Protection by the Most Holy Mother of God. Served the Liturgy without consecration. Explained the meaning of this feast. Carried presanctified gifts to the house of an ailing woman and gave her the sacraments. Although I already had given her last rites a few times, she wanted to partake in them again, and added, "I will die on the day of the Feast of Protection." So she did. At 2 o'clock in the afternoon she passed away.

October 3. I sang a funeral service for this woman.

October 6. Performed the Hours, a customary prayer service, and married two couples. Then I left the redoubt, and I stayed in my small cabin in the woods for the whole week.

October 13. Served the Liturgy without consecration and delivered a sermon. Thank God, the epidemic has ended. Fortunately, only two people died from this disease. Yet everybody lay ill.

October 27. Served the Liturgy without consecration. The Kenaitze hunters who had gone to the mountains, returned to the redoubt. As it turned out, all of them also fell sick, but, by the mercy of God, none died. I told the natives, "God sends a punishment for human sins." I celebrated such a fortunate outcome with performing a thanksgiving customary prayer service.

October 29. Deep snow fell, which means that winter has arrived.

November 3. Served the Hours. It is already cold. Visited the Chkituk village to give last rites to an ailing woman.

November 8. The Feast of St. Michael the Archangel. Served the Liturgy without consecration. Before the service I anointed with myrrh a Finn who earlier belonged to the Lutheran heresy, and who then joined the Orthodox Church. Explained to the Kenaitze the importance of guardian angels. Performed a customary prayer service in honor of St. Michael Archangel.

November 9. I visited the Kenai native village to give last rites to their *toion*. In the evening in the redoubt I gave last rites to a boy.

November 10. Served the Hours and a requiem service. The songleader visits the Chkituk village each day to change a plaster for a woman who suffers from a terrible abscess.

November 13. At 1 o'clock in the afternoon Zazubovich, who was the company's chief manager here, died.[22] It was clear that his health was fading away, but he never thought about death and never talked about it. It is a pity that before his death he was not able to join in the holy mysteries. Before Zazubovich died my songleader frequently visited his house and during conversations reminded him of his Christian duty. Yet the manager postponed this important business until, as he said, he felt worse. I myself stayed with Zazubovich for two hours, and again told him to accept the last rites, but he kept on repeating that he would do it when he felt really worse. Worse when? When I was visiting him, Zazubovich was already hardly able to speak.

There is a problem. Who will replace him now? Zazubovich had sent his assistant to the Kniks [Kniki, Knik villages, thus in original] for the whole winter, and there is no reliable person here among the company workers who might take over administration of the redoubt. To lock and seal off his office means everybody will suffer from hunger, because it will terminate all native trade and disrupt the company work. If we do the latter, the company workers will have to go away to hunt animals in order to feed themselves. After long deliberations, I decided to put the burden of management of the redoubt on my own shoulders, while awaiting further instructions from the office of the chief administration. At worst, if it happens that my arbitrary decision somehow does not please the company and its chief authorities, I will console myself with the thought that I made the right decision and sacrificed my own tranquility for the common good.

November 14. Visited the Chkituk village, where I sang a funeral service for a diseased woman. As soon as I reached the village, it started snowing, and the snow is now very deep.

November 15. Sang a funeral service for the manager. We have wept a little about the poor fellow. Then I treated all the company workers and the Kenaitze who came for his funeral with food and drinks and put these expenses to his account, and then brought all his belongings to the trade store. Having mourned a little, we returned to our homes.

November 17. Served the Liturgy without consecration. Instructed the Kenaitze about the worldly life and the afterlife. Then I performed a requiem service for the manager. Now I have to attend to the company's business. Well, since I put myself in this situation, I will have to manage this work as best I can.

November 18. I sent a letter to the company's head office about the death of the manager.

November 21. The Presentation in the Temple of the Mother of God. Served the Hours. Too cold. For this reason, I could not serve the Liturgy without consecration.

December 6. The Feast of St. Nicholas, the Wonderworker. Served the Liturgy without consecration. By their presence the people who came for this service warmed the air in the church, and this helped me to perform the Liturgy. I instructed the faithful about the need to glorify God by veneration of the saints. Saints reached holiness through their superhuman deeds and by defeating worldly temptations, flesh and the devil, certainly with God's help. Therefore, when we venerate a saint we simultaneously glorify God. I also told the faithful about some miracle works, which St. Nicholas achieved. Then I performed a customary prayer service. After the end of all services, I treated all who were present with drinks and food as far as I could afford, because today I celebrate my name day.

December 8. I served the Hours. There is a snowstorm today.

December 15. Performed the Hours and a customary prayer service. Very cold. It is a pity that I do not have a thermometer anymore, but I assume it is more than thirty degrees below zero [Celsius].

December 22. It became warmer, and I was able to serve the Liturgy without consecration, a requiem service, and also baptized an infant.

December 24. Served vespers in a regular manner as prescribed by the church regulations.

December 25. The Nativity of Our Lord Jesus Christ. Served the Liturgy without consecration, spoke about this feast, and performed a customary prayer service. I also treated with food and drinks everybody who came to celebrate this feast.

December 26. Served the Hours and then a requiem service for the deceased manager, for he did not have anybody to pray for his soul. In Kenai he had neither close relative nor distant relatives nor friends. For the Kenaitze, whom I invited for his funeral feast, I cooked a requisite memorial meal of cereal. The fact that my letter about the death of the manager was returned undelivered offended me very much. In his letter of response the chief of the Mountain Expedition asked me to help him with *baidarkas* and paddlers. If I had had all these things, I would not have disturbed him and would not have asked him to deliver the mail to Kodiak. I sent the letter back to the chief of the Expedition and let him decide whether to deliver my mail or not, but requested that he not send it back.

December 27. Performed the Hours, then a customary prayer service, and requiem services at the request of the Kenaitze who celebrated their name days. Today many natives came for the services....

December 28. Performed the Hours, a customary prayer service. Praised the Kenaitze for regular attendance at church services and praying during feasts.

The year is coming to an end. Will I be able to find something that might console my mourning spirit? Alas! Most probably, not. In my daily life I cannot even notice anything that might raise my hopes. Only trifles and daily routine. I pray to the prophets and beg them to give me wings. I would have flown away and rested in peace at some holy cloister awaiting the mercy of a saving God!

Unworthy, Missionary Hegumen Nikolai.

1864. January 1. The New Year came, but I am still a decrepit creature and cannot renew myself. I do not know what the coming year will bring me. It is hard to describe the melancholy and sadness that now eat away my heart. Well, let God decide everything! Performed the Liturgy without consecration and a customary prayer service. In my instructive sermon I told the Kenaitze about the meaning of the New Year.

January 6. Epiphany. Served the Liturgy without consecration, performed the rite of water blessing and also instructed the natives how to store the holy water and when to use it.

January 12. Performed the Hours and a customary prayer service for a person who celebrated his name day.

January 19. Performed the Liturgy without consecration and a customary prayer service. I suffer from a toothache. It might be the result of a cold I caught earlier.

January 26. Served the Hours. The toothache is unbearable, and it does not leave me. I try to use various means to somehow relieve the pain.

February 2. The Feast of Purification. Served the Liturgy without consecration and delivered a sermon. The weather is bad. Although it is not so cold, it is snowing heavily.

February 3. I have a headache. The right side of my head especially hurts, and I cannot hear from my right ear.

February 9. Performed the Hours, a customary prayer service, and a requiem service. Although I do not feel a pain in my ear, I still cannot hear.

February 16. I could not perform services because I applied a plaster to the back of my head. The songleader replaced me today and sang the Hours.

February 19. I performed the royal prayer service [*tsarskii moleben*].

February 23. Served the Hours and instructed the natives to tell other Kenaitze from distant villages to come to fast by the first week. Here in Kenai we do not keep Shrove-tide feast in high esteem, and therefore the local people do not celebrate it.

March 1. The Day of Mutual Forgiveness [*Proshchalnii Den'*]. Served the Liturgy without consecration and read a sermon, in which I told the Kenaitze that we should forgive each other, if we want Our Lord to forgive us. In the evening a few redoubt residents and Kenaitze, before leaving the redoubt, visited me to say good-bye, as they are accustomed to do.

March 2. We started to perform church services, and people who will partake in the rites of fast and penance are gradually coming.

March 3. We prayed. Baptized six infants.

March 4. We prayed again, and I also instructed the Kenaitze. Today I began hearing native confessions, and slowly proceed, waiting for when all of them return from their hunting trips. I do not want to hurry the Kenaitze in such important business. That is why I decided to start hearing confessions earlier.

March 7. Saturday. Served the Liturgy without consecration. Before giving communion I delivered a sermon, which was addressed to everybody, but especially to the Kenaitze. 137 people received communion.

March 8. Served the Hours, and delivered a sermon. Performed a thanksgiving customary prayer service on behalf of the communicants. Then I blessed the present natives and dismissed them.

March 9. Visited the Kenaitze village in the vicinity of the redoubt to give last rites to an ailing *toion*. He could not partake in the rites of fast and penance because of his poor health.

March 15. Served the Liturgy without consecration and a requiem service. Then the Kenaitze left for their hunting expeditions.

March 22. Served the Hours and told the Kenaitze about the necessity of partaking in the sacraments of confession and communion. Those Kenaitze who were not able to partake in the rites of fast and penance during the first week, have now returned and came for the service.

March 25. Served the Liturgy without consecration, during which forty-eight people received communion. I delivered a requisite word of address to the communicants, and instructed them how they should behave after receiving communion.

March 29. Performed the Hours, a customary prayer service and requiem.

April 1. We are occupied with writing letters and reports. Besides, I am busy trading with the Kenaitze in the company store. Could I ever have imagined that I would have to become a trader? Well, now I am!

April 5. Served the Hours and told the Kenaitze through an interpreter to pray to God diligently, make the sign of the cross, and bow in the correct manner. I also added that they should pay attention not only to the outward manifestations of religion, but also to turn their inner world to God. I instructed them to set their hearts and minds and to imagine that they stand in front of Almighty God. Otherwise, what is the use of simply making the sign of the cross and bowing, if your mind often flows away somewhere else, and even turns to something inappropriate at such a solemn moment. Such empty praying will be unpleasant to God. God will respond to inner reverence, not to outward demonstrations.

April 10. I visited the Kenaitze village in the vicinity of Kenai and sang a funeral service for the deceased *toion*. Then I instructed the Kenaitze about the worldly life and afterlife and reminded them not to concentrate too much on the first. It is better to care about the afterlife, to live according to God's testaments, and to revere God with your good behavior, which will eventually bring eternal life. Indeed, here in this world everything is temporary, but there in the afterlife there will be eternal existence.

April 12. Palm Sunday. Served the Liturgy without consecration. I related to the Kenaitze how the Savior had entered the temple in Jerusalem, and how people welcomed him with palm branches, and how some threw their clothes under His feet to show that they revered Him as their king. In the same way, our hearts should also be turned to the Savior. Although we cannot see with our eyes the coming Savior, we can see many people around us, who are either poor or do not have anything to cover themselves with, and shiver from cold. Take pity on the poor and unprotected and homeless, feed the hungry in the name of the Savior, and by doing this one will please the Savior Himself, for He once said that by helping the poor brethren people helped Him. For such good deeds He will glorify you before the Heavenly Father. I performed services in the order prescribed for the Passion Week.

April 19. Holy Easter. Served the Liturgy without consecration. We are lucky: the weather is good. My only regret so far is that nobody has come from Kodiak to replace the deceased manager. Trading in the store, which is not my business, already bores me.

April 20. Served, celebrated the feast, and baptized an infant. The visiting Kenaitze pilgrims who came for the feast services departed today.

April 22. The assistant manager, who wintered in a few Knik villages, has returned to Kenai. Although formally the assistant still cannot take over the management of the redoubt, at least he will partially lift from my shoulders the burden of trading.

April 26. Served the Hours and told the Kenaitze about God's grace.

May 2. Baptized an infant.

May 3. Served the Liturgy without consecration and married two couples.

May 4. Finally the company's representatives came from Kodiak to take over the management of the redoubt. What surprises me is that the chief manager at Kodiak did not respond to my letter. They did not even thank me for taking care of the company's business for half a year. I may assume that in their eyes I did something wrong. From their silence I also may conclude that apparently it would have been better to leave everything as it was. Well, it will be a good lesson for me in future!

May 9. The Feast of St. Nicholas. Served the Liturgy without consecration, read the sermon, and performed a customary prayer service.

May 17. Performed the Hours, a customary prayer service and a requiem, and also married a couple.

May 24. Served the Liturgy without consecration, read a sermon and baptized an infant. My teeth still disturb me very much. People advised me to smoke tobacco, and indeed, as soon as I smoked a little the pain subsided. *Toions* from the Knik villages arrived, and ask me to visit them. They say that old women, especially those who are ill, regret that I am going to leave them. They hope to receive my blessing at least for the last time. Listening to the *toions'* words I could not keep myself from tears.

May 28. The Feast of Ascension. Served the Liturgy without consecration and read a sermon. In the evening I departed with the purpose of visiting the Kenaitze villages.

May 31. When I reached the mouth of the Susitna River, I found gathering there natives from Susitna and Kniks, who were very glad that had I arrived.

June 1. I began performing services. A large number of the Kenaitze gathered here in order to participate in the services and to pray. The weather is very hot. I hardly can breathe. The smell from the fish they hang out in the sun to dry makes this sweltering heat unbearable. Small fish called *telkha* stink especially bad. They pile this fish in large pits and keep it there until the fish rots, after which the fat gets separated from the meat . Then they squeeze this fat and put it into large leather bags. Afterwards they eat this fat. It seems that nobody but the Kenaitze themselves can appreciate this delicacy.

June 2. Performed a service, baptized five infants, and heard confessions.

June 3. Performed a service again. Baptized ten infants and also heard confessions.

June 4. Served the Liturgy without consecration. The total number of the Kenaitze to whom I gave communion is 134, except for four small children. I also married four couples. Sang funeral services for the deceased natives. I feel extremely tired, not from the work, but more from the suffocating heat. In the evening I left these natives. At least en route there will be a chance to breathe a gulp of fresh air. At this time of the year nights are not dark here, and one even can see the crimson disk of the midnight sun, only without rays.

June 5. The Tyonek village. Arrived here early in the morning, and served the Hours for those local natives who had gathered here from various neighboring camps, where they usually stay, fish, and prepare their winter supplies. I noticed that the local *toion* has a good garden, where he grows potatoes and turnips. This *toion* also owns a decent good-sized house.

June 6 Again performed services, and also baptized twelve infants.

June 7. Trinity Day. Served the Liturgy without consecration, where I gave communion to 115 natives. After dinner I departed.

June 8. The Kustatan village. Performed services and baptized six infants. I reprimanded a Kenaitze who, as I was told, shamanized. This native does not deny this, and says, "I am not familiar with any devilish power, but simply tell people whatever comes to my mind, and also jump and hop, as I saw old men do in the old days. It happens that, as a result of this, people sometimes recover and they pay me for my work. But sometimes they die. In this case I might make up some story why it happened and people believe me." In response I said, "So you only deceive people," and he admitted that he did. For such deception, according to the rules of the Christian church, I had him kneel down during the whole service. After this I firmly warned him to stop shamanizing, and he promised to leave off his trade.

June 9. Performed services and heard confession.

June 10. Performed services and gave communion to seventy-four natives from two villages. Sang a funeral service for the deceased people whose names the Kenaitze gave me.

June 11. The Titukil village. Performed services. There are so many mosquitoes here that one can hardly stand them and it is impossible to escape their stings.

June 12. In Titukil I performed services and heard confessions from the inhabitants of three other small settlements, which took place on this side of the Inlet, where the redoubt is located.

June 13. Performed services and gave communion to sixty-three natives, and also conducted a requiem service for the deceased. Then I left for the redoubt.

June 14. Performed the Hours, a customary prayer service, baptized an infant.

June 16. A steamship arrived and stayed at the harbor. The ship brought the Most Reverend Petr, who came to the shore and drank tea with me at my house. Six hours later the steamship sailed off to the sea. The ship also brought to us Vladimir Stafeev, the new redoubt manager, who is young, single, and apparently inexperienced. It will be hard for him to control the local people. Who makes such unwise decisions among the company's authorities? To such remote areas as Kenai they should send married people, who possess some administrative experience to a certain extent.

June 21. Performed the Liturgy without consecration and a customary prayer service. Had dinner with the new manager at his house. It is raining today.

June 22. Served the Hours, and also reminded the Kenaitze about the necessity of going to church on a regular basis and storing their food supplies in advance. Observing the carefree nature of this people, one would not err in wishing that the authorities would introduce some sort of inductive measures that might make the Kenaitze more disciplined.

June 29. The Feast of St. Peter and St. Paul. Served the Liturgy without consecration, and read a sermon. Then I performed a customary prayer service and a requiem for the late Zazubovich. Otherwise, who else will remember this person, who did not have any friends and relatives.

July 1. I am occupied with preparations for another expedition.

July 5. Served the Liturgy without consecration, read a sermon, performed a customary prayer service, and completed preparations for the journey.

July 6. Today I found out that the new manager cancelled my trip. His excuse is that he cannot find paddlers for me, and I believe him. The Kenaitze have already noticed that Stafeev has a weak character, and decided to see what would happen if they did not listen to him.

July 12. Served the Hours, read a sermon. Earlier I had a toothache, and now one of my ears cannot hear. I had to apply a patch behind my ear.

July 14. I was able to serve the Hours, and the pain has calmed down a little, but I still hardly can hear.

July 26. Served the Liturgy without consecration and baptized an infant. An Iliamna *baidarshchik* [Savva Riktorov] along with his team arrived at the redoubt. He talked me into performing services for them, for they want to partake in the rites of fast and penance. He says that the Nushagak priest does not visit them. I certainly cannot reject such an important request.

August 2. Served the Liturgy without consecration, where I joined in the holy mysteries these visitors from Iliamna, of which there were fifteen people. I instructed these visiting Kenaitze to behave decently at work, home, and everywhere.

August 4. Baptized an infant.

August 6. Transfiguration. Served the Liturgy without consecration, read a sermon and told the Kenaitze about the meaning of the Transfiguration. Baptized two infants.

August 9. Performed the Hours and a customary prayer service. Told the Kenaitze that there is nothing wrong with feeling anger, but instructed them to avoid committing a sin. Some of the natives are still rather vindictive in their savagery. They certainly do not think that vindictiveness is a sin.

August 11. Began services for the visiting Iliamna people, who are fasting, and also for some residents of the redoubt.

August 15. The Feast of Assumption. Served the Liturgy without consecration and gave communion to twenty-nine people. Read a sermon. Performed a customary prayer service.

August 16. Served the Hours and baptized an infant.

August 18. Again the steamship arrived and brought the Most Reverend Petr, and here I am: almost deaf and with the patch on the back of my head.

August 19. The Most Reverend visited our church and my house.

August 23. The Most Reverend performed a service which was attended by a large number of the Kenaitze. When the Kenaitze learned that the Most Reverend would perform a service in our church on August 23rd, they notified all nearby villages and by the day of the service everybody had arrived, either on foot or by *baidarkas* across the Inlet. Many brought their children. During the service the church could not accommodate all the faithful, and many Kenaitze stood on the portico or crowded outside of all the windows. All the natives watched the rites of the service with rapt attention. After the Liturgy without consecration all the Kenaitze approached the Most Reverend asking for his blessing. After the service how they talked about what they had seen! With special pleasure they repeated to each other what they had seen and how the priests were dressed and what they did. In short, everything looked new to them, and the natives remained very satisfied. After the service his Grace stopped in my house, where we drank tea and also had some snacks.

August 24. At 2 o'clock in the afternoon the ship sailed off and the Kenaitze departed as well. It again became quiet in our redoubt and life returned to the same old routine. I sang a funeral service for a deceased person who drowned. No sooner had I returned to my house than it started to rain heavily.

August 25. Performed a customary prayer service and the Hours. Now I can hear with my right ear.

August 31. Performed a customary prayer service for the manager, who is going to Nuchek to get married.

September 4. Our manager returned and has decided to postpone his marriage. Our portage route that we usually use to go to Nuchek scared him very much. No doubt this route looks scary to any new arrival. These great hulks of mountains, which one meets en route and whose peaks covered with snow, may make even people with strong hearts lose their nerve.

September 6. Performed the Hours and a customary prayer service. These days people in Kenai are mostly collecting their potato harvest. My own garden brought a good crop.

September 8. The Feast of the Nativity of Most Holy Mother of God. Served the Liturgy without consecration, read a sermon, and performed a customary prayer service.

September 9. Performed a requiem service. Married a couple. So much trouble did this wedding cause me. It was Panfilov [Pamfilov], the assistant manager, who was married, and it was his second marriage. Of course, the most honored guest of this wedding was the manager Stafeev, a young man and a reveler. Unfortunately, there was plenty of vodka, so they got completely drunk and behaved improperly. But I am glad that there were no complaints from anybody. And besides, who would complain? Among the guests nobody remembers anything. When they invited me to this wedding dinner I somehow felt that nothing good would come of it, and excused myself by saying that I had to collect my potato crop as soon as possible.

September 10. I reprimanded Stafeev for his behavior, but he says he does not remember anything.

September 13. Served the Hours. I also punished the songleader Pamfilov by forcing him to perform low bows for his drinking. Like his father, he is very addicted to vodka. Panfilov asks to be discharged from his duties as reader. I ordered him to send a formal petition as required. It seems unrealistic to expect any improvements in his behavior, and again, the reason for this is an everlasting vice—drinking.

September 14. The Feast of Exaltation. Served the Liturgy without consecration and delivered a sermon and also stressed to what indecent behavior drunkenness may lead people.

September 18. Performed a customary prayer service for those who were ready to leave for the [Mountain] Expedition to deliver there a supply of potatoes.

September 20. Performed the Hours and a customary prayer service, and a requiem. All our Kenaitze are away and occupied with hunting in the mountains. The redoubt workers sailed off to the Mountain Expedition. For these reasons, there are few faithful in church today. Word recently reached us that some deadly epidemic was coming. I remind the Kenaitze that everything is in God's hands, and one cannot escape from God's will.

October 1. The Feast of the Protection by the Mother of God. Served the Liturgy without consecration. I treated the faithful with food in my small cabin in the woods. I always celebrate this feast day in the woods.

October 4. Served the Hours. It is not snowing yet, and the weather is humid. I am suffering from a toothache again.

October 7. Much snow fell.

October 11. Served the Hours and delivered a sermon. The *baidarka* with the redoubt workers returned from the Expedition. Stafeev brought for himself a native girl, but I reprimanded him a little, and ordered him to take the girl back, and he did as I said. People told me that the manager regretted having to do this, but he is afraid of me. Were I a compliant missionary, who knows what would have happened here in Kenai.

October 18. I served the Liturgy without consecration, read a sermon, and baptized two infants.

October 22. The songleader visited the Kenai native village to sing a funeral service for an infant.

October 24. Gave last rites to a sick woman in the redoubt, who has suffered from tuberculosis for a long time.

October 25. Served the Hours. Praised the Kenaitze who recently returned from their hunting expeditions in the mountains, for coming to church to address their prayer to our Lord, and to thank Him for the good hunting and for their safe return. I also added that everything comes from God, both our luck and health, and all our life is in God's hands.

November 1. Served the Liturgy without consecration and delivered a sermon, during which I pointed out to the Kenaitze that they still do not commemorate their deceased people in a Christian manner. Sang a funeral service for an infant. Then I performed a requiem service and later blessed the songleader's newly built house.

November 12. Gave last rites to an ailing woman in the redoubt.

November 14. Served a prayer service for a person who celebrated his name day.

November 15. Served the Hours, delivered a sermon and sang a funeral service for the deceased woman.

November 21. The Feast of the Presentation in the Temple of the Mother of God. Served the Hours, but could not perform the Liturgy without consecration because it was very cold. Delivered a sermon and performed a customary prayer service.

November 22. Did not perform any service, because of the freezing weather, and besides, my songleader is ill.

November 29. I again suffer from a terrible toothache, and cannot go outside in the cold. The songleader sang the Hours for me.

December 6. The Feast of St. Nicholas. Fortunately, it became warmer, and I was able to perform the Liturgy without consecration. Delivered a sermon, where I told the Kenaitze about St. Nicholas and how this saint lived all his life in a holy manner, and how God rewarded St. Nicholas with blessed power to help human beings who live in poverty and misery and who address to him their prayers. Performed a customary prayer service. Today I celebrate my name day. On this occasion, having finished the church service, I treated all natives who came for the service with food. The Kenaitze remained very pleased with my treat.

December 13. Performed the Hours, a customary prayer service, and two requiem services.

December 20. Performed services. Sang a funeral service for a deceased infant. Reminded the Kenaitze that death comes unexpectedly, and even youth does not protect us from this. One cannot rely on a strong build and good health. It is better to try to live a virtuous life, and always be ready for death. Served a requiem service. The songleader visited the Kenai native village to sing a funeral service for a deceased Kenaitze woman.

December 22. Read prayers [*molitvoslovil*] for a woman who has given birth.

December 24. Was occupied with the usual chores both at home and in the church. Served vespers. Many natives came to this service. The Kenaitze remember the feast [of the Nativity of Christ, or Christmas] well, and come from distant villages to pray and to sing carols to glorify Christ and maybe to receive something for this. We treat with tea and bread those Kenaitze who sing carols. Then we cook some food for them. During the first day I make for the natives something myself. Next day it is the company that usually treats them with food. Thus, the Kenaitze not only celebrate this feast, but also have a chance to eat their fill, for at this season they do not have enough food. As a matter of fact, the latter occurs mainly because of their own unreasonableness. The natives do not want to parcel out their supplies and to extend them for the whole year. Instead they eat very much and voraciously until all the food is gone. And this is repeated each year.

December 25. The Feast of the Nativity of Christ. As required I performed the service in a solemn feast manner. I told the Kenaitze what this feast means, and how Christians should celebrate it. Performed a customary prayer service. Having finished the services, I treated with food my neighbors, residents of the redoubt, and the Kenaitze.

December 26. Served the Hours, and delivered a sermon. Afterwards, the manager treated everybody with food. In the evening he and a few others took a notion in their heads to put on masquerade dress and masks and go around visiting the shacks of local people.

December 27. Served the Hours. Explained to the faithful that it is indecent for Christians to wear masquerade dress. By turning oneself into some scarecrow one distorts the human image endowed upon us by God. I also performed a customary prayer service for those Kenaitze who celebrated their name days. Then Stafeev came to me with his head hanging, and asked me to forgive him for his foolishness. I gave him a long instructive talk, which he kindly listened to, and then said, "I heard that you are very demanding, and I would not have started putting on masks if I had not been drunk." I responded that it is not me who is demanding. It is the Christian law itself that forbids such foolish things. This evening and the next ones there was no noise anymore and everything was quiet. It is amazing how this man, who is said to have belonged to high St. Petersburg society, never heard from other priests that it is shameful to do such things. Baptized an infant. It is cold. I again suffer from a toothache, which most probably was caused by the cold.

One more year has passed and reduced the time of my worldly presence. My God, what will finally await me? My sinful heart is full of deep sorrow because it did not feel anything good and promising during the past year. I started to browse various instructive books on my shelf and ran across one useful article, which I read with pleasure and which consoled me a little. Here is one passage from this article: "My son! I am more satisfied with patience and humility rather than with great joy and happiness. Why are you so upset about petty things? Even large troubles should not bother you. Let it go, small and large troubles are not the first and not the last to come. They will be with you as long as you live. If you always take things close to your heart, everything is gone for you. Remember that you are neither God nor angel, but a simple human being. How can you be so content all the time, when neither angels nor the first man in the Paradise were? Oh, Lord! Blessed be Thy word, which is sweeter than honey to my lips. Grant me a good end, help me quietly to leave this world. Remember me, God, and guide me by a straight route to Thy Kingdom."

Missionary of the Kenai Mission Hegumen Nikolai.

Description of the Kenai Area[23]

Kenai Region

No one has exactly defined the borders of this area and measured its size. It is impossible to say with certainty about the amount of fertile and infertile soil because the whole area is still very much wilderness. So far there have been no attempts to cultivate the local soil except in the vicinity of the redoubt, where people plant potato and turnip gardens, which produce abundant crops without any fertilizers.

Natural Wildlife

The local mountains are mostly of sandstone. However, large rocks also can be found. Not much is known about minerals. Opposite of the redoubt two volcanoes can be seen with the smoke coming from the tops of these large hills, but with hardly any fire. Forests occupy the greater part of this land. Trees are not to be found on the hilltops and mountain ranges and spots dominated by the tundra. Among the most widespread trees one can single out the spruce, birch, and close to rivers, the poplar, alder, and willow. Here and there rowan and cherry trees grow along with other small bushes. On mountain ranges one can see juniper. A fair number of animals roam the local forests, specifically the moose, deer, mountain sheep, river beaver, black and brown bears, wolves, black and red foxes, otter, mink and ermine. Birds: geese, swans, cranes, ducks of different kinds, seagulls, and loons. In the local woods one can find hazel hens, ptarmigans, eagles, hawks, eagle owls, and little owls. Fish run from the sea upstream. From second half of May to the second half of August king and silver salmon red fish run. Having spawned their eggs, they die. Yet, such fish species as the salmon and the loach move up to rivers and lakes and winter there. In spring these fish go down to the Inlet. As for reptiles, there are few except worms, leeches, and frogs in lakes. Insects: mosquitoes, wasps, flies, bumblebees, red, white, and yellow butterflies.

Inhabitants

As of 1864 the number of all inhabitants of the Kenai parish was 806 males and 807 females. Therefore, their total number is 1,613. These native inhabitants are divided into the Kenaitze, Chugach, Ugalentsy, and Mednovtsy. Although the Kenaitze and Mednovtsy speak different languages, they can understand each other because of their frequent contacts. The Chugach are almost the same people as the Aleuts. By origin and language and even by their appearance the Ugalentsy stand close to the Kolosh. Local natives do not have a very developed spiritual life. All their activities are directed to only one goal: how to feed themselves. The local inhabitants, especially those who live close to the sea, have a very low birth rate. They usually subsist on mammals and other products of the sea, and when these natives become ill they almost always cough blood and have tuberculosis. On the other hand, those Kenaitze who live far from the sea and eat the meat they find in inland areas are usually healthier than other peoples. If inland natives die, it is mostly from natural causes such as injuries and colds.

Dwellings

In this area one will not find towns or even villages in the usual sense of the word. In summer on the seashore or on riverbanks the Kenaitze usually set up some sort of barns, where they dry their fish, which serves as their food supply for the whole year. When they finish drying the fish, the natives wander off wherever they want. During cold winters and severe frosts natives gather somewhere in a dense forest, where they build winter dwellings and stay here until it becomes warm. As soon as warm weather returns, they again wander off. Some Chugach who live a settled life on the seacoast reside in permanent dwellings.

Life Ways and Manners

Almost all local peoples practice a wandering lifestyle. By now I have baptized them, and they are all Christians. Yet there is a small number of those whom I was not able to convert. These are the Mednovtsy and the Kolchane, who reside in remote areas. There is no way to penetrate to their remote habitats, especially to Kolchane country. As was mentioned earlier, local inhabitants build their dwellings carelessly and only for temporary use. The Mednovtsy people as well as the far-off Kenaitze who live in Knik do not even have such temporary shacks. Where the animals go, they usually move as well. Where hunting is successful, these natives usually stay in huts covered with skins. Their clothing is also made of skins. Those who live close to the redoubt are used to the Russian cloth and live a more regular life.

I have not noticed any special customs they might observe on the occasion of a birth or a marriage. When the priest is not around, they usually weep hysterically during funerals. Earlier, all relatives of the deceased singed their heads, whereas the closest kin tortured themselves by slashing their bodies. Nowadays they have abandoned this custom and only cut out their hair in a circle. All the belongings of a deceased person are divided among the kin, and nothing is usually left for a wife or for children. Festivities, amusements, music, and feasts are done in the following manner. People from one village go to another village for a treat. No matter how many people come, all eat to an extreme and dance to exhaustion. Dancing is accompanied by sounds of a wooden hammer. Usually one of the natives beats on a wooden board with this hammer, while others roar and tap their feet on the floor. Here is all their amusement. Then guests receive gifts: beads, deer skins and so forth.

Industry

Local peoples pursue one kind of industry: hunting. If natives kill extra animals they usually bring the meat to the company. Gardening among the natives hardly exists. Only those who live in the vicinity of the redoubt plant some potatoes and turnips. The crops happen to be abundant here, even without any fertilizers. If encouraged and provided with extra seeds, more natives will learn gardening.

Fishing

In the second half of May fishing season begins. Offshore in the bay people usually set up a stick fence [*zapor*] about seventy feet in length. People sit down on this fence and keep a basket trap [*sok*] made of roots. The fish come upon the fence and move along the fence and get into the traps. In rivers natives set up fish traps made of osier [*mordy*]. The most widespread fish specimen here is the king salmon, whose weight reaches seventy-four and more pounds depending on the season. In the last days of July some fish reach 110 pounds, but by then they are not so tasty. Natives dry the fish and store it as their food supply for the rest of the year. Russians living in the redoubt usually salt this fish. If necessary, the company buys king salmon from the natives at thirty kopecks per fish.

Trade

The company controls all trade operations here. The natives are not satisfied with the prices they receive for furs, and for this reason they do not especially desire to go hunting. It is only when he needs tobacco or some trinkets that the savage goes after fur-bearing animals. If the meat had not been a major part of their diet, the natives most certainly should have procured ten times less animal skins than they do now. For example, there are plenty of sables in the Kenai area, and their furs are of good quality. Yet the natives hardly hunt them. Only boys catch them for amusement. The natives usually use good sable furs to make clothing, while they carry low quality furs to the company store. When asked why they do this, natives usually respond, "The company does not have eyes and all the same will give us a ruble for any pelt."

Enlightening of Natives

All local inhabitants who have been baptized now belong to the Orthodox Church. Yet there still exists a small number of unenlightened natives, who live very far away. The word of the Gospel has not yet been heard there. Those savages who accepted the Christian faith have changed for the better and have abandoned their bad customs. Even impudence, which is so characteristic of a savage's behavior, has disappeared. The Kenaitze became quiet, humble, and harmless. Living under the constant supervision of a spiritual shepherd, it might take only ten years before the morality of the newly baptized improves to the level of good faithful Russians. Even now their moral life is quite decent.

Government

Within their clans natives are headed by *toions*. Each village has its own *toion*. Incidentally, with the exception of trade, Russians do not exercise any control over administration of the Kenaitze whatsoever. Moreover, the Kenaitze's own *toions* possess little power. What these natives practice is very far from subordination. One would rather call it reliance on yourself [*samovlastie*]. The Kenaitze like to repeat, "Why should I listen to a *toion*? Does he feed and clothe me?" Furthermore, they do not have a system of punishment for those who do wrong. Natives occasionally might threaten a wrongdoer that they would report on him to the Russians. Yet, these mischief-makers know very well that the Russians, like their own *toions*, will hardly do anything to them. Things would be better if the company developed some system of light punishments for the natives.

CHAPTER TWO

Hieromonk Nikita (Nikita Marchenkov)

A Report to the Alaskan Ecclesiastical Consistory, May 27, 1885[24]

I HAVE THE HONOR to report to the Ecclesiastical Consistory that for the past year within the borders of my mission everything was well except for some disease that struck us and whose major symptom is coughing. This disease started in Kenai as early as 1883. In the past year twenty-nine children below the age of eight have died from it. The disease turned into an epidemic and continues to ravage the entire Kenai population, touching not only children, but also adults. I myself could not avoid the common lot, and was ill for a long time. The disease is especially dangerous for pregnant women. All the pregnant women who became ill died right after giving birth.

I performed all ministrations in time as far as I could, although in those villages which are located far from Kenai, some people unfortunately do die without receiving last rites and are buried without a funeral service. Yet, upon receiving information about their death, I conduct funeral services for these people either in absentia or during my regular visits to these villages. Working in the position of songleader, Creole Nikolai Sorokovikov has always been diligent and shrewd in fulfilling his duties, for which he has good skills. As for the school, which we talked so much about, I cannot say anything promising. Despite my sincere desire, I shall hardly be able to establish a permanent school in Kenai. The teacher, whom I hired practically at my own expense, taught children reading and writing quite successfully all summer. However, later being afraid of the severe winter and boring life in Kenai, he returned to Kodiak. I personally cannot teach because I spend much time traveling to various localities of my parish. When I stay home, I have to work for myself, because to hire somebody in summer is practically impossible. Everybody who is able to work at this season, from small children to adults, are employed either by Alaska Commercial Company to salt fish right on the spot in Kenai, or by the fish cannery in Kasilof. Therefore, upon return from my first regular trip I have to fish on my own in order to make some food supplies for winter. Carrying water to wash this fish, and also cleaning and salting these fish, I do by myself.

Besides, my eyesight grows worse and worse, and I have not been able to hear from my left ear for a long time, and on top of this, my right ear is in severe pain. I also have constant headaches, which make me lose consciousness from time to time. All this does not allow me to concentrate on something or perform writing work any length of time. And finally I honestly want to admit that even if I had the relevant knowledge, I am not the right person to work with children. For this work one has to possess both habit and experience. As for me, working with them for two or three weeks exhausts me and makes me completely sick. The school guidelines, which were released by the Holy Synod and approved by his Imperial Majesty, are nice in theory, but unfortunately not applicable to the local conditions of the Kenai area, because classes can meet here on a regular basis only in winter.

A Trip to Tyonek and Kustatan to Perform Various Ministrations, 1885[25]

June 16. *Baidarkas* arrived from Tyonek to fetch me. I started to prepare myself for the trip, but had to postpone my journey because of the strong wind that continued until June 19th.

June 19. Having performed a customary prayer service for my safe trip, I left the redoubt (or in other words Kenai) and by crossing the Inlet set out directly for Tyonek, which is about thirty-five miles away and which took us about seven hours to reach. As soon as I arrived in Tyonek I immediately instructed the natives to begin performing rites of fasting and other preparations for communion. I also strongly reprimanded the natives for some serious drawbacks on their behavior, which I will explain below.

June 20. The service proceeded as required in the local chapel. Then I had to conduct various investigations and cross-examinations. I also wrote birth certificate records and checked confessional rosters. Given the uncooperative and cunning nature of the Kenaitze, this is a hard and depressing procedure.

June 21. Before the beginning of the service I anointed three infants with myrrh. After the service I performed a funeral rite for the deceased at the village cemetery. During the Liturgy I commemorated these deceased people. After dinner I began hearing confessions. The total number of confessed people is [blank space]. The evening service immediately followed the confession, which usually continues for a long time. Thus, the whole day I was occupied with performing services.

June 22. Always trying to prevent the Kenaitze, especially their women, from breaking the rules of abstinence, I woke them up as early as possible, made them dress and be prepared for communion and then did not dismiss them until the very end of the Liturgy. After having sung together a requisite prayer, I prepared the communion wine and bread right away and celebrated the liturgy, during which I gave communion to 150 natives.

From the beginning of the Liturgy to the moment when everybody was about to receive communion I imposed genuflection on three young native men and one woman in front of all the people as a model punishment. These four people violated abstinence by ridiculing the relevant instructions I gave after the vigil. So they had to stand embarrassed on their knees and with their heads down. Yet I allowed them to receive communion.

June 23. Wind and rain prevented us from immediate departure, and only in the evening were we able to leave. By nighttime we arrived in Kustatan, where I encountered the same problems and concerns. I forgot to mention that before leaving Tyonek I joined in holy matrimony three young couples.

June 24. Early in the morning we set up the church tent and began services. Today is the feast day of the Nativity of St. John the Forerunner. To protect our service from the rain I had the residents of the village set up the cover in front of the church tent.

June 25. I continued to perform services, and as usual I verified various church documents. Nothing special happened in Kustatan except that this village, whose population has already shrunk, has now lost six of its residents. One of them, a young man, was ripped apart by a bear. After the matins I baptized an infant and then sang a funeral service for those who died during the winter. After dinner I heard confessions. During this trip I had to work without an interpreter. Therefore, I had to use gestures to make myself clear. In this manner before I started confessing people, I instructed them as much as I could.

June 26. After the matins, we gathered for a requisite prayer in the beginning of the Holy Communion. Then I served the Divine Liturgy during which I gave communion to twenty-seven natives.

June 27. This day we had to idly sit or lie in a log cabin with a low ceiling, where I could not even stretch out. Because of the torrential rain we could not perform services or do anything else. Yesterday, when I was giving communion service, I could already feel how my feet were submerged in mud and water. Then we noticed puddles both inside the tent and especially outside where the faithful stood, and whose feet were in mud up to their ankles. Yesterday, I also joined one couple in holy matrimony.

June 28. Today is the feast day of Venerable Sergius and Herman of Valaam, the Wonderworkers. This day is also memorable because of an incident that happened on the same day last year, when we were going to Knik to perform various ministrations. While crossing the harbor called "Portage" in the Knik area, we were caught in a terrible storm, which wrecked our *baidarka* and we narrowly escaped death. Another feast day came: to commemorate Saints Paul and Peter.

Although it was still foggy and rainy, after a short prayer, we set out back home, where, thank God, we safely arrived by evening.

A Trip to Knik and the Susitna River to Perform Various Ministrations, 1885[26]

July 6. On this day *baidarkas* arrived from the Susitna River to take us, and we immediately started to bake communion bread, and prepare ourselves for this trip.

July 8. Having prayed to God, we set out from Kenai and as always at first went directly to Tyonek, where we arrived after dusk. When we were leaving Kenai the weather was quiet, but before sunset the wind and waves rose. As a matter of fact, the wind was favorable, and it would not have been dangerous to sail farther, but we had planned to land in Tyonek, where there was a chance of being caught in the surf. Unfortunately, we did not let anybody in Tyonek know that we were coming, and there was nobody on the shore to await us. To call people to come and help us we signaled by two gunshots, while keeping ourselves far from the shore. In the fog we lost sight of two of our other *baidarkas*. Later, when the Tyonek people finally heard and helped us, we had to start a fire on the shore before these two *baidarkas* finally saw us. In Tyonek the rain, wind, and surf delayed our departure until July 13, and only on this day were we able to depart, and only because there was a favorable wind.

July 13. On this day we reached the place called Sushnikakh,[27] which is located in the mouth of the Susitna River. Here we stayed for a night. It rained heavily and the wind blew strongly. Now we had to move upriver against the current.

July 14. Water rose and the same favorable wind blew. The rain drizzled, and we proceeded farther. Installing on our *baidarkas* improvised sails made from blankets and such like we moved upriver toward the so-called "Small Island," where we found all the natives gathering. By the time we reached Small Island, all my clothing had gotten wet and I had to change. The only dry and clean clothes I had on were trousers and a long blue jacket which served me for a cassock. In this dress I performed all services. There was no place to wash myself except the river water. As far the Kenaitze's steam baths, I absolutely cannot put myself there. To me these bath shacks look like doghouses. As for our rivers here, their water is so cold that, given my poor health, I did not risk washing myself there.

July 15. Upon arrival we immediately set up the tent and put there the box with church items. Then we started performing services after which we gave the Kenaitze various instructions, which we usually provide while visiting their villages. I did not feel well, and only with great difficulty did I deliver a sermon. My heart was beating so fast that it was hard to speak. I was sweating and felt feverish. My head seemed to be breaking from pain, and my right ear was in severe pain. During this day I baptized three infants. Most important, I was able to verify all church registers.

July 16. In the morning, after the service, I performed a funeral rite for the deceased. After the Liturgy without consecration I performed the rite of blessing water at the request of the inhabitants of the village. After dinner I heard confessions.

July 17. As always after the matins I prayed along with the natives who were preparing to partake in the rite of communion. Our prayer was accompanied by the terrible howling of numerous Kenaitze dogs, whom their owners tied up at my insistence, because native dogs usually follow their owners everywhere, even to church. These dogs howled so loudly that I could not hear my own weakened voice.

Incidentally, similar inconveniences and trifles always accompany me during church services in other Kenaitze villages. Besides, dogs will either fight or even bite each other for some small piece of dried fish they steal when their owner is not at home. Moreover, I saw many times how throngs of dogs will attack two or three of their unfortunate comrades, which leads to a general fight, where one cannot tell who attacks whom. It should be noted that a Kenaitze village normally has many dozens of dogs. An average Kenaitze native often owns more than ten animals. Such dogfights and howls, which make you shiver, silence everything around, and I have to interrupt my talk during the service for a minute and wait until they end. This day I served the Liturgy, where I gave communion to 110 natives. Then I joined one couple in holy matrimony. On the same day we left Small Island going downstream and stopped at the mouth of the Susitna River, where we set up a travel tent. Here we stayed waiting for Knik *baidarkas* that were expected to take us. Our former paddlers were dismissed.

July 18. The *baidarkas* did not arrive until the next evening. Having no intention of postponing our departure until the next morning and trying to use good and quiet weather, we immediately set out for Knik "Island" [Marchenkov put this word in quotation marks]. At dawn the next day we reached this place. Upon arrival, we had natives set up the church and travel tents, and, first of all, began examining how our written registers from this village reflected the real picture. Nikolai Sorokovikov, a songleader, does all the work of examining villages and making regular entries in a travel journal during our trip. Sorokovikov is a long-time local resident, who was born here and who is more experienced in dealing with the Kenaitze than myself. More than anybody else he knows all features of the Kenaitze's character, these half-Indians who belong to my mission. Sorokovikov helps me very much, and I am very grateful to him. In the afternoon I baptized three infants and anointed another one with myrrh. Then I sang a funeral service, and later served vespers.

July 19. After the matins I performed a rite of baptism over an adult Mednovtsy native. Converted from paganism, he received the name of Nikolai after the name of his godfather. Then the service continued in a requisite order.

July 20. I continued performing the service. Then I heard confessions. The weather was gloomy, but the drizzly rain somehow did not disturb us. And besides, the natives erected a cover in front of the church tent.

July 21. I performed the Liturgy during which 159 natives received communion. After the service I joined in holy matrimony the newly baptized Mednovtsy native with a Kenaitze woman. As far as I could, I instructed this Mednovtsy how to behave after receiving communion. Incidentally, I addressed these instructions to all the other natives. Although I do know their language, the rest of the day I tried to converse with the Kenaitze. A few natives are more or less familiar with some Russian words, and we were able to understand each other. That is how we communicated in rather an original manner.

July 22. Today we set out back home. Safely crossed the notorious "Portage" harbor. Then we passed Knik "Island," which is below the Kondratieff cape, and by the evening being filled with a feeling of satisfaction for the completed mission we returned to Kenai.

Kenai Missionary Hieromonk Nikita.

CHAPTER THREE

Priest Nikolai Mitropol'skii

Report to the Alaska Ecclesiastical Consistory, July 22–August 3, 1888[28]

I HAVE THE HONOR to report to the Alaska Ecclesiastical Consistory that after I left San Francisco on May 10–22,[29] I arrived at Kodiak Island on May 19–June 2, where I spent the whole month waiting for an opportunity to sail to Kenai. I reached Kenai on June 20–July 2. Renting an apartment in Kodiak and traveling to Kenai required some extra expenses.

The Kenai church needs repairing. I made the most urgent repair at local expense. I postponed repairing other things until the arrival of his Grace or until my personal trip to San Francisco. The priest's house still remains unfinished, although during archpriest Vechtomov's tenure $1000 was spent on its construction, and I will hardly be able to spend the winter in such a house. The local teacher said to me that last winter he and his students almost froze in this unfinished building. Now I understand why the late Father Nikolai preferred to spend winters in Kodiak. With our limited local church resources it will hardly be possible to complete repairing this house to accommodate a family priest, when in winter the temperature outside is usually between thirty and forty degrees below zero Celsius. It will require $400 or $500, the sum we hope to receive from our highest superior, his Grace. We are sure that, as an ardent supporter of missionary work in general, he will not refuse to allocate these crumbs for the benefit of the local mission.

Having spent ten days in Kenai, in three *baidarkas* with three manholes each, I and my reader set out to visit the southwestern and northwestern areas of the parish to acquire a better knowledge of the parishioners' life and to fulfill my priestly duties. The first village that I visited is called Kustatan. It usually takes eight hours to reach this village from Kenai, provided one travels without any stops and is helped by a favorable current and good weather. The overall number of the Kustatan population is thirty-four persons including children. I stayed in this village for three days performing matins, vespers, Liturgy without consecration, hearing confessions, and giving communion. On Sunday, after the Liturgy, I continued on, sailing to a village called Tyonek, which is located forty or fifty miles from Kustatan. In Tyonek I gave rest not only to my body, but also to my soul. When I was nearing the village, I was afraid that I would find the Tyonek chapel in the same miserable condition as in Kustatan. There, in Kustatan, I had to perform church ministrations in a structure that represents four bare walls without a ceiling, a roof, a floor, windows or a door. During my services I did not know if I should pray or brush away the mosquitoes, hosts of which haunted us here. Unlike Kustatan, in Tyonek, considering local conditions, the chapel is maintained very well, for which we should credit Mr. Stafeev, a former trade agent of the Alaska Commercial Company. The chapel looks neat and well-maintained and gives you the feeling that you perform services in the Lord's church rather than in a barn. Tyonek has 130 residents including children. During the three days of my stay there, I fulfilled all my priestly duties and then on the fourth day left for the village called Susitna. This trip was tiring. We traveled by sea to the mouth of the Susitna River for seven hours. Then we made a short stop to drink tea and throughout the whole night were moving upstream and finally reached the village at 4 o'clock in the morning. The Susitna chapel is in the same condition as in Kustatan. More natives live here than in the other two villages. Following my instructions, by the evening of the same day the Kenaitze had covered the roof with birch bark. We hung our travel icons on the walls, set up the altar [*prestol*] and the communion table [*zhertvennik*], after which I joined in the holy mysteries seventy-five people of both genders and of all ages. By the evening of the third day I departed from here and sailed to Knik village, where I spent sixteen hours. The Knik chapel is not well-maintained either. A local reader told me that during Father Nikita's last visit to the village, they promised to build a decent chapel. I asked them why they did not fulfill their promise, and the Kenaitze responded, "We thought that we would not have Father anymore." Having fulfilled all necessary ministrations, I convinced the natives to set up a decent prayer house by September. If God helps me, I intend to spend the coming winter in this village. By word of mouth I learned that for a long time the neighboring Mednovtsy have been eager to hear the Gospel and accept holy baptism. Yet, in summertime, when the priest visits Knik, they cannot come here, while in winter, when groups of the Mednovtsy gather in Knik for trade, it is the priest who cannot come. After I complete all ministrations in my parish, in order to spread the word of Gospel among those who long for it, I made a decision to return to Knik and stay here for the whole winter. I hope that our Lord God will bless my plan. At church expense I bought a house in Knik, which became church property. This house will accommodate me, my songleader, and interpreter. If the Lord blesses the project of spreading His word among these sheep longing for spiritual food, we should visit this place once every two winters. Who knows, it might turn out that there will be a way for the priest to visit the Mednovtsy in their mountains. In this case, we might need this house I bought in Knik. In Knik I confessed and joined in the holy mysteries 110 people.

I tried to persuade the residents of the villages where the chapels are still not put in proper order, to work on these structures to make them look like God's temples, and explained to the parishioners what they needed to do. On my part, I promised to bring icons for these chapels during my next visit. They willingly agreed. Next year during my second visit I will see what they have done.

The Kenai parochial school is accommodated in the house of the priest. Seven boys and five girls study there. Classes meet each day from 9 o'clock in the morning to 12:30 noon and from 1 o'clock to 3 o'clock in the afternoon. Children learn Russian, English, and mathematics, and boys are also taught to read Church Slavonic, which will prepare them as readers for the church.

Tomorrow, if a favorable wind blows, I will start another trip, now to the eastern part of the parish. When I return from this trip, if opportunity permits, I will report to you again.

Missionary Priest Nikolai Mitropol'skii.

Report to the Alaska Ecclesiastical Consistory, 12–24 August 1888[30]

I have the honor to inform the Alaska Ecclesiastical Consistory that on August 4 of this year I completed my journey to the southern section of the Kenai parish. This time I visited three villages: Aleksandrovsk, which is located ninety miles from Kenai, Seldovia, which is in the vicinity of Aleksandrovsk, and Ninilchik, which is half of the travel distance between Kenai and Aleksandrovsk. In all these villages the chapels are very well-maintained. The Aleksandrovsk one even has an icon-screen. These chapels were built and are maintained at the expense of their residents, the Aleuts and the Kenaitze, who are headed by the Creoles living there. These Creoles are Ivan Munin from Aleksandrovsk, Ivan Aleksandrov from Seldovia, and Aleksei Oskolkoff from Ninilchik. All these three men act as readers. During the feasts and on Sundays they serve the Hours, baptize infants, bury the deceased, and take care of the needs and maintenance of the chapels. I must to add that they do all this work because of their own zeal and absolutely free of charge. In the Seldovia village Ivan Aleksandrov translated into their native [Dena'ina] language the Creed, the Lord's Prayer, and hymns in honor of the Most Holy Mother of God, which the village inhabitants now sing together and quite harmoniously. Residents of these three villages deserve credit for good religious and moral life. To be true, in some places one still can see old superstitions and prejudices, sometimes even shamanism. Yet all these drawbacks are hardly visible, and it is noticeable that faith in God makes good progress among them. It would be helpful if the ecclesiastical consistory would send me three or four books with some easy-to-read sermons and instructions. I would distribute these books among the chapels, where people read them on Sundays. In the Seldovia village I convinced Ivan Aleksandrov to organize a school, and people there agreed to pay him twenty-five cents from each procured beaver pelt. I already sent to Seldovia some ABC books. It would also be useful for the whole parish if we bring a boy from each village to Kenai for education, but the lack of resources prevents me from doing this. However, this idea came to my mind after I had returned from this missionary trip, and I still have not thought enough about this. Next year, if God blesses me, when I visit my parish again, I will talk about this with residents of each village, and maybe, with God's help, something will come of it. This winter I decided to spend in Knik village, around 100 miles from Kenai, with the sole purpose of beginning to propagate the Gospel among the mountain residents known by the name of Mednovtsy. For this purpose, I have already bought in this village a house for myself for $70 and gave orders to begin building a chapel. I will go there in September on a schooner and will return to Kenai, if the Lord allows me, not earlier than August.

About this I have the honor to report to the Alaska Ecclesiastical Consistory. The Kenai missionary Priest Nikolai Mitropol'skii.

Report to the Alaska Ecclesiastical Consistory, March 1889[31]

I have the honor to inform the Alaska Ecclesiastical Consistory that I spent the winter of 1888–1889 not in Kenai, the location of the church, but in Knik village, which is located in the northern part of the Kenai Bay 120 miles from Kenai. I decided to winter there for the following reasons:

(1) Visiting this part of my parish I found out that in such villages as Kustatan, Susitna, and Knik, the chapels, which are designed for performing services, are chapels only by name. In reality, these are log frames without ceilings and roofs, without windows and doors and without floors. Moreover, there is not a single icon there. Thus, in Knik I had to perform services under an open sky. Fortunately, it was not raining there. To my question why the chapels were kept in such miserable conditions, I always heard one response. The Kenaitze assured me that they had started to build the chapels in fulfillment of the instruction given by Father Nikita. But when they heard about his death, they stopped construction, thinking that again they would be left without a priest. However, I felt that there were also some other reasons involved, such as the poverty of the natives and their mental infancy and inability to take the initiative. Without guidance they are unable to make even a step. To make the chapels more or less decent in appearance, I needed to undertake some measures as soon as possible.

(2) Deep in their souls the Kenaitze are religious-oriented, attentive to the instructions given to them by a priest, and extremely humble, but at the same time they are very infantile, with a weak understanding of church services and rituals. Many of them never saw the Divine Liturgy. During my trip around the

parish I performed services in a small travel tent that accommodated only the priest and the songleader, whereas the others had to stand outside. Many Kenaitze do not know how to make the sign of the cross or how to approach the priest to receive blessings. Moreover, some of the natives, when meeting the priest, made the sign of the cross at him. They are not aware of the Orthodox feasts. Although they have wooden calendars, where they mark down with crosses the dates of the feasts, they have no idea of the meaning of these feasts and why these feasts were established. It is hardly surprising that the Kenaitze are so ignorant. When Kenai missionary Hegumen Nikolai passed away, this parish did not have a priest for more than twelve years. The last missionary, Hieromonk Nikita, stayed here only two or three years. Besides, a missionary can hardly accomplish anything during his short visits (from three to four days) to a native village in summertime, when he has to confess people, give them communion, baptize, marry and sing funeral services for the deceased. In wintertime it is impossible to visit these areas, because from October to the end of March the Kenai Bay is covered with moving ice, and to reach the opposite side of the bay is practically impossible. The only way out is to winter there.

(3) It was Knik village that I selected for my winter stay, because this is the place where so-called Mednovtsy descend from the mountains. Although the Mednovtsy are a wild and unruly people, who two years ago killed an agent of the Alaska Commercial Company, in the words of Knik residents, they express a desire to hear the word of Gospel and accept holy baptism.

Considering all this, I ventured to spend a winter on the other side of Kenai Bay. So on September 1–13 of the last year, having prayed to our Lord God and having asked God to bless those who remained in Kenai, I and Sorokovikov, my songleader, set out for Knik on the schooner *Kodiak*, which was carrying to Knik a trade agent and his goods. We took with us all necessary materials for performing church services and for complete the building of a chapel, particularly wooden boards, nails, window frames and so forth. We arrived in Knik on September 3–15. After our arrival, first of all, we started to rebuild the chapel, which by the month of October, with God's help and due to the efforts of the songleader Sorokovikov, was ready. So on October 1 [the date illegible, might be 7] at the day of the feast of the Protection of the Most Holy Mother of God, we were able to perform the Divine Liturgy without any difficulties. During that winter the chapel services were conducted each Sunday and on feast days, and the services were always accompanied by short, easy-to-grasp sermons. Besides delivering sermons in the chapel I frequently conducted personal talks at my house. Rarely a day passed without somebody's visiting me, and I used these opportunities to insert in such talks some information about the holy mysteries or Orthodox rules concerning home life, family or social life. Therefore, during this winter natives discovered for themselves religious and moral principles and, in general, learned many things they were not aware of earlier. By

Christmastime the Kenaitze had gathered for a customary prayer service. Despite a long distance some came from Kustatan and Susitna villages. For the first time they had a chance to see a solemn church service in a well-equipped chapel, and I joined all those who came in the holy mysteries. On the feast day of Epiphany I performed the rite of blessing of water and explained to them the meaning and significance of the holy water and how the faithful should use it. I visited all houses with the cross. For the Kenaitze all these things were new, and they will remember them for a long time. Those who came from Kustatan and Susitna promised to build the same kind of chapels in their villages as in Knik. It is a pity that there is now nobody among these Kenaitze who could sing or read something for them during Sundays or on feast days. Nevertheless the natives promised to visit their chapels regularly for a collective, though silent, prayer. To help organize the Kenaitze I found among them a boy of seventeen years old, who lived with me for the whole winter, and now this boy has begun to understand Russian and he already can read and write. But I did not dare to take him with me to Kenai without his Grace's blessing and also because I still do not know about my own next assignment. I promised this boy that if I stay in Kenai I would bring him to study at the parochial school.

I enlightened eighty-eight Mednovtsy with the holy baptism, and anointed six of them with myrrh. To communicate with them, I had to rely on two interpreters: one translated from Russian to the Knik tongue, and another from Knik to the Mednovtsy tongue. Yet I overcame this obstacle without much difficulty. The Mednovtsy kept on coming to Knik in small parties and families and stayed there no more than four or five days. However, even during this short time, I was able to give them basic instructions, and baptized and joined them in the holy mysteries. Those who came with wives I married. In their words, the total number of Mednovtsy living up the Copper River is 500. They added that the rest of their fellow tribesmen would like to come to see me, but cannot do it, because of the great distance. They said; "If you go to us and stop somewhere halfway, all of us would accept baptism." I promised, if God allows, to visit them. Further dissemination of Orthodoxy and strengthening of the faith among the new converts depends on decisions of his Grace. To visit these mountain residents a missionary should have his own dogs and sleds. Also, for successful propagation of the Gospel at least one chapel should be built amid the Mednovtsy lands. We could buy and store in this chapel all items necessary for performing services. Such a project will certainly require expenses on our part, because to rely on material help from the newly converted is impossible. In Kenai itself we should have two songleaders. One cannot leave the church without a parish priest for six or seven months. As a temporary solution, for the time when we were away in Knik, we selected one person from the parishioners, who agreed to act as a churchwarden and reader for a salary of three dollars a month, but this sum is nothing, and we cannot provide more due to the scarcity of our local resources.

I have the honor to report to the Alaska Ecclesiastical Consistory about the above-mentioned. *Acting Kenai Missionary, Nikolai Mitropol'skii.*

An Excerpt from a Letter to the Most Reverend Vladimir, Bishop of the Aleutians and Alaska, Circa 1891[32]

On the fourth day after my return from Nuchek, I set out to visit the villages of the Kenai area. In my parish, thank God, everything continues to go well. In Seldovia village I performed a water blessing prayer service at the place designed for the building of a new chapel. The Seldovians have already prepared the logs and boards. In Ninilchik village, due to the efforts of the elder, who supervises the chapel, its building is now in good order. It would be very helpful if Your Grace could in some way draw Your archpastoral attention to the efforts of this elder, named Feodor Kvasnikov. Residents of such villages as Kustatan, Tyonek, and Susitna have informed me with deep regret that they have no person who could perform services for them during the feast days and on Sundays. They particularly said, "We built the chapels as you ordered. Still, we do not hear any services in them. The only bright day is when you visit us." I could not console them in their sorrow. Moreover, due to their poverty, they are not able to support a reader even if such person were available. Would you, please, Your Grace, think about doing something that might console them.

Asking for Your Grace's archpastoral prayers for myself and my flock, Your humble novice, Missionary Priest Nikolai Mitropol'skii.

Nikolai Mitropol'skii to Nikolai, Bishop of Alaska and the Aleutians, April 12, 1891[33]

Relying on Your kindness and mercy, I dare to write You this private letter. Thank God, I reached Kenai safely. On the way to Kenai our ship stopped for three days not far from Nuchek. In this village a man, who is in charge of the local chapel, came to me and asked me to stay longer, complaining that no priest had visited them for three years. However, I did not accept this offer and instead only promised to visit them in May. I will try to fulfill my promise despite the fact that such a journey will bring to me many inconveniences and put me in danger. I will have to travel by *baidarka* across the entire Kenai Gulf, then drag the *baidarka* through mountains and then cross Prince William Sound. On the whole, it will be more than 300 miles one way. They say that dragging the *baidarka* through the mountains is especially dangerous: one can fall into snowdrifts. I hope that by Your prayer God will bless my journey. Upon my return from Nuchek I will certainly report to Your Grace. There are 392 people in Nuchek, and all of them are Russian Orthodox.

Thank God, in the Kenai area, both in the Kenai church and local chapels, everything goes well. Yet I have reason to be concerned, which requires Your word of advice. The problem is that three Americans, who wintered in Knik this year, hanged there one Mednovtsy native, who had killed another American five years ago. Father Nikita had baptized this Mednovtsy native. Each year this native kept on coming to Knik and did not try to escape from justice, saying, "I am responsible for the murder and ready to be tried." These three Americans, who did not have any legal authority, dealt with him in their own way. These are the facts as I know them. I am not in a position to decide whether they are right or wrong. However, the other day two of these Americans approached me asking me to marry them to two of my parishioners. As long ago as before I began serving in the Kenai mission, these Americans took these women and lived with them as though they were their wives. What should I do in this situation? To give them access to the holy mystery of matrimony means to go against the rules of our church, for I consider what they did went against the law. On the other hand, to refuse to marry them will raise their hostility against me, which means for me a life of a constant fear expecting a bullet. Second, denying them holy matrimony might indirectly encourage illicit cohabitation in general, against which I have been fighting since the moment of my arrival in Kenai. Mr. Miller, one of the grooms, visited me with a gun in his pocket. When I informed him that I might not marry him, he said that, all the same, he would continue living with the native girl. Miller also added that he does not recognize any Russian rules and that he is law to himself, and he would do whatever he wants to do and told me to be careful. After such words, how can one live in the Alaskan wilderness where protection does not exist? Meanwhile, the agreement between the Russian and American governments about the sale of Alaska plainly says that Russians *will be maintained and protected in liberty, property and religion* [the italicized phrase is written in English].

In this extreme situation, I am inclined to marry them if a local judge, who himself is afraid of them, will give me a paper that says that these two did not break the law by hanging that Mednovtsy native. If I do not receive such a paper, I will certainly not marry them and therefore will have to be prepared for all kinds of consequences before appropriate instructions from Your Grace reach me.

Your Grace, I humbly ask You to permit me to come to San Francisco again for the winter. I understand that to You it might look as though I just came to Kenai and already want to return. In reality, my Father, the chief reason for my request is that communication here is very rare and I will hardly have the opportunity to write to You until the fall. As far as summer is concerned, I might not be in Kenai because I will try to use any available vessel to visit Nuchek and the rest of my parish before August. Please, Father, do not think that by asking You to let me winter in San Francisco I am trying to avoid work. Not at all, I will have worked much this summer. As for winter, it will be a waste of time for me just to stay in Kenai with ten parishioners amid snow and ice. I would be able to do much more staying with You. Besides, I would have a chance to rest surrounded by my family. Please, give me Your appropriate instructions and bless my parishioners.

Asking for Your holy prayers and archpastoral blessing, I remain Your humble novice, Missionary Priest Nikolai Mitropol'skii.

Report to Vladimir, Bishop of Alaska and the Aleutians, June 10, 1891[34]

I have the honor to inform Your Grace that my reader Nikolai Sorokovikov died in June of 1891. Until now I was able only to hear confessions from the residents of Kenai during Holy Week and give them communion. After Easter I visited Ninilchik village, where after performing church ministrations, we contracted an epidemic disease, which, as word of mouth says, ravaged Alaska. I and my songleader became sick. I recovered in five days and had sufficient hope and an energy to come back to Kenai. The songleader was still weak and I wanted to leave him in Ninilchik to recover. But he did not want to stay and decided to go with me in the hope that the sea air would help him. Unfortunately, en route he caught cold, and in ten days he was gone. In Kenai everybody was sick too, and there was hardly anyone to bury Sorokovikov. With a help of one man I somehow built a coffin and alone sang funeral services for him. Twenty-five people, or may be even more, died from the epidemic in surrounding areas. We still do not have exact information from other localities. After the death of the songleader I have only myself to ring the bell, read, and sing on Sundays. My churchwarden is still sick. Aleksei Ivanov, the teacher, helps me, but he cannot be in charge of the choir alone. His major drawback is the lack of a good voice. After the death of the songleader I was able to serve the Divine Liturgy only three times and with major gaps especially while singing "Mercy of Peace." It unlikely that I will be able to go to Nuchek this year. Yet I think about visiting other villages of my parish, although without the songleader it will be very hard. Moreover, in winter there will be absolutely nothing to do here in Kenai. Let me, my Father, come to San Francisco.

Asking for Your Grace's prayer and Your archpastoral blessing for me and my flock, I remain a humble novice of Your Grace, Missionary Priest Nikolai Mitropol'skii.

Nikolai Mitropol'skii to Nikolai, Bishop of Alaska and the Aleutians, September 7–19, 1892[35]

I have the honor to inform Your Grace that the current year I started the inspection of my parish from its southern part by visiting Ninilchik village. Residents of this settlement, around fifty people of both genders, are all Creoles. All adult villagers are responsible for church services here. Specifically, an elder, Feodor Kvasnikov, supervises the local chapel. He is very meticulous and eagerly takes care of the chapel. This year he informed me that Ninilchik residents had resolved to extend the chapel building ten more feet in order to set up an icon screen. They also need four icons to complete this project. On Sunday I officiated at the Divine Liturgy after which everybody received communion. I also anointed with myrrh a few infants, who had been earlier baptized by a Creole, Aleksei Oskolkoff. This village is located fifty miles from Kenai.

From Ninilchik I went to Aleksandrovsk. People of this village take good care of their chapel. To complete its decoration they need only icons for the Royal Gates. The village consists almost exclusively of people from the Aleuts. The chapel is supervised by one Russian elder who also acted as a songleader until the present year. This year, because of his illness, this elder was not able to assist me during services, and I had to ask a songleader from a neighboring Seldovia village to help me. This man assisted me in church services when I was giving sacraments to more than 150 people.

The Seldovia village is populated by the Kenaitze. Individuals who work in the local chapel are Ivan Aleksandrov, a Creole from Kodiak who serves as a reader, and Zakhar Balashov, who is also a Creole. Earlier the village chapel was small and was not able not accommodate all the residents. Last winter the above-mentioned Creoles and other Seldovians themselves built a new chapel with an icon screen. To be sure, the building is not yet completed, but one can already conduct church services there. For their chapel, Seldovians need icons with images of Our Savior, the Most Holy Mother of God, and St. Nicholas, after whom the chapel was consecrated. When I arrived at this village, I performed a customary prayer service and also blessed water. Then for four days I performed various ministrations, and on the fifth day, which was Sunday, I celebrated the Divine Liturgy during which more than 100 people of both genders received communion. I also churched a few infants, earlier baptized by Creole Ivan Aleksandrov, performed a few marriage ceremonies, and sang funeral services for those who died during the past year.

Upon returning to Kenai, I performed a few Liturgy ceremonies during which a few Creoles assisted me, especially Aleksei Ivanov, a graduate of the school attached to the Consistory of San Francisco Bishopric. Then in July I set out for a trip to visit the villages of Kustatan, Tyonek, Susitna, and Knik, located north of Kenai. There is a chapel without an icon screen in Tyonek. It is hard to say when exactly this chapel was built. I think it might be about ten years ago. In the other three villages, Kenaitze themselves built their prayer houses after my arrival in Kenai. None of the four villages has any trained people, and because I had no one to help me during the services I had to use presanctified gifts. As for baptisms, marriages, and funeral services, these rites were conducted according to the requisite order. The poor inhabitants in these four villages do not have any money to pay to their own readers. At the same time, they constantly feel a need to pray to God. The Kenaitze have their own improvised wooden calendars that allow them to check on which Sunday is Holy Easter, Trinity Day, Ascension into Heaven or other feasts. In Tyonek it is a reader who keeps track of the feasts on these calendars. During Orthodox feasts all village residents gather in their prayer houses and in silence expose to God their deep inner feelings. They ask me to send them one or two songleaders, but I am not in a position to do something in this respect. I was only able to promise them that I would approach the ecclesiastical authorities on their behalf. In my view, some of the graduates of the school organized by Bishop Vladimir might make good candidates for these positions. All these villages together number about 500 residents.

Upon returning to Kenai, I received confession from and gave communion to the residents of Chkituk, Kasilof, and Titukil as well as to the people of Kenai. The first three villages are located ten to fifteen miles from Kenai and together number about 100 inhabitants. Four of the families live permanently in the vicinity of the church. In winter the inlet is frozen and almost all communication normally is terminated until April. I did not visit Nuchek because no one from this village came to pick me up, and I myself could not hire anybody to bring me there.

Humble servant of Your Grace, Missionary Priest Nikolai Mitropol'skii.

The Kenai village, the center of Orthodox activities among the Dena'ina, with the Church of the Holy Assumption at the background (1911–1912). Courtesy of the Anchorage Museum of History and Art (B91.9.90).

Pavel (Paul) Shadura, a missionary and a priest in the Cook Inlet area from 1907 to 1952. Courtesy of the Anchorage Museum of History and Art (B90.3.24).

Ioann Bortnovskii, a missionary to the Dena'ina from 1896 to 1907. Courtesy of the M. Z. Vonokouroff Collection, Alaska State Library Historical Collections (PCA 243-93).

The Church of the Holy Assumption in the Kenai village. Courtesy of the O. G. Herning Collection, Alaska and Polar Regions Department, University of Alaska, Fairbanks (86-095-38).

Old building of the Orthodox chapel in the Dena'ina village of Eklutna (New Knik). Photograph by the author, summer of 1998.

Dena'ina Indians in the Knik area. Left to right: Evan Wasilly [Ivan Vasilii] and his wife, John Ivan with his wife, and "Bear" Ivan with his son, c. 1900. Courtesy of the Anchorage Museum of History and Art (B82.52.267).

Seldovia village in 1908 with an Orthodox chapel on the left. Courtesy of the Anchorage Museum of History and Art (B82.52.213).

Alexander Iaroshevich, a missionary in the Cook Inlet area from 1893 to 1895. Courtesy of the M. Z. Vonokouroff Collection, Alaska State Library Historical Collections (PCA 243-88).

Vladimir Stefeev, a Russian from Estonia, an American Commercial Company trade agent and a lay Orthodox leader among the Dena'ina of the Tyonek village in the 1880s. Courtesy of the Kodiak Historical Society.

Susitna Station of the Alaska Commercial Company that conducted trade with the Dena'ina, c. 1905. Courtesy of the Anchorage Museum of History and Art (B91.9.176).

Dena'ina Indians from the Tyonek village, 1898. Courtesy of the U.S. Geological Survey Photographic Library, Denver (Mendenhall WC 14).

Konstantin Sorokovikov, a mixed-blood songleader pictured during his visit to Seldovia, 1900. Courtesy of Alaska State Library Historical Collections (PCA 243-1-105).

A burial at the Russian Orthodox cemetery at Tyonek in 1898. Courtesy of the O. G. Herning Collection, Alaska and Polar Regions Department, University of Alaska, Fairbanks (86-095-132).

Ioann Bortnovskii (center) with his Seldovia parishioners; from left to right, Vasilii Baiiu (churchwarden), Anisim Aleksandrov (member of the St. Nicholas Temperance Society), Nikolai Fomin (a songleader), and Iakovlev. The last one was most probably a relative of Old Iakovlev, who served as an interpreter for Iaroshevich during his trips to the Dena'ina. Courtesy of Alaska State Library Historical Collections (PCA 243-1-90).

CHAPTER FOUR

Priest Aleksandr Iaroshevich

Report to Vladimir Donskoi, the Dean of Clergy of the Sitka District, August 2, 1893[36]

AFTER MY ARRIVAL at the place of my work, I immediately set off on a trip to familiarize myself with my parish. The Kenai parish numbers ten settlements. Among them, seven villages have their own chapels. Having inspected these chapels, I found out that all of them need to be repaired and redecorated. To be specific:

(1) Aleksandrovsk village chapel consecrated after Saints Serguis and Herman, Wonderworkers from Valaam. The residents of this village want at their own expense to cover the interiors of the chapel with boards and to paint the roof with oil paint. The boards, 600 pieces, have already been bought. Also, the residents are currently collecting money to purchase the paint.

(2) Seldovia village. St. Nicholas chapel. Although this brand-new chapel has been built in a proper manner, it remains unfinished. The interior of the chapel needs to be covered with wooden boards and wallpaper. The roof needs to be covered with tile. And an icon screen needs to be painted in white oil paint. The Seldovians have boards and tile. Also, they are currently collecting money to buy the other necessary materials. All work they will do at their own expense.

(3) Ninilchik village. The Transfiguration of Christ chapel. According to instructions of Priest Nikolai Mitropol'skii an altar was added to the chapel, but it was left unfinished. [...] This work was conducted without permission from his Grace. Therefore, the Dean of Clergy promised the Ninilchik Creoles to petition his Grace to receive his blessing to continue this work. [...] All work and the purchase of all necessary materials the parishioners will conduct at their own expense, as soon as they receive the archpastoral permission of his Grace.

(4) Kustatan village. The chapel has not been consecrated. It was built last fall. This chapel has been built without a ceiling. The residents of this village promised to make the ceiling for their chapel, to cover all walls with calico, to install windows, and repair the roof. The residents will conduct all the work by themselves.

(5) Tyonek village. The chapel has not yet been consecrated. This chapel was built in a disgusting manner in a steam bath style [*skvernim bannym uglom*]. Due to the clumsy construction, there are big chinks. The logs do not match up

and rain freely comes through the gaps between them. The roof is covered with birch bark, and the supporting beams are all unstable. Water also easily comes through this roof. I instructed them to dismantle the chapel and rebuild it in a proper manner, with the floor and the roof remade. The residents agreed to conduct all work at their own expense.

(6) Susitna village. The chapel has not been consecrated. Like the Tyonek chapel, this one has the same drawbacks and similarly was built in a clumsy manner. I gave the local people the same instructions to rebuild the chapel. The residents themselves will conduct the work.

(7) Knik village. The chapel has not been consecrated. Like the other three chapels, this one, although a little bit better, was also built in haste. I convinced the local natives to rebuild the floor, to caulk the walls, and if they have a chance, to cover the walls with wallpaper.

In each village I assigned all chapel-related matters to three persons: *toion*, *zakazchik* and churchwarden. All three are to maintain the chapels. Specifically, the *toion* is the chief treasurer who keeps chapel money, the *zakazchik*, as a headman responsible for village hunting and fishing, is obliged to collect donations and to turn them over to the *toion* for safekeeping. The churchwarden is in charge of the sale of candles and cleaning the chapel. He is also to encourage people to donate to the chapel. Money acquired from the sale of candles and other church items the churchwarden is obliged to turn over to the *toion* in the presence of the *zakazchik*. In general, these persons will supervise all church-related matters not separately, but together. Thus, in Aleksandrovsk village, one Aleksandr Shagi is the *toion*, Nikolai Shukhi is the *zakazchik* and Dionisii Maltsev is the churchwarden. The former churchwarden, Stefan Aginiia, was removed from his position by the Dean of Clergy for negligence of his duties. In addition, there is a songleader, Ivan Munin, in this village. In Seldovia village, Feodor Berestov is the *toion*, Nikolai Baiiu is the *zakazchik*, and Zakhar Balashov is the churchwarden. This village does not have a songleader. Therefore, I advised [Mikhail?] Balashov and Nikolai Baiiu to come to my place in Kenai for the winter to be instructed, and they agreed to this suggestion. Ninilchik village is completely a Creole settlement, and therefore they have neither *toion* nor *zakazchik*. The position of churchwarden is occupied by Feodor Kvasnikov. One experienced old man, Aleksei Oskolkoff, was assigned to baptize infants. The chapel has two songleaders: Grigorii Oskolkoff and Ioann Panfilov [Pamfilov]. The first one conducts church services, another one teaches children praying and singing. In the Kustatan settlement, Petr Chickalusion occupies the position of *toion*, Gavriil Achitliklukt is the *zakazchik*, and Konstantin Takache is the churchwarden. In the Tyonek settlements, Konstantin Kundukuliashin is the *toion*, and Petr Unikhliachguliakhliak is both *zakazchik* and churchwarden. In this village a Kenaitze native, very fluent in Russian, Aleksandr Shichkatakhin, is responsible for baptism of infants. In Susitna village, Petr

Tikhkunukhtilusion is the *toion*, Ivan Tutauekhshtukhta is the *zakazchik* and Stepan Kichtagan [Kachtagan] is the churchwarden. And finally, in Knik, Petr Kunachtukhta is the *toion*, Afanasii Tukchun is the *zakazchik*, and Mikhail Tishdilusion is the churchwarden.

Informing Your Reverence about these facts I humbly ask Your Reverence to approach his Grace, Bishop, to ask for his archpastoral permission and blessing for repairing and rebuilding the above-mentioned chapels.

Missionary of the Kenai Mission, Priest Aleksandr Iaroshevich. 2 August 1893, Kenai.

Act Concerning the Establishment of the Kenai Protection Brotherhood[37]

On October 1, 1893, we, the undersigned, parishioners of the Kenai Missionary Assumption Church, residents of St. Nicholas Redoubt [Kenai], upon the advice of our missionary priest Aleksandr Iaroshevich, expressed a desire to join the newly established Brotherhood [this word is underlined in the original] named in honor of the Feast of the Protection of the Most Holy Mother of God in order to assist the priest to provide material support for the church, school, poor parishioners and maintenance of the cemeteries. For this purpose, during a general meeting that took place today on the above-mentioned date, after a customary prayer service devoted to the Mother of God, it was unanimously resolved to donate each month no less than twenty-five cents to the Brotherhood fund, which we confirm with our own signatures.

Members of the Brotherhood [St. Nicholas Redoubt]

Priest Aleksandr Iaroshevich (signature)
Songleader Aleksei Ivanov (signature)
Starosta Ivan Ivanov (signature)
Aleksandr Demidov (signature)
Ioann Sorokovikov (signature)
Anton Ivanov (signature)
Makar Ivanov (signature)
Evgeniia Iaroshevich (signature)
Filipp Ivanov (signature)
Marfa Ivanov (cross)
Lavrentii Mishakoff (cross)
Faddei Ukotli (cross)
Sergei Mishakoff (cross)
Stepan L'tatel'tisha (cross)
Nikolai Iukisat (cross)
Petr Kal'khinekhutakha (cross)
Innokentii Shakai (cross)
Nikanor K'iul'khkish (cross)
Evfimii Kal'chakakhutaka (cross)
Vasillii Kliakva (cross)
Nikolai Makuloff (cross)
Nikifor Mishakoff (cross)
Stepan Mishakoff (cross)
Antonii Bakel'chushin (cross)
Innokentii Tatutliutmia (cross)
Stepan L'kankata (cross)
Feodor Chuljin (cross)
Daniil Kal'khnish (cross)
Petr Mishakoff (cross)
Dmitrii Priskokin (cross)

Nikolai Kalifornskii (cross)
Nikolai Balitaeliush (cross)
Avel' Vutkatakha (cross)
Nikolai Bakhketuliktukta (cross)
Petr Kinga (cross)
Stepan Mishakoff (cross)
Aleksei Pamfilov (cross)
Ivan Oskolkoff
Konstantin Sorokovikov

I thereby confirm that the information provided is true, Priest Aleksandr Iaroshevich.

By-Laws of the Kenai Village Church Brotherhood Named After the Protection of the Most Holy Mother of God, the Alaska Territory, United States of America[38]

(1) *The Name of the Brotherhood*: the brotherhood shall receive the name Church Brotherhood named after the Protection of the Most Holy Mother of God. For purposes of brevity, the brotherhood may be called the Kenai Protection Brotherhood.

(2) *The Major Goals of the Brotherhood*: (a) to maintain the local church; (b) to care for the local parochial school; (c) to provide help to the poorest parishioners; (d) to maintain the cemetery.

(3) *Secondary Goals of the Brotherhood*: to promote the spiritual and physical well-being of the whole people as well as separate individuals. For this purpose members are (a) to absolutely stop brewing vodka and restrain themselves from excessive alcohol consumption; (b) to spread education in the parish including young children in Kenai village for which members of the brotherhood are obliged to send their children to the Orthodox parochial school; (c) to use any opportunity to visit church services and non-service talks.

(4) *Who Can Be a Member of the Brotherhood and Who Cannot.* Individuals may be members of the brotherhood if these persons are: 1. of Orthodox faith; 2. fulfill their Christian duties diligently; 3. honest; 4. physically healthy; 5. not younger than eighteen and not older than fifty years old; 6. sober; 7. not involved in brewing beer or vodka. Therefore, individuals cannot be members of the brotherhood if they are 1. not Orthodox; 2. not willing to raise their children in the fear of God and send them to the Orthodox parochial school; 3. not honest, specifically: (a) those who do not go to church; (b) those who brew beer and vodka and other alcoholic beverages; (c) those who drink alcohol, offend people with words, and gossip, fight, and publicly misbehave; 4. suffering from incurable disease; 5. younger than eighteen and older than fifty (a note: those who joined the brotherhood before October 1, 1893, shall remain its members even if they fit this stipulation about the age limits).

(5) The parish priest, even if he is not a member of the brotherhood, has the right at his own consideration to influence the affairs of the brotherhood, to be present during its meetings and to see that the brotherhood by-laws are observed correctly by the members.

(6) A person who wishes to become a member of the brotherhood must first of all apply in writing about his desire through the brotherhood secretary to the chairman of the brotherhood. The latter shall present this paper for consideration at the brotherhood meeting. If the person is accepted, he has the right to participate at the next brotherhood meeting and after this is considered a member.

(7) The brotherhood begins to provide help to its members starting from January 1, 1896.

(8) Due to the lack of a physician in Kenai, the brotherhood sets up its own first-aid kit with all necessary regular medicine modeled after the school first-aid kit initiated by the Most Reverend Illarion. The brotherhood will receive medical services from this pharmacy.

(9) (a) In addition, the brotherhood provides its members material help, for example, during illness. If someone from the brotherhood becomes seriously ill and will not be in a position to work or find food, this member shall be provided during a six-month period with $4 per month. The next six months such a brotherhood member shall be provided with $2 per month. The monetary allowance shall not be available for more than one year; (b) In case of an accident. If a brotherhood member injures himself at work this person shall be provided by the brotherhood with a monetary allowance on the same terms as in case of an illness; (c) however, if a brotherhood member due to drunkenness, fight or simply carelessness injures himself, in this case he is denied any allowance. Moreover, upon recovery this person shall be obliged to pay a fine to the brotherhood. In case of his death, his family shall not be provided with any allowance and such a deceased member will be denied a solemn brotherhood funeral ceremony.

In case of death. If a brotherhood member passed on to the eternity at God's will, his remaining widow, provided she is a member of the brotherhood herself, and the orphans shall receive a lump sum allowance. To provide this help each member of the brotherhood shall pay an additional fifty cents each. In this case the lump sum allowance shall not be allocated from the permanent brotherhood fund. If the widow does not belong to the brotherhood, she shall receive half of this allowance, and therefore each member of the brotherhood shall pay in this case only twenty-five cents. It should be stressed that the family of a brotherhood member who commits the sin of suicide shall be completely denied any allowance and the deceased himself shall not receive a Christian funeral.

To commemorate any fellow-brother member who died in a Christian manner, the priest shall perform requiem litanies at his house, and during the day of a funeral the liturgy, with the exception of the days when liturgies are not permitted according to church rules. The name of the deceased shall be written down in the brotherhood list and shall be commemorated at each mournful [*zaupokoinoi*] Saturday Liturgy. During the liturgy and the funeral rite all brotherhood members shall stand keeping lighted candles.

(10) Brotherhood Officials. (a) Supervisor of the brotherhood, Priest of the Kenai Missionary Church; (b) Chairman; (c) Treasurer; (d) Record-Keeper.

(11) Responsibilities of the Officials. 1. The responsibilities of the supervisor are outlined in paragraph 5. 2. Chairman: (a) selects a day and a month for meetings; (b) manages all brotherhood-related matters on behalf of members and if necessary contacts other societies and institutions; (c) monitors voting procedures during meetings. (d) All members shall obey the words of the chairman. (e) The chairman is confirmed in his position by the *arkhirei* of the see and therefore, only the latter can dismiss the chairman from his position. (f) All members must honestly obey his decisions. (g) If the chairman does not fulfill his duties, he shall be obliged to pay a fine, which is to be three times as much as the fine paid by a regular brotherhood member.

2. Assistant to the Chairman. (a) He fulfills the duties of the chairman, if the latter is not in a position to fulfill them; (b) he replaces the chairman without any elections if the chairman dies or moves away; (c) he acts as Treasurer of the brotherhood, or, in other words, is responsible for the brotherhood fund and (i) receives from the Secretary the monthly dues, (ii) allocates money, what the brotherhood or the chairman allows to be paid, (iii) is also nominated and dismissed by the Ecclesiastical *arkhirei*. An explanatory note: after each monthly meeting during the first Sunday he is to come to the house of the chairman for the auditing of the brotherhood fund.

4. Secretary. (a) He keeps the journal of the brotherhood meetings and financial records; (b) he does a roll call; (c) he collects monthly dues, which he transfers to the Treasurer after meetings; (d) at the end of the year he composes an annual report and presents this report to brotherhood members on the first day of October during the general meeting. Explanatory note 1: After each monthly meeting during the first Sunday he is to come to the chairman's house and bring the brotherhood journal and the financial records for auditing and signing. Explanatory note 2: Supervisor Priest, Chairman, and Secretary, if the brotherhood expresses this wish, may calculate and examine the brotherhood money kept by Treasurer.

(12) Responsibilities of Members.

1. All brotherhood members are to demonstrate love to their neighbors and especially to their fellow-brotherhood members. Each member is to help each other as far as he can. Yet they shall not hide the misdemeanors of brotherhood members. They are expected to disclose them at the brotherhood meetings.

2. Christian duties members are to fulfill honestly, namely: (a) each Sunday and feast day to come to the temple of God, (b) shall participate in collective singing of prayers, (c) shall behave in a seemly fashion in the temple of God, (d) shall confess and receive communion once a year, (e) to obey church authorities and their spiritual father, (f) raise their children in a Christian manner, and for this reason, they themselves should live their lives in a Christian manner, avoid alcohol abuse and quarrels both at home and especially on Sundays and during feast days, when the most appropriate pastime for the faithful is to read books on spiritual and moral topics or converse on soul-saving themes, (g) shall take off his hat when in front of the church and make the sign of the cross remembering that the church is the place of God's presence, (h) members are to pay their dues to the brotherhood fund on a regular basis; those who do not pay dues for six months shall be expelled from the brotherhood and lose all brotherhood rights, (i) all brotherhood members are to show up for meetings, various festivities, and for the funeral of a fellow-brother in decent clothing and have seemly appearance, (j) those who do not show up for a festivity or a funeral or a brotherhood meeting without any serious reason, those who demonstrate indecent behavior, shall be obliged to pay a fine to the brotherhood of from twenty-five cents to $1. Explanatory note: An exception is made for women who are burdened with large families, and therefore cannot always be present at brotherhood meetings or festivities. (k) To the list of the feast days when brotherhood members are to come to church Thanksgiving Day and Independence Day (Fourth of July) must be attached. On the feast day of Protection by the Most Holy Mother of God, during the liturgy all brotherhood members are to stand in the temple in the first row keeping lighted candles.

(13) Brotherhood meetings.

1. There shall be three kinds of meetings: monthly, annual, and special ones: (a) monthly meetings shall be held each month on the first Wednesday after the first day of each month. If a meeting does not take place for some reason on that day, the gathering shall be held the next Wednesday, (b) annual meetings shall always be held on the feast day of the Protection by the Most Holy Mother of God which is on October 1 in the evening or after dinner, depending on circumstances. During this meeting an annual report shall be read and brotherhood officials shall be elected, (c) The chairman may initiate special meetings for consideration of a matter of large significance.

2. Each meeting begins and ends with a prayer. In the beginning brotherhood members shall sing the *troparion* to Protection of the Mother of God, and at the end there shall be a *kontakion* and a dismissal prayer read by the priest.

3. During meetings each member has a right to speak up, but with the permission of Chairman, and shall stand while speaking. Each member shall speak in a decent and businesslike manner. Talk in an assailing and offending manner

must be avoided, and shall be punished by fines, dismissal from a meeting or even by exclusion from the brotherhood, (a) if a speaker talks in a decent and businesslike manner, nobody has the right to interrupt him except the chairman and only for a serious reason, (b) if a meeting does not reach mutual consent in certain matters, the problems shall be resolved by a majority vote. The chairman shall never vote, but if a tie vote occurs, the priority shall belong to the side supported by chairman, (c) if somebody does not talk on business, the chairman may ask him to remain silent, and if this speaker does not obey, the chairman may impose a fine on him; if the speaker does not obey in this case he is dismissed from the meeting, (d) no member shall speak about, announce or converse on outside of the brotherhood (namely, at home, in company or on the street) those matters and problems discussed during brotherhood meetings. If members violate this rule once, they shall pay a fine of twenty-five cents, if twice: fifty cents, three times: $1, and if they violate this rule for a fourth time, they are expelled from the brotherhood, (e) each member shall always show up for brotherhood meetings (the explanatory note: concerning women see paragraph 12 under letter (j)); those who do not come, shall explain the reason for their absence; those who miss meetings without any serious excuse shall be fined: first time: ten cents, second time: twenty-five cents, third time: $1, and on the fourth time they are expelled from the brotherhood (explanatory note: brotherhood officials are fined twice as much as the regular members); (f) during meetings each member shall speak in a simple and decent manner and must not talk again on the same matter after the meeting is dismissed; (j) those who offend the chairman during a meeting without a serious reason shall be expelled from the brotherhood; if the reason was serious, this person shall pay a fine of $1.

(14) Punishments.

1. A monetary fine shall be paid by those who: (a) do not come to meetings without a serious reason; (b) behave indecently; (c) offend a fellow-brother or officials or in general; (d) do not fulfill their duties outlined in paragraphs 11 and 12.

2. Members who shall be expelled from the brotherhood are those who: (a) do not visit the church, (b) do not obey church authorities and lie and gossip about them and generally do not live in a Christian manner.

(15) (a) Each brotherhood member shall have a good knowledge of the by-laws. Lack of knowledge of these by-laws must not be used as an excuse; (b) if the brotherhood ends its work for some reason, all its money and property shall be transferred to the Kenai Assumption Missionary Church; (c) those who wish to join the brotherhood again, after they have left the brotherhood or lost their membership for nonpayment of monthly dues, shall pay $2 for the right to be admitted and other dues as other new members, but those who are expelled from the brotherhood shall never be admitted again.

Travel Journals of the Kenai Missionary Aleksandr Iaroshevich for 1893 and 1894[39]

June 22. At 8:30 o'clock in the morning I, along with Father Vladimir Donskoi, Dean of Clergy, and songleader Aleksei Ivanov, set out to visit the southern part of the Kenai parish including Aleksandrovsk, Seldovia, and Ninilchik villages and some other localities. The weather was favorable for our trip. The only inconvenience we experienced was extreme tiredness from sailing in a *baidarka*, for we were not accustomed to sitting in the same position for several hours. By evening we reached Ninilchik village, which is located in thirty miles from Kenai. The local people met us with loud gun shooting. To my question as to what it meant, they responded, "That is how, Father, we salute a priest." Indeed, later in every other settlement that we visited people welcomed us in a similar manner. Ninilchik inhabitants gave us quite a hospitable reception. First of all, we went to examine the chapel. My fellow travelers and I were astonished that inside the chapel it was very clean and neat. It is due to the zeal of Feodor Kvasnikov, an acting churchwarden, that the chapel looks like new. I asked Kvasnikov to show me the chapel's money and the churchwarden readily responded to my request. We found $57.10 in cash. As for candles, I found out that the chapel did not have them. The churchwarden explained, "We ran out of them." I immediately supplied the chapel with this and other items they needed at a cost of $36.50. Kvasnikov and other parishioners asked me to send them two regular icons and six icons for Royal Gates as well as a copy of the Gospel. I promised to help them. I also tested how well a few local children knew basic prayers, and found out that they are quite good in this. Having spent a night in Ninilchik, the next day at 7 o'clock in the morning we proceeded farther, using a favorable current and a low tide and hoping to reach Laida village.

June 23. At 1 o'clock in the afternoon we arrived at Laida. A seventy-five-year-old man, who is still strong and vigorous for his years, met us here. Twenty people temporarily live in this settlement. They asked me to prepare them for and to give them communion as soon as possible. They were afraid if they went to some nearby village in order to perform rites of preparation for communion, they might not be able to fish, which would leave them without any winter supplies. I promised to accommodate their desire on my way back from Seldovia, and in the meantime I asked them to find in Laida a decent place for performing the Divine Liturgy. At 4 o'clock in the afternoon we proceeded farther and by the evening arrived at Kachemak Bay, which is located approximately forty-five miles from Ninilchik. Here Mrs. Kennedy, a woman who is a member of a large local Orthodox family, also wanted to partake in the rite of penance to prepare herself for communion, and asked me to let her do it right here. Being overburdened with a large family, she cannot leave the place. In a similar manner I promised her that on my way back from Seldovia, I would stop by, and asked her to prepare a decent tent and clear a place for performing the Divine Liturgy. On this trip I did not carry a tent with me, for I did not plan to stop in these two places. Usually people from small settlements come to the closest larger village to conduct the rites of penance and fast in order to prepare themselves for communion. However, this time they did not expect me to come so suddenly. Aleksandrovsk, Seldovia, and Ninilchik villages have chapels, so that there is no need to carry a church tent while traveling on this side of Kenai Bay. Having spent a night at Mrs. Kennedy's home, we left for Seldovia.

June 24. We left Kachemak at 9 o'clock in the morning. The weather was gloomy and it was drizzling, but the sea was quiet. Yet, when we reached the middle of the strait, a strong wind rose and our *baidarka* started to jump from one wave to another. For the person like me, who was not earlier exposed to the sea, all this was far from a joke, and I was quite scared. Amid the general silence a helmsman, who noticed my fear, suddenly said, "Father, do not be afraid, it is not a wind, it is just a breeze." I did not want to look like a coward and tried to cheer myself up. By 2 o'clock in the afternoon we were able to get to Seldovia village, where a salute of gun shooting that sounded like thunder welcomed us. After giving a blessing to those people who came to meet us, we then proceeded to the house they provided for us. A little later *toion* Feodor Berestov visited us and reported about conditions in his settlement. To my question if they were still drinking as before Berestov responded that they are gradually quitting. He also added: "Since your last visit there were only two drunks." At 6 o'clock in the evening I performed the all-night vigil of the Nativity of St. John the Forerunner. During the psalm reading part of the service when the faithful sat [*kathisma*] I instructed people about repentance. There were about ninety praying people. After the all-night vigil the weather grew quieter, and the Dean of Clergy left for Aleksandrovsk to perform ministrations there. I heard that some shamans still exist here, and in the evening I called for Berestov and inquired about them. Berestov promised to bring two of these shamans who reside here in Seldovia.

June 25. In the morning I served the Hours along with the pro-liturgy, where I continued my instructions about repentance. After the pro-liturgy I celebrated a water blessing prayer service. Then carrying the Cross and holy water I visited local houses. After dinner I talked with the *toion* and a churchwarden about conditions in the village. They were reminded to be attentive to the well-being of their own people, and to restrain the young and the inexperienced from any wrongdoing. At 2:30 in the afternoon all the people of the village gathered in the *toion*'s house, where I composed new confessional registers. At 6 o'clock in the evening I served vespers followed by a customary prayer service to the Most Holy Mother of God. During vespers I instructed the Seldovia residents about the necessity of mutual forgiveness. I also spoke about shamanism because recently shamans have again become active among the Kenaitze. Driven by motives of profit these shamans have begun to confuse people's minds. Some residents of the village directly asked me to stop this ungodly [*bogomerzkoe*] business. Having finished vespers I called for one shaman and began to persuade him to leave his shameful trade. After my admonition he promised to quit shamanizing and added in particular: "Father, I am grateful to You for opening my eyes. Now I clearly see all the misery of shamanism, and from now on I will try to take care of my soul and will start to live in a Christian manner." I imposed on him a church punishment, which he accepted willingly because he knew that he deserved it.

June 26. At 8 o'clock in the morning I served matins. During this service in my sermon I spoke against drunkenness. After matins there was the litany for the deceased performed. From 12 noon to 6:30 o'clock in the evening I heard confessions. All-night vigil at 7 o'clock in the evening, where I instructed the Kenaitze about a proper preparation for the Holy Mystery of Confession. Then I read a requisite prayer designated for all who prepare themselves for communion. After this prayer I finished confessions.

June 27. The matins at 8:30 o'clock in the morning, then a requisite prayer for communicants followed by the Divine Liturgy, where I gave communion to seventy-six adults and about thirty children. After the liturgy I delivered a requisite welcoming address to the communicants. Particularly, I stressed that the holy mysteries, which they joined in today, should serve as a key for renewal of their life in the Christian spirit. Then I served a customary prayer service to St. Nicholas, the Wonderworker, whose name a local chapel carried. At 3 o'clock in the afternoon I performed the Great Vespers service that included singing a prayer glorifying the Most Holy Mother of God. After this prayer I explained how Orthodox Christians should live and behave, when a priest is not around. Reminded them to take a good care of the appearance of their chapel and also asked them increase their donations. At 5 o'clock in the evening I invited all residents of the village to the *toion*'s house to discuss various questions concerning the maintenance of the chapel and the personal life of parishioners. Incidentally, during this meeting people unanimously resolved that all Seldovians donate to the chapel fund five cents of each earned dollar. In addition, due to the extreme poverty of the Kenai church, the Kenaitze supported my suggestion to establish a special fund to collect money for decorating the Kenai church. Moreover, they rendered the Dean of Clergy an annual allowance for travel expenses.

The *toion*, *zakazchik* and churchwarden were instructed to restrain all the faithful from drinking. Alcohol abuse is widespread in this village beyond all belief. I used all available means trying to make Seldovians stop drinking vodka, but reached only partial success. Thus, I was able to convince them to promise to drink vodka moderately. I view this only as the beginning and hope that Our Lord himself will make them aware of the miserable conditions in which they put themselves because of vodka. On the whole, drunkenness has developed in the Kenai parish to a great extent. Erasing this evil that hinders people's well being from Kenaitze life has become my goal. When they drink, the Kenaitze know neither moderation nor time, and as a result, the population of the Kenai parish decreases year by year. I will be fighting this scourge of alcohol as much as I can.

At 5:30 in the evening Father Donskoi returned from Aleksandrovsk, and brought with him a couple to perform for them a marriage ceremony. He also brought a boy whom he intends to take to Sitka for instruction. At 11 o'clock in the evening four couples were married and, at the request of the Kenaitze, two persons were appointed as *zakazchiks*. Local natives have a wonderful tradition of not doing anything without a priest's blessing. Therefore, nomination of the *toion* and *zakazchik*, who are elected by a community, is always confirmed by a priest's blessing.

June 28. At 8 o'clock in the morning, accompanied by continual gun shooting, which Seldovians enjoy very much, we left Seldovia for Kachemak Bay, where the Kennedy family lives. Strong wind and rain made our trip very unpleasant. The *baidarka* and our clothing got wet, and for this reason I felt very uncomfortable. We arrived at Kachemak at 1 o'clock in the afternoon. After a short rest, Father Donskoi continued the trip, while I stayed at the Kennedys' place in order to perform all necessary ministrations. I joined in the holy mysteries both the Kennedys and a few other people from Ninilchik village, who came here to perform some temporary jobs. During matins I instructed these people about the great importance of confession and communion.

June 29. At 7 o'clock in the morning, a morning prayer and the Divine Liturgy, where I confessed and gave communion to nine adults. At 10 o'clock in the morning, having instructed these people about the proper behavior of Christians when a priest is absent, we continued our journey. The weather is bad. It rained heavily, our *baidarka* got wet, and we have to sit amidst this dampness. How unpleasant! About 12 noon the sky cleared a little. We reached Laida village at 3 o'clock in the afternoon. About twenty people came out to welcome us. Having found out that two shamans live in Laida, I wanted very much to meet and to talk with them. So I told Old Iakovlev to invite them in. The shamans came. I communicated with them through Iakovlev, who speaks the Kenaitze language very fluently. I questioned them, trying to learn what prompted them to return to the old faith. I also explained to them what a great sin shamanism is and how shamanism contradicts the Christian law. During our talk I exposed all the falsity and shallowness of their trade and stressed that in case of illness and various calamities, which Our Lord sends to us for our sins, we should pray to God rather than calling upon some spirits and appealing for help to the devil, the enemy of humankind. I told them about the punishment the church imposes on apostates from the holy faith, and especially on those who name themselves

Orthodox Christians and wear crosses, but at the same time call themselves shamans, servants of the devil, and confuse people who so rarely see priests.

My words affected the shamans and they sincerely repented, and also added that they had shamanized exclusively for material profit, because people generously pay for their magic. The shamans gave a firm promise not to shamanize anymore, and later during vespers both of them announced in public that they were not shamans anymore and asked people not bother them with various requests, because they realized the falsity of shamanism, and from now on they wished to take care of their souls, since they were already in old age. After they finished speaking, I told everybody that anyone who would dare to shamanize or ask a shaman to perform magic would surely be subjected to church punishments. All Kenaitze have been considered Orthodox Christians for a long time, and it is high time that they leave behind their old beliefs and delusions. For the edification of the other Kenaitze, I laid on both shamans a church punishment. At 7 o'clock in the evening I served vespers and matins.

June 30. At 7 o'clock in the morning, prayers and the Divine Liturgy. I served the Liturgy in a tent. During the Liturgy about twenty people joined in the holy mysteries. After the service I delivered a short address to the communicants. I also asked that they fence the place where, during the service, tables substituting for the Holy Altar had been placed, and that they erect a holy cross in the center of this spot. I also instructed them to burn these tables and throw the ashes into sea. The same instructions were given to the people of Kachemak. At 10 o'clock in the morning we moved on. The weather was excellent. A favorable current and wind made our trip wonderful. At 1 o'clock in the afternoon we reached Ninilchik, where people had finished the Liturgy without consecration just before we came, and everybody joined in the holy mysteries. Carrying the cross and holy water Father Donskoi visited the parishioners' houses.

According to instructions of the priest Nikolai Mitropol'skii, the village residents are now in the process of building an extension to the chapel. After the work is completed, the sanctuary is to be moved from the chapel to the altar. Father Vladimir Donskoi, the Dean of Clergy, was not in a position to grant them permission to conduct this work without the agreement and blessing of the Bishop. Therefore, he had to ask the parishioners to interrupt their work for a while and promised to secure the permission of his Grace as soon as possible. In any case, permission is needed because they have slightly changed the whole building project. Father Donskoi instructed them to dismantle the extension designated for the altar and to move it to the opposite side of the chapel, which will extend the chapel building itself. In addition, he advised them to add a small belfry with a cupola to this new extension. Father Donskoi did not allow them to remove the sanctuary from the old place. Instead, at a distance of four and a half feet from the altar he recommended that they build an icon screen (before their chapel did not have an icon screen), which will make natural altar. The residents of the village eagerly agreed to his suggestion and promised to start work as soon as they received the permission of his Grace. We spent the night at Aleksei Oskolkoff's place, and the next day at 7 o'clock in the morning, accompanied by good wishes from the Ninilchik residents, we departed for Kenai, where we arrived at 4 o'clock of the same day.

July 9. Today Father Vladimir Donskoi and I again set out for a trip to visit the villages of the Kenai area. Now our destination was the northern part of the parish. On the evening of the same day we arrived at Kustatan village, which is located on the opposite side of Kenai Bay within thirty-five sea miles of Kenai. As usual we traveled by *baidarkas*, and as always inhabitants welcomed our arrival by gun shooting. The population of Kustatan is very small. Having provided my blessing to everybody, we went to sleep to a Kenaitze *barabora* that had neither a table nor chairs nor a bed. There was no end of mosquito attacks. A host of them chased us both inside and outside the cabin. We had to fill our *barabora* with smoke in order to get rid of them.

July 10. At 9 o'clock in the morning I performed a customary prayer service with water-blessing, and also provided the local chapel with all necessary items. After dinner, while Father Donskoi was busy serving ministrations, I collected all the village residents and composed a new confessional roster, because the old one was prepared so carelessly that it was hard to read. Then I heard confessions from thirty-eight people. At 7 o'clock in the evening Father Donskoi performed the all-night vigil and then read the evening prayer.

July 11. At 8:30 in the morning I read requisite prayers for the communicants, and then Father Donskoi performed the Divine Liturgy, during which all village residents received communion. After the Liturgy he served a customary prayer to Holy Equal-to-Apostles Olga, and delivered a requisite address to the communicants, and also explained the great meaning of confession and Holy Communion. At 7 o'clock in the evening I married three couples, but refused to marry the fourth couple without the permission of Father Donskoi. He did not grant his permission either because the bride has not yet come of age. Father Donskoi advised the groom to wait until next year in hope that by this time the question about native marriages would be resolved.[40] Since this Kenaitze native was involved in an illicit cohabitation with his bride, who is under the legal age, I ordered the bride to be brought back to her mother in Tyonek. During the marriage ceremony I spoke about the meaning of marriage. I also instructed all Kenaitze not to dare to take their wives without a priest's permission because the illicit cohabitation contradicts Christian teaching and therefore must be avoided by Orthodox Christians.

July 12. Having spent the night in the same dirty *barabora*, the next day we were glad to move farther on. However, the weather was bad, and in order to reach our *baidarkas* we had to get through the muddy clay. We were stuck up to our knees in this mud. On top of this, it was raining. From all this dampness, one feels indisposed all through one's bones. By dinnertime the rain finally stopped. In the meantime, I caught cold, worn out by three days' stay in the dirty Kustatan *barabora*. Therefore, by the time we came to Tyonek, I had a strong headache and had begun shivering. Hardly had we reached Tyonek that people told me that in a small settlement located six sea miles from Tyonek, there lived a very sick old man. Despite the aggravating headache and fever, I immediately departed to give him last rites. As luck would have it, en route we were caught in high waves, and one of the waves completely covered our *baidarka*. Almost half of the *baidarka* was filled with water. Everything became wet: our clothing, and shoes, and I seriously feared that after returning to Tyonek I might fall ill. Having given last rites to the sick man, still drenched all over I came back to Tyonek. Fortunately, having drunk a few glasses of tea, I felt better. Next morning I woke up feeling absolutely all right.

In Tyonek the chapel was built of logs, but in very clumsily and badly. Large chinks in the walls. Although the floor is new, the way the natives made it shows sloppy work: the boards of the floor were laid unevenly. The walls are covered with simple calico, the ceiling with a gray one and the roof with birch bark. I audited the chapel books, which show that they have $18. I also provided the chapel with all necessary items.

July 13. At 9 o'clock in the morning I performed a customary prayer service with a water-blessing during which I also talked about the meaning of confession. After the service Father Donskoi baptized six infants and read a cleansing prayer to the women who were preparing to become mothers. In the meantime, I collected all the people of the village to the house of the local *toion* and prepared a new confessional roster. In Tyonek people also drink heavily. For this reason, before hearing confessions I delivered a word of address about the evil of drunkenness, and explained to them the harmful effects of vodka on the health and well-being of people. I forced the *toion* to give me a promise in public that the Kenaitze would not drink vodka at least until my next visit. Moreover, I reminded him that as the *toion* and headman of his village he must be a good example of Christian behavior, and, therefore, for the sake of his own people, he should completely quit drinking vodka. The *toion* agreed. Then I extracted from each native individually a promise to restrain himself from consumption of alcoholic beverages. The *Zakazchik* immediately started to thank me for caring so much about his people. He also stressed that so far no priest had ever enlightened them about such things, and for this reason, they surmised that drinking vodka and drunkenness did not contradict the Christian teaching. He also added that they would take my words seriously.

At 3 o'clock in the afternoon Father Donskoi and I started to hear confessions. At 7 o'clock in the evening, after performing the all-night vigil, we renewed confession. At the end of the day evening prayers were read.

July 14. At 8 o'clock in the morning, prayers for communicants. Then I served the Divine Liturgy, where I joined in the holy mysteries about 140 souls including children. After the prayer read from the pulpit, I delivered a requisite address to the communicants, and also spoke about the necessity of fulfilling promises we make. At 3 o'clock in the afternoon I collected all the village residents at the *toion's* house in order to discuss various matters concerning church life and the people's well-being. During the meeting I said that God's temple should be a decent and a clean-looking place, which reminds us of God's presence. I also stressed what people usually say about the place where a chapel or church is dirty and unattractive: "Here live bad people because they do not care about their church. The soul of these people must be as dirty as their church." On the contrary, people whose church is clean and nice-looking are usually praised and spoken of as follows: "These people are good, they care about God's temple, which means that they love God." In conclusion, I instructed the Tyonek residents to pay more attention to their chapel. Specifically, I advised them to dismantle the chapel and rebuild it, because the building was built in a clumsy manner. Any Kenaitze house is built better than the chapel in Tyonek. Regarding removing the sanctuary from its place, I talked with the Dean of Clergy. He promised to petition his Grace and secure the necessary permission. I also instructed the Tyonek people to fence the cemetery. All residents of the village promised to donate to the chapel five cents from each earned dollar, and I gave them a special cup to collect church donations. In order to support the Kenai church, which is currently falling apart, the Tyonek people also agreed to contribute money to a separate cup with the inscription: "For the Maintenance of the Kenai Temple." In Tyonek I again had to speak about drunkenness, and again all residents confirmed their promise not to drink. Each year on communion day it has been customary for the *zakazchik* to treat everybody with a small glass of vodka. This year for the first time a glass of vodka was replaced with a cup of tea. God help them in this good beginning!

Everybody left the meeting in a good mood and promised to fulfill what I asked them to do. The *toion*, *zakazchik* and the churchwarden were put in charge of the chapel. As for other villages, I prepared for Tyonek a special credit book, which records all items acquired by the chapel from the Kenai church as well as the amounts of money that they paid for these items, along with an indication of the amount of remaining debt. Having finished our business in Tyonek we were prepared to move farther, but an unfavorable wind kept us in the village another day. At 6 o'clock in the evening Father Donskoi performed the all-night vigil of the Holy-Equal-to-Apostles Prince Vladimir. After the service I taught a Kenaitze native who speaks Russian fluently how to conduct baptism of infants.

July 15. At 8 o'clock in the morning, Father Donskoi first performed the Divine Liturgy, then he served a customary prayer service of Holy-Equal-to-Apostles Prince Vladimir with a requisite wish of many years of life. Having finished this service, Father Donskoi told people a short story about the life of the holy prince Vladimir. At noon we parted with everybody, and having provided the last-minute instructions along with blessings, we proceeded further to Susitna village. Seven hours later we reached a settlement called Sushnikak, but did not find anybody there. We had to stay here for a night in some *barabora* without a roof, right under the pouring rain. Using all our ingenuity we tried somehow to fix the roof. Father Donskoi and I occupied the *barabora's* corner, where it was not leaking so much. We wanted to make tea, but found out that there was no good drinking water around. As a result, we had to drink tea made from local muddy river water that looked like milk. Somehow we were able to spend a night here, and next day moved up the river to Susitna village.

July 16. At 8 o'clock in the evening we finally reached Susitna. Having blessed the local people, we went to the *toion*'s house. Our interpreter has not arrived yet. He is on his way carrying his merchandise, and is expected tomorrow.

July 17. A customary prayer service with water-blessing in the morning. Then I baptized eleven infants and read cleansing prayers for the women who were preparing to become mothers. I also sang funeral services for all those who had passed away, and prepared new confessional rosters. At 6 p.m. I served the all-night vigil, visited by 150 faithful who prayed.

July 18. I served the Divine Liturgy, where I joined in the holy mysteries forty infants. Then through a local interpreter, who barely speaks Russian, I delivered a sermon about the meaning of repentance. After our arrival at Susitna Farther Donskoi and I started inspecting the chapel. In all fairness, we expected more from this chapel. It is known that Susitna village is the most prosperous among all the Kenaitze settlements. At the same time, the chapel structure looks the most miserable compared to other Kenaitze chapels. Susitna people are very much addicted to drinking and donate little to the chapel. It is shameful what we found out: that they donated only $19 to the chapel for the whole year. After dinner I gathered all Kenaitze in the chapel and gave them instructions on how to prepare themselves for mysteries of Confession and Holy Communion. Then I spoke about drunkenness and stressed how harmful this habit is both for the soul and the body. I vividly described the miserable condition of a drunk and asked them to stop consuming vodka. The *toion* and *zakazchik* gladly agreed with my words and said to me the same things I already had heard in Tyonek: "We have heard such words for the first time." The rest of the people responded: "Let the *toion* and *zakazchik* watch us, and we will try to do as the priest said." Father Donskoi and I thanked them for their attention to the words of the priest, but at the same time stressed that they should keep the promises they give before God. We also added that it would be better not to promise God anything rather than to promise and not keep one's word. At 3 o'clock in the afternoon we performed confession. The total number of people who received confession was 100 persons. At 7 o'clock in the evening I served the all-night vigil of Holy Elijiah the Prophet. After the vigil we read an evening prayer and gave a short talk on how people who prepare themselves to accept the holy mysteries should behave and how they should spend their time after joining in these mysteries.

July 19. At the appropriate time I read a prayer for communicants and started the liturgy, where I joined 110 persons in the holy mysteries. After a prayer, which was read from the pulpit, I delivered my welcoming address, in which I said that the day of holy communion should be one of the greatest events for the Kenaitze because they live so far away and have a chance to see a priest and to receive from him this divine prerequisite for eternal salvation only once a year. Then I scheduled a meeting of village residents for 2 o'clock in the afternoon. During the meeting I encouraged the natives to donate to the chapel. As a result, all participants at our gathering came to an agreement to set aside five cents from each earned dollar into a special cup. When they found out about the miserable condition of the Kenai church, Susitna residents decided to donate the same amount of money for the renovation of the Kenai church. Some of these Kenaitze, who are good Christians, immediately started to make their contributions during the meeting, and at the end $8.50 had been collected. Thank God! It is obvious that the Susitna Kenaitze feel for the poor Kenai church. May Our Lord God help them! In addition, during the meeting it was resolved that the local chapel itself be rebuilt and put in proper order. For this purpose, village residents asked me to order two icons drawn on a canvas at the cost of no more than $10 each along with a cross and a small book of Gospels. After the meeting, in the presence of Father Donskoi and other witnesses, the churchwarden Stepan Kachtagan paid me $33.10 for candles, small body crosses, icons, and other items I took with me for this trip and also provided the Dean of Clergy $5 for travel expenses; the total sum is $38.10.

Having blessed everybody, at 6 o'clock in the evening we proceeded further up to Knik village. Before it took us only two-and-a-half hours to descend to the mouth of the river. Now we spent thirteen hours going upriver due to the extremely strong head current. For a night we stayed at the mouth of the river in a half-demolished *barabora* without a roof. A strong wind blew at night, but fortunately it was not raining. Otherwise our situation would have been awful. Because of the cold he had caught somewhere before, Father Donskoi suffered from a bad toothache. Hardly having any sleep, we woke up at 3 o'clock in the morning and sailed further.

July 20. Spent the whole day en route. We could have reached Knik on the same day, but the rowers were very tired. Since the weather was good, we decided to stay for the night, when the village was about thirty miles distant. Besides, we had to stop because the *baidarka* in which Father Donskoi was sitting broke. We have sent people to the nearest Kenaitze summer camp, which is located six miles away, to bring needles and threads to fix the boat. Next day at 4 o'clock in the morning we left the place where we had stayed for the night and reached Knik at 9 o'clock in the morning

July 21. Found few people in Knik. The *zakazchik* promised that he would gather everybody by the next day. As a matter of fact, not many people live in Knik permanently. The same could be said about all other Kenaitze villages. All the people who are considered Knik residents live in various localities scattered around the village two, three, and six miles away, and father. There are only three residential houses in Knik and one company trading post. Knik village itself is located up the river twelve miles from its chapel. Therefore, reaching the village takes the whole day. On the same day that we came to Knik, in the evening I served a customary prayer service with water-blessing and all-night vigil. During the service Father Donskoi delivered a sermon on the responsibilities of faithful Christians.

July 22. At 7 o'clock in the morning I performed the liturgy, after which I served a customary prayer service of Equal-to-Apostles Holy Maria Magdalene accompanied by requisite wishes of many years of life to all the faithful. After the Liturgy without consecration I baptized four infants and sang funeral services for five deceased people. On the same day I prepared a new confessional roster. At 2 o'clock in the afternoon Father Donskoi and I heard confessions. The all-night vigil at 7 o'clock in the evening. An evening prayer after the service and instructions on how to prepare oneself for confession and communion and also on how one should behave after partaking in these rites.

July 23. At the appropriate time a requisite prayer for the communicants, then the liturgy, where I joined all Knik residents in the holy mysteries. After the liturgy I delivered a welcoming word of address to the communicants. At 2 o'clock in the afternoon while performing two marriage ceremonies, I instructed the people about the importance of the rite of holy matrimony. Until recently the Kenaitze usually took their wives without securing any church blessing and simply lived with them, postponing the marriage ceremony itself for the time when a priest visited them. Regarding this I had to instruct all Kenaitze in all villages which I visited, that those who intended to be married should wait for the arrival of a priest instead of taking women and living with them without the church's blessing. Those who for some reason cannot wait for a priest's visit should come to Kenai themselves. At 3 o'clock in the afternoon there was a village meeting, where we talked about taking good care of the chapel's appearance. For this purpose, participants unanimously elected Mikhail Tishdilusion to the position of churchwarden. Along with the *toion* and *zakazchik* Mikhail was assigned to supervise the chapel, encourage donations to the chapel, collect these donations and so forth. All Knik residents unanimously agreed to contribute five percent of each earned dollar to the needs of their chapel.

Also, without any reprimands on my part the *toion*, *zakazchik* and the churchwarden by themselves promised to stop drinking vodka. Vodka is the curse of the people. People continue to die from addiction to this evil habit. If for the next ten years the Kenaitze keep on drinking as heavily as they do now, their population will decrease considerably or might be gone completely. All Kenaitze people along with their headmen gave me following promises. Some announced that they would stop drinking completely. The others said that they would restrain themselves from drunkenness as much as possible. During the same meeting, one native who has two wives promised in public that he would live only with one wife. At 11 o'clock in the evening, using a favorable current, we left Knik and set out for Kenai. Having sailed thirty miles, we stopped at a small island to wait for the next favorable current.

July 24. At noon, we were able to move on. It is impossible to sail struggling against the current in Kenai Bay. The speed of the current here reaches eight knots an hour, and in the Knik area it is even higher. Even a steamer with all its sails up and helped by a favorable wind barely "crawls" against this current. Under these circumstances, sailing by a *baidarka* is out of the question. Therefore, each time one has to sit and wait for a favorable current for about six hours, until the next current arrives. Today we were able to reach Kondrashka [Kondratieff] Cape, where we stayed for a night. The trading store in Knik is usually closed in summer, and for this reason we had to buy a little flour and dried fish from the Kenaitze. En route we found out that the dried fish was infested with worms, while the flour got wet. Having no other choice, we had to accept our lot and used both for our meals. The remaining part of the route we found a small consolation in drinking tea. Thank God, the water on this side of Kenai Bay is of better quality. On the opposite side the water is so muddy that one has to drink what could literally be called clay dissolved in water.

July 25. This morning we sailed on further. However, hardly had we covered thirty miles than we had to stop and again wait for a favorable current. Within three miles from the place where we stopped, the Kenaitze village Nikishka[41] is located. To stretch our legs Farther Donskoi and I decided to visit this settlement. It turned out that the village had only three small houses and nothing else. When a favorable current returned, we were able to continue our journey, and at 4 o'clock in the afternoon we noticed the cupolas of the Kenai church on the horizon. I took off my hat and sent my prayer to the Mother of God thanking her for giving me a chance to safely complete my first trip over my parish. I also prayed asking her to protect me in my future journeys. Thus, having covered 600 miles by *baidarka*, today we finally returned home.

Travel Journal of the Kenai Missionary for 1894, My Impressions and Notes. The Survey of the Southern Part of the Kenai Parish.

This year I have to visit my parish much later than I planned. More than twenty days have already passed since the day arranged with the Kenaitze from Seldovia, who were supposed to send a few *baidarkas* to bring me to their village. Yet, the Kenaitze have not come. Visiting the northern part of the parish, where I am going now, usually takes more time than the southern section. Unfortunately, I am already short of time. For this reason, I myself had to hire *baidarkas* in Kenai and use them during the whole trip. Word reached me that a trade agent in Seldovia village made the Kenaitze leave the village to go to procure beaver furs in order to pay back their debts. It should be noted that trade agents in my parish behave like masters and harass the natives in all respects. Seven or eight years ago a few trade agents, who wintered in Knik, hung an Orthodox Mednovtsy native. At present, these people remain unpunished, although Father Nikolai Mitropol'skii reported this incident to the American authorities.

July 6. Today at 5 o'clock in the morning along with my songleader Aleksei Ivanov I left Kenai. Before the departure I served a customary prayer service for those who travel on water. By 7 o'clock in the evening, we arrived at Ninilchik village. At the shore the people of the village met us, and I gave them my blessing. Of course, as always they welcomed us by gun shooting. To rest from my trip I went to the place of Aleksei Oskolkoff, a respected old man. In the meantime, the churchwarden, I. Kvasnikov, was already hurrying to report to me about chapel finances. Everything is going on well in the village. The Ninilchik Creoles repaired their chapel, which I inspected a little later.

The Ninilchik residents indeed should be credited for having done such excellent work. Aleksei Oskolkoff especially contributed much effort to making an icon screen. The churchwarden is also doing good work keeping chapel finances in proper order. The sale of candles was conducted honestly, and all donated money was reported. From the sale of candles they received $69.70, and $9.50 came in as donations. I supplied the chapel with new candles, small body crosses, and icons at the total amount of $42.95, which I received immediately along with the money they owed for the last year. After all these expenses were deducted, there was $34.75 in the chapel fund. The appearance of the chapel produced the most favorable impression on me: everything was neat, clean, and kept in proper order. After inspecting the chapel, I checked on how the acting songleader, Gerasim Oskolkoff, performed chapel services on Sundays and on feast days. Later on I announced to the people that beginning on Monday they were to start preparing themselves for holy sacraments, and promised them that on my way back to Kenai I would come by again to confess them and provide communion. Having spent a night at Aleksei Oskolkoff's place, the next day at 3 o'clock in the morning we proceeded further, helped by a favorable current.

July 7. Reached Laida village at 7:30 in the morning. The population of Laida is even smaller than Ninilchik's. For this reason and because it was already late, instead of staying here I encouraged the Laida people to go to a larger neighboring settlement to perform rites of preparation for holy sacraments, and everybody agreed. I had to wait for a favorable current, and then accompanied by Old Iakovlev and two Kenaitze boys set out for Seldovia at 1 o'clock in the afternoon. In order to get to Seldovia without going through Kachemak one has to cross a large bay, which is thirty miles in width and has frequently turbulent waters. Although there was hardly any wind, huge waves rose in the bay. The entire route to Seldovia we sailed in constant fear, and finally reached the village at 8 o'clock in the evening.

Sad feelings filled my soul as I neared Seldovia. I had heard that Seldovians still did not want to restrain themselves from alcohol, and continued drinking. What made me feel even worse was that Seldovia is the only village in my parish that carries the disgusting nickname of a "drunk village." As far as the northern settlements of the Kenai parish are concerned, such as Kustatan, Tyonek, Susitna, and Knik, people in these villages have completely stopped drinking vodka. This year a Knik trade agent twice came to Kenai and thanked me himself and on behalf of a Tyonek trade agent for making the natives quit drinking. I am not sure to what extent the traders' gratitude is sincere, but I am glad that the Kenaitze took my words so seriously from the very beginning. Ironically, the same Knik trade agent held me up to ridicule, when he heard earlier that I had made the Kenaitze promise me that they would stop drinking vodka. During the talks with his drinking companions the trade agent said that it would never happen. Yet, time proved that what at first seemed to be impossible, according to sense, became possible with the assistance of God's grace. During his stay in Knik, Mr. Washburn, the chief manager of the Alaska Commercial Company, thanked me earnestly as well.

Therefore, the above-mentioned alcohol abuse was the chief reason for me being so worried, as I entered the Seldovia village. We had a chance to see right away that the rumors about Seldovians' behavior that had reached us are true. On the shoreline, a half-drunk Feodor Berestov, the local *toion,* met us. He could barely stand. Nevertheless, he tried hard to show us that he was sober, which was amusing to watch. Since nobody expected that I would come in my own *baidarkas*, all the inhabitants were away on hunting trips. The *toion* promised to bring everybody by the time when I returned from Aleksandrovsk. After we landed, I went straight to the chapel. The walls, the ceiling, and the floor of the structure are covered with grooved boards. The villagers also installed new windows and bought enough new tiles for the roof. Although the work has not yet been completed, the chapel already looks nice. The Kenaitze were going to paint the walls and the ceiling with white oil paint after my departure. Seldovians bought all these materials at their own expense using chapel donations, which increased this year to more than $70. Despite their drawbacks, Seldovians look after their chapel very carefully, for which we should thank them very much.

July 11. At 6 o'clock in the evening I started to perform the all-night vigil, during which I delivered a sermon about the harmful effects of drunkenness, trying to convince the Kenaitze to listen to their priest and quit drinking. I expanded on this subject for a long time, and in conclusion instructed them to think seriously about my words, when they go back home, and to give me tomorrow a positive response. Incidentally, I found it necessary to point out to them that to my shame it is only Seldovia village that carries the disgraceful nickname of a "drunk village" and ruins the prestige of the entire Kenai parish. When I ended the all-night vigil, everybody left silently and sullenly.

July 12. At 7 o'clock in the morning I served the Hours and then typical psalms. In my sermon I talked about the necessity of genuine repentance. I also returned to the same theme I raised yesterday, simply because in Seldovia people become literally and hopelessly drunk [*s krugu spilsia*]. Characteristically, the *toion* of the village, whom I tried to convince to stop drunkenness, said to me: "Father, we cannot live without vodka." Yet, yesterday's sermon appears to have affected the Kenaitze, for today when I asked them: "Well, what did you decide?," a few natives told me in a straightforward manner that they would completely stop drinking vodka. To my surprise, among them were people from whom I absolutely did not expect such a response. However, the majority of the people remained indecisive and simply stood in silence. To break this silence, I stressed that I would not leave the village without receiving a positive response, and also added that I would not let this drinking spree continue as earlier. Thus, for about five minutes I had to stand at the pulpit in complete silence. Realizing that people were having a hard time and did not know how and what to respond, I offered my listeners the following word of advice. If they cannot stop drinking vodka, I suggested that they at least eliminate drunkenness. So I said that it would be permitted to heavy drinkers to consume vodka at the amount of half of a cup, provided that such drinking takes place very rarely and serves as a prevention for drunkenness. To those who did wish to listen to their priest and want to make their bodies and souls healthier, I suggested they quit drinking vodka completely. In order to restrain them from breaking their promises, I suggested a fine of one dollar for anybody who is noticed to be drunk, which shall be contributed to the needs of the chapel (one cannot be drunk from half of a cup of vodka). Now to my question: "What will you say to this?," all of them responded: "All right, let's make it so." In offering this word of advice, I tried to impose on the Seldovia Kenaitze at least some moderation in drinking, for it is known that the natives usually do not restrict themselves to one shot, but drink at once from three to four glasses. Even a person with an iron constitution after a few of such drinking sprees might damage his health. It is natural that one hardly can say anything positive about the health conditions of the Seldovia Kenaitze. In this village almost all young people at the age of twenty-four or twenty-five cough blood. One seriously wonders what they will pass on to the next generation. The mortality rate is always higher in Seldovia than in other villages, and the major cause of these deaths is tuberculosis. A large number of infants, before they reach three or four years, also die, for which their drunk parents should be blamed. Unfortunately, this year in Seldovia the Alaska Commercial Company built its trading store, and by now the village has two trading stores, which compete with each other and try to lure the Kenaitze by getting them drunk. Yet, I firmly believe that this time the Lord will not let the Seldovians fall again. At least in their words the natives express a desire to become sober.

July 13. I performed the Divine Liturgy of St. John Chrysostom, during which seventy-nine adults and thirty infants partook in the rites of confession and communion. At 2 o'clock in the afternoon I went to give last rites to a sick woman, and later on carrying the Holy Cross and holy water visited the houses of the parishioners. Seldovian people accompanied my visits to their houses with loud gun shooting, which they enjoy very much. At [blank space] o'clock in the evening in the *toion*'s house I gathered a village meeting. After a requisite prayer in the beginning, I spoke on the same subject as in Aleksandrovsk village [about establishment of the brotherhood]. As a result, all Seldovia hunters, of which there were twenty-three people, joined the Kenai Brotherhood named after the feast of Protection by the Mother of God. Each member promised to pay monthly dues of twenty-five cents, which will be $3 per year. By the beginning of the school year Seldovians also promised to send to Kenai one of their boys, to receive education at the parochial school. At 7 o'clock on the seashore, at the people's request, I performed a thanksgiving customary prayer service to St. Nicholas, the Wonderworker, during which I sprinkled with holy water their *baidarkas* along with all their hunting and fishing gear. Using this favorable moment, I reminded the natives that before they started anything they must seek help from above. I also advised hunters to appeal to St. Nicholas, the Wonderworker, more frequently and ask him for help, for this saint is considered a protector of those who travel at sea.

July 14. At 9 o'clock in the morning using a favorable current, we left Seldovia village. Although a fresh wind blew, we safely crossed the strait, which is thirty miles in width. En route we were dressed in *kamleikas*.[42] At 4 o'clock in the afternoon we reached the cape where Laida village is located and had to stay here until 2 o'clock in the morning waiting for a new current. At 2 o'clock in the morning we set out for Ninilchik. En route one more *baidarka* joined us. It carried a family that was going to Ninilchik to fulfill their Christian duty of partaking in the rites of confession and communion.

July 15. At 7 o'clock in the morning we came to Ninilchik. No sooner had I taken a short rest than residents of the village flocked to me with complaints about each other. Thus, suddenly I found myself in the role of "justice of peace." To my regret, the time I had planned so carefully in advance was wasted in "trials" and "investigations." Although they are related to each other by kinship, Ninilchik

Creoles, like the Creoles from Kenai, do not live in peace. As I noticed in Sitka, Kodiak, and Kenai and also heard from people in the northwestern villages of Alaska, animosity, gossip, and disagreements are a characteristic feature of the entire Creole population. It is surprising that the native populations, thank God, are not familiar with these vices despite their frequent contacts with the Creoles.

At 2 o'clock in the afternoon I served a customary prayer service with water-blessing, during which I consecrated the renewed chapel. During the service, using the Scripture verse "Make every effort to live in peace with all men" [Hebrews 12:14], I said that all the faithful should live in peace. At 6 o'clock in the evening I conducted the all-night vigil, which included the blessing of bread and anointment with holy oil. The service was devoted to the Equal-to-Apostles Prince Vladimir. During the service I delivered a sermon, in which I explained to the people that Christian brotherhood and unanimity serve as necessary foundations of the entire Christian life. In my sermon I also suggested that the Ninilchik Creole establish in their village a brotherhood like we did in Kenai. The inhabitants accepted my idea.

July 16. At 10:30 in the morning I gathered all residents of the village in the house of Aleksei Oskolkoff for a talk. The talk started with a prayer. Then I described to the residents in detail why they should open a brotherhood in Ninilchik. When my speech ended, people again expressed a desire to have such a brotherhood in their village. After this I prepared the text of an agreement about the opening of the brotherhood. The agreement indicated the following major goals of the brotherhood: (1) to unite all residents of the village in one tight brotherly circle, (2) to spread education among the children of the village, (3) to take care of the chapel house, (4) to help the poorest in the village, and (5) to maintain a local cemetery. To pursue the above-mentioned goals it was resolved to introduce monthly dues at the amount of no less that twenty-five cents from each member. All the male population of the village (fifteen people) joined the brotherhood. In addition, Ninilchik now has its own school. Creole Grigorii Oskolkoff volunteered to teach Russian and Church-Slavonic, while another Creole, Ioann Pamfilov, will teach God's Law and church singing. For some time classes will meet at a private house, and then this winter the brotherhood will build a special schoolhouse. In the end I wished the newly opened brotherhood good luck in their work, and added that I would inform the ecclesiastical authorities about what we had just discussed. I will send the text of the agreement to his Grace for approval through the Dean of Clergy. During the same meeting Aleksei Oskolkoff was elected chairman of the brotherhood, while Feodor Kvasnikov became treasurer, and Petr Oskolkoff was appointed record-keeper. The meeting ended with a collective singing of the prayer "It is truly meet and right."

July 25. Today at 8 o'clock in the morning, accompanied by the songleader Aleksei Ivanov, I again set out to visit the northern part of my parish, and by the end of the same day I arrived safely at Kustatan village. As always, all residents of the village met me on the shore. Having blessed everybody, I went to the *toion*'s place. The *toion* gladly reported that all his people are now completely "dry." Moreover, nobody mentions alcohol at all. I praised them for this achievement and added that the Kenaitze should always live the same sober and good life as they did during the past year. Thus, on their own, the natives realized that it is possible to live without vodka.

I spent the entire evening talking to the *toion* and other Kenaitze. The *toion* was so glad that the Kenaitze stopped drinking vodka that during the whole evening he continually returned to the same subject. Incidentally, the *toion* told me a story that vividly shows that among the Kenaitze there exist people who sympathize very much with what the priest tries to do for them, and firmly follow his word of advise. Here is one story: In Tyonek village a *toion*, an old man, died. A large number of residents from all the villages gathered to pay their last respects to the deceased. Among those who came was the Susitna *zakazchik*, who suggested that the Kenaitze, according to earlier custom, distill and drink vodka in honor of the dead man. This suggestion was very tempting, and the Kenaitze were hesitant to reject it. But a few people suddenly came up and turned down the *zakazchik*'s suggestion. Moreover, they convinced people to keep the promise they had given to the priest, who cares about the Kenaitze's well-being. So plans to distill vodka were dropped. The *toion* stressed that if these people had not stopped the Susitna *zakazchik*, the Kenaitze little by little would have again been involved in drunkenness. With all my heart I enjoyed listening to this good news.

July 26. At 7 o'clock in the morning I served a customary prayer service with water-blessing. The *toion* and a churchwarden informed me that for the past year there were few donations and those not from everybody. Therefore, during the service I asked the natives to bring more donations to the chapel,

July 27. At 2 o'clock I gathered the Kenaitze for a talk, which was opened with the prayer "To the Heavenly King." Then I explained to them in detail why in Kenai we opened the brotherhood. Then I invited the local Kenaitze to become members of this society. Also, I suggested that they send a boy from their village to Kenai for schooling. The Kenaitze eagerly responded to my invitation, and immediately seven people joined the brotherhood. Then, having provided the Kenaitze with my final instructions about Christian life and blessed everybody, at 4 o'clock in the afternoon we left for Tyonek, helped by a favorable current.

En route a strong wind suddenly came up. Persistently and for a long time, we struggled against the powers of the sea. Yet, thank God, we overcame them and by 10 o'clock in the evening we reached Tyonek. Given such bad weather, nobody expected us here. Constantly moving breakers pushed us back to sea and there was no way to reach the shore without outside help. To let people know about our arrival, my paddlers started to shoot off their guns. For a long time there was no response from the shore. Finally, the Tyonek people heard the shots and also started signaling to us by shooting back. Thank the Kenaitze for helping us reach the shore. Otherwise, the waves would have surely turned us over. The poor Kenaitze had to walk in water up to their necks in order to catch and hold our *baidarkas*. The natives literally carried out to shore. The Knik trade agent who lives here in summer met me with open arms, which surprised me very much. Last year, when Father Donskoi and I visited Tyonek, he insulted us for no reason, and now such a sudden change. I do not know what made him change his behavior in such a way. Then this agent invited me along with my songleader to his place, and during my entire stay in Tyonek he was very kind and considerate. After the busy trip, we enjoyed our first quiet and good night sleep.

July 28. At 7 o'clock in the morning I audited the chapel's finances. I found out that the churchwarden had conducted the sale of candles and the collection of donations dishonestly, for which he was strongly reprimanded in public. I was ready to dismiss him from this position, but decided to allow him to stay for another year for lack of any other suitable candidate. At the same time, I pointed out to the churchwarden that I would be watching him carefully, and if I noticed in future any misuse of money, I would remove him in disgrace as a person who cannot be trusted. Having inspected the chapel, I served a customary prayer service with water-blessing, during which all people stood holding lighted candles. During the service I talked about the importance of keeping one's vows (concerning what I had heard in Kustatan about the suggestion of the Susitna *zakazchik* to distill vodka).

After the prayer service I announced that after dinner there would be a general meeting. However, at the appointed time an incident happened that disrupted our plans. Here is the story: In Tyonek there lives a Kenaitze native, a family man, who regularly suffers from attacks of some unexplained fear. During these attacks of fear he becomes afraid of everybody and runs away to the woods, where he stays without any food from two to ten days. Completely unconscious he wanders through the woods and mountains. That is what happened with him during my visit. No sooner had we left the chapel than this Kenaitze started to complain to people around him about a bad headache. Ten minutes later he was seen running away to the woods. Everybody dashed off trying to catch him, but all in vain. It was not until 7 o'clock in the evening that we came back to the village completely worn out and still unable to find this man. After his escape his relatives asked me to perform a customary prayer service to the Mother of God and to St. Nicholas, the Wonderworker, to help return their nephew (that is how everybody calls him here). I certainly fulfilled their request. During the service I talked about virtuous Christian life, and also praised the Kenaitze for completely quitting drinking vodka, and asked them to continue living a sober life as they do now.

July 31. At 9 o'clock in the morning I along with my songleader proceeded further. Reached the mouth of the Susitna River at 2 o'clock in the afternoon. The current was not so strong. Therefore, at this time it was a little easier to move up the river. Having sailed about thirty-five miles, my paddlers felt very tired. Yet, fearing bears, which are abundant here, they decided not to take any chances on staying for a night in the woods. Instead, they tried to use all their efforts to reach one village that is located halfway to Susitna.

August 1. We arrived at Susitna at 10 o'clock in the morning. There was hardly anybody left in the village. All the people were away either fishing or hunting. I immediately ordered a boat to be sent to a nearby camp to inform people that the priest had come. The Susitna residents repaired the chapel, but, for lack of any experience, they did this very poorly. All day until evening, the songleader and I worked in the chapel building the new altar. The old one, which had been made simply from a large storage box taken from a store, barely stood on its legs. It was impossible to perform the Divine Liturgy on such a table. In addition, there was a strong spring river flood here. As a result, all houses, including the chapel, were flooded with water halfway up their walls. Water damaged the altar, communion table, pulpit, and other items very badly. So I and the songleader had to do some carpentry work. Fifteen years ago, when the water rose especially high, the whole village was literally washed away and some Susitna houses were seen floating in the vicinity of Kenai. Now, due to the severe frost, the houses remained where they belonged. Having finished the repair work, I audited the churchwarden. The sale of candles was conducted honestly. As for donations, there were very few compared to the number of people. Despite their promise, not a single cent was donated to the Kenai church. When I asked the churchwarden why there were so few donations, he responded that the Susitna Kenaitze surmised that if somebody donated to the chapel, it was like throwing money into the water. Because of this response, before my departure from the village, I decided to hold a general meeting of all parishioners to check personally if what I just heard was true or not. By 7 o'clock in the evening people gradually started to gather. By 9 o'clock in the evening I was able to perform a customary prayer service with water-blessing. During the service sixty-five faithful stood holding lighted candles. I introduced this ritual in all villages to make services more solemn. During the prayer service I delivered a sermon on a Gospel theme from Mathew 10:11.

August 2. At 7 o'clock in the morning I verified the confession registers and then performed various ministrations. During my sermon yesterday, I said a few words about the necessity of donating to the chapel, and also expressed my regret that the Kenaitze did not fulfill their promises. After I completed ministrations, an interpreter visited me and said that he had come by at the Kenaitzes' request. To my question: "What is the matter?," the interpreter responded: "The Kenaitze asked me to tell you that during the whole year they continually donated to the chapel as much as they could. Now they have learned from your yesterday's sermon that very few donations were found in the chapel. Therefore, they think that the churchwarden hid the money." After dinner, I called the churchwarden and told him what I heard from the interpreter. The churchwarden admitted that he had lent for himself $13, and added that he had not told me anything about it, because he was afraid. Having reprimanded him, I instructed the churchwarden to conduct the chapel business honestly, and added that otherwise I would have to remove him from this position. Now I am completely convinced that one should constantly watch the Kenaitze churchwardens. The Kenaitze churchwardens do report the money received by chapels from the sale of candles, because they all know very well that I wrote down in my book the amount of money the chapel spent to purchase candles and other materials. Therefore, during auditing they must show either money received for the sold items or the items themselves. It is impossible to cheat here. As for the donations, it is difficult to control them and some of the churchwardens take advantage of it. Now I have decided to make two cups for each chapel: one for chapel donations and another for the donations to the Kenai church. Each cup will be sealed with the seal of the Kenai church. I announced this to all the people and asked them to put their donations personally into these cups. I also forbade anyone to open these cups before my arrival, and warned them that I would use a church punishment if they disobeyed. I said that I would open these cups myself in the presence of witnesses.

At 6 o'clock in the evening I performed vespers and matins. Almost all the people took part in the service except a few persons, who still had not come back from their hunting and fishing trips. These remaining people will come to Knik this year to partake in the rites of penance to prepare themselves for communion.

August 4. At 6 o'clock in the morning, a morning prayer and the Divine Liturgy of St. John Chrysostom, during which ninety-six adults and thirty infants joined in the holy mysteries. At the end of the service I spoke about the worthlessness of shamanism, to which some of the Susitna people are still attracted. After the service I joined in holy matrimony two couples, including one Mednovtsy man. This is the first Mednovtsy native I have ever married. At 3 o'clock in the afternoon I gathered the Kenaitze for a talk. I spoke about how useful education might be, and also explained the purpose of the opening in Kenai of the brotherhood and invited the Susitna Kenaitze to become members of this society. Twenty people immediately volunteered to join the brotherhood with an obligation to pay monthly dues of twenty-five cents. They also promised to send to me in Kenai one of their boys for training.

We came to Knik at 6 o'clock in the evening. As in Susitna, we found hardly any people here. For all this I blame the Seldovians, who did not send *baidarkas* for me in time. The Knik *zakazchik* immediately sent word to a neighboring camp, which is located within twenty-five miles from Knik, to inform people that the priest had arrived. Having rested a little I audited the Knik churchwarden. He conducted honestly the sale of candles and reported all money. Donations to the local chapel exceeded what I found in Susitna, although nothing was contributed to the Kenai church. After auditing the chapel, I felt very tired. Still, I served the all-night vigil.

August 6. By evening people gradually started to gather. At 7 o'clock in the evening I served the all-night vigil. I devoted my sermon to the responsibilities of faithful Christians and explained the meaning of confession.

August 7. At 7 o'clock in the morning the Divine Liturgy of St. John Chrysostom. During the liturgy all the infants in village joined in the holy mysteries. At the end of the service there were requisite prayers before confession. From 9:30 o'clock in the evening I served vespers and matins, during which I talked about the great holiness of the rite of communion. After this I sang a requisite series of prayers, and then continued to confess people. Confession ended at 8 o'clock in the morning. As in other villages, in Knik I confessed people through an interpreter. During the whole day I did not have a chance to have a seat and rest. So when the confession was finished, I felt completely worn out and, besides, thirsty.

August 8. At 7 o'clock in the morning, the morning prayer and the Divine Liturgy of St. John Chrysostom, during which all residents of the village joined in the holy mysteries. At the end of the service I delivered a requisite address to the communicants, and then announced that I intend to spend this winter in Knik. The inhabitants were glad to hear this news. The *zakazchik* of the village offered me a small room at his house. Besides, the residents of the village promised that in winter they would deliver the necessary number of logs, which I might need to build a house to live in. As for boards, tiles, and other necessary items, the natives told me directly that they would not be able to acquire them at their own expense.

Given the Kenaitzes' slovenliness, God only knows how I will be able to live in the tiny room with all my family. Not having a house is inconvenient for a single person. More so for a family man. Now I become completely convinced that the missionary work among the Mednovtsy will be successful only when the priest stays in Knik each year. For this reason, we need a convenient house in this village. It ought to be remembered that a priest should stay in Knik from the first days of September to the last days of April, which comprises eight full months. To live permanently in a Kenaitze's house is inconvenient both for a priest and for a Kenaitze himself, who is overburdened with his family. This winter I along with my family consciously decided to endure all misfortunes in order to begin missionary work among the Mednovtsy. For this is the will of God.

At 2 o'clock in the afternoon I finally parted with the Kenaitze, promising to return soon, and helped by a favorable current, left Knik. The weather seemed to be good, but as it turned out only in the Knik Arm. The Knik Arm is very conveniently protected against winds: nearby mountains shelter this harbor from the strongest eastern wind, and all other winds hardly penetrate it. We proceeded smoothly, and did not even guess what awaited us further. No sooner had we left the Knik Arm than we were met by a strong wind and waves. May the Lord save you from such trouble! It was useless to turn back and, therefore, we had to continue our route. Only after four hours of hard work were we able to reach an islet, where we spent the night.

August 9. At 9 o'clock in the morning using a favorable current, we left the islet. The wind that stopped us yesterday subsided. When we were crossing the harbor known as Turnagain Arm, we were again caught in a strong wind. In Kenai I heard seasoned sailors say that they would rather withstand the strongest storm in open sea than be caught in this harbor in a strong eastern wind. The waves were irregular, and one did not know from what side to expect them. Water was boiling as in a pot. That was the situation we got in, while still about six miles from the nearest shoreline. And besides, it was now too late to turn back to the islet without the risk being carried out to sea. The only way out was to move forward entrusting our fate in God's hands. My paddlers were very scared. Indeed, our lives were in grave danger. I ascribe my and my travel companions' being saved exclusively to the protection of the Mother of God and to our prayers to St Nicholas, the Wonderworker. I promised to myself that, if we reached the shore safely, I would perform a customary prayer service to both of them upon returning to Kenai. From our own experience we learned the validity of the Russian proverbs: "one who has not been in sea, does not know what fear is" and "having experienced what sea is all about, one always feels like praying to God."[43] I do not wish even my enemies to go through what we had to survive. Amid this turbulence we lost sight of the *baidarka* that carried the songleader, whose boat was heavier than mine, and besides, had inexperienced paddlers. I was seriously concerned for his life. It was practically impossible to pass through the irregular waves. So we had to let the current carry us, and the paddlers just tried to keep a balance. After four hours of such struggle, the current finally threw us onto to the shore. The same happened with the second *baidarka*. I was drenched all over, and did not catch cold only due to the care of my diligent wife. She supplies me for my trips with all necessary items of clothing and in necessary quantity. Fortunately, the tide carried us close to the river. So we had a chance to get fresh water to make tea. I have to admit that at that time the tea we made tasted like the best tea I had ever drunk. Everybody was completely exhausted. Taking a good rest, we renewed our route and reached Nikishka by 11 o'clock in the evening. Here we stayed for the night.

August 10. At 9 o'clock in the morning, using a favorable wind, we left Nikishka. Coming close to Kenai, I noticed the log frame of our new church, which is now under construction. Although the new church will be located far from the seashore, one can see the building very well from the seaside. When the roof and cupolas are completed, the view the temple will command will be wonderful. My only regret is that we do not have any materials to gild the cross with.

So, God let me safely complete my second visit to my parish. Arrived at Kenai at 2 o'clock in the afternoon. The same evening I performed a customary prayer service to the Queen of Heaven and to St. Nicholas, the Wonderworker, to thank them for saving my life and the lives of my travel companions.

Aleksandr Iaroshevich to Vladimir Donskoi, Dean of Clergy of the Sitka District, September 6, 1894[44]

I have the honor to report to Your Right Reverence the following information. During my visit to Knik I conversed with its residents about building a rectory where the priest and his family can live in wintertime; the village inhabitants promised to deliver logs and willingly agreed to participate in the construction work. As for the other building materials, namely regular and grooved [*shpuntovie*] boards for the ceiling and a floor as well as nails, windows, doors, tile for the roof and other things necessary to complete the work, the residents of the village are not able to buy them on their own.

Considering missionary work a sacred and important cause, and also believing that the success of the propagation of the Gospel might be achieved only if the missionary stays at Knik each winter, I hope that the Alaskan Ecclesiastical Consistory will take all this into consideration and support the speedy construction of the suggested rectory with its resources. How many of these resources we will need I cannot say for the time being. In view of this, I humbly ask Your Right Reverence to place the trouble of the calculation on Yourself.

I would like to see this house as a structure of thirty feet in length and seventeen feet in width. The most desirable thing is to design the house inside in the manner that will make it convenient place for a family priest. To everything I mentioned above, I feel obliged to add that we need a carpenter, whom we will have to pay $1.25 per day. As Your Right Reverence knows, the Kenaitze do not understand anything about construction work. In the meantime, as soon as I come to Knik again, I will try to build a foundation for this rectory. Also, when I see the Mednovtsy I may ask them to help too. Although I think it will be a little premature to do so.

Kenai Missionary Priest Aleksandr Iaroshevich.

Missionary Trip to Knik, Winter of 1894, from Aleksandr Iaroshevich's Attachment to the Church Service Journal[45]

September 15. At 6 o'clock in the morning I departed from Kenai. We had to face an unfavorable wind, and for this reason it was only by evening that we were able to near the Nikishka settlement, where we stayed for the night. In this village, in the house of a Kenaitze native named Innokentii Chadalushaia, I baptized an infant. The father wanted me to give him the name Mark, and I did so.

September 16. At 9 o'clock in the morning, helped by a favorable current, I left Nikishka. My travel companions were a Kenaitze paddler and a boy named Stepan Sorokovikov. The latter came back from Knik in order to accompany me. Although the wind barely blew, it was unpleasant. It was hard to move forward. The rower had to maneuver the *baidarka* the entire time and we covered no more than eighteen miles during the whole day. To be exact, it was not us who covered this distance. Rather, it was the favorable current that carried us forward. When the current changed its course, we reached a beach and spent the night there.

September 17. In the morning we continued on our route. Now a side wind had started to blow, and it was quite chilly. Yet, this wind helped us to cover about thirty miles during this day. Thus, we safely crossed this choppy harbor [Knik Arm], where we experienced so much fear last year. We spent the night on a small island. It was raining hard.

September 18. Early in the morning accompanied by a slight breeze we left the small island. Then the weather grew so calm that after sailing only five miles, we lost our chance to catch a favorable tide. Therefore, we had to stop and wait for a new tide. We were not able to reach Knik, the point of my destination, until 6 o'clock in the evening. To my regret, I did not find any natives in the village except a very old Kenaitze woman. All Kenaitze along with their families were away hunting and fishing. What a surprise for me. I was naive enough to think that after my arrival here I would be able to organize a school right away. Eventually, this old woman also went away somewhere, and Knik literally became empty.

September 19. At 8 o'clock in the morning I performed a customary prayer service devoted to the Mother of God and St. Nicholas. All faithful are represented only by my own family and by Stepan Sorokovikov, the acting songleader.

September 20. At 5 o'clock in the evening I celebrated vespers and matins. Participating: the same people as yesterday.

September 21. At 7 o'clock in the morning I celebrated the Divine Liturgy of St. John Chrysostom. Today three native hunters came back to the village and brought their furs to the trading store. Then they again left.

September 23. At 5 o'clock in the evening I celebrated vespers [mournful vespers] and matins. The praying faithful were again represented by my own family and S. Sorokovikov.

September 24. At 7 o'clock in the morning I celebrated the mourning Divine Liturgy of St. John Chrysostom. Afterward, I served the great requiem for those missionaries who worked to advance Orthodoxy in America. At 5 o'clock I performed the all-night vigil accompanied by blessing of loaves of bread and anointment with myrrh. The service was devoted to Our Venerable Father Sergius, Wonderworker of Radonezh. It appears that today, when Orthodoxy in America celebrates its 100th anniversary, Our Lord God decided to bring to the village some Kenaitze to celebrate this great event. And indeed, to my great joy, five minutes before the beginning of the service two native hunters returned to the village. During the service I gave them small body crosses and small icons with images of St. Sergius of Radonezh.

Although I wanted to stay in Kenai until September 25 to celebrate this anniversary, I could not do it because by this time strong winds usually start blowing, and in these weather conditions to set our for a water journey across the Kenai Gulf would have been unsafe. To make things worse, these winds keep on blowing the whole winter without pause. Therefore, I decided to perform the ceremony of celebration later in Kenai when I come back home from Knik.

September 25. One Hundredth Anniversary of Orthodoxy in America. At 8 o'clock in the morning I performed a rite of the lesser blessing of water and then the Divine Liturgy of St. John Chrysostom. The praying faithful were represented by my own family, two Kenaitze, and Sorokovikov. At 3 o'clock in the afternoon I celebrated a great vespers. Due to the absence of the faithful in Knik, I omitted some parts of the service. When I come back to Kenai, I will fill this void and repeat the solemn service itself. I gave Ivanov, the songleader who remained in Kenai, detailed instructions on how to celebrate this anniversary.

September 27. Today again four more hunters came from the forest and having sold their furs to the trading store they went back to the forest. Yet before they left the natives called on the chapel, prayed, and also brought some donations. At 5 o'clock in the evening we served vespers and matins, in which the above-mentioned hunters participated too.

September 28. At 7 o'clock in the morning I celebrated the Divine Liturgy of St. John Chrysostom.

September 30. Today another hunter returned to the village. Yet tomorrow he is again planning to leave. At 5 o'clock in the evening I celebrated the all-night vigil accompanied by the blessing of loaves of bread and anointment with myrrh.

October 1. The feast day of Protection by the Most Holy Mother of God. At 9 o'clock in the morning the Divine Liturgy of St. John Chrysostom, during which two infants (my own children) joined in the holy mysteries. After the Liturgy I performed a customary prayer service, accompanied by kneeling, and devoted to the Most Holy Mother of God. At 5 o'clock in the evening I celebrated the all-night vigil. The praying faithful were represented by my own family and Sorokovikov.

October 6. Today another hunter with his family came back to Knik.

October 7. At the usual time in the evening I served vespers and matins. All those who were at Knik at this time participated in the service.

October 8. The Divine Liturgy of St. John Chrysostom at 7 o'clock in the morning. The same people participated in the service. The all-night vigil at 5 o'clock in the evening.

October 9. At the usual time I performed the Divine Liturgy of St. John Chrysostom. The praying faithful were represented by four persons. At 3 o'clock in the afternoon I celebrated the great vespers with *akathist* in honor of St. Nicholas, the Wonderworker. After the *akathists* one more hunter with his family came from the forest.

October 10. Today a Kenaitze *toion* with his people came to Knik from a settlement located twenty-five sea miles from here. He intends to winter in Knik. The natives are gradually gathering. Among those who arrived was Ruf Stepanov, a local interpreter.

October 11. In the morning I and the Kenaitze who have just arrived went to the forest, where we cut trees and stockpiled logs for building a rectory. We cut seventeen trees, and each log is eighteen feet in length. In the evening I served vespers and matins. Twenty-six faithful of both genders participated in the service.

October 12. The Divine Liturgy of St. John Chrysostom at 7 o'clock in the morning. There were twenty-six praying people. Today at 3 o'clock in the afternoon we again cut trees in the forest and prepared fifteen logs.

October 13. From the morning on we were again occupied with cutting trees and making logs. Today the Knik churchwarden along with his family returned from his hunting trip. They brought from the forest Foma, an old man who felt ill. Then Foma's family also arrived. Since the Kenaitze gather little by little, today I decided to start special religious talks with them, and I plan to do this each Thursday and Tuesday. The first talk took place at 4 o'clock in the afternoon. The meeting started with the collective singing of the prayer "To the Heavenly King." Then I explained to the Kenaitze the concept of God. When I ended my talk, they recited and learned by heart words of the basic prayers such as "Glory to the Father" [and to the Son and to the Holy Spirit]. I also explained to them how to make correctly the sign of the cross. We also learned how to sing "Lord, have mercy on me." Although this year we celebrate the 100th anniversary of Orthodoxy in America, in religious respects the local Kenaitze still remain literal savages. They do not know a single prayer and have only a vague idea of the holy faith in general. The natives only know that there is God, whom one needs to believe in, and that one has to perform the rites of fast and penance when a priest comes. The ignorance of the Kenaitze was the major reason why I decided to start my regular religious talks with them. All Kenaitze who were at the village participated in this first talk.

October 14. We continued cutting trees and making logs. So far we have stockpiled fifty pieces. These logs are stockpiled deep in the forest and to bring them to the site of construction will be quite difficult. For this reason, we plan to chop trees in some other places which are close to water, to make it easier to transport the logs. At 5 o'clock in the evening I served vespers and matins. There were forty-four praying faithful.

October 15. At 7 o'clock in the morning the Divine Liturgy of St. John Chrysostom. There were forty praying faithful. The all-night vigil at 5 o'clock in the evening with forty-two participating faithful.

October 16. At 9 o'clock in the morning the Divine Liturgy of St. John Chrysostom, where I joined six infants in the holy mysteries. At the end of the Liturgy the priest talked about and explained to the faithful a Sunday reading from the Gospels. There were forty-two praying people. At 2 o'clock in the afternoon I gathered the Kenaitze for a religious talk in the chapel and told them about God and how He created the world. Then we repeated the prayer that they learned during the last meeting, and we also started learning a new prayer, to the Holy Spirit. At the end of the meeting we sang simple litanies. After the meeting I celebrated the great vespers with an *akathist* in honor of Our Lord Jesus Christ. During the service the Kenaitze sang together. It was their first attempt and they have not yet learned a necessary harmony in singing. There were forty-four praying faithful during this service.

October 17. At 7 o'clock in the morning I served the requisite customary prayer service celebrated on this day with wishing many years of life to the reigning Imperial family. There were many praying people during the service. Then I delivered a sermon, where I stressed that we should pray for all people, and especially for the Russian czar, who promotes the advance of Orthodoxy in America by sending priests and providing them with a necessary assistance. Today I opened a school for the Knik Kenaitze. So far only six children have showed up for classes.

October 18. I was occupied with teaching my classes. Specifically the children were learning a few basic prayers up through "To the Heavenly King." In Russian language class they learned vowels and at the end of classes we sang together "Lord, Have Mercy on Me." Vespers and matins at 5 o'clock in the evening. Forty-three faithful participated in the service.

October 19. At 7 o'clock in the morning the Divine Liturgy of St. John Chrysostom, then classes. Today a Kenaitze man cut his hand with an axe, and I visited him to stop the bleeding and put on a bandage. The wound is not dangerous.

October 20. Classes in the morning. After classes I again visited the sick Kenaitze to wash his wound and change the dressing. At 4 o'clock many Kenaitze gathered for my regular religious talk. After all sang together the prayer "To the Heavenly King," I repeated the creation story, which I had told them before, and I also spoke about how the first people appeared. Everything is new to the Kenaitze, and they are very interested in holy history. Then we learned the prayer to the Holy Spirit and recited the prayers they learned earlier. At the end of the meeting the Kenaitze sang together. They love collective singing very much and usually sing with great enthusiasm. The meeting ended with reciting the prayer "It is truly meet and right."

October 21. At the appointed time classes in the morning. Again visited the Kenaitze who cut his hand. The wound starts to heal. I washed it with an extract of chamomile and put on a bandage from "Russian [the next word is illegible]" toolkit. At 5 o'clock in the evening I celebrated vespers and matins, where forty faithful participated.

October 22. At the usual time the Liturgy of St. John Chrysostom. Then I celebrated the lesser litany in honor of those who have passed away. After the service I taught classes at school and then visited the sick Kenaitze. The all-night vigil at 5 o'clock, where forty-eight faithful participated.

October 23. At the appointed time the Divine Liturgy of St. John Chrysostom, where I joined ten infants in the holy mysteries. Then the priest related and explained a Sunday reading from the Gospels. There were forty-eight praying people. At 2 o'clock in the afternoon I conducted a religious talk. The talk started with a singing of the prayer "To the Heavenly King." Then I continued my talk, in which I told the Kenaitze about the fall of our ancestors. After this I asked them to learn the prayer "To the Heavenly King." At the end of the meeting we sang together. Specifically, we sang the *akathist* to the Assumption of the Most Holy Mother of God and simple litanies. I noticed that the natives show more harmony in their singing. After the talk I celebrated the great vespers with an *akathist* to the Assumption of the Most Holy Mother of God.

October 24. In the morning I taught classes. During the last week the children learned all the basic prayers very well, and in addition, they know how to write and pronounce their vowels. After the classes I visited the sick Kenaitze.

October 25. At the usual time I taught classes, and then visited the sick native. At 5 o'clock in the evening I served vespers and matins. There were more than forty praying people.

October 26. The Divine Liturgy of St. John Chrysostom at 7 o'clock in the morning. Forty-three faithful came for this service. Then classes and a visit to the sick Kenaitze. Today, two more Kenaitze fell ill.

October 27. Classes at school. A few more people fell ill. Now the total number of sick people is thirteen. After dinner I visited these sick natives. Those who got sick yesterday now feel better. After I gave them a laxative, they felt much better. I also regularly change the dressing on the wound of the native who cut his hand. At 4 o'clock in the afternoon more than forty Kenaitze gathered for the religious talk. After the usual beginning I continued relating the stories from the Old Testament, specifically about Adam's children. Then we learned the prayers including "To the Heavenly King." At the end of the meeting we sang simple litanies.

October 28. Classes in the morning, then visits to the sick. Vespers and matins at 5 o'clock in the evening. Fifty-seven faithful participated in the service. Because of a lack of houses not all the inhabitants of the Knik Arm winter in the Knik village. Some of them live in another settlement, which is located twenty-five miles from Knik. Although many Kenaitze from that settlement did come to Knik to winter, not many people stay in Knik itself. The same can be said about other Kenaitze villages. In no locality natives live a settled life. Instead, they live by wandering around.

October 29. At 7 o'clock in the morning the Divine Liturgy of St. John Chrysostom, after which I served the lesser litany in honor of those who have passed away. Seventy-seven faithful participated in the service. Then classes and later on visits to the sick. The all-night vigil at 5 o'clock in the evening. The same number of praying people as yesterday.

October 30. At 9 o'clock in the morning the Divine Liturgy of St. John Chrysostom, during which I joined eight infants in the holy mysteries. At the appointed time I explained to the faithful a Sunday reading from the Gospels. The same number of praying people as yesterday. At 3 o'clock in the afternoon I celebrated the great vespers with an *akathist* to St. Nicholas, the Wonder-worker. After the *akathist* I held a religious talk with the Kenaitze. The priest continued relating stories from the Old Testament, specifically about the corruption of humankind and the keeping of the true faith in Noah's family. Then we repeated basic prayers and started learning "The Most Holy Trinity, Have Mercy on Us." At the end of the talk we sang simple litanies and the prayer "To the Heavenly King." The meeting was dismissed after a collective singing of the prayer "It is truly meet and right." Today fifty Kenaitze participated in the talk.

October 31. Classes in the morning as usual. Children come eagerly to classes and do their home assignments diligently. They work especially hard on Russian writing. After dinner I visited the sick natives.

November 1. Classes from morning until noon, then visits to the sick natives. I continue washing with an extract of chamomile the wound of the Kenaitze who cut his hand with an axe. Today Foma, the little old man who is a longtime local resident, became seriously ill. The big toe on his left foot got completely black. All this does not look good. Foma complained that he could not feel this toe, and I made a mustard bath for his feet. At 5 o'clock in the evening I served vespers and matins. Fifty-two faithful participated in this service. Now all participating Kenaitze can sing together simple litanies.

November 2. At 7 o'clock in the morning I celebrated the Divine Liturgy of St. John Chrysostom. More than fifty faithful participated in the service. Then I was occupied teaching classes and after dinner again visited the sick. It seems that old Foma feels a little better. Today he could feel his toe, although it is still black.

November 3. As always, classes in the morning and then visits to the sick. Old Foma feels neither better nor worse. He complains about a fierce pain in his toe. At 4 o'clock I conducted a religious talk with the Kenaitze. After a collective singing of the prayer "To the Heavenly King," the priest continued relating stories from the Old Testament. He spoke about the Great Flood and the life of people after the flood. Then the Kenaitze repeated basic prayers and completed learning a new one, "The Most Holy Trinity, Have Mercy on Us." After reciting prayers and singing litanies, we sang "God with Us" and "To the Heavenly King." All residents of the village took part in this religious talk.

November 4. At 9 o'clock in the morning classes at school. After classes I visited the sick. Old Foma feels worse. Now his entire left foot has become black and he complains of the severe pain. I think if we had a physician here, he would cut off the old man's entire left foot, because the black tumor keeps on growing and moving. Vespers and matins at 5 o'clock in the evening. During the service I related the story about the Tower of Babel and about Abraham, who had been elected to maintain the true faith in God. Fifty people participated in the service.

November 5. At 7 o'clock in the morning I celebrated the Divine Liturgy of St. John Chrysostom, and after the Liturgy I served the litany in honor of those who have passed away. There were many faithful who showed up for this service. After the service I was occupied with classes. At 2 o'clock in the afternoon I visited the sick. The black tumor on the old man's leg keeps moving up, which increases his pain. All simple remedies such as poultices, mustard plasters, and rubbing with turpentine have not relieved his pain and the tumor grows worse and rises higher. The poor old man now is in a pitiful condition, and I absolutely cannot do anything to ease his sorrows. The all-night vigil at 5 o'clock in the evening. During the all-night vigil I told the natives a story about the manifestation of God to Abraham in the shape of three guards. More than fifty people came to this service.

November 6. At the usual time I celebrated the Divine Liturgy of St. John Chrysostom during which the priest did a Sunday reading from the Gospels and explained the meaning of what he read. There were more than fifty faithful at the service. A religious talk with the Kenaitze at 2 o'clock in the afternoon. The talk was opened with singing the prayer "To the Heavenly King." Then the priest told the natives a story from the Old Testament about the birth of Isaac and his sacrifice. After this all those who participated recited prayers that they had learned, including the prayer "Holy Trinity, Have Mercy on Me." At the end of the meeting we sang simple church litanies and learned another prayer. Then I celebrated the great [*torzhestvennaia*] vespers with an *akathist* in honor of St. Nicholas, the Wonderworker. The same number of faithful as this morning.

November 7. At 7 o'clock in the morning I was invited to see sick old Foma. From severe pain and sleeplessness Foma has lost consciousness many times, which very much scares the Kenaitze. I brought the old man back to consciousness by giving him liquid ammonia to smell. Now all his leg up to the knee is black, and the skin on the bottom of his foot is peeling from a strong fever. The old man is in a horrible condition. When Foma regained consciousness I advised him to cleanse his soul tomorrow by confession and accepting last rites. The old man agreed. Later I taught classes at school. At 5 o'clock in the evening the all-night vigil with blessing of loaves of bread and anointment with myrrh. There were more than fifty faithful at this service.

November 8. The feast of St. Michael the Archangel. At 9 o'clock in the morning the Divine Liturgy of St. John Chrysostom during which I joined ten infants in the holy mysteries. At the requisite time I delivered a sermon in which I spoke about the significance of this feast. After the Liturgy I served a customary prayer service devoted to St. Michael the Archangel. There were more than fifty faithful at the service. Before the Divine Liturgy I visited old Foma and gave him last rites. The black tumor has now risen above the knee and, on top of everything, he cannot urinate. At nighttime the old man absolutely cannot fall asleep.

November 9. Taught classes in the morning and after dinner visited the sick. The Kenaitze who cut his hand with an axe is now recovering. Foma, on the contrary, feels worse and worse.

November 10. At the usual time classes at the school, then visits to the sick. I think the life of old Foma will end soon. All the time during our talks, since he has been sick, the old man repeatedly said that he was not afraid to die and knew that he would soon pass away. In his words, it was the only unbearable pain he suffered that tortured and scared him so much. A religious talk with the Kenaitze at 4 o'clock in the afternoon. After singing the prayer "To the Heavenly King," the priest continued relating stories from the Old Testament. This day he spoke with the Kenaitze about Joseph. Then the natives repeated basic prayers and sang hymns [*Elitsi vo Khrista Krestiteliia*]. Then we practiced singing together *akathists* to the Savior, to the Mother of God, and to Nicholas the Wonder-worker. The talk ended with collective reciting of the prayer "It is truly meet and right." All village inhabitants participated in this meeting.

November 11. Classes in the morning. The children make good progress. After dinner I went to visit old Foma, who is now completely in very bad shape. Mournful vespers and matins at 5 o'clock in the evening. Many faithful participated in the service. After the service I again called at old Foma's and read the prayer for the dying. At 10:30 in the evening a Kenaitze came in and informed me that old Foma had just died. I immediately went to him and served the first litany.

November 12. At 7 o'clock in the morning the mourning Divine Liturgy of St. John Chrysostom. After this I sang a great requiem service for all who have passed away and specifically for Foma, a newly presented servant of God. After this service I went to the house of Foma to perform the litany. Then I taught classes. The all-night vigil at 5 o'clock in the evening. During the vigil I continued my talk about Joseph. There were fifty-one faithful at this service.

November 13. At 8 o'clock in the morning I served the litany at Foma's house, and then we went by procession from the house to the church. At 9 o'clock in the morning I celebrated the Divine Liturgy of St. John Chrysostom, during which

I delivered a sermon in which I explained to the faithful where the souls of the dead stayed until the Judgment Day. After the Liturgy without consecration I sang a funeral service for God's servant, Foma, and then we went to the cemetery in a solemn procession. A religious talk with the Kenaitze at 2 o'clock in the afternoon. After the usual beginning the priest told the natives a story from the Old Testament about the life of the Hebrews in Egypt, about the birth of Moses and his exodus. Afterwards we repeated the prayers which the Kenaitze learned earlier and they started learning the Lord's Prayer. At the end of the meeting we sang various litanies, the prayer "To the Heavenly King," and refrains to *akathists* that are usually sung during a prayer service in honor of the Mother of God. Then I celebrated the great vespers with an *akathist* in honor of the Savior. More than fifty faithful participated at the service. At 5 o'clock I baptized an infant, who received the name Daniil.

November 15. Taught classes in the morning. I now have fourteen students. One boy even came from Susitna to study. Vespers and matins at 5 o'clock in the evening. Forty-eight faithful came for this service.

November 16. Divine Liturgy of St. John Chrysostom at 7 o'clock in the morning and then classes.

November 17. Classes in the morning. The Kenaitze meeting at 4 o'clock in the afternoon. After the usual beginning, the priest told the natives about the entrance of the Jews into Canaan. The Kenaitze continued to learn the Lord's Prayer and also repeated the prayers they have already learned. At the end of the meeting we sang together.

November 18. Classes in the morning as usual. The children now can write simple words which I dictate to them. They also can read a little in Russian and Old Church Slavonic, and do some simple arithmetical problems. Also, they have already learned many prayers. Vespers and matins at 5 o'clock in the evening. Forty-nine faithful participated at the service.

November 19. The Divine Liturgy of St. John Chrysostom at 7 o'clock in the morning, then the litany in honor of those who have passed away. After this I taught classes. The all-night vigil at 5 o'clock in the evening. During the vigil service I continued to enlighten the natives about the Old Testament, particularly about kings David and Solomon. There were more than fifty faithful who came for the service.

November 20. At 9 o'clock in the morning I celebrated the Divine Liturgy of St. John Chrysostom during which I related and explained a Sunday reading from the Gospel. A meeting with the Kenaitze at 2 o'clock in the afternoon. After singing the prayer "To the Heavenly King," the priest told the Kenaitze about the prophets in general and specifically about the prophet Elijah. Then the natives learned by heart the *troparion* in honor of the feast of the Nativity of Christ and repeated all previous prayers. The Kenaitze also sang the "Lord's Prayer," "Lord with Us" and simple litanies. After the meeting I celebrated the great vespers with an *akathist* to St. Nicholas the Wonderworker. Fifty faithful participated in the service. The all-night vigil at 5 o'clock.

November 21. Classes in the morning. Today is the feast day of the Presentation in the Temple of the Mother of God. At 9 o'clock in the morning the Divine Liturgy of St. John Chrysostom, after which I performed a customary prayer service in honor of the Mother of God.

November 24. Classes in the morning. A religious talk with the Kenaitze at 4 o'clock in the afternoon. After singing the prayer "To the Heavenly King" the priest told the natives the rest of the history of the Hebrew people, from the time of the division of the Hebrew kingdoms to the Nativity of the Most Holy Mother of God. Then the Kenaitze continued learning by heart the *troparion* in honor of the feast of the Nativity of Christ and also repeated all prayers they had learned earlier. At the end of the meeting we sang.

From November 28 to December 3 I was busy working in the chapel. I was covering the walls with calico and wallpaper, and now the chapel has already acquired quite a decent appearance. The delighted Kenaitze now look at the chapel and keep on repeating, "Now it is a real church, a real church." The days when I was busy with this work my boy Sorokovikov was responsible for teaching classes.

December 5. Taught classes in the morning. At 5 o'clock in the evening the all-night vigil with blessing of loaves of bread and the *akathists* in honor of St. Nicholas the Wonderworker and anointment with myrrh. About sixty faithful came to this service.

December 8. Taught classes in the morning. Today I have sent some Kenaitze to Susitna to inform those in that village who did not perform the rites of fast and penance this summer to hurry down to Knik and fulfill their Christian duties of partaking in confession and communion. I held the Kenaitze meeting at 4 o'clock in the afternoon. After the usual beginning the priest told the natives about the Annunciation of the Most Holy Mother of God. Afterwards all Kenaitze repeated the prayer "Rejoice, O Mother of God Full of Grace, the Lord Is with Thee" and other basic prayers. At the end of the meeting we practiced singing.

December 11. At 9 o'clock in the morning the Divine Liturgy of St. John Chrysostom, during which I delivered a sermon based on a reading from the Gospels. The Kenaitze meeting at 2 o'clock in the afternoon. After singing the prayer "To the Heavenly King" the priest told the natives about the Nativity of Christ. Then all Kenaitze together recited the prayers and the *troparion* in honor of the Nativity of Christ, a composition that they earlier learned by heart. It looks as though the local Kenaitze enjoy collective singing very much. Both men and women and the children usually sing with great enthusiasm. Besides, the Kenaitze are very pleased that now they know their prayers. I often heard the Kenaitze saying, "Well, thank God, now when Father leaves, we will not have to pray to God silently anymore as we did before. Now we will be able to sing and even to read something, since, thanks to Father, we have learned certain things." After the religious talk I celebrated the great vespers with an *akathist* to St. Nicholas the Wonderworker. More than fifty faithful came for this service.

December 16. From today on I have to cancel my classes temporarily because fifty Kenaitze have come from Susitna. The Knik natives have given them accommodation in the available village houses. As a result, Knik has become so crowded that I do not have the facilities to meet my classes. Besides, starting tomorrow these Susitna Kenaitze will begin performing the rites of fast and penance, and I will have to conduct services for them each day. Vespers and matins at 5 o'clock. More than sixty faithful participated in the service.

December 17. At 7 o'clock in the morning the Divine Liturgy of St. John Chrysostom, after which I served the litany in honor of those who have passed away. More than 100 faithful participated in the service. The all-night vigil at 5 o'clock in the evening. More than 100 faithful came for this service. It was unbearably hot in the crowded chapel.

December 18. I celebrated the Divine Liturgy of St. John Chrysostom at 9 o'clock in the morning. The religious talk with the Kenaitze at 2 o'clock in the afternoon. Since so many Kenaitze came from Susitna, who absolutely do not know anything about the prayers, after the usual beginning specifically for them I decided to repeat briefly stories from the Old Testament up through the period of Abraham. At the end of the meeting we practiced singing. The newly arrived natives noticed the progress their fellow Knik tribesmen have made in prayers and church singing, and now the Susitna Kenaitze literally pursue me everywhere asking me to teach them. After the religious talk I celebrated the great vespers with an *akathist* to the Savior. More than 100 faithful came to this service.

December 24. Today at 4 o'clock in the afternoon the Mednovtsy, about thirty people, finally came to Knik. At 6 o'clock I celebrated the great vespers with blessing of loaves of bread and anointment with myrrh. There were about ninety faithful at this service.

December 26. At 7 o'clock in the morning the Divine Liturgy of St. John Chrysostom, after which I performed a customary prayer service in honor of the Mother of God. There were seventy-five faithful at this service. At 6 o'clock in the evening I gathered the Susitna Kenaitze and asked them to help the Knik Kenaitze to chop trees for building the rectory. Unfortunately, except for three of them, the Susitna natives talked their way out of this, saying that they were busy. With regard to the Knik Kenaitze, they decided to go to the forest to chop trees the day after tomorrow.

December 27. This morning I gathered the Mednovtsy for a talk and advised them to take advantage of my presence here to fulfill the Christian duty of fast and penance, to confess and to receive communion. All Mednovtsy willingly agreed to do this except a shaman who has two wives. The latter directly said that he did not want to perform these rites. I began persuading him to take care of his soul and not to do such stupid things. Yet he still did not want to listen to me. Finally, he said, "The reason I do not want to perform the rites is that I do not want you to take from me my second wife." I told him to think it over carefully and repent, and that I hope that we will continue talking about this matter next time. This was the end of our talk. I told those Mednovtsy who expressed a desire to perform the rites of fast and penance not to listen to those people who live in sin, but, as Orthodox Christians, to listen to their priest and always to do what he says.

December 28. On this day the Knik Kenaitze were about to go with me to the forest to chop trees and prepare logs for building for the rectory. However, for some reason the trade agent Krison did not like it at all that the Kenaitze wanted to work for me. To disrupt our plans he started running around the village threatening to beat everybody and shouting, "I will smash the head of anyone who would dare to work for the Father." This Krison tried to harass me in every way, but I absolutely could not understand the source of his animosity, and what he wanted from me. To find out the reason for his interference in our project, which is absolutely none of his business, I went to his place and in a polite manner quietly asked him, "Tell me, why do you not let the Kenaitze work for me?" In response I heard a whole stream of most disgusting curses. He blamed me for keeping the Kenaitze from their hunting trips and acting against interests of the company [ACC]. Then he went on and on in a similar manner by saying various nonsense and tall tales. I told him that the company had nothing to do with my work in Knik and that I do not feel any need to go against its interests. I also explained to him that our Orthodox feast had not yet ended and asked him to give me two days by promising that after the New Year I would definitely send the Kenaitze on their hunting trips, which is absolutely not my concern. This scoundrel did not even want to listen to me and said, "If you yourself go with the Kenaitze to work I will smash your head too." And then he added, "The Kenaitze owe my trading store about $100. Make sure that they pay this money and then you can take them to work for you." What could I do with this scoundrel? I did not have any other choice except completely postponing the whole project. That is how this renegade disrupted all my plans to build the rectory. Incidentally, his words that it was supposedly hunting season did not make any sense. After this incident the Kenaitze stayed in their homes almost the whole month doing nothing, and the agent still did not tell them anything. At the same time, he did not want to give me even two days. I informed Krison that I would complain to Mr. Washburn. This made the agent absolutely furious, and he refused to sell me any food from his store. The Kenaitze were also on edge, and if it were not for me, they would have brought Krison many troubles. ACC trade agents persistently try to convince the natives that they are the only masters in their villages. Yet, in reality, it does not work this way, and the natives listen more to the priest, which aggravates the agents so much that they want to stop at nothing to spite the priest. It is so frustrating. The priest cannot do anything without making the agent angry. Therefore, my hopes to build the rectory by the next year were left unfulfilled.

January 1, 1895. At 9 o'clock the Divine Liturgy of St. Basil the Great, during which the priest delivered a sermon, in which he explained how Orthodox Christians should greet the New Year. More than eighty faithful came for the service. At 2 o'clock in the afternoon I renewed my religious talks. On this day the talk was opened with a singing of the prayer "To the Holy Spirit." Then the priest enlightened the Kenaitze about the meaning of the Circumcision of our Lord Jesus Christ and also explained why after birth all people receive their guardian angels from God. I also instructed the Kenaitze in what they should do to maintain close relationships with their guardian angels. After this the Kenaitze repeated the prayers they learned earlier. During this talk the natives were also learning the *troparion* in honor of the Nativity of Christ. At the end of the meeting we practiced singing. When the talk ended, I celebrated the great vespers with an *akathist* to the Mother of God. The same number of faithful as in the beginning of the day.

January 2. At 7 o'clock in the morning I celebrate matins for the Mednovtsy who were performing the rite of penance. During the matins I also spoke about God as the creator of the world. Twenty-nine Mednovtsy performed the rite of penance. At 5 o'clock in the evening I served vespers and matins. The old man named Jacob, that Mednovtsy who has two wives, did not want not perform this rite because he fears that I will make him abandon one of his wives. I already wrote about this Mednovtsy in my church service journal for 1894. I have never seen such a stubborn native, and, on top of it all, this old man is a shaman. Although not regularly, the other Mednovtsy do diligently visit the temple. The trading store stands as the major obstacle to their visits to the chapel. The Mednovtsy stay bartering there literally the whole day and also a major part of the night. They do listen to my religious instructions very attentively.

January 7. At 7 o'clock in the morning I read requisite prayers before communion for the natives who were performing the rite of penance. Then I celebrated the Divine Liturgy of St. John Chrysostom and confessed the faithful except that fanatic shaman, who did not show up for the confession. At the end of the Liturgy I delivered a welcoming address to the communicants. After the Liturgy, at the request of a Kenaitze, I performed a customary prayer service in honor of St. Basil the Great. More than fifty faithful participated in the services. I celebrated the all-night vigil at 5 o'clock in the evening. About eighty faithful came to this service.

January 9. Today I found out that the Mednovtsy are going home, and decided again to converse with Jacob, the old shaman, who did not fulfill the Christian duty of partaking in the rites of confession and communion. I went to the place where the Mednovtsy stayed and found the shaman at home. He came forward to accept my blessing. Then through an interpreter I explained to him the purpose of my visit. I said that since the time he had accepted holy baptism, he was expected to change his way of life and to live as an Orthodox Christian. I also told Jacob that a Christian should not have two wives and especially must not shamanize, which confuses fellow tribesmen who have only recently accepted the Christian faith. Since he belongs to the Christian church I was concerned about saving Jacob's soul and ordered him to submit himself to all requirements of the priest, namely, to leave one of his wives, to marry another one according to Orthodox law, and to abandon shamanism forever. Otherwise, I added, I will cross his name off the list of Orthodox people. It seems that my threat affected him, and besides, for the past few days the shaman himself has somehow changed. He no longer shows arrogance, pride, and pomposity. The good behavior of his fellow tribesmen apparently makes him more submissive and reasonable. The shaman told me that he wants to remain an Orthodox Christian, and that it was the reason he adopted baptism. The old man also said that he did not remember everything I taught him about. I asked him to come to my place after dinner and I would teach him. At 3 o'clock in the afternoon Jacob came and we went to the chapel together. There in front of the image depicting the Judgment Day I told him in detail about the fate of sinners and righteous men in the afterlife. The shaman looked completely confused and right in the chapel started to thank me for saving him in time from unavoidable death. Jacob promised to change his life completely. In addition, he asked me to permit him to confess, and, of course I gladly let him do this. The woman whom he wanted to marry according to Orthodox law was not with him, and he promised he would definitely join her in holy matrimony next time. He also promised to abandon the second woman as soon as he returned to his village. On the whole, I felt greatly comforted that all Mednovtsy fulfilled their Christian duties and went back home with renewed souls.

January 14. The Divine Liturgy of St. John Chrysostom at 7 o'clock in the morning. Afterwards, I performed a customary prayer service in honor of the Holy Equal-to-Apostles Nina Enlightener of Georgia. Thirty-eight faithful came to this service. The Kenaitze again are leaving the village for their hunting trips, and the number of people in Knik decreases with each day. The all-night vigil at 5 o'clock in the evening. Thirty-eight faithful came for this service.

January 16. Today *zakazchik* Afanasii with his family and all the other Kenaitze who live at his house left for a hunting trip. I decided to renew my classes. Six children now regularly study in my classes. All others have left the village with their parents, who have gone on hunting trips.

January 17. Classes in the morning. Vespers and matins at 5 o'clock in the evening. Nineteen faithful came for the service. Each evening from 6 to 8 in the evening I instruct two Kenaitze, Ruf Stepanov and Nikolai Kuliktukta (from Tyonek). I am training them to become readers at the chapel. They can now read and write in Russian and do simple arithmetical problems. Yet, doing readings in Church Slavonic during services will be their major task. They can recite all basic prayers for church services, and now they are learning how to read the Hours.

January 31. Taught classes in the morning. The Kenaitze keep on wandering off. Only a few people remain in the village. A religious talk with the Kenaitze at 3 o'clock in the afternoon. After the usual beginning I repeated the whole story of the sufferings of Jesus Christ beginning from the Last Supper. The Kenaitze listen to all these stories with intense attention and frequently make me repeat this or that episode. We spent the end of the meeting by practicing collective reading and singing of prayers. Nineteen faithful participated in this talk.

February 9. Taught classes. A religious talk with the Kenaitze at 2 o'clock in the afternoon. After the collective singing of the prayer "To the Holy Spirit," the priest told the natives how Christianity had spread in the first centuries and how Russia had been baptized. Then in order to find out what the Kenaitze remember from the stories I have related to them in the past six months, I started to ask some of them about various episodes from the Old and New Testaments. To my great joy, the natives remember perfectly well the greater part of what I told them.

February 10. Taught classes in the morning. Today the Mednovtsy again came to the village and called on me. I promised to talk with them by inviting them to come to the church in the evening. Vespers and matins at 6 o'clock in the evening. After the service I talked with the Mednovtsy about the holy faith, and all five of them decided to accept holy baptism.

February 18. At 7 o'clock in the morning I went to an ailing woman to give her last rites. When I was leaving her house, holding the presanctified gifts in my hands, a sorrowful incident happened, which forced me to postpone the Divine Liturgy until tomorrow. To make the reader of this journal aware of the mean and dirty trick the local Americans played on me, I have decided to describe everything in detail. Besides my family and myself, two Americans lived in Knik this winter: A. Krison, a trade agent of the Alaska Commercial Company, and a miner named George Palmer. On December 19, 1894, the latter took Pelageia Chanilkhiga, a local Kenaitze girl, as his concubine. As it turns out, this Kenaitze girl at first did not want to live with him in an illicit manner. She told him that this was a very bad idea, that the priest would not allow them to live in this manner, and suggested that they marry in the church. Palmer did not want to be married in the Orthodox Church. I am sure that the agent Krison egged him on to make this decision. Palmer and Krison calmed the girl by telling her that I supposedly already knew about everything and had nothing against this illicit cohabitation. By spreading this lie about me they simply wanted to add more weight to their words and lure this Kenaitze girl to live with Palmer. I certainly had no idea what was going on, and when I heard about the whole incident two days later I was about to go to the trading store to find out exactly what had happened and if possible to correct the problem. Afanasii

Talchun, the Knik *zakazchik*, tried to persuade me not to go there because they would not listen to me and I might only get into trouble. Then Afanasii added that since this disgraceful incident had happened in his village, he, the *toion* and a few more natives would go there themselves. He did as he said. Five of them went to the trading store but without any result. To the question of the *zakazchik* why he, Palmer, did not want to be married, Palmer and Krison started to shout saying that they did not want to listen to anybody and that they could live as they want and that this was nobody's business. Palmer and Krison also told the Kenaitze that if I wanted to talk with them about this matter, I should come to the store alone without any witnesses. After such a response, I certainly did not go there, and simply did not say a word to Palmer about this, because I had already seen what kind of people I had to deal with. At first I thought to postpone this matter until spring, when navigation begins, and to report it to the proper authorities. Yet, it did not turn out this way. Yesterday in the evening, Palmer's concubine visited me for confession, and I firmly reprimanded her regarding her illicit life, which was my duty as a priest.

This morning, as I already wrote, I went to visit an ailing woman. While I was out, Palmer came to my place and asked my boy Stepan Sorokovikov where I was. The boy told him where I had gone to. Palmer came to this house, where I served the ministration, and waited until I came out. In the meantime, Krison stood in the middle of the road, cutting off the entrance to the house where I was. The natives who were around immediately guessed that these two were up to something bad and wanted to go to help me. The first one who tried to help was the *toion* Petr Teiko, but the agent Krison grabbed his shoulder and pushed him back, saying, "We don't need any more people there." My boy S. Sorokovikov ran toward me by the other route, but Krison noticed him and also pushed him back. All this proves that they were plotting against me in the most disgusting manner. When I finished the ministration and, suspecting nothing, went outside, Palmer blocked my way and said, "What right do you have to interfere in the life of American citizens, and what did you say to that woman yesterday?" I answered that I did not say anything bad to that woman. I told her what I thought, as a priest, was best for her, since she is my parishioner. I also added that I spoke to her during her confession, when she attended a church service. Palmer, who called me by the most disgusting words, which I do not want to reproduce here, grabbed me by the throat and using all his force punched me in my left eye. What made it worse, he hit me with a ring he wears on his finger and cut all along my left cheek. Stepan Kachin, who was there, and another Kenaitze named Evfimii Votchapalan, who rushed from his house to help me, seized the scoundrel, but before he was stopped Palmer was able to punch me again in the upper part of my forehead. Ruf Stepanov was also here, but he acted like a coward and did not do anything. My eye got swollen and now is all black, and the cheek cut by Palmer's ring is bleeding. It is hard to describe my wife's horror when she saw my face. A little later Krison came running and started offering his help, medicine and so on. I could not stand the complete hypocrisy of this man. Nevertheless, I politely thanked him for his offer, but refused to accept any medicine from him. I could not remain any longer in Knik after what happened to me and considering such a hostile attitude toward me.

February 22. Today on sleds and under the guard of five Kenaitze I and along with my sick wife and little children left Knik for Tyonek, which is located 100 miles from the village. It is hard to find the words to describe this winter trip we attempted on sleds in a freezing weather of minus forty degrees [Celsius]. We had to sleep practically under open sky.

February 24. At 6 o'clock in the evening we reached Susitna village.

February 25. I gave last rites to two ailing people. We decided to spend this day in Susitna to give ourselves a rest after a three-day trip.

February 27. After suffering numerous hardships during last six days at 10 o'clock in the evening we finally reached Chuvitna[46] village, which is located four miles from Tyonek. In Chuvitna Mr. and Mrs. White, a wonderful and good couple, invited us to stay with them. Here we lived almost a whole month awaiting the opportunity to get to the Kenai side. During that trip my wife and children got cold and were sick. For all the reasons mentioned above, I had to cancel the Divine Liturgy and leave Knik.

Trade agents of the ACC harass Orthodox parishioners, church, and clergy. It is horrible what is going on here in the Kenai Gulf area, especially in wintertime, when the gulf is frozen. These agents bully the local people, and the priest and generally do whatever they want. In Kenai itself the trade agent does such disgraceful things in winter, that the hairs rise on my head from fear. Yet we do have no authorities to restrain such ruffians, and that is why life in the Kenai Gulf is so bad. I am afraid that the situation might get out of control if all these incidents drive the local people to the edge of desperation.

Aleksandr Iaroshevich to Vladimir Donskoi, Dean of Clergy, May 14, 1895, About the Results of his Trip to Knik[47]

I have the honor to report to Your Reverence the following information. On September 15 of 1894 I, as promised earlier, left Kenai and set out for Knik with the intention of wintering there for the purposes of missionary work. My family departed from Kenai a few days earlier on the schooner *Kodiak*. Before my departure I turned all church responsibilities and money over to a churchwarden and a songleader in the presence of witnesses from the ranks of parishioners. In addition, I provided the songleader with detailed instructions on what he was supposed to do during my absence. A brotherhood treasurer, Aleksandr Demidov, also received instructions and was also assigned to serve as the temporary chairman of the brotherhood.

On the above-mentioned day, having served a customary prayer service for travelers, I left Kenai and in four days arrived at Knik. Except one enfeebled old woman I was not able to find any people here because everybody, along with their families, had left the village for their hunting trips. So I was not able to open the school immediately after my arrival as I had planned earlier, although I warned the local people during my last stay in Knik not to take their children on hunting trips. Later I found out that they cannot do this. The natives usually go away hunting for a long time and do not want to part with their children for so long. During the whole month nobody returned to the village. Therefore, the great event, the 100th anniversary of the Orthodox Church in America, I celebrated almost alone. Yet, it seemed that God took mercy on me: by chance two hunters came back and together we celebrated this anniversary. Next day they again left [into the mountains]. It was only at the end of October that people gradually started to return. So the whole summer, from the day of my arrival to the end of October, I was busy training a boy, Stepan Sorokovikov, preparing him for performing a songleader's work. I left my songleader Ivanov at Kenai to substitute for me for the time when I am away. At the end of October I started teaching classes. We did not have a special place to accommodate the school, so I had to teach at the house where I was staying with my family. Because the Kenaitze do not live together in one place, but are scattered around, with great difficulty I was able to collect thirteen students. I paid the most attention to learning prayers and singing. Neither the children nor the adults here have any idea of the prayers. Not a single person can make the sign of the cross along with the accompanying prayer words. And this is despite the existence of Orthodoxy in America for 100 years! This was what prompted me to teach them how to pray to God. In addition, in my school I taught the children the Russian language along with Slavonic reading. As far as the Holy History is concerned, I introduced this subject during a general gathering in the chapel, for it was impossible to make an interpreter stay at school each day because he also had to take care of his own family. After more natives returned to the village, during Sundays before vespers I conducted regular talks on Orthodoxy-related topics. I gave the same talks on Thursdays. During these talks I taught them prayers, explained the basic tenets of the faith and related the Holy History from the Old and New Testaments. The talks always ended with collective singing, of which the Knik residents are very much fond. Here everyone sings and with great enthusiasm. I performed all church services without any changes and replacements, and everything was conducted according to the instructions of the Alaska Ecclesiastical Consistory. On Sundays, feast days, and also on many regular days through Ruf Stepanov, the interpreter, I always delivered sermons to the natives. So my work with the Kenaitze proceeded well. Yet the major purpose of my visit here was missionary work, which I had no chance whatsoever to start until almost Christmas. It was only on December 22 that the Mednovtsy descended from the mountains. The first time thirty-two people came. Of these Mednovtsy I enlightened thirteen natives with the holy baptism. The others had already been baptized by Father N. Mitropol'skii. Therefore, the first four months I spent in Knik were absolutely useless for missionary work. During this time, by remaining in Kenai, I would have been able to do a lot. Unfortunately, the Mednovtsy never come down before the end of December, awaiting the severe frosts. After Christmas, during January and February at different times, only fifteen Mednovtsy visited Knik. Of them I baptized five people. The others had already been baptized. With the beginning of March, or when the thaw begins, the Mednovtsy do not come anymore, for traveling by river at this season is very risky. Therefore, few Mednovtsy came to Knik during the past winter, and their total number was about fifty people of both genders. Of this number I baptized only eighteen people.

Thank God, all Mednovtsy who visited Knik fulfilled their Christian duties of confession and holy communion. I also joined in holy matrimony seven Mednovtsy couples. The Mednovtsy live very far away, and like the Kenaitze, are also scattered around. The only difference between them is that the Kenaitze do have settlements, while the Mednovtsy absolutely do not have them. Literally for a whole year they keep moving from one place to another and hunting. They do say that their nearest settlement is located within twelve to fifteen days of travel, but this settlement is nothing but the place where the Mednovtsy gather during summertime for fishing. As for settlements in the full sense of the word, they do not have them. Mednovtsy country is very rich in fur-bearing animals, especially black foxes and so-called "silver gray" [this expression is written in English] foxes. Not only Mednovtsy men, but also women and even children bring these furs for trade. For these foxes the ACC pays up to $50. Yet, if we take into account the high prices the company charges for its merchandise, these furs are sold for almost next to nothing. Other trade stores on the Nuchek side and along the Yukon River pay the same price for these furs. In former years many Mednovtsy used to come to Knik because, with the exception of Knik, there were hardly any trade stores available in the area.[48] But since the influx of Americans to Alaska, trade stores have mushroomed, especially along the Yukon River. Quite a few stores on the Prince William Sound. As a result fewer Mednovtsy now come to Knik. Thus, in 1888 almost 100 heathen Mednovtsy came here, of whom Father Nikolai Mitropol'skii baptized about eighty people. In 1890 fewer Mednovtsy came to Knik and so forth. Finally, in 1894 during my stay in Knik, there were few Mednovtsy, only about fifty people. Polygamy is widespread among the Mednovtsy, and it cost me much time and effort to convince those who accepted holy baptism to live in a Christian manner. Among the Mednovtsy one might even meet such characters who live both with their wives and their own daughters. I had special preliminary talks with those who volunteered to accept holy baptism, and decided not to baptize those who disagreed with my arguments concerning the Christian way of life and morality. I believe that not the number of the converted is important, but the quality of the internal disposition of those people toward Christianity. Fortunately, nobody disagreed with my arguments and all Mednovtsy with whom I had such talks accepted holy baptism according to their internal conviction.

The Mednovtsy still believe in shamanism, but, as I had the chance to note, the status of shamanism among them is shaky. And among the Kenaitze the traces of shamanism are also noticeable, but exclusively in the northernmost part of the parish and very rarely. So there is hope that it will be completely eradicated. First, the distant location of this area from the church and, second, the lack of any special person who can teach them the basics of faith explain the survival of shamanism. The Kenai Protection Brotherhood made it their special priority to correct this latter situation.

In conclusion, I have to mention that the missionary work among the Mednovtsy is hindered by various circumstances. First, the Mednovtsy, harassed by agents of the ACC, come to Knik reluctantly, and each time fewer and fewer, especially after trade agent along with a few other persons hung an Orthodox Mednovtsy in Knik. During the past winter only forty-seven Mednovtsy visited Knik and on different days. Of them I baptized eighteen people, which is the only result of my seven-month missionary stay in Knik. The rest of them had been already baptized earlier. Second, the Mednovtsy find good deals for their furs in other trade stores located in Prince William Sound, and along the Copper River, which is also located closer to the Mednovtsy than Knik. Third, these savages come to Knik only for a very short time, only for three or four days, and sometimes even for less, and they spend almost all their time in the trade store. It is natural that during such a short time the priest is not in a position to teach them something substantial. One has to restrict himself to only teaching them how to correctly make the sign of the cross, and telling them the basic rules of Christian faith, life, and morality. Fourth, the Mednovtsy never come before the second half of December. Therefore, despite my seven-month stay in Knik with missionary goals, I was able to work with them only during two months. Yet, if one were to take into account only the days when the Mednovtsy were present in Knik itself, there would hardly be three weeks. And finally the presence of the priest himself in Knik always entails great hardships and troubles. When the harbor becomes covered with ice, the priest has to live here in isolation from the rest of the world. In addition, the local trade agent plays the role of an unrestrained master in all respects. If he wants to do nasty things to you, he might stop selling you food from his store. That is exactly what happened with me this winter. Fortunately, I was able to buy everything necessary in advance, otherwise I would have died from hunger. Driven by hatred of me and Orthodoxy, the trade agent also refused to serve my interpreter, only because he was my interpreter. So I had to support this poor fellow and his family at my own expense. In December the Kenaitze wanted to prepare logs to build a house for me. Krison, the trade agent, did not like this idea and threatened to smash the head of the first native who dared to work for me. When I came to Krison and asked him why he did all this, the agent responded that he would smash my head too if I went to work together with the Kenaitze. Krison also added, "The Kenaitze owe my trade store almost $100. Let them pay this debt first, and then go to work for you." I would like to ask what connection exists between me as a priest and the Kenaitze's debt to the store. I cannot see in such attitudes anything except hatred, ill will, and the desire to rule in the village. In February the trade agent along with his friend, George Palmer [in original Georgii Parmer], did such a nasty thing that I together with my family had literally to escape from Knik under protection of a few armed Kenaitze. Only God knows what misfortunes and hardships I, my wife, and my little children had to go through. All evils that befall both for the parish and the mission come from these scoundrels the trade agents. Sometimes I simply feel desperate. The oppression that the local priest and Orthodoxy have to suffer is awful. And this happens not only in Kenai, but all over Alaska. Trade agents of the ACC (certainly not all of them, there are good people among them) are tyrants. The reason why one of them was murdered might be explained by the brutal treatment of natives by the trade agent himself. This is true and one cannot dispute this truth. In a word, our conditions here are so awful that it is hard to describe. One must speak up and protect his independence from these scoundrels. The clergy themselves are not in a position to do anything. Yet the United States government, under persistent requests from Orthodox authorities, can do a lot. Help us, for God's sake, help!!!

All this information I present to the kind consideration of Your Blessed Reverence. Kenai Missionary Priest, Aleksandr Iaroshevich.

CHAPTER FIVE

Priest Ioann Bortnovskii

"Kenai Mission"[49]

THE KENAI MISSION RECEIVED ITS NAME from the Kenaitze, the native tribe that resides on the coast of the Inlet of the same name and among whom our Orthodox messengers started to work. In 1841 at the St. Nicholas Redoubt, which is located on Kenai Bay, the Russian-American Company built a small chapel at its own expense. A layman, A. Kamkov, who supervised the company's trade business in this area, conducted church services here in a simplified manner [*po mirskomy chinu*]. In 1845 ecclesiastical authorities found it necessary to send a special missionary to Kenai. To this position they appointed Hieromonk Nikolai, who worked earlier as a housekeeper at the *arkhirei* place at New Archangel (Sitka) from 1841. On March 7, 1849, his Grace, the Most Reverend Innocent, Bishop of Kamchatka, Kuriles and the Aleutians sent regulation number 158 to Hieromonk Nikolai, who by this time was already the Kenai missionary. The regulation said in particular: "Time and experience have shown that there is no better place than St. Nicholas Redoubt at Kenai for establishment of a permanent Orthodox mission, which is to work along the coasts of the Kenai and Chugach Bays. Thereby we bless you, Hieromonk Nikolai, to turn the existing chapel into a church by installing there an icon screen and altar [*prestol*] of the size of twenty-eight inches in height and ten and a half inches in length and width as much as the place allows, along with the holy corporal named after the feast of Assumption of the Most Holy Mother of God. After completing the work you are to consecrate the church and report to me about the work you have done." The document is signed: Humble Innocent, Bishop of Kamchatka, Kuriles and the Aleutians.

From this time on, or to be more specific, from 1849 onward when the church was completely established here, the Kenai mission began living a full religious life. In this area there was a vast field in which to plant the seeds of the Lord, for in addition to the Kenai region, the missionary supervised Konstantinovsky Redoubt (Nuchek) and the Nushagak Church. It was obvious that the newly appointed missionary could not sit idle. His work demanded a great deal of hard, selfless labor in order to move forward at least a little toward the defined goal. And indeed, a few years of such labor brought excellent results. Thus, confession registers of the Kenai mission for 1859 indicate that by this time the Kenai area already numbered

1,432 Orthodox souls (664 males and 750 females) of various *inorodtsy* tribes: 801 souls (360 males and 444 females) of the Kenaitze, 450 (227 males and 223 females) of the Chugach, 148 people (seventy-three males and seventy-five females) of the Ugalentsy, five people (four males and one female) of the Aleuts and eighteen people (seventeen males and one female) of the Mednovtsy.

Ecclesiastical authorities highly appreciated the fruitful labor of this committed missionary. In 1849, for his zealous work of converting people of other beliefs to Orthodoxy, he was awarded a thigh shield, and in the same year he received a formal blessing from the Holy Synod. On May 3 of 1859 he was awarded the pectoral cross [*naperstnii krest*]. In addition, in November of the same year the Holy Synod raised his rank to Hegumen. In 1857 he was awarded a bonus of 400 rubles, and on April 17, 1857, received the order of Holy Anna of the Third Rank. To increase the quality of his evangelical work Father Nikolai established a small school, which he supervised and where he personally taught. Some graduates of, as they call it here, the "Hegumen's school," are still alive. Thus, tirelessly and fruitfully did Hegumen Nikolai work in the field of propagating of the word of the Gospel for more than twenty years, from 1845 to 1867. On July 21, 1867, this servant to our Lord departed to eternity, to Him who judges both the dead and living.

From 1867 to 1881 the Kenai mission lived the life of a miserable orphan. All these years the position of the missionary remained vacant. These were hard years for the young and not quite strong Kenai mission: the decline of religion and morality, neglect and other flaws were evident everywhere. Finally, 1881 came, which became fertile year for Orthodoxy in Kenai. In this year the mission was revived. A special missionary was again appointed here. This was Hieromonk Nikita, who arrived at the place of his appointment on June 3, 1881. The new missionary tried as much as he could to clean and decorate the local temple, which he found in a state of total neglect. Nikita's petitions for material help to the Kenai church received a favorable response from the Alaska Ecclesiastical Consistory. In 1883 the roof of the Kenai church was covered new tile, the floor was completely repaired, the walls were covered with calico, and the icon screen was painted in oil paint. A few other repairs were also made. During Nikita's tenure the Most Reverend Nestor also had a new house built for the priest by his order, because the old one was not suitable for living. Unfortunately, after the death of his Grace and for lack of resources, construction stopped and the house remains unfinished. Father Nikita also paid a great deal of attention to upgrading the morality of his flock. He also organized and taught parochial school for a while.

On September 12, 1886, Hieromonk Nikita was relieved of the missionary duties at his own request, and on April 14, 1888, the priest Nikolai Mitropol'skii replaced him. Father Nikolai worked as a missionary until 1892. His tenure was especially marked by enlightening the Indian savages by the word of the Gospel. In 1893, by his special instruction, the Most Reverend Nikolai, Bishop of the

Aleutians and Alaska, appointed Aleksandr Iaroshevich as the new missionary to Kenai. With his arrival the life of the Kenai mission became more active. The rise of the parishioners' morality, revival of the parochial school, and the opening of brotherhoods serve as good illustrations of this regeneration.

Church

When opportunity allowed the parishioners sometimes repaired the local church. Yet by the time Father A. Iaroshevich received his appointment to Kenai, the building was in state of decay. It was decided to build a new building. Father Iaroshevich and his parishioners along with the priest Vladimir Donskoi, Dean of Clergy of the Sitka district, petitioned his Grace, the Most Reverend Nikolai, to grant permission to start building the new church in Kenai. The petition received a favorable response and on May 8, 1894, the Dean of Clergy informed Father Iaroshevich that the Holy Synod had approved the construction project at St. Nicholas Redoubt [Kenai] and allocated for this purpose $400.

On June 13 of 1894, with the Lord's help, under supervision of a special commission composed of a local priest and a few elected reliable parishioners, construction began. By 1895 the church was completed, and on June 9 of the same year, having received a blessing from his Grace, the Most Reverend Nikolai, Hieromonk Anatolii, Dean of Clergy of the Sitka District, consecrated the temple after the feast of Assumption of the Most Holy Mother of God. Unfortunately, the priest Iaroshevich, who initiated the construction, was not able to participate in the solemn ceremony of the consecration. By this time he had already been transferred to the town of Juneau at his own request, where he worked for the Kolosh mission. To replace him the priest Ioann Bortnovskii was appointed to Kenai. This is the short history of the Kenai mission and its status.

The new Kenai church was built in the form of a ship. This wooden church, built of logs, has an icon screen, looks decent and accommodates up to eighty people. The icon screen and the Royal Gates have new icons, which the local brotherhood purchased for $100. The walls of the temple are covered with wallpaper, and the icon screen and the ceiling were painted in oil paint. The portico is divided into two small rooms: one for the vestry and the other for archives and church supplies. Yet the walls are still not covered on the outside. The roof was covered with tiles and painted in oil paint. There is not yet a bell tower, so three bells hang on the beam under the awning in front of the entrance door. Both voluntary donations of parishioners and the Alaska Ecclesiastical Consistory financed the construction of the church and installation of the icon screen. Brotherhood members also built a decent fence around the church cemetery. In addition, the Kenai brotherhood members eagerly participated in the construction of the church building itself. In particular, they freely delivered all logs necessary for the construction, worked for free or for a small fee at the construction site, and donated money. The old church building now temporarily accommodates the local parochial school.

The Kenai mission included the following villages: St. Nicholas Redoubt or Kenai with 167 residents (the Kenaitze and Creoles), Ninilchik with sixty-six Creole residents, Seldovia with 120 Kenaitze residents, Aleksandrovsk with 100 Aleut residents, Kustatan with forty-eight Kenaitze residents, Tyonek with eighty-four [Kenaitze] residents, Susitna with 197 [Kenaitze] residents and Knik with 109 Kenaitze residents. St. Nicholas Redoubt or Kenai is considered the center of the mission, because both the church and the priest along with the songleader are located here. In all other villages residents themselves have built chapels. Chapels in Ninilchik, Seldovia, and Aleksandrovsk are better designed and equipped than those in other villages. In these three settlements, where people take better care of their chapels, the living conditions of the residents are usually better than in other localities. In Ninilchik, Seldovia, and Aleksandrovsk literate people who serve as readers perform services in a simplified manner [*po mirskomu chinu*] on Sundays and feast days. On the whole, in these villages the presence of Orthodoxy is more noticeable.

In other villages, namely Kustatan, Tyonek, Knik, and Susitna, there are no special readers attached to the chapels, the chapels are opened rarely, and the general level of Orthodoxy is therefore not so advanced. The latter is a matter of major concern for the present missionary. The missionary works to train and raise literate people in these settlements, who will be able to perform services in a lay manner [*po mirskomu chinu*] and baptize the newborn, and also supervise schools of literacy, and eventually to instruct and lead the local Kenaitze toward a good moral life. Incidentally, recently in Susitna, the most populated village, which is located far from Kenai, the situation has partially improved. A former graduate of the Sitka school [Ivan Soloviev] was appointed to this village to work as the reader and teacher. Also, a boy, who is the son of the Kustatan *toion*, is currently studying at the Kenai one-year parochial school. In the future he will be able to work in his village as a reader. With the help of God, we gradually raise the level of piety in other localities as well.

During my visits to Kenaitze villages in 1897 I already noticed the good aspects these people's character. Thus, they show absolute loyalty to their spiritual father, especially in matters that concern the common good, which is a prerequisite of successful missionary work. And besides, one easily notices that the Kenaitze are people of a peaceful and guileless nature, devoid of feelings of flattery and envy. Improvidence and laziness are their major drawbacks. It is not surprising that because of this they sometimes starve, especially by spring. Lacking foresight, the Kenaitze are prone to gluttony and as a result of this passion for food they feel content only when they have all they want to eat. If he notices food, the Kenaitze native tries to eat as much as possible, and indeed, he usually eats during one meal a huge amount of food, especially meat, such as an average

European would never eat even in ten days. They especially like grease, which is plentiful in the meat of local animals. As a matter of fact, the addiction of the Kenaitze to grease can also be explained by the harsh conditions of this country. It is known that fat keeps the bodies of these poor people warm. In some villages Kenaitze now plant gardens, but on a very limited basis. The potato is the major vegetable they like to plant. The Kenaitze's dwellings hardly differ from those of the Kolosh: the same dirt, waste, stench and so on.

The Kenaitze mission also encompasses another tribe of savages called Mednovtsy. The latter reside in the mountains, which are located 300 miles from Kenai. Communication with the Mednovtsy is very inconvenient, and one can reach them only from the Knik village and only in wintertime. The Mednovtsy themselves sometimes descend in wintertime to the Knik village for trade purposes, and if they have the opportunity they gladly accept holy baptism. No missionary has ever climbed up to the Mednovtsy villages. One cannot say with certainty when these natives were enlightened with the Christian faith for the first time. In confessional roster for 1849 we may find that fourteen Mednovtsy (twelve men and two women) were registered as members of the Orthodox Church. Having compared confessional rosters for later years, we may find that the number of Orthodox Mednovtsy at times increased and at times diminished. Thus, the 1882 roster lists only two Orthodox Mednovtsy men. From 1884 their number again increased. In 1884 there were ten Orthodox Mednovtsy, next year: eleven people (seven men and five women), and in 1886 twelve people. In 1887 the number of Orthodox Mednovtsy remained the same, but the next year it jumped up to 110 people (sixty-nine men and forty-one women). This was the year when priest Nikolai Mitropol'skii wintered in Knik with the sole purpose of enlightening this tribe. The confessional roster for 1894 lists 127 Orthodox Mednovtsy (seventy-seven men and fifty women). Until the end of 1897 this number remained unchanged. On the basis of these facts we may conclude that the Orthodox mission among the Mednovtsy has entered only the first stage of its development.

To the Kenaitze's credit, it should be said that this people is steadfast in their Orthodox faith and no temptations will make them change their religion. As for the frivolous Creoles, who live in Kenai, one cannot be so sure about their loyalty to the holy faith.

School

The establishment of a school in Kenai goes back to the time of Hegumen Nikolai, who conducted missionary work here. Although available church documents in Kenai do not contain information about this school, its graduates who are still alive serve as good evidence of the existence of this school. The curriculum of this school was church-oriented and tailored according to the program of our old deacon [*diachkovie*] schools. God's Law and Church Slavonic were the only subjects that were taught and old methods of education were practiced. The nickname, "Hegumen's School," which the school received, directly corresponded to the goal of its curriculum. It was not a surprise that the school produced extremely zealous Orthodox graduates.

With the death of Father Nikolai the school ceased to exist and was not reopened until 1883 by Hieromonk Nikita. Yet he taught the school only for a short period of time, specifically only one year. Father Nikita maintained this school exclusively at his personal expense, and his personal resources were probably not enough to support education in Kenai on a permanent basis, which might explain such a brief period of its work. In 1887, according to the order of Archpriest Vladimir Vechtomov, the school was restored. Father Vechtomov appointed a special teacher, Aleksei Ivanov, a graduate of the Orthodox school in San Francisco, with a monthly salary of $15. At the present time Ivanov is a songleader at the Kenai Church. Unfortunately, the Kenai school again functioned only for a short time. In 1889 the teacher's salary was terminated, and consequently the school was closed. From 1893 onward the Kenai school started to live a more regular life. At the present time classes meet on a regular basis and are not interrupted anymore. Now the curriculum of the Kenai school in everything resembles that of parochial schools in Russia. The curriculum is structured according to the Holy Synod's regulations for parochial schools, with English as an additional subject.

In addition, there is a school in Ninilchik village, housed in a special structure built by members of the local Orthodox brotherhood. This is a very solid building that stands near the chapel and fully corresponds to its major purpose. The subjects taught at this school are God's Law, Russian and Church Slavonic, mathematics, and lessons in singing. From 1887 to the present schools of literacy [*shkola gramoty*] were opened in such villages as Seldovia, Aleksandrovsk, and Susitna. In Seldovia Ivan Tepenok, a graduate of the Kenai school, is responsible for teaching classes, for which he receives $4 a month, provided by the local brotherhood. In the Aleksandrovsk school Nikolai Munin, a graduate of the Sitka Orthodox School, works as a teacher and receives a salary accumulated from the donations of local residents. In Susitna, Ivan Soloviev, also a graduate of the Sitka Orthodox School, works as a teacher and receives for his work $4 a month from the Kenai Orthodox Brotherhood.

Travel Journals for 1898–1903[50]

March 23, 1898. Today, accompanied by Mr. Ryan, I left for Seldovia by boat to fulfill my pastoral duties. On the way to Seldovia we visited Kasilof and had to stay there until midnight waiting for a low tide. We reached Seldovia about 8 o'clock in the morning of the next day, right on the eve of the Annunciation Feast. From a distance before entering the village, we could already see that the chapel was decorated for this feast and filled with the praying faithful. I stayed at Nikolai Baiiu's place, who serves here both as a local songleader and a coastal *zakazchik*. Until very late I conversed with the *toion*, *zakazchik*, churchwarden and reader about village life. They had a great deal of interesting information to share with me. As it turned out the living conditions of the Seldovians have grown worse. The company [Alaska Commercial Company] stores have stopped providing goods on credit. Furthermore, to prolong the existence of their trading stores and maintain profits, the agents continually push the Kenaitze to aggressive hunting. The Kenaitze were certainly able to procure something this winter. They even delivered more furs than during earlier winters. Yet this active hunting hardly improved their desperate economic situation, for the agents bought these furs at the lowest prices. Moreover, against the Kenaitze's wish, instead of money the trade agents paid the natives with goods.

These unexpected conditions harmed the chapel's income and the finances of the local St. Theodosius Brotherhood. Besides, the constant absences of the Seldovians on their hunting trips did not allow them to start building a new house for the school. Moreover, this winter all classes in the Seldovia school had to be canceled for lack of any resources to support the school. For me as a spiritual mentor of the Seldovians and their supervisor, it was painful to hear such sad news. To correct somehow all these shortcomings, I decided, if God sends me health, to winter in Seldovia next year in order to start the school by myself. All the more so, because Seldovia is a convenient place to observe what goes on in Aleksandrovsk, a neighboring village, which also has many problems, again as a result of the domination of the same companies. It should be also noted that Seldovia has many children of school age and I hate to see how they roam around unattended. Only a few of them, who are the most diligent, did not put aside their books, although classes were canceled.

March 25. Feast of the Most Holy Mother of God. At 9 o'clock in the morning the Hours followed by the liturgy without consecration. At the end I performed a customary prayer service in honor of the Most Holy Mother of God and wished many years of life to the members of the local St. Theodosius Brotherhood. I delivered a sermon on a Gospel theme and greeted all faithful on the occasion of this feast. The whole chapel was filled with praying people. All the faithful sang marvelously, and at the end of the service I thanked everybody for this excellent job, especially the local reader Nikolai Baiiu, who put so much effort into teaching people proper singing. I also thanked Zakhar Balashov, a churchwarden, for keeping the chapel perfectly clean.

In the fall of 1897 Seldovia parishioners donated money to the chapel for purchase of two new bells. Therefore, they now have three bells. They also built a large fireplace to keep the chapel warm during wintertime. After dinner I audited the chapel finances, and then at 6 o'clock in the evening I anointed nine infants with myrrh. In Seldovia only one woman had died. Therefore, the population increased by eight more people.

March 26. At 9 o'clock in the morning I served Great Lent hours and vespers. After dinner I was occupied with some writing. Great Vespers and matins at 6 o'clock in the evening. After service I supervised choir practice for the coming feast of Palm Sunday.

March 27. Great Lent Hours and vespers. At 2 o'clock in the afternoon we again practiced singing. The children and adults who know how to sing also participated. Matins at 5 o'clock in the evening. This service was in honor of the resurrection of Lazarus. After the service I confessed children.

March 28. At 8 o'clock in the morning prayers for those who prepare themselves for confession, then the rite of lesser blessing of water and the Divine Liturgy of St. John Chrysostom. During the liturgy I delivered a sermon on the Gospel theme about the resurrection of Lazarus. All children who came for confession as well as infants received communion. Before confession I read the prayer from the pulpit, then thanksgiving prayers. After serving the Divine Liturgy I sang funeral services for two persons who passed away during the past year. I left the chapel at 12:30 in the afternoon and after a short break during which I had a glass of tea I started to perform confession of adults. At 5:30 in the evening confession was interrupted and at 6 o'clock in the evening I started serving the all-night vigil with the litany blessing of breads and incensing the Sanctuary, icons, and the people, and the church. I also blessed willow branches and distributed them among the faithful. Marvelous singing and the magnificent illumination of the chapel along with well-dressed praying faithful provided appropriate solemness and holiness to the whole service. After the service I continued to perform confession and completed it at 11:30 in the evening. On the whole, seventy-four people received confession.

March 29. Palm Sunday. At 8:30 in the morning prayers for those who prepare themselves for confession, then the Divine Liturgy of St. John Chrysostom. Using the Gospel I delivered a sermon where I explained why our Orthodox Church had introduced the tradition to hold branches of the pussy-willow tree and lighted candles. All those who came for confession received communion. After dinner, carrying the holy cross and holy water, I visited houses of parishioners.

At 6 o'clock in the evening there was a brotherhood meeting. All members, whose total number is thirty-five, were present. After an introductory prayer, Nikolai Baiiu, the brotherhood record-keeper, informed members about the brotherhood's finances for the last months. As a supervisor of the brotherhood, I audited Baiiu's books and found out that by March of 1898 the brotherhood fund had only $68.58. We also discussed those members who have not paid their dues for a long time. I found out that the delays were caused not by careless attitudes, but because people were simply unable to put aside some money for this purpose. The brotherhood let these members defer payment of their dues. During this meeting I secured a new well-arranged house, where we can accommodate a future school. It was resolved that all villagers shall help build another house for the owner of this structure. Incidentally, this owner had already prepared all necessary building materials. Of course, everyone agreed with this arrangement. The meeting ended with collective singing of "It is truly meet and right" and with a dismissal prayer. Therefore, in Seldovia everything goes on even better than I expected.

March 30. At 9:30 in the morning Mr. Ryan and I left Seldovia and the next day at 6 o'clock in the evening we were back in Kenai.

August 19. Using a *baidarka* I set out to visit the villages of Susitna, Tyonek and Kustatan. As far as Knik is concerned, I performed all ministrations there in the spring. Therefore, now there is no need to go there. I wanted to start my trip right after Assumption of the Mother of God, the feast after which the Kenai church was consecrated, but bad weather me kept here until now. We left Kenai about noon, but could not use a favorable current to reach Tyonek. Instead we had to struggle again the head current. My paddlers became exhausted, and we had to come by a small settlement, Chilikhna [also Chubutna or Chuvitna], which is located seven miles from Tyonek. Only the next day at 3 o'clock in the morning did we reach Tyonek.

August 20. To my joy, from the Tyonek inhabitants I learned that all Susitna residents have stayed at home. People of the latter village built a camp around their chapel and impatiently waited for me. Moreover, Susitna natives sent a *baidarka* to Tyonek, just in case, to fetch me if I needed it. I was so happy that I made an immediate decision to use a favorable current to sail to Susitna because I did not want to keep the Kenaitze waiting for me, which might hinder their coming hunting trip. From Tyonek I took with me Ivan Kvasnikov who would serve as a reader and interpreter. We departed from Tyonek at 11 o'clock in the morning and by night we reached the first Susitna village, or the so-called "village of Aleksandr." Here the natives have only four well-built houses with various extensions. I also noticed gardens planted with potatoes and turnips.

August 21. Clear day. Fresh southern wind that will be favorable to us. After having tea, we proceeded further. Because of frequent rains the Susitna River is full of water and the current is very rapid. It is very hard to sail up river. Nevertheless, by 3 o'clock in the afternoon we came to our destination. People of the village cordially welcomed us. In Susitna we found about twenty American miners, who stay there ready for various ventures. Having audited the chapel finances, I found out that the churchwarden performed his job not very honestly. He refused to admit this for a while, but then pressed by a few witnesses had to confess. I will probably have to relieve him of his duties. Yet I found that inside the chapel looked well-maintained: no dampness, dirt or dust. The natives also built a new floor for the chapel. However, from outside the building still looks unattractive. If not for a small cross on the roof, one could never have told this structure from local Kenaitze *barab-oras*. Having examined the chapel, I pointed out to the *toion*, *zakazchik* and church-warden all its defects, and asked them to remove them. They agreed with me and promised that by Christmastime they would prepare boards if they received a church saw from Tyonek. I promised to send them this saw as soon as the Tyonek school-house was completed. I also promised to send them Ivan Kvasnikov (a teacher in Tyonek) to stay in Susitna for Christmastime and supervise all repair work.

Gardening is well developed in Susitna, primarily because of the fertile soil. Besides, this area, located far from sea winds, is quite warm. No wonder that people even collect abundant wheat crops, which for us in Kenai is hard to imagine, although Kenai is situated farther south than Susitna. Susitna natives complain about poor fishing. This year they stored few supplies of dried fish. Now they put all their hopes on the coming hunting trips. Yet in appearance everybody looks joyful, healthy and well-fed. I did not see any sick people among them. Neither did I notice the presence of vodka and beer.

August 22. I did not perform any services in the morning because the Kenaitze have the habit of taking a steam bath before partaking in the rites of contrition, penance, and fast. Besides, not all people returned to the village. I spent the whole day attending to numerous problems and questions accumulated for two years. To the Kenaitze's credit, in preparing themselves for communion, they try to do away with all their disputes and arguments, and do this only through a priest. At 5 o'clock in the evening I baptized five children and anointed with myrrh ten more. Then I served vespers, where I spoke about peace, love and unity between a shepherd and his flock. The service ended at 10 p.m.

August 23. At 8 o'clock in the morning I blessed water, then performed the Divine Liturgy of St. John Chrysostom and gave communion to fifty infants. From 2 o'clock in the afternoon I confessed thirty-four children of school age. Vespers and matins at 6 o'clock in the evening. All services were accompanied by instructive talks.

August 24. At 8 a.m. morning services, then the Divine Liturgy of St. John Chrysostom. All those who came for confession received communion. At 2 o'clock in the afternoon I continued to confess the faithful. At 6 o'clock in the evening I interrupted confession and began performing vespers and matins. This service ended with reading evening prayers. Then I continued confession and finished it at 4:30 o'clock in the morning of the next day. On the whole, eighty-six people were confessed. An interpreter assisted me during confessions.

August 25. After the liturgy I performed requiem services for those who had died since my last visit to Susitna. In the past two years seven people died here and eighteen were born, which shows an increase in population of eleven people. After dinner, carrying a cross and holy water, I visited the houses of parishioners. At

4 o'clock in the afternoon I performed a marriage ceremony for two couples. At 6 o'clock in the evening there was a meeting of Susitna's St. Metrophanes Brotherhood, in which brotherhood members participated. The Brotherhood mutual fund has $39.40. There was talk about repairing the chapel. The meeting resolved to prepare wooden boards by Christmastime, and devote all time at the end of December and in the beginning of the January Christmastide to repairing the chapel, to make the building look neat and have a proper appearance. Ivan Kvasnikov, who will have come from Tyonek to Susitna by this time, will supervise all the work. At the present time, Susitna numbers twenty-three brotherhood members.

August 26. I completed all my work here. Yet we cannot leave: it is raining cats and dogs.

August 27. Fresh southern wind. There is so much water in the river that it now floods the island where Susitna village is located. To avoid the flood we descended to the lower settlement, the so-called "village of Aleksandr." Although here the water has also flooded all the banks, the houses, which are situated on a hill, are not in danger, We decided to stay in this village and wait for quiet weather.

August 28. A clear quiet day, but the water in the river is still rising. One house is completely surrounded with water. At 7 o'clock in the morning we finally got in our *baidarkas* and left for Tyonek, where we arrived at 6 o'clock in the evening. In the village all the Kenaitze had already gathered and were waiting impatiently for us. Incidentally, this area did not avoid flooding either. In Chubutnu village (five miles from Tyonek)[51] the pressure of the river water washed out a barn with everything that was inside. It was a great loss for its owner. In addition to the barn, there were new empty barrels, three small tugboats, ten fishing nets and some other materials. All this property belonged to Mr. Lad, who always helps our Orthodox church and the local Kenaitze.

August 29. The Beheading of St. John the Baptist. At 9 o'clock in the morning I performed a morning service and delivered a sermon, in which I reminded the praying Kenaitze to treat with love the school that will soon be opened and also its teacher. After the morning service men gathered at a designated spot and piled all wooden boards that will be used for repairing the schoolhouse. After the liturgy without consecration, we inspected the local chapel. The building is perfectly clean, without a single piece of dust. All chapel finances were handled correctly and punctually. On the whole, the local churchwarden's zeal and diligence had a considerable effect on life in the village. This person certainly deserves an award. At 6 o'clock in the evening I conducted the all-night vigil. A large crowd of natives visited this service and prayed. Irina, a daughter of Ivan Kvasnikov, also took part in reading and singing. I noticed that during the service almost all the faithful sang correctly and in harmony, which proves that Kvasnikov is doing a good job here.

August 30. Quiet and clear day. At 9 o'clock in the morning I performed a rite of the lesser blessing of water, then the Hours and a midday service the liturgy without consecration. I did not have a chance to celebrate the liturgy because of the lack of communion bread. The one I brought from Kenai was already old and not good. Having finished the service, I performed a customary prayer service in honor of St. Nicholas at the request of a Kenaitze native. Then I anointed two children with myrrh. Vespers and matins at 6 o'clock in the evening. At the end of the service I explained the meaning of the prayer. Among the people who prayed were many Americans.

August 31. It has been raining since morning. In the afternoon the sky cleared. The Hours in the morning, then confession. Vespers and matins at 6 o'clock in the evening, evening prayers and again confession until 11 o'clock in the evening. Total number of people who received confession is seventy-three. I heard their confessions through an interpreter.

September 1. At 7 o'clock in the morning prayers, then the Divine Liturgy of St. John Chrysostom. Upon finishing requisite prayers, I instructed the natives about holy communion. All faithful who confessed as well as infants joined in the holy mysteries. After the prayer, which I read from the pulpit, thanksgiving and dismissal prayers. Then, I joined two couples in holy matrimony. After dinner a local brotherhood meeting. The Tyonek St. Innocent Brotherhood has twenty-four members. There is $21.70 in its mutual fund. All these facts let us hope that in Tyonek the brotherhood cause will be advanced or at least partially justify its purpose. I visited Chubutnu village and stayed there for three hours. At 7 o'clock in the evening Medgee, a respected old American, invited me for a dinner.

September 2. Fresh western wind with rain. It means that we cannot continue on our route and have to stay in Tyonek.

September 3. Bad weather again. Yet at 6 o'clock in the morning, with an ebb tide, we decided to start out for the next village, Kustatan, where we arrived at 1 o'clock in the afternoon. We found only a few people in the village. They are mostly women, who stay at home while all the men are away.

September 4. We inspected the chapel. The building looks neglected and in some spots leaks. We may have reason to expect that Kustatan village will soon be abandoned. In fact, there are few inhabitants left here. And besides, because of the lack of jobs the remaining natives have become extremely poor and cannot support their chapel. Hunting here has also declined. All these factors together force the local Kenaitze to think about moving to some other villages. Some of them want to settle in Kenai, while the others plan to move to Tyonek. For my part, I find that leaving the village is the best that the Kustatan residents can do under the present circumstances.

September 5. I served the liturgy without consecration and then baptized two infants. Starting at 3 o'clock in the afternoon, I confessed twenty-three people. The all-night vigil from 6 o'clock in the evening. Evening prayers after the vigil.

September 7. It is getting colder. The ground is frozen down to more than an inch. At 4 o'clock in the morning, with an ebb tide, I left the Kustatan village and arrived at my home in Kenai by midday. Ivan Kvasnikov, who accompanied me during this trip, will have to return to Tyonek with the next tide. From September 8 to September 14 I stayed at home.

September 15. Today at 1 o'clock in the afternoon I departed for Ninilchik, but before we reached Kasilof a strong wind stopped us, and we had to turn to a nearby shore. However, we found out that it was harder to reach the shore than to stay on water. Only because of our skillful paddlers did everything turn out all right.

September 16. The wind calmed a little. At noon, with an ebb tide, we sailed on and about 8 o'clock in the evening safely reached Ninilchik. Here we stayed at Stepan Daryin's place.

September 17. In the morning, after the Hours, I served the liturgy without consecration, then anointed an infant with myrrh, and after this audited the chapel. As always, in Ninilchik the chapel has been found in a perfect order. They covered the ceiling in the sanctuary with new wallpaper, and attached two new bells to the chapel. All chapel finances were handled in the best manner. After the inspection, we visited the house of Feodor Kvasnikov, a local churchwarden, who also supervises our parochial school. This venerable elder likes to talk. He always finds a large number of topics to talk about, but mostly he likes to converse with people about the chapel and school-related matters. I agree with those Americans who have nicknamed him "lawyer." Besides, Feodor is a perfect choice to supervise all kinds of noble projects concerning the well-being of the whole village. As the churchwarden he belongs to that rare type of man in Alaska who may serve as a role model to others. It is impossible not to love and respect him.

September 18. After the service there was choir practice. Then, in the schoolhouse, Ninilchik's Holy Trinity Brotherhood held its meeting. I have to admit that the brotherhood here is falling apart. Therefore, the most energetic steps are required to prevent it from further decline. In addition to scanty resources and the inability to pay membership dues, the major reason why this brotherhood is disintegrating is quarrels among the residents of the village. The present meeting was mainly devoted to discussing steps that might support and strengthen the brotherhood. After discussion, members resolved: to elect new leaders of the brotherhood, to reduce the membership fee from twenty-five cents to fifteen cents and also reduce the allowances to sick members from $4 to $3 a month.

September 21. At 9 o'clock in the morning I opened classes at the Ninilchik school, divided all the children (thirteen students) into groups and defined a curriculum for each one for the entire 1898–99 school year. I also assigned Ivan Ivanovich Kvasnikov (a son of the Tyonek teacher Ivan Kvasnikov) to act both as a teacher and songleader with a salary of $10 a year paid by the residents of the village. Tomorrow, if weather allows, I am planning to return to Kenai.

September 22. The weather is good. At 7 o'clock in the morning I left Ninilchik village and set out for Kenai, where I arrived safely about 9 o'clock in the evening.

March 26, 1899. Very clear day. About 5 o'clock in the evening we safely reached Seldovia. At the present time Seldovia accommodates a postal station. Moreover, the convenient geographical location of the village now makes it important for all of Kenai Bay. Seldovia is accessible year-round for navigation and naturally serves as a vital center for transportation and communication in this part of Alaska. I would like to note that the Seldovians spent this winter in extreme need, frequently roaming the mountains searching for wild game and trying to feed themselves. At the same time, they lived this season quietly in a sober and peaceful manner, and generally were better-behaved than during the previous years. In Seldovia I received my first mail package: mainly newspapers and magazines. I spent the rest of the evening looking through them.

March 27. The weather worsened. It started to snow and a strong wind blew. At 9 o'clock in the morning I anointed four infants (one boy and three girls) with myrrh, then inspected the chapel. Seldovians donated little money to the chapel and to its maintenance. I found the building in the most miserable condition. One notices everywhere dust, untidiness and general neglect. Of course, I drew the churchwarden's attention to all these drawbacks. He tried to excuse himself by saying that he had spent most of this winter away from home, and promised to put the chapel in proper order. Vespers at 6 o'clock in the evening. The whole chapel was filled with praying natives. I want to admit that those who sang together did it very well. Before the dismissal prayer I delivered a sermon on the following Gospel theme: "Man does not live on bread alone but on every word that comes from the mouth of the Lord." Everybody listened with great attention and in silence. With few exceptions, all Seldovians speak Russian and, therefore, I did not have to seek an interpreter's assistance when instructing them.

March 28. At 8 o'clock in the morning I performed the rite of lesser water blessing, then the Divine Liturgy of St. Basil the Great with instructions. Gave communion to all infants and one adult who was prepared to deliver a baby. Yesterday, after vespers, I heard confessions. Having finished the liturgy, I conducted a funeral service for one infant who died this winter, and then, carrying a cross and holy water, visited the houses of the Seldovians. I noticed in the village four new houses built since my last visit to the village. At 6 o'clock in the evening I celebrated vespers with singing a requisite *prokeimenon*, "Turn not away Thy Face." Before the dismissal prayer I talked about the meaning of the sign of the cross.

March 29. The weather is stormy. Today is a new moon. At 9 o'clock in the morning I served the Hours. After the service there was choir practice. I mostly taught them to sing hymns from the Divine Liturgy because they are not quite familiar with them. At 6 o'clock in the evening I performed vespers and matins. At the end I delivered a sermon in which I talked about some disorderly behavior I had noticed in the Seldovian community. For example, there are people who leave services before they end. Some young people behave improperly on the portico of the chapel during services and so forth. I spent the evening with John Smith, an agent of the Alaska Commercial Company, who invited me to his house. A few words about him. John Smith is far different from the majority of the company's trade agents in Alaska. The good qualities of his character absolutely set him apart from his colleagues. The Seldovians like Smith very much. He also enjoys great respect from whites. Many people stress that this winter, he eagerly and with great success worked to make local people live a sober life. John Smith's efforts deserve sincere recognition and cordial gratitude.

March 30. Continued to perform services in the same order as yesterday. The arrival of *Dora* is expected here daily. Looked into controversial incidents that concerned a few adopted children, who often simply leave their guardians, even if the latter are their close relatives, and, attracted by handouts, come to live with completely unrelated people. There is no doubt that this practice harms social life in general and the lives of these children in particular. Therefore, I used all kind of measures to eliminate this evil. I also threatened that if these runaways do not cooperate, I will start taking them to Kenai and raising them under my personal supervision.

April 1. A warm and clear day. At 9 o'clock in the morning I served Great Lent Hours, then typical psalms and vespers. A meeting of the local brotherhood at 1 o'clock in the afternoon. The meeting was opened with a prayer "To the Heavenly King." We discussed the ways to speed up fencing the cemetery, chapel and school, and found a satisfactory solution to this problem. As it turned out, the natives had already prepared all necessary building materials. In addition, we discussed some other problems. Thus, much attention was devoted to such questions as the proper upbringing of children, especially orphans, and the responsibilities of the *toion*, *zakazchik* and churchwarden. We also talked about how to eradicate card playing and so forth. At 6 o'clock in the evening Great Vespers and matins, then confessions, and at the end a talk with the children about the meaning of confession. I confessed twenty-nine people, who are mostly children of school age, including two adults.

April 2. A clear and warm day. At 8 o'clock in the morning I gave last rites to Anna, a sick Kenaitze woman. During the liturgy I gave communion to all who came for confession. Beginning at 1 o'clock in the afternoon I heard confessions from adults. The total number of people who received confession today is sixty-six.

April 3. Prayers at 8:30 in the morning, then the Divine Liturgy of St. John Chrysostom. All who confessed received communion as well as two infants. After the service I was invited to bless one new house. At another house I performed a customary prayer service in honor of our Savior. About 2 o'clock in the afternoon I left Seldovia for Aleksandrovsk, where I arrived at 5 o'clock in the evening.

April 27. Today at 8 o'clock in the morning with the rising tide, I set out for Knik to perform my regular priest's duties. Knik is the northernmost village of the Kenai parish, and is located 115 miles from Kenai. At first, I had no intention to go there so early. The most convenient time to visit Knik is after the end of fishing season. But this time, Knik residents themselves came to Kenai by sloop to pick me up, and I had to postpone all other urgent matters at home and to depart with them to their village. Hardly had we started when we had to come back because of a strong headwind.

April 28. The wind still did not allow us to depart.

April 29. The wind changed and the weather became more favorable for our trip. By 9 o'clock in the evening we had safely reached Tyonek. This village stands apart from the direct route to Knik, but I came by this place in order to take Ivan Kvasnikov, who accompanies me each year as a songleader and an interpreter. In Tyonek everything was quiet and peaceful. There was no turbulence or agitation, and everybody lives in harmony with each other. Although about fifty miners wintered here, all of them behaved very well, and did not do anything shameful. Due to the tremendous energy and efforts of Ivan Kvasnikov, the local songleader and teacher, chapel life of the Tyonek Kenaitze has not only revived, but has also improved considerably compared to earlier years. The following facts confirm what I just said. This winter Tyonek Kenaitze demonstrated genuine brotherly feelings toward each other. It is especially noticeable by spring, when practically everyone is short of food. I frequently saw how a Kenaitze native, after he had returned from a hunting trip, shared everything with his fellow-villagers. On top of this, total sobriety, rejection of card playing, and zealous attendance of chapel services clearly prove that Tyonek Kenaitze have changed significantly. They do not remind me at all of the former Kenaitze, with their old worldview and heathen way of life.

April 30. At 2 o'clock in the morning when the tide rose, we left Tyonek and sailed on. By 8 o'clock in the evening we had already reached Old Knik. This village, when I visited it last time, had two or three native houses [*baraboras*], and two small trade stores. Now Old Knik has completely changed. One can see many new houses, larger trade stores and even a saloon. In a word, any spot more or less convenient for living is now occupied by a house or at least by a tent. This winter about 100 American miners stayed in Knik as well as a few soldiers with an officer. Because of the presence of the soldiers, the miners had to restrain themselves and no incidents happened. As a matter of fact, the American government sent these soldiers to build a road from Knik to Yukon. Last summer they laid 250 miles of this road and reached the Mednovtsy villages. This summer the soldiers plan to build farther, and eventually they intend to reach the Yukon River. This means that Knik will surely become the gate to Yukon. For this reason, all kinds of people are now flooding Knik. Various commercial enterprises fill with their businesses this once half-forgotten slum. Trade stores have also penetrated Mednovtsy country. As a result, not a single Mednovtsy visited the Knik villages[52] this winter. They say that crowds of Americans now literally swarm areas populated by the Mednovtsy. Driven by self-interest, these newcomers widely use unscrupulous methods in dealing with the natives. For these intruders, alcohol certainly serves as their major tool. Thus, recently they got a Mednovtsy drunk to death: this native drank for a whole week and then died. As recently as last winter the Mednovtsy still knew nothing of whiskey. This is only the beginning, and it is easy to predict what soon will happen with these natives. In all fairness, a large number of white people have also perished in Mednovtsy country. According to recent information, about 100 of them died there from various misfortunes. A very convincing lesson to all other daredevils!

May 1. Today I am already in New Knik. I found here only a few Kenaitze. The majority of them are still away, roaming in forests and mountains. As soon as I came, a few natives were sent to alert all others who were out of the village that the priest had come. I have not been to both Kniks for more than a year. In 1897–98 I spent the whole winter in Knik, therefore the last summer I did not come here. Now I notice that the morality of the Knik residents has declined. In March one woman hung herself. The reason was the death of her husband. A few Kenaitze women (four) illicitly cohabit with Americans. Alcohol abuse also occurs. American newcomers represent the major temptation for local natives [*inorodtsy*]. Intruders use any kind of unscrupulous methods to turn the Kenaitze into convenient tools to satisfy their own, frequently vicious goals.

At 6 o'clock in the evening I celebrated vespers. Only those whom I was able to find in the village participated in the service. With a heavy heart I conducted the service. I felt emptiness and desolation in everything and everywhere. Since my last visit the chapel remains unfinished. Many have forgotten how to sing hymns. Moreover, some of them do not know how to make properly the sign of the cross. So much time and energy did I invest that winter in drawing them at least closer to the way of life all Christian faithful are expected to follow. When I left them the first time (March of 1898) I was convinced that I had partially reached my goal. Therefore, with happy feelings and light heart did I leave the Kenaitze. However, during my present visit I have found that all my efforts were in vain. They again started moving around and settling far from the village in small camps, forgetting what they learned at school. Cold feelings everywhere. For the past year the chapel was opened only two or three times. It is hard to write about all these things, but it was even harder for me to see them when I was visiting the village. Both Kniks need a special person who will teach school, perform chapel services and keep up public morality. The Kenaitze themselves stressed that they want to obtain such a person.

At the end of my service I gave a sermon, in which I expressed all my sorrows concerning all the sinful things I found among them.

May 2. The Divine Liturgy and ministrations.

May 3. After the service, the men started to repair the chapel and the women washed the chapel floors. It is a clear and nice day except for mosquitoes, which plague us. One cannot hide from these annoying insects either by day or at night. The Kenaitze are beginning to gather. Vespers and matins at 6 o'clock. After performing the service I taught everybody church singing.

May 4. At 8 o'clock in the morning I served the Hours, then typical psalms. At the end of the service I explained to the natives the meaning of prayer. One American also visited the service. Then I anointed three infants with myrrh. The men again worked near the chapel. Vespers and matins at 6 o'clock in the evening. In my sermon I talked about a few wicked habits I have noticed among local Kenaitze. For example, after taking a steam bath, men go outside absolutely naked to cool themselves off and do not feel ashamed in the presence of women and even their own daughters. I also noted that they tend to copy the American manner of cursing and whistling. Two Americans visited the service. Later on, I taught the natives church singing.

May 5. The Hours at 8 o'clock in the morning, then typical psalms. After "Blessed be the name of the Lord henceforth and forever more," instructions before confession. After this, I explained to the natives what is required from those who prepare themselves for confession, who should confess and why God needs our repentance. After the service I baptized one infant. Then starting at 1 o'clock in the afternoon I heard confession. Vespers and matins at 6 o'clock in the evening, then evening prayers. Later on, continued confession. Total number of confessed people is seventy-six.

May 6. At 7:30 in the morning prayers and the Divine Liturgy of St. John Chrysostom. During the liturgy 100 people, including infants, received communion. Upon finishing reading a prayer at the pulpit I delivered a sermon about how Christians should organize their lives in order to deserve eternal life. After the Divine Liturgy, I performed a customary prayer service devoted to the birthday of his Majesty Russian Emperor. Then I served a funeral service for those who died during the past year (three adults and three infants), and also spoke about the afterlife. At 2 o'clock in the afternoon a brotherhood meeting. During this meeting members discussed brotherhood-related matters accumulated for the past year. At 6 o'clock in the evening I united one couple in holy matrimony. Tomorrow I plan to leave Knik.

May 10. Today at 9 o'clock in the morning I returned to Kenai.

July 26. Two days after the departure of the Most Reverend from Kenai, when the water rose again about 11 o'clock in the morning I sailed by *baidarka* to Susitna, Tyonek, and Kustatan to fulfill my regular pastoral duties. Because of favorable weather we quickly reached Tyonek, where we arrived at 5:30 in the evening. The first thing that pleasantly surprised me in this village was a new fence that natives had built around the cemetery. It was our Most Reverend Tikhon who during his visit to Tyonek suggested that the parishioners fence the cemetery. I was so glad that his words had such an impact on the Kenaitze. I plan to stay in Tyonek for only one night. Tomorrow, God willing, I will set out for Susitna. I have to be there as soon as possible in order to catch the Susitna natives before they wander off to the mountains. I invited Kvasnikov, a former teacher, to accompany me on this trip, of course for a fee, but he flatly refused. So I had to rely on the help of my Stepka [Stepan], a Susitna boy whom I teach at Kenai and who acts both as a reader and an interpreter.

July 27. About noon, when the tide rose, we left Tyonek. By the evening we reached the mouth of the Susitna River and stopped there for the night.

July 28. A clear and nice day. After we woke up and drank tea, we sailed on. Going up the Susitna River is hard work. In some places one has to literally struggle with the current. The mouth of the Susitna River is located only thirty miles from the chapel. Yet it took us thirteen hours to cover such a short distance. En route we took only one thirty-minute break. When we reached the village, I found there only two or three Kenaitze families. All the others are wandering in neighboring forests and mountains. Today a *toion* sent messengers to let them know that I had come. I expect that the Kenaitze will start gathering tomorrow.

July 29. A very hot day. By the evening the weather changed. At first, we heard thunder and saw lightning, then it started to rain. About 2 o'clock in the afternoon the Susitna churchwarden, along with the *zakazchik* and my Stepka came from Tyonek. I audited the chapel finances and found out that some money was missing because the churchwarden did not do his job properly. I took some steps to correct this situation. The chapel building itself still remains neglected and unrepaired. Matins at 6 o'clock in the evening The number of the faithful who came to the service and prayed is forty.

July 30. At 9 o'clock in the morning I served the Hours, then the liturgy without consecration. The Susitna residents are gradually returning to the village, and today more people came for the service than yesterday. After the service I visited the opposite bank of the river to examine the place designated for the new chapel building. The problem with Susitna is that because of the frequent floods, as, for example, last fall, the present village, located on a small island, will soon be abandoned and removed to the opposite bank, which is much higher. A trading store and some Kenaitze have already moved to the new place. Because of this, the chapel will also have to be removed. In fact, the chapel should be completely rebuilt at the new place. The present structure was built carelessly, without any symmetry, and reminds one of a cattle barn rather than a prayer house. Besides, time has damaged the building material. I hope his Grace will grant permission to start work on the new chapel. The Kenaitze have already prepared wooden boards for the roof. For this purpose the natives spent $4.50 of the chapel money, while a local brotherhood donated $4. Also, boards from the old chapel can be used to build a new floor and ceiling. All this allows me to conclude that the building of the new chapel will not require too much labor.

After dinner I baptized four infants (boys). Vespers and matins at 6 o'clock in the evening. Eighty natives participated in the service and prayed. After the service a requisite prayer and instructions before confession, then I heard children's confessions. Confession was preceded by a sermon (through an interpreter) about a righteous Christian life. Today I confessed sixteen natives.

July 31. At 8 o'clock morning prayers for those who perform rites of fast and penance, preparing themselves for communion. Then, the Divine Liturgy of St. John Chrysostom, where I gave communion to about forty infants and children who came for confession. Then I read a prayer from the pulpit followed by a short requisite prayer service before confession for adults. I ended this service with a short sermon, in which I stressed that human beings come to this earth to prepare themselves for the Heavenly Kingdom. I started hearing confession of the adult faithful at 1 o'clock in the afternoon and finished about 6 o'clock in the evening. Sixty-three people is the total number of natives who came for confession. This number does not represent all Susitna residents. Some natives had already left for the mountains, and therefore this year they will not be able to partake in the sacraments. All-night vigil at 7 o'clock in the evening and then evening prayers.

August 1. At 8 o'clock morning prayers, the lesser blessing of water, and the Divine Liturgy of St. John Chrysostom. During this service I delivered a sermon devoted to cleansing our bodies and spirits. I gave communion to all those who had been to confession. After the prayer read from the pulpit, I sang thanksgiving and dismissal prayers. Having finished the Divine Liturgy, I sang funeral services for seven infants who died since my last visit to Susitna (one of them was baptized, but not anointed with myrrh). After dinner, carrying the cross and holy water, I visited the houses of the village residents.

At 3 o'clock in the afternoon I held the meeting of local brotherhood members. I audited the brotherhood's finances, and found out that only $19.20 remained in the mutual fund. Due to their poverty, members did not pay a large part of their dues for the past year. The brotherhood also bought dried fish, grease, and other foodstuffs to help those who were starving. While one brotherhood member canceled his membership, another person joined. So at the present time the membership of Susitna's St. Mitrophanes Brotherhood remains the same: twenty-three people. I suggested that members buy an icon with an image of St. Mitrophanes, but they still cannot make up their minds. I instructed the brotherhood to supervise the building of the new chapel. For this purpose, we elected three brotherhood members, who are familiar with carpentry, to act as a sort of construction committee.

After persistent requests of the *toion*, *zakazchik* and his mother, I had to leave my Stepka in Susitna for the winter. I entrusted him with teaching prayers, basics of religion, and church singing to local children. On Sundays and feast days he is expected to read prayers in the Susitna chapel in the way that I instructed him. Unfortunately, Kvasnikov warned me that I might not catch him in Tyonek. So I have to drag my Stepka to Tyonek to help me in interpreting. Then, when I do not need him anymore, I will have to bring him back to Susitna.

At 5 o'clock in the evening we left Susitna and stayed for the night at the mouth of the river with the same name.

August 2. Strong wind with rain. We have to submit ourselves to the forces of nature, and stayed on shore waiting for the weather to improve.

August 3. Foggy morning. In the afternoon the sky cleared a little, and we felt a light southern wind. We certainly used this opportunity and without wasting time moved on. We arrived at Tyonek at 6 o'clock in the evening. All Kenaitze were at home, but Kvasnikov was gone. He had boarded the ship *Perry* and gone somewhere on his own business. For that reason, the presence of my Stepka was very handy.

August 4. Rainy and windy. By noon the wind grew even stronger and turned into a real storm. I have never seen such huge breakers in my life. At 9 o'clock in the morning I served the Hours and then the liturgy without consecration. All the natives sang very well and held many lighted candles. At the end of the service I thanked the Tyonek residents for building a fence around the local cemetery and, most of all, for their obedience. After the service, I anointed with myrrh five infants (three boys and two girls). Then I inspected the state of the chapel and its finances. The sale of candles and other church materials was conducted honestly and all money was reported. At 6 o'clock in the evening I served vespers and matins. The Kenaitze sang very well, and again there were many lighted candles. Nikolai Kuliktukta, a Kenaitze native, read six psalms at the beginning of matins. This Kuliktukta asks me to give him permission to perform regular chapel services on Sundays and feast days. For lack of any other experienced people, I have to satisfy his request. Kuliktukta reads slowly, but correctly. Besides, he is somewhat familiar with church singing. All in all, permitting him to act as a reader will be better than to locking the chapel completely and thereby denying the local Kenaitze a chance to gather for prayer. After the service twenty-nine children received confession. Before confession I offered a short sermon devoted to the Ten Commandments.

August 5. At 7:30 in the morning a requisite prayer before holy communion. After this, as always, the Divine Liturgy of St. John Chrysostom. I also gave communion to about forty infants and to all twenty-nine children who had received confession. After "Blessed be the name of the Lord henceforth and forever more" I read a requisite series of prayers before confession for the adults. At the end we together recited the Creed. At 1 o'clock in the afternoon I started hearing confessions. At 6 o'clock in the evening an all-night vigil devoted to the

Feast of Transfiguration of Christ. After the service I read evening prayers and then continued to hear confession. The total number of people who received confession today and yesterday is 105. Among the natives who came for confession there were also a few families from Susitna.

August 6. The Feast of Transfiguration of Christ. At 7 o'clock in the morning requisite prayers before holy communion. After this, I performed the rite of the lesser blessing of water, and then the Divine Liturgy of St. John Chrysostom. Using readings from the Gospel I explained to the natives the meaning of this feast and also instructed them. All who came for confession received communion. Upon finishing the prayer "Blessed be the name of the Lord henceforth and forever more," I read thanksgiving and dismissal prayers. After the liturgy, on a private request, I performed a customary prayer service in honor of the Mother of God. Then carrying a holy cross and holy water, I visited the houses of parishioners. Then I performed a second customary prayer service in honor of the Mother of God at another private house. A gathering of Tyonek's St. Innocent Brotherhood at 3 o'clock in the afternoon. All registered members (twenty-four people) participated in this meeting. Members examined the state of finances of their brotherhood for the last year. Tomorrow, at 6 o'clock in the morning I plan to sail to Kustatan.

August 7. Early in the morning, when the tide subsided, I left Stepan in Tyonek for Kustatan. When the tide rises again, he will have the opportunity to come back to Susitna. I arrived at Kustatan about 9 o'clock in the morning and found here only half of the village residents. All others had departed for Kenai to celebrate Assumption of the Mother of God, the Kenai church feast [*khramovii prazdnik*]. After dinner I baptized one infant and gave him the name Nikolai. Then performed funeral services for those who had died, and inspected the chapel and its finances.

On the whole, the finances were handled honestly. Yet, as for the chapel building itself, its conditions are deteriorating. Incidentally, the village itself is in state of disintegration. By next winter three more families plan to move to Kenai. It might be expected that both Kustatan village and its chapel will soon be abandoned. All-night vigil at 6 o'clock in the evening. Those who still remained in the village (twenty people) participated in the service and prayed. After the service I read requisite prayers before confession. Total number of those who received confession is sixteen people, including children. After confession, I read the evening prayers.

August 8. At 8 o'clock in the morning requisite prayers and then the liturgy without consecration. All natives who confessed received communion. After a prayer, "Blessed be the name of the Lord henceforth and forever more," thanksgiving and dismissal prayers. About 4 o'clock in the afternoon I left Tyonek to return to Kenai. When I returned I found everything in Kenai in good and proper order.

August 25. Today, in two Seldovia *baidarkas*, I along with Aleksandr Demidov left for Seldovia. From here I plan to sail to Aleksandrovsk and Ninilchik. Recently, his Grace appointed Demidov, who had completed a course of studies at our Kenai school, to be a teacher in Seldovia. This will be my second trip to the village this year. The major purpose of this trip is visiting my flock in Seldovia one more time before the beginning of the long annoying winter. I also want to deliver to them words of consolation and instruction. Besides, I want to participate personally in the opening of the new school here and arrange accommodations for the new young teacher. It was quite hard for me to watch Demidov weeping when he left his parental home in order to plunge himself into an unfamiliar life. This incident reminded me of my own childhood, and my departures from my home, at first, to both schools, and finally overseas, to America. We all walk under God, and thank Him for everything!

September 1. At 8 o'clock in the morning I performed a customary prayer service to celebrate the opening of the Seldovia school. Twenty-four students along with their parents participated in the service. I ended the prayer service by wishing many happy years to the Russian Imperial Family, the Holy Synod, the Most Reverend Tikhon, teachers and students and to all Orthodox Christians. At the request of the Seldovia residents, at 10 o'clock in the morning I performed the rite of the lesser blessing of water in the chapel. There were sixty praying people.

March 6, 1900. Today about 5 o'clock in the evening I sailed from Kenai to the southern part of my parish to visit Seldovia, Aleksandrovsk, and Ninilchik villages. Although the wind and the current favored us, we interrupted our route near Kasilof village because of nightfall and also the blocks of ice, which are still abundant in the water at this season. Trying to be cautious, we decided to drop anchor and to spend the night by simply staying on water in a safe place.

March 7. Early in the morning we continued our route. The wind again helped us, and we proceeded without any troubles, although one sailor became seasick. About 8 o'clock in the morning we neared Ninilchik and were prepared to drop anchor, but a sudden wind and rising waves pushed us back to sea and we missed the village. About 8 o'clock in the evening we entered the mouth of Seldovia harbor. Because of the darkness and the head current we had to stay at anchor before reaching the village.

March 8. Bad day with a drizzling rain. Now the wind has turned into a deadly calm, and we cannot move because we do not have any paddles. Somehow we dragged ourselves to the village and by 7 o'clock in the morning we were among our people. As I expected, all Seldovians stayed at home impatiently awaiting my arrival, and they were very glad to see me again. I found everything in the village in proper order. Seldovians live peacefully, quietly and without any misdeeds with the exception of the known sinner Mr. N. who still illicitly lives with a woman. I have already reported this incident, but nothing came of it. All the people of the village are healthy except two feeble old men. The material well-being of the Seldovians improved during the winter, especially since January, when the majority of them were hired to work for the Kachemak Coal Company at Homer.

Fortunately for the Seldovians, McPorson, the company's local manager, turned out to be a wonderful person. He sympathized with the miserable conditions of the local natives, and took their needs to heart. Driven only by humanitarian motives, McPorson decided to help the natives. During January and February he provided the Seldovians and people from the Aleksandrovsk village with permanent jobs. He also gave Seldovians special days off to perform rites of fast and penance, and promised to provide them with more jobs in future. It is nice to know that these lucky circumstances raised the economic well-being in at least these two villages. There is no doubt that the improvement in living conditions of these people will have a positive effect on their chapel and parish life. Chapel income will increase, brotherhoods will revive their activities, and other needs will be satisfied. McPorson indeed acts as a real benefactor of the local residents, and deserves the most sincere gratitude from those who take the interests of natives close to their hearts. When I finish my work here, I immediately plan to visit Homer and personally thank him for his benevolence. Incidentally, McPorson himself wants to meet me. Earlier, when I stayed in Seldovia, he already twice sent me a written invitation asking that I visit him in Homer.

Great Vespers and matins at 6 o'clock in the evening. The chapel was completely filled with praying natives. Before the dismissal prayer I delivered a sermon, in which I talked about the benefits of peace, love and truth both in one's personal and social life. Everybody listened with rapt attention.

March 9. At 8 o'clock in the morning I served Great Lent hours, typical psalms, and then vespers. There were about 140 praying people, all of whom now partake in the rites of fast and penance. The natives sing very well, which I had already noted before. After the end of the service, I asked all the men to stay for a talk. There is a problem. Earlier I reminded the Seldovians on several occasions that the chapel needed some repairing. Of course, as always, they had promised to do this (the Kenaitze are very generous with their promises), but did not go beyond that. So now the Seldovia chapel is falling into disrepair and decay. For example, the altar cloths they made five or six years ago from some cheap painted fabric remain unreplaced. In short, one notices that everything in this chapel looks cheap, worn-out and unattractive. Of course, poverty is not a drawback [*bednost ne porok*], and parishioners could be excused if they had been poor, but when one sees how the Kenaitze wives buy not only new but even expensive dresses that cost between five and ten dollars, one unavoidably becomes outraged at such neglect of God's sanctuary. In my talk with the natives I shared with them all these concerns and tried to convince them to change their attitudes. As an example I used some Kodiak parish villages they are familiar with. I also pointed to the neighboring Aleksandrovsk village, where the people are poorer than the Seldovians, but who care about their chapel. Finally, I threatened that if they remain stubborn and unconcerned I will treat them like misbehaving children, who neglect the advice of their father, and stop visiting them. As a result, all of them announced that by Easter the chapel will be put in proper order.

After this I anointed five infants (four boys and one girl) with myrrh. During the winter one native died, therefore the increase of the population is four people. Upon finishing the rite of anointment, I churched the infants. After this I audited chapel finances and found out that $24.75 was missing. To my question about the missing money a churchwarden casually remarked that he had hardly stayed at home this winter, and therefore did not know about anything. For explanations I had to turn to the *toion*, *zakazchik* and other more authoritative people. In their turn, the headmen came to the conclusion that it was the churchwarden who should be blamed for the embezzlement, and also for neglecting the chapel's maintenance. The *toion* claimed that there were many natives who volunteered to work on the chapel, but the churchwarden kept asking them to wait. For this reason, the Kenaitze asked to elect a new churchwarden, and decided to discuss the missing money at a general meeting of all adult parishioners. I certainly agreed with this suggestion.

Great Vespers and matins at 5 o'clock in the evening. After the service we remained in the chapel to elect a new churchwarden. All participants unanimously voted for Vasilii Baiiu, a resident of Seldovia. Baiiu is an honest, reliable man, zealous in his faith and attentive to the conditions of the chapel. The newly elected took an oath and received the necessary instructions. The problem of the $24.75 will be discussed tomorrow.

March 10. At 8 o'clock in the morning I served Great Lent hours, then typical psalms and vespers. There was the meeting about the missing money. After a long discussion we came to the following conclusion. Since it is the community that elects a churchwarden and entrusts him with the responsibility to supervise the chapel and chapel-related matters, the community itself should be responsible for all missing money. In order to fill the shortage, the meeting unanimously resolved that from April 1, 1900, everybody who returned to work for the Kachemak Coal Company would donate ten cents from each dollar to reimburse the embezzled money and also to cover repair work in the chapel and school, and also to support the poor in the village. To guarantee that this money would be safe, it was resolved to approach the chief manager of the Coal Company and ask him to deduct ten cents from each earned dollar. Then each month the manager shall transfer the money to the *toion* who, in the presence of witnesses and a clerk, will put it in the mutual fund. The resolution of the meeting written in English was signed by all participants of the meeting (thirty-seven people). The residents of the village delegated me to deliver the document to the chief manager.

Great Vespers and matins at 6 o'clock in the evening. After the end of the service requisite prayers before confession, after which I explained the meaning of the Ten Commandments. I heard confession from thirty-two children of school age. After confession evening prayers.

March 11. A requisite prayer at 8 o'clock in the morning, then the Divine Liturgy of St. John Chrysostom. All children who came for confession received communion as well as all infants (fifty souls). After the prayer "Blessed be the name of the Lord henceforth and forever more," requisite prayers before confession for adults. We ended with a collective reciting of the Creed and with a talk about genuine repentance. After dismissal prayer, requisite thanksgiving prayers preceding holy communion. After this I read a cleansing prayer for women on the fortieth day after childbirth, churched infants, and performed a funeral service for a person named Nikolai, who died this winter. From 1 o'clock in the afternoon I started hearing confessions. At 6 o'clock in the evening the all-night vigil with the ceremony of carrying of Lord's Holy Cross out of the chapel. After all-night vigil I read evening prayers and then I continued to confess people, the total number of which was seventy-nine persons.

March 12. At 8 o'clock in the morning teacher Aleksandr Demidov read a requisite prayer, while I was visiting two feeble old men in order to give them last rites. After the morning prayer I performed the rite of the lesser blessing of water and then the Divine Liturgy of St. Basil the Great. At the liturgy using a Gospel phrase "take up the cross and follow me" [Mark 10:21], I delivered a sermon devoted to the meaning of the Lord's Cross. All adults who came for confession received communion along with one infant. After the prayer was read from the pulpit I read the thanksgiving and the dismissal prayers. Then I conducted a customary prayer service at the request of the new churchwarden, who needs the Lord's help to successfully perform his new duties. Everybody visited this prayer service. After dinner I visited the houses of local parishioners with a cross and holy water, and found all dwellings clean and neat. In one house I served another customary prayer service in honor of the Mother of God.

March 13. At 9 o'clock in the morning members of Seldovia's St. Theodosius Brotherhood held their general meeting. Members studied the annual report of the brotherhood. In the past year the brotherhood lost two members: one died and the other was expelled. At the same time, another person joined the society. At the present time the Seldovia brotherhood numbers twenty-nine people. By April 1, 1899, the brotherhood's fund had $61.21. For the past year members donated $38.50, which gives an increase of the total fund to $99.70. Also, of this money the brotherhood spent for the past year: (1) $11 to help sick brotherhood members; (2) $4.85 to help the poor; (3) $4.25 for the funeral of one of the deceased members. In total, $20.10 was spent. Therefore, by April 1, 1900, the brotherhood mutual fund had $79.60.

During this time the brotherhood held four meetings. At the present meeting, the brotherhood elected a new treasurer. I also spoke, explaining to the members a few brotherhood by-laws. Members also discussed the measures they should take to upgrade the work of the brotherhood in general. As an example of how things should be done, I pointed out to them to some good traditions we have in the Kenai brotherhood. Finally, the gathering resolved to correct all existing mistakes. God help them. All their meetings usually began and ended with a prayer.

After dinner I tested the children of the local school. They showed the best results in reciting prayers by heart and reading Russian and Church-Slavonic texts. Singing is satisfactory. At the same time, I have to mention that the natives already knew how to sing fairly well long before the school was founded here. The children's performance in mathematics, English and Russian writing was very poor. According to the local teacher [Demidov], a poor or complete lack of knowledge of Russian and also a shortage of the textbooks on English are the major hindrances to the children's progress. He hopes that next year some of these drawbacks will be eliminated. In addition, only one student in this school was able to show some knowledge (although poor) of Holy History as well as Old and New Testaments.

In my view, the lack of any order and discipline represents another serious defect of the school. While examining the children I had to remind them to behave and be silent. The lack of discipline and self-restraint, disrespect for older people, and other examples of misbehavior copied from white people are the major drawbacks of all Seldovian youth. No wonder these weaknesses affected the performance of the students, who are supervised, incidentally, by a teacher who is still himself immature. Yet, the teacher kept a school journal properly and diligently. From this journal I learned that classes were taught from September 6, 1899, to March 8, 1900, the day of my arrival here. There was a short Christmas break from December 19 to January 15. Classes met 131 days. The journal shows that each day classes started at 8:15 in the morning with a morning prayer, which was read by three students in turn. Also, each class began and ended with a collective reciting of a prayer. In the beginning of the class they sang "To the Heavenly King," and at the end "It is truly meet and right." During the day classes met as follows: (1) from 8:30 to 9:30 a.m.: God's Law; (2) from 9:45 to 10:45 a.m.: Russian and Church Slavonic languages; (3) from 11 a.m. to 12 noon: mathematics (on Thursdays and Saturdays); (4) from 1 to 2 p.m.: English language. The number of students at the Seldovia school was sixteen in September, twenty-four in October. All other months their number was stable: twenty-three students. The children never missed classes. Students themselves collected wood for the fireplace, warmed the building, and cleaned the school and the chapel. Nobody forced them: the children did everything voluntarily. This vividly proves that the children love the school, which also greatly pleases their parents.

June 26, 1900. After I had visited all the local summer fishing camps to notify the natives about my arrival today, by 5 o'clock in the evening, I finally reached Knik and its chapel. I had left Kenai on June 19. In addition to fishing camps, I visited such miners' towns as Hope and Sunrise. I usually move around by *baidarka*. Ivan Soloviev, a Kenaitze native, accompanies me on this trip. Soloviev is a good find, and I can save some money on him. He acts both as a paddler and an interpreter, and also as a reader. The Knik chapel still remains unrepaired, and by its unattractive appearance produces a depressing impression on a visitor. With a heavy heart and deep sorrow did I enter this prayer house, which, incidentally, was never opened since my last visit (May 1–May 7, 1899). On the same evening I demanded that the local *toion*, *zakazchik* and churchwarden come and provide their explanations concerning the miserable condition of the chapel. They found all sorts of excuses. Thus they told me that everybody was supposedly away the whole winter, that they starved all the time, and had to stay in the mountains to hunt wild animals and so forth.

Of course, these are the usual Kenaitze excuses, which they use all the time. Finally, Knik headmen assured me that by Christmas the chapel will definitely be put in proper order.

June 27. At 9 o'clock in the morning I served the Hours and then the liturgy without consecration. After "Blessed be the name of the Lord henceforth and forever more," I delivered a sermon in which I shared with the natives my concerns and gave them a few words of advice regarding a genuine Christian life. Ivan Soloviev translated my words, and everybody listened attentively. After the service I asked all the men to stay for a final discussion about repairing the local chapel. I started the meeting with a talk about the significance of the church building for Christians, and stressed that not only headmen of the village, as the Kenaitze usually think, but everybody should take care of the prayer house. Then, I encouraged all those who were present to get seriously engaged in repairing the chapel. I also added that in addition to contributing their labor, they need to collect money to buy windows, calico, wallpaper, and paint, and finished my talk by asking them to donate as much as they could right there. As a result of this talk, immediately during the meeting all the natives volunteered to contribute their labor and money to the project. We collected $9.20 right on the spot. Many of those who did not have money promised to bring their donations as soon as possible. Moreover, I was surprised to learn that without any request on my part the Knik Kenaitze decided to contribute $3.25 to the building of the Kenai bell tower, which is now under construction. Accordingly, I do expect the Knik chapel to acquire an appropriate appearance by Christmas. After the meeting I baptized an infant and anointed three others with myrrh. In Knik five people including one infant died in the past year. Having finished the rite of anointment, I audited the chapel finances and found that there were hardly any donations. I attribute it to the fact that the Knik natives always spend much time away from their homes. During their wanderings they even reach the Mednovtsy camps, despite the hardships of such a journey. Last winter eight Knik natives visited the Mednovtsy. They left Knik on September 1 and traveled fifty-five days carrying all their belongings on their backs. They returned to Knik only on May 1.

From 3 in the afternoon to 5 o'clock in the evening I supervised choir practice. I taught them to sing hymns from the Divine Liturgy. Vespers and matins at 6 o'clock in the evening. At the end of the service I noted that everybody who comes to pray also should participate in collective singing during a public worship. For this reason, I continued, natives should make an effort to learn hymns. After the service I blessed a house.

June 28. At 9 o'clock in the morning I performed a rite of the lesser blessing of water, then Hours and the liturgy without consecration. During the ceremony of blessing the water I spoke about the healing power of the blessed water, and all faithful stood holding lighted candles. After "Blessed be the name of the Lord henceforth and forever more" requisite prayers before confession. Then everybody recited the Creed. After the service we again had choir practice. As a result, during the next service they started to sing better. At 1 o'clock in the afternoon I began confessions. At 6 o'clock in the evening I served the all-night vigil with the Polieley.[53] The service was devoted to apostles Paul and Peter. Afterwards, the evening prayer, and continued hearing confession. The total number of natives who came for confession is sixty-six.

June 29. At 7 o'clock in the morning a requisite prayer, then the Divine Liturgy of St. John Chrysostom. I delivered a sermon based on the Gospel stories about holy apostles, whom we commemorate today. All natives who came for confession as well as twenty infants received communion. The Divine Liturgy ended with thanksgiving prayers to the All-Russia Imperial Family, the Holy Synod, the Most Reverend Tikhon, members of the local brotherhood, and all Orthodox Christians. After this I performed a funeral service. At 2 o'clock in the afternoon there was a meeting of the Knik St. Sergius Brotherhood (twenty-three members). The brotherhood mutual fund had $29.45. Using the low tide, we left for Old Knik at 8 o'clock in the evening in order to give two sick people confession and communion.

June 30. Early in the morning, having finished our business in Old Knik, with a low tide we proceeded further, moving towards Susitna. But soon a strong wind forced us to stop at the first summer fish camp build by Knik natives. We stayed here waiting until the weather changed.

July 1. Today we are again en route. Stopped for the night at the mouth of the Susitna River. Here we ran across the Susitna *toion*, who informed us that many people in his village are ill, but even more people are starving. As in Knik, the fish still have not reached Susitna, which explains why the natives starve.

Dogs are also starving along with people. It is hard to watch these animals that look like moving skeletons.

July 2. Although today is Sunday, which is supposed to be a day off, we sail on. Any day Susitna natives expect a fish run, and we want to catch them before they are occupied with fishing. Today I had a chance to see with my own eyes how well Susitna women, and only Susitna women, handle small boats and *baidarkas*, which they row as skillfully as native men. By the evening we reached Susitna itself and its chapel. I found about twenty Kenaitze in the village. As for the rest, I will have to gather them. Tomorrow the Kenaitze will send messengers to notify those who have left the village that I have arrived. Susitna now has three trading stores that belong to different companies: two stores in this village, where we are staying, and one more in the lower Susitna village. On one of the tributaries of the upper Susitna River gold was found, but the works will start next summer. Our Stepan has grown up, looks healthy, and seems to have completely turned into a Kenaitze. Today one American, who is a local agent of ACC, expressed a desire to marry to a Knik Kenaitze woman with whom he has already lived for a long time and with whom he has a bunch of children.

July 3. At 9 o'clock in the morning the Hours and the liturgy without consecration. There were about thirty praying people. They belong to the natives who remained in the village. After the service I audited the chapel's finances and found everything in the best order. Evidently, last year's reprimand on my part brought the churchwarden to reason. However, the chapel income is still very miserable. When there was only one trading store in Susitna, the chapel had a higher income. Now, when the Susitna natives have three stores the income has completely dropped.

The chapel was opened only twice for the whole year: during the Feasts of Nativity of our Lord Jesus Christ and Epiphany. Although "our Stepan," who was entrusted with conducting public worship in the chapel, teaching the basics of religion to local children, and church singing and praying, wintered here, he did absolutely nothing. Moreover, children forgot those things they knew before. I was going to take this Stepan back to my Kenai school to complete his education and bring him back later to work here as some sort of a teacher or a reader. However, his mother, obviously because of her feeble-mindedness, rejected my good offer. She said that he is her only son and that she is old and weak (which is not quite true), and if he leaves there would be nobody to help her carry firewood and water, although the village is encircled by woods on all sides and the water literally washes the houses from underneath. For a whole hour I tried to convince her to change her mind, but all in vain. It means that all my expectations regarding Stepan are gone. Being put in such an unfavorable situation, I am now absolutely lost and I do not know what to do in order to raise somehow the level of Orthodoxy among the Susitna inhabitants. Obviously Stepan himself is no better than his mother. He spent only one winter in Susitna, and it is already hard to recognize the former Stepan. Now he has become lazy, vulgar and negligent of his clothing. In short, he has completely turned into a savage, and what is even worse, he has lost any inclination for studying. For this reason, I have to admit that the Susitna life with its ignorance and dullness fits him better. Like his mother, Stepan himself rejected my offer to continue his education either in Kenai or at the Sitka school.

At 6 o'clock in the evening vespers and matins. There were many lighted candles. The chapel was crowded with praying faithful. Because of the presence of so many people, I felt an unbearable sweltering heat inside the chapel. At the end of the service I talked about a few abnormal phenomena I had noticed in the life of Susitna inhabitants.

July 4. At 9 o'clock in the morning the Hours and the liturgy without consecration. Right after the service there was a general meeting of all the men from all Susitna settlements. I talked about those bad developments that I have found in this village which do not fit the behavior of a Christian true believer: frequent arguments and quarrels that neared fighting, card playing, attempts to distill vodka, abduction of a Copper River native girl by two local youths, disobedience of the *toion*, poor chapel income, and lack of regular chapel services. We also discussed problems pertaining to the building of the new chapel. The natives mentioned that all the necessary building materials were already prepared and, therefore, after the fishing season ends, the natives will begin construction of the chapel. We also reached positive decisions on all other matters.

At 3 o'clock in the afternoon I baptized eleven children and anointed with myrrh five others. Two people died in the past year. The increase in population is fourteen people. At 6 o'clock in the evening vespers and matins. After the service I explained in an accessible form the meaning of confession rite to children of school age and then heard their confessions. The total number of children who confessed was thirty-seven. I also tested how well they had learned their prayers. Susitna children know, although partially, only the Lord's Prayer and "Rejoice, O Mother of God Full of Grace, the Lord Is with Thee." It is a pity that so many children here remain without proper instruction. Personally I cannot improve this situation. Moreover, the very way of life of the Susitna inhabitants does not encourage their enlightenment. Endless wanderings in mountains and forests by entire families are the major hindrances to organizing a proper church and religious life. Only the establishment of a boarding school may pull their children of nomadic wanderings and promote successful education here.

July 5. At 8 o'clock in the morning, prayers and then the Divine Liturgy of St. John Chrysostom. All those who confessed received communion as well as sixty infants. After "Blessed be the name of the Lord henceforth and forever more," requisite prayers before confession for adults. After the dismissal prayer, requisite prayers before the rite of holy communion. Afterwards, at a private request I performed a customary prayer service in honor of the Mother of God. At noon I started hearing confessions. Then I performed vespers, matins and read the evening prayer. After the service I continued confession. Today eighty-eight people came for confession. The total number of natives who received confession, including those whom I confessed yesterday, is 125.

July 6. At 7 o'clock in the morning, requisite prayers before holy confession, blessing of water and the Divine Liturgy of St. John Chrysostom. During the ceremony of water blessing I delivered a sermon appropriate for this occasion. All faithful who confessed received communion. After the prayer "Blessed be the name of the Lord henceforth and forever more," I delivered a welcoming address, then thanksgiving prayers and the dismissal prayer. Afterwards, I sang a funeral service.

At 2 o'clock in the afternoon I joined in holy matrimony A. McConahay, an American, and Mapoy, a Knik Kenaitze girl, who lived with him in an illicit manner for more than seven years. The good proof of their illicit connection is their older daughter, who is already eight years old. This couple has four children total. Mr. McConahay paid me $5 for performing the mystery of holy matrimony, and also treated to tea all Kenaitze who showed up for this ceremony.

At 3 o'clock in the afternoon Susitna's St. Mitrophanes Brotherhood (twenty-three members) held its meeting. I was also occupied with putting into proper order the brotherhood's finances. From the past year there remained $23 in the brotherhood mutual fund. In addition, $20.30 was received as membership dues. In total, at present the Susitna brotherhood has $40.30 in cash. There were no expenses. The Susitna inhabitants also asked me to approach the Alaska governor on their behalf, and to inform him that they starve each spring because of the enormous shortage of fish. They also asked me to stress that the major cause of these sad developments is the advancement on the Kenai Bay of cannery factories (at present there are three factories), which catch almost all the fish using various devices. I heard the same complaints in Knik. These statements and concerns are quite justified. The fishing season is already coming to an end, but the Susitna inhabitants have caught only four fish! At 6 o'clock in the evening I left Susitna and sailed down the river to its mouth, where I stopped for the night.

July 7. At 9 o'clock in the morning using the low tide, I continued my trip and reached Tyonek about 6 o'clock in the evening. This was the busiest time for the local Kenaitze. I found them occupied with drying fish for themselves for their winter supply and to sell. Now there is high demand for dried fish. It is delivered to Yukon and other gold-mining areas as a feed for sled dogs. God blessed the Tyonek natives with a large catch, even more than they could store. This summer, in a settlement called Chubutnu, which is not far from Tyonek, a new cannery factory was built. The factory operates four fish tanks and has sixty fishermen along the shoreline in the Tyonek area. The governmental project of building a road to Yukon through Susitna led nowhere, because it entails enormous expenses. The army barracks are now empty. Soldiers and horses have been moved to Valdez (north of Nuchek). The American government decided that Valdez would be the most convenient starting point for the road to Yukon. Construction work here is now in full swing. And besides, rumors circulate that a railroad might be built in the future.

July 8. The absent Kenaitze gradually begin to arrive. All-night vigil at 6 o'clock in the evening. Forty faithful participated in the service and prayed.

July 9. At 9 o'clock in the morning I performed a ceremony of water blessing, then the Hours and the liturgy without consecration (there was no regular liturgy for lack of communion bread). One American family also visited the service. Then audited the chapel's finances. Everything was reported diligently. Order and cleanness in the chapel are superb. Besides, due to the churchwarden's efforts, the altar has beautiful new cloths, and the floor in the vestibule is covered with a rug. In a word, the efforts and work of the Tyonek churchwarden deserve appreciation and the most sincere gratitude. At a private request I performed a customary prayer service in honor of St. Nicholas, the Wonderworker. Then vespers and matins.

July 10. At 9 o'clock in the morning the Hours and the liturgy without consecration. After the service I anointed with myrrh three infants. In the past year nine people including infants died of influenza in this village.

July 11. At 9 o'clock in the morning the Hours and then the liturgy without consecration. After the service, I called a general village meeting in the chapel, where I tried to convince the natives to stop brewing a kind of Kenaitze beer, which they call "*makula*," and also to abandon card-playing. The Americans who wintered in Tyonek filed a complaint concerning the brewing of "*makula*" and the disgraceful behavior of the Kenaitze when intoxicated with this "*makula*." With deep regret I have to admit that, as it turned out, the respected Tyonek *toion* named Peter was more than anybody else involved in this drinking spree. For this reason, I did not give to him a church certificate of merit that he had been awarded, and decided to keep the award until next year. In addition, right in the chapel in front of everyone I strongly reprimanded him. As a result, the *toion* himself and his subordinates apparently promised that they would stop brewing "*makula*" and reduce their card playing.

When the meeting was over, at a private request I performed a customary prayer service in honor of St. Nicholas. At 1 o'clock in the afternoon requisite prayers and instructions before confession, and then confession. At 6 o'clock in the evening vespers and matins and the evening prayer for those who are preparing themselves for communion. Then I continued confession. On the whole, sixty-six people received confession. A few natives (ten people) expressed a desire to come instead to Kenai to perform rites of fast and penance during the feast of Assumption of the Mother of God.

July 12. At 8 o'clock in the morning a requisite prayer before holy communion, the Divine Liturgy of St. John Chrysostom, thanksgiving and dismissal prayers. All faithful whom I confessed along with thirty infants received communion. After the prayer "Blessed be the name of the Lord henceforth and forever more" I delivered a sermon, in which I taught the natives how Christians should behave in order to gain eternal life. Upon completing the Divine Liturgy, I sang the funeral service for those who died in the past year. At 1 o'clock in the afternoon I joined one couple in holy matrimony. At 2 o'clock in the afternoon there was a brotherhood meeting. At present, the brotherhood mutual fund has $26.10. The brotherhood also provided significant material help to its sick members. Thus, $18 was spent for this purpose during the winter. During this meeting I handed over to them over $10 donated by our most benevolent Father, the Most Reverend Tikhon. In response, all at once the Tyonek brotherhood members stood up, bowed very low, and all together said in Russian, "Thank you." Naive childish smiles and an especially happy mood noticeable on their faces long after the meeting was over showed how the natives were touched, and how deeply they were grateful for such archpastoral attention.

About 5 o'clock in the evening I parted with the Tyonek inhabitants and moved to Chubutna, a neighboring settlement, where I need to give confession and communion to a few sick people.

July 13. At 8 o'clock in the morning I confessed and gave communion to three men and one woman. From Chubutnu I was going to Gope [Hope], where I was expected to baptize three children. Then, from Hope I planned to proceed to Sunrise to purchase there some medicine for our Kenai brotherhood drugstore. Yet, en route strong unfavorable winds made my progress very slow. We came back to Kenai on July 23.

August 21, 1900. Today I departed from Kenai in order to visit Seldovia, Aleksandrovsk and Ninilchik villages, the second time in this year.

August 26. [Seldovia] At 9 o'clock in the morning the Hours, then the liturgy without consecration, and finally the lesser blessing of water. After the service there was a general meeting of all Seldovians at the chapel house. People elected and confirmed in their new positions the new *toion* and *zakazchik*, who replaced those who passed away this spring. We also talked about how to improve the moral life of the village youth. The newly elected headmen took an oath and received appropriate instructions. Afterwards, I performed a customary prayer service at the request of the newly elected.

Under the new churchwarden (who was elected this spring) the chapel has significantly improved. The interior of the cupola tower has been covered with grooved boards, and the building itself has been repainted in oil paint. New cloths were put on the altar and on the lectern. The natives also built a platform in front of the entrance to the chapel. For all these efforts I expressed in public my gratitude to the churchwarden. Anointed with myrrh an infant. After dinner I was occupied by helping to resolve various local problems and listening to people who came for my advice. At 6 o'clock in the evening the all-night vigil. All inhabitants of the village participated in the service. After the service, ten people, mostly pregnant women, came for confession. I also read the cleansing prayer for these women.

August 27. At 8 o'clock in the morning a requisite prayer, then the Divine Liturgy of St. John Chrysostom. Then I read from the Gospels and explained to the natives a parable about the vineyard. There were ten adult communicants along with forty infants. After the dismissal and thanksgiving prayers I handed out church certificates of merit to those people to whom they had been issued. At 1 o'clock in the afternoon I started to perform marriage ceremonies individually for each couple. On the whole, today I married six couples including Adam Bloch, the known agent of the Alaska Commercial Company.

Incidentally, I feel it my pleasant duty to add a few words about this gentleman. Everybody knows that this spring the epidemic disease of influenza visited Alaska. In some villages, especially in Seldovia, all the inhabitants became sick. Moreover, there was nobody to take care of such daily necessities as hot water and firewood. It was during these days that Adam Bloch showed his humanity and magnanimity toward his neighbors irrespective of who they were, both friends or non-friends. At the same time, although being himself very ill, Bloch nevertheless visited the houses of all sick villagers several times a day, providing people with various drugs, meals, firewood and other necessities. He did it absolutely for free, driven only by humanitarian impulses. When Bloch was not able to move himself, he sent his children to help the people. For those who died, and again for free, Mr. Bloch supplied everything that was needed for decent burials. Such help, especially provided during the time of the epidemic, is really invaluable. Seldovians themselves realized this very well and now they point out that if it was not for the help provided by Bloch, more people would have died.

No need to mention that this type of behavior is very rare in Alaska. We indeed should praise Our Lord for sending His blessing through this kind man. In addition to the above-mentioned, Mr. Bloch also contributed much effort to put the interior of the chapel in proper order. He donated half of the paint used for painting the whole building, and himself took part in the work. Bloch also paid half of the price of the cloth that now covers the altar.

August 28. At 9 o'clock in the morning at the local school I performed a requisite prayer service to celebrate the beginning of the school year, and wished many years of life to All-Russia Imperial Family, the Holy Synod, the Most Reverend Tikhon, teachers and students. When the participating faithful kissed the Holy Cross, I sprinkled them with holy water. I also delivered the word of instruction, which both Seldovia students and their young teacher equally needed. For this school year we have twenty students, which is four students less than the last year. The major reason of this decrease is that adolescent boys do not stay for long in the village because they have to participate in hunting trips and, as a result, fail to attend classes.

After the prayer service there was a brotherhood meeting. During this meeting brotherhood members elected Lubov Berestov as the new head to replace the deceased chairman of the brotherhood. Mrs. Berestov is a widow of the late *toion*, and she is a very serious and prudent woman. Zakhar Prokopiev became the new treasurer, and Vasilii Baiiu was elected as the record-keeper. Members also agreed to admit two new members. In addition, it was resolved to repair the school building. The meeting ended with the collective singing of the prayer "It is truly meet and right." Afterwards, at the local cemetery in the presence of a large number of praying people I sang a funeral service for those who died this spring, of which there were twenty-four people including infants.

March 8. Today, at 7 o'clock in the evening I departed for Seldovia in two *baidarkas* which had been specially sent on March 6 to bring me. I am going to this village without any church helpers because in Seldovia they have their own readers. A fresh northern wind blew the whole day. About 5 o'clock in the evening we reached Ninilchik. We hardly made it to the shore: rather than landing we were literally thrown out by a breaker. There is nothing special that has happened in Ninilchik that deserves to be reported. Everybody is alive, healthy, and busy doing daily chores.

March 9. We sailed on: the weather is a little better than yesterday. Stopped for the night at Anchor Point. Here we ran across five *baidarkas* with Seldovians, who had come here to check if there were any sea otters left, but in vain.

March 10. At 7 o'clock in the morning all seven *baidarkas* proceeded further. Reached Seldovia about noon. I found everything here in proper order. The Seldovians spent this winter away on hunting trips. At 6 o'clock in the evening the all-night vigil visited by all inhabitants of the village. The natives sang very well. After the service I read a cleansing prayer for the women.

March 11. At 8 o'clock in the morning the lesser blessing of water and after this as required the Divine Liturgy of St. Basil the Great. I delivered a sermon on a Gospel theme that prayer and fasting represent the best tools against evil spirits. Gave communion to about twenty-five infants. The schoolchildren sang hymns and sang very well. Adults also participated in the singing. All Seldovians and one American with his wife came for the service. After dinner, carrying the holy cross and holy water, I visited the houses of villagers. At 6 o'clock in the evening vespers with singing of the *prokeimenon* "Turn not Thy Face." At the end of the service I spoke about how the faithful should spend their Sundays and feast days. It must be mentioned that the way Seldovians spend holy feasts is not always according to the requirements of the Lord's commandments. After the service I gave requisite cleansing prayer to women and churched an infant.

March 12. At 8 o'clock in the morning I served Great Lent Hours, then the typical psalms, and vespers. After the service a parish meeting at the chapel house. The subject of our talk was a *zakazchik* who was elected and confirmed in his position last fall. The majority of the Seldovians have come to the conclusion that this *zakazchik* has turned out to be irresponsible and also prone to drinking. As a result, a new *zakazchik* was elected and sworn in. His name is Vasilii Baiiu. Baiiu simultaneously serves as the churchwarden.

Later on, I investigated one serious incident. As a matter of fact, this case is not so much complicated as odious. On December 17, 1900, Hans Sivertsen, an American, made two local Kenaitze women drunk. Pavel Baiiu, a young Kenaitze who is eighteen years old, also took part in this drinking bout. They were drinking in a house that belongs to another local Kenaitze, who was away at that time and who is a husband of one of these two women. Moreover, the doors of the house were locked, and the light was shut off. Later on, when people forced the doors open, they saw that this youth Pavel Baiiu was dead, one of the women was deadly drunk, while the other woman, although not so drunk, was scared to death. Unfortunately, the people who entered the house at first did not pay special attention to Pavel Baiiu thinking that he was only sleeping or had fainted from a heavy drinking. Therefore, they only took from the house the children of the drunk Kenaitze woman who was unconscious. Only at 11 o'clock in the evening did they notice that Pavel did not move, and had large bruises on his neck, under his chin and on one of his temples. The Kenaitze woman who was not so drunk assures everyone that it was this American Hans' doing. Although she could not see anything because it was dark, she was able to hear. Here they are, the deeds of the local civilizers, who boast about their cultured manners.

After dinner I audited the chapel's finances, and found everything in perfect order. The chapel is clean and neat. At 6 o'clock in the evening the Great Vespers and matins.

March 13. From 8 o'clock in the morning Great Lent Hours followed by typical psalms and vespers. I used the free time for writing. At 6 o'clock in the evening the great vespers and matins.

March 14. At 8 o'clock in the morning all services in the same order as yesterday. At 4 o'clock in the afternoon an infant named Maroa died. She hit her head and suffered for a long time. After the service I tested the children from the local school. Sixteen children came for the examination including five girls. They showed very poor results and were very poor in all subjects. Among the first group of children only one is able to read and write. On basics of religion the first group of children knows prayers very poorly and nothing about Holy History. In mathematics three boys can write and read digits up to 100, while the others know nothing. In English, they cannot write at all, and know only the alphabet, but only in sequential order. The second group reads prayers well, but has no idea of Holy History. In Russian, three students can read, including one who also reads Church Slavonic. As for the others, they know almost nothing. They also showed very poor results in English and mathematics.

As far as the third (senior) group is concerned, it is represented only by one student, who demonstrated the same results as the first two. I also want to mention that this senior student was able to read fairly well even before his admission to the Seldovia school. In singing hymns the students' results are quite satisfactory. Generally, I have to admit that the Seldovia school produced a miserable impression on me, although it has existed for almost two years. The teacher, Aleksandr Demidov, argued that the children supposedly did not attend classes on a regular basis, which is the major hindrance to successful and proper schooling. In his words, there were some days when only three students showed up for classes. Then, argued Demidov, there were some students who came for classes only two or three weeks for the whole year and now showed up for my examinations. Be that as it may, it is sad to see and to hear about such drawbacks in this benevolent project. I feel especially sad because the former *toion* (now deceased) predicted such a bright future for the Seldovia school, when we worked together to open it. Now it turns out to be just the opposite.

During the village meeting, which we held in the chapel on March 12, the present *toion* and other headmen complained that the teacher, Aleksandr Demidov, treats the children too harshly and does not care about their education. As a result, in the eyes of Seldovians, the school now stands as some sort of horrible and hated monster.

The school journal shows the following information. On average, from three to sixteen children came for classes. There were three age groups. During the winter they studied:

(1) Basics of Religion. First Group (six boys and three girls): they know prayers up to a ten-psalm unit done in the monastic order of prayers [*desiatislovie*]. From the Holy History of the Old Testament they finished up to the Tower of Babel. Second Group (four boys and three girls): the same prayers; from the Holy History of the Old Testament they studied the period up to the Prophets. Third Group (one student): the same prayers and from the Holy History the student studied Old and New Testaments using the book *Uroki Po Zakonu Bozhiju* [*Lessons on Basics of Religion*] by Archpriest Smirnov.

(2) Russian and Church Slavonic (two groups). The first group studied reading and writing using the ABC book by Grigorovskii. They used the same book to study Church Slavonic. The second group (one student): reading along with retelling stories, memorizing and copying from a book titled *Rodina* [Motherland]. For studying Church Slavonic this student performs the same tasks using *Chasoslov* [an Orthodox prayer-book].

(3) Mathematics (three groups). The first group studied how to count orally and in writing up to 100. The second group did formulas by using the textbook by Tenishev, chapter one; subtraction and addition up to ten. The third group learned the same chapter from the same textbook along with subtraction and addition up to 100.

(4) English (three groups). The first one: the alphabet, the second one: reading and writing using the book *Primer*. The third group: reading, writing and spelling using *Primer* by another compiler.

(5) All groups together also learned church singing. Vocal singing of hymns from Sunday services, Divine Liturgies, and Great Lent hymns. From September to March classes met 444 times during 128 days.

After dinner I was occupied with writing my journal. At 6 o'clock in the evening matins with reading the Great Canon of St. Andrew of Crete.

March 15. In the morning I performed divine services in the same order as yesterday. After the service, the meeting of the members of Seldovia's St. Theodosius Brotherhood. All brotherhood members (twenty people) participated. After the usual prayer in the beginning, we studied the annual report of the brotherhood, which give us the following information

By March 1, 1900, there remained $79.60 in the mutual fund of the Seldovia brotherhood. In addition, dues were paid: for March: $3; for May: fifty cents; for September: $17; for November: $5; for January of 1901: $2.25; for February: $2.75. The total amount of dues is $30.50. Overall, the brotherhood fund contained $110.10. Of this sum, from March 1, 1900, to March 1, 1901, the *toion* Feodor Berestov spent $3 for the teacher's salary, $4 for repairing the school, $16.35 for a brotherhood member's funeral, $1 for the funeral of an infant, $2 to help sick Praskovia Balashov, $2 as an allowance to the widow Lubov Berestov for Christmas. Overall, $28.35 was spent. Therefore, by March 1, 1901, there remains $81.75 in the mutual fund.

During the above-mentioned meeting one member terminated his membership, while another person joined the brotherhood. As a result, the number of members did not change. It was resolved to provide an allowance of $2 to Maria, a poor widow. During the meeting we also arranged an exchange of an old schoolhouse for a newly built structure, larger and more solid, of thirty feet in length and twenty-two feet in width. Now it will be easy to accommodate about fifty children. In the new schoolhouse it only remains to replace a hay roof with another one. The brotherhood promised to do this by next fall.

May 8. [...] At 4 o'clock in the afternoon I parted with the good and simple-hearted people of Aleksandrovsk, and went to Seldovia, where I stopped for the night. In Seldovia I found only women and small children. All the men had left the village to hunt wild animals (bears). Today ships *Bertha* and *New Port* which deliver mail stopped in Seldovia.

May 11. I am staying in Seldovia because of the wind and rain.

May 12. I let the *baidarka* and the rovers go. Instead, I am going by a small passing boat that lifts anchor this evening.

May 13. The Week of the Holy Fathers of the Council of Nicea. At 9 o'clock in the morning I served the Hours followed by the liturgy without consecration. Using a reading from the Gospels in my sermon, I instructed people that we should make ourselves firm in our Holy Orthodox faith and by this faith. Today primarily women came for the service. After the liturgy I sang a funeral service for two infants, who died this spring. Unfortunately, the boat on which I was expected to depart did not leave Seldovia yet. Finally we hoisted anchor. I had to spend every day from May 14 to May 18 on this small boat, which put in at many localities on Kachemak Bay for various purposes. Arrived at Kenai about 5 o'clock in the evening on Max 18.

June 18. Today at 7 o'clock in the morning I set out to visit the northern settlements of the Kenai parish. As during the last year, the same man, Ivan Soloviev, accompanies me on this trip both as an interpreter and a songleader for the same pay, $1 a day. I traveled to Tyonek on a rented boat that belongs to an American named Edelman. In order to reach other villages I will have to find somebody else in Tyonek to pick me up.

June 19. Our route was quite long due to a slow wind, and we arrived in Tyonek only about 3 o'clock in the afternoon. I found that the Tyonek Kenaitze were doing all right or, to be exact, at this time they had nothing to do. The captain of our longboat, who did not see anybody in the shallows, made the following observation, "It looks like they celebrate Sunday here today, and the natives are busy reading the Bible." This do-nothingness is explained by the fact that the first fish run has ended, and the second one will not start for two or three weeks. For this reason, our stay among the Tyonek inhabitants, as the natives put it themselves, will be timely and quite desirable. From the information I received it follows that the Tyonek people spent last winter quiet decently: by living in a sober, peaceful, and quiet manner. The natives were mainly occupied with hunting for wild animals and with other noble pursuits, which had a favorable moral and economic impact on their daily life. As a result, people did not starve this spring and more people were born than died.

At 6 o'clock in the morning I audited the chapel finances. The chapel income turned out to be very poor. This is because Nikolai Kuliktukta, a Kenaitze native and the only person here who knows church reading and singing to some extent, was away for the whole winter. Therefore, services were not held and candles were hardly sold. Yet, I found the chapel and the schoolhouse clean and in proper order.

June 20. At 9 o'clock in the morning the Hours followed by the liturgy without consecration. In my address I spoke about the proper preparation for confession and holy communion. All Tyonek inhabitants attended the chapel service.

Then, I gave cleansing prayers to two women. At 6 o'clock in the evening vespers and matins. In my sermon I stressed that holy matrimony is a sacred union and that lechery is a great sin. The reason I decided to talk about it is an incident, in which a local Kenaitze woman left her legal husband, a Kenaitze native, and went to live with an American.

Today for a long time I also conversed with a Sunrise police marshal and reported to him that in Kenai some Americans were involved in the illegal sale of strong alcoholic beverages. They supply the Kenaitze natives with this liquor for $2 per bottle. The marshal promised to consult the district court regarding this.

June 21. At 9 o'clock in the morning the Hours followed by the liturgy without consecration. I offered a sermon about the proper raising of children, for I noticed a few abnormalities in the life of the old and young generations. It is raining and windy today. Yet, everybody is glad. Here in Tyonek and in Kenai the rain has been a long-awaited "guest." It has not rained here for more than a month. At 6 o'clock in the evening vespers and matins.

June 22. As usual, the Hours followed by the liturgy without consecration. In my sermon I explained to the natives the meaning of the sign of the cross, and also some other prayer symbols. After the service I anointed a newborn with myrrh. The rest of the day I was occupied with writing my journal and resolving a few family disputes. Today, at 6 o'clock in the morning the ship *Excelsior* dropped anchor in Tyonek. At 6 o'clock in the evening I performed the all-night vigil devoted to the Vladimir icon of Mother of God. Having finished singing the *slavoslovie* [doxology] I explained the meaning of the prayer. After the service requisite prayers before confession. Then I confessed children of school age and provided them with requisite instruction. Today twenty-five people came for confession.

June 23. At 8 o'clock in the morning requisite prayers before holy communion. After this I performed the rite of the lesser blessing of water and the liturgy of St. John Chrysostom in accordance with the prescribed rules. Gave communion to twenty-five adults and about thirty infants. Also, I offered a sermon in which I explained to the natives what a church means for the faithful, and how the Christians should behave during a church service. After the prayer "Blessed be the name of the Lord henceforth and forever more" requisite prayers for those who were preparing themselves for confession and thanksgiving prayers for communicants. From 1 o'clock in the afternoon to 5 o'clock in the evening I was occupied with hearing confessions. Today thirty-four people received confession.

June 24. At 8 o'clock in the morning a morning prayer, then the Divine Liturgy of St. John Chrysostom. At the liturgy I delivered a sermon based on the Gospel story about Gadarene demoniac [Luke 8:26–39]. All those who came for confession received communion (fifty-four people). After the communion and the prayer read from the pulpit, I recited requisite series of prayers after the communion. At 1 o'clock in the afternoon there was a brotherhood meeting. Members heard the brotherhood's annual report, which looks as follows. By July 1900 $26.10 remained in the brotherhood mutual fund. $8.50 was received as membership dues. $11.70 was spent on help for sick members. Therefore, by July 1901 $22.90 remains in the brotherhood mutual fund.

After the brotherhood meeting, I joined one couple in holy matrimony, sang the funeral rites for the dead and at a private request performed two customary prayer services in honor of the Mother of God. The rest of the day I was occupied by visiting the houses of parishioners, and afterwards, invited by an American named George Madison, spent the evening with his family.

June 25. I planned to leave Tyonek early in the morning, but rain delayed me, and we had to stay waiting for the next tide, which came later the same day. Now we are moving to Susitna by dory (a small boat with a flat bottom). By 11 o'clock in the evening have neared the mouth of the Susitna River and stopped there for the night. First of all, at this place we had to withstand a fierce attack of mosquitoes. No other locality can match Susitna in the number of mosquitoes.

June 26. At 8 o'clock in the morning we sailed on the same route, moving upriver, which is very difficult because of the rapid current. Having covered half of the distance, we had to leave our "flat bottom boat" and borrow a *baidarka* from the Susitna inhabitants, which significantly sped up our journey. We arrived at the village about 10 o'clock in the evening, and found only a small number of inhabitants in the village. The majority of them are still scattered around.

June 27. There are still few Kenaitze in the village. The churchwarden is also away. Accordingly, the chapel is locked. I visited the other bank of the river, where the Susitna inhabitants now are building their new settlement. Here, on one of the hills, they also built a new chapel, which looks like a regular house. The size of this chapel is the same as the old one, the walls are made of logs and the roof is covered with planks. The building still does not have a floor, windows, or doors, and therefore still cannot be used for church services. In general, compared to the old structure, the new chapel produces a favorable impression. I am glad with all my heart that finally I can see the new chapel in this village after waiting for so long.

In Susitna, as in other areas (Kenai, Kasilof, Knik and Seldovia) the Alaska Commercial Company is now in the process of terminating its trading activities. Instead, to fill the void various petty exploiters have mushroomed all over. Very hot today, and it seems that thunderstorm might come, which is quite common in this area. In general, Susitna summers are far different from what we are used to seeing down in Cook Inlet. In Susitna, the summer season is usually a summer in the literal sense of the word, which is explained of course by the geographical location of the village. Situated far from the sea, Susitna is surrounded by mountains, which are covered with mighty forests. As a result, the vegetation here is abundant. Raspberries, cloudberries, viburnum and other berries ripen early.

Gardens here also bring abundant crops. A local trading agent collected last year in his garden several turnips which weighed about fourteen pounds each. Moreover, grain crops are successfully raised here, which is still impossible in Kenai. Before July rains rarely happen in this area, but when they come they look like real rainstorms. In winter in Susitna, deep snow falls, which sometimes forces people to stay at home. The only disaster that hits Susitna in summer is mosquitoes, which make life unbearable. For this reason, Susitna Kenaitze spend their summers by the sea, where they also dry fish and store it for their supplies.

At 5 o'clock in the evening I audited the chapel finances and found everything in order. The chapel income looks very good. At 6 o'clock in the evening vespers and matins. After singing a prayer glorifying the Savior I delivered a welcoming address. In this address, I expressed my joyful feelings concerning the completion of the new chapel, spoke about the significance of the prayer house for Christians, and explained to the natives how to cleanse their conscience when they prepare themselves for communion. Spoke through an interpreter, and the natives listened to me attentively. The evening time was devoted to resolving various cases.

June 28. In the morning I confessed and gave communion to three ailing people. After this, I served the Hours followed by the liturgy without consecration. I delivered a sermon, based on a Gospel theme, about the power of prayer and the sign of the cross. After the service, I called a meeting of parishioners, where we discussed a few misunderstandings between the *toion* and the other headmen. Came to a favorable solution. Right after the meeting, at a private request I sang a requiem service. Today I do not feel well: dull ache in my bones and some sort of general indisposition.

At 3 o'clock in the afternoon I baptized five infants and anointed with myrrh five others. At 6 o'clock in the evening the all-night vigil service devoted to saint apostles Peter and Paul. The chapel was crowded with praying faithful. Sweltering heat from the presence of so many people. After the service I conversed with school-age children, and then confessed them. On the whole, thirty-six people came for confession. Our Stepan, a former Kenai student, again did not do anything to advance Orthodoxy in Susitna. Children absolutely do not know anything. During confession many children stated that they had themselves approached Stepan and asked him to teach them how to pray, but each time Stepan, this evil person, turned down their noble requests. As a result, one has to admit that it is not worth taking the Kenaitze children away to distant schools and wasting money on them. You try to do good things for them, but they pay you back in the most ungrateful way. Native children are absolutely useless for the Lord's Church. Stepan from Susitna represents the third case of what I have already seen during my work in Kenai. The Susitna chapel was opened only three times during the whole year: during the Feasts of Nativity of Jesus Christ, New Year's Day, and Epiphany of Our Lord. And all this time, Stepan was staying in the village doing nothing. His behavior might well illustrate the Russian saying: "No matter how much you feed a wolf, he keeps on looking into the forest."

June 29. At 8 o'clock in the morning a morning prayer for those who are preparing for confession. Then, the Divine Liturgy of St. John Chrysostom. I delivered a sermon about raising children in the Christian spirit. All people who came for confession as well as sixty infants received communion. After I sang a prayer from the pulpit, I read requisite prayers before confession, and then after the dismissal the adult faithful listened to thanksgiving prayers. At 1 o'clock in the afternoon I started confession that ended about midnight. Today 105 natives came for confession, including five Mednovtsy: four men and one enfeebled old woman, who had been baptized by Hegumen Nikolai and who has not had a chance since then to confess and receive communion. Having heard about the arrival of a priest in Susitna, she did everything to come here and join in these holy mysteries, maybe for the last time in her life. At 6 o'clock in the evening I performed matins, which ended with the evening prayer required for those who prepare for holy communion.

June 30. At 8 o'clock in the morning the morning prayer, then the lesser blessing of water and the Divine Liturgy of St. John Chrysostom. One hundred and five natives received communion. After the prayer read from the pulpit, I offered the faithful relevant instructions and read thanksgiving prayers. After finishing the Divine Liturgy, I performed a customary prayer service in honor of the Mother of God. The chapel service ended very late and I felt extremely tired.

After dinner, there was a brotherhood meeting. By present, this brotherhood numbers eighteen members. During the meeting members paid their annual dues, and then heard the general report. By July 1900, in the mutual aid fund of the brotherhood there was $43.30. During this meeting $24.30 more was collected as dues. Only $2 had been spent for the past year. Therefore, by July 1901 there remains $65.60 in the mutual fund.

During the same meeting the members also resolved: (1) After the death of a brotherhood member, his wife, and if he did not have a wife, his children, and if he does not have children, his close relatives, shall receive $10 allowance from the mutual fund; (2) Each new member shall pay a $2 introductory membership fee. Before the dismissal the meeting ended with the collective singing of the prayer "It is truly meet and right." Then, two customary prayer services at private requests, and requiems for the deceased for the past year (three people).

July 1. At 8 o'clock in the morning the Hours followed by the liturgy without consecration. After the service, in the presence of the majority of the Kenaitze, I joined three couples in holy matrimony. Before the dismissal I spoke about relations between husband and wife. After dinner we went down to the mouth of the river and found a sloop from Knik awaiting us. At 7 o'clock in the evening we continued our route, but soon ran aground and had to stay here for the night.

July 2. Early in the morning, about 3 o'clock, we sailed on. Our progress was very slow because of the total calm. Moved by rowers, the sloop went as slow as a turtle. For this reason, we still were not able to reach Knik today, and had to stop for the night five miles from this village.

July 3. Today we finally reached the place. Most of the Kenaitze are out of Knik. They are only now beginning to return from their summer camps. The natives ask me to proceed with my ministrations as soon as possible, for they expect a fish run from day to day. The bulk of the fish run through this area for only three days. To miss these three days means to be left for the whole winter without dried fish. This is a very serious reason and I have to take it into consideration.

New Knik is famous for its berries: red currants and viburnum. All over, the entire place looks literally like a garden.

At 3 o'clock in the afternoon auditing of the chapel finances. Everything is in proper order. Incidentally, the interior of the chapel now looks more attractive than before. At 6 o'clock in the evening I served the matins. Twenty-five natives were present at the service.

July 4. At 9 o'clock in the morning the lesser blessing of water, then the Hours followed by the liturgy without consecration. After "Blessed be the name of the Lord henceforth and forever more" prayers recited in a monastic order [*desiatislovie*], then requisite prayers before confession, and at the end the Creed recited by all present natives. About seventy people attended this service. Afterwards, I baptized one infant and anointed with myrrh four others. At 1 o'clock in the afternoon confession. Fifty-seven people were present. At 6 o'clock in the evening the all-night vigil devoted to Venerable Father Sergius, Wonderworker of Radonezh. After the vigil, the evening prayer for those who are preparing themselves for communion.

July 5. At 8 o'clock in the morning a morning service, after this the Divine Liturgy of St. John Chrysostom. All people who came for confession as well as up to twenty infants received communion. After the prayer read from the pulpit, I delivered a welcoming address and then gave communion to the faithful as required. After completing the Divine Liturgy, I sang a requiem for a woman who died this winter. After dinner there was a brotherhood meeting, during which members paid their annual dues and heard the brotherhood's report. By July 1900 there was $29.45 in the mutual fund of the Knik brotherhood. $9 was donated and, therefore, there remained $38.45. Of this sum $7.50 was spent for assistance to ill members. So that, as of July 1901, they have $30.95. The meeting ended in the usual order. After the meeting I performed a marriage ceremony for one couple. On the same evening, having said good-bye to the Knik inhabitants, who accompanied my departure with loud gun shooting, I left Knik and set out again for Tyonek. I came to Tyonek about 9 o'clock in the morning on July 7.

July 7. At 6 o'clock in the evening I performed the all-night vigil at the Tyonek chapel. There were about thirty praying natives. These were all the people who remained in the village at this time.

July 8. I do not have communion bread. For this reason, I perform the Hours with the sequence requisite for the liturgy without consecration. The same number of praying people as yesterday. Immediately after this service, I baptized an infant who was born three days ago. The newborn received the name "Olga." Afterwards, I performed a water blessing prayer service in the new house of the local *toion*.

July 9. About 10 o'clock in the morning I set out by *baidarka* for Kustatan. Upon arrival, I performed the matins and the liturgy without consecration, and gave communion to nine people. Due to strong unfavorable winds I had to stay in this tiny village until July 13. On Saturday, July 14, we took the risk of crossing the Inlet to the Kenai side, and, thank God, reached the shore safely. By 12 noon of the same day I was at home. Upon arrival in Kenai I learned that all the children are suffering from diarrhea and sharp stomachache. The most upsetting news was that in my absence the large bell in our church cracked. My heart bleeds when I hear its soundless ringing, which reminds me more of painful moaning rather than church bell ringing. The fact that there is no money at all to buy a new bell aggravates our sorrows. My parishioners, who are still contributing money to cover the building of an extension to the church, cannot afford any new expenses. Here they are, our miserable conditions![54]

April 25, 1902. At 9 o'clock in the morning...I set out for Seldovia, where I arrived about 1 o'clock in the afternoon. All Seldovians are healthy, and besides at this time they stay at home. At 3 o'clock I baptized Pavel, the infant son of an American who is married to a Kenaitze woman. After this I anointed five other infants with myrrh. Then, auditing the chapel finances I found a few irregularities that had been already reported by a person who acted last winter as a temporary churchwarden and substituted for the permanent one. The chapel itself is clean and neat, and very well maintained. They also made some repairs. On the whole, it looks like the churchwarden is doing a good job and diligently cares about the maintenance of the chapel.

At 6 o'clock in the evening the all-night vigil. The whole chapel was filled with praying faithful. When I finished reading the expanded prayers glorifying the Savior [*velikoe slavoslovie*], I delivered a sermon based on the phrase from the Gospel: "Repent and Believe the Good News!" [Mark 1:15]. I noticed some ugly things in the Seldovians' behavior, and this was the reason I selected this topic for my sermon.

April 28. The Myrrh-Bearing Women week. Before the beginning of the chapel service, I read the cleansing prayer for women and then churched a child. Then, as required I performed the Divine Liturgy of St. John Chrysostom. During the liturgy I gave a sermon, which I based on the Gospel's instructions that we should zealously serve the Lord like the Myrrh-Bearing Women, who are now praised by the Holy Church, had served Him. Thirty infants received communion. The Divine Liturgy ended with requisite prayers before confession. Confession started at 1 o'clock in the afternoon. Matins and the evening prayer at 6 o'clock in the evening After this, I continued hearing confession. Overall, eighty-seven people came for confession.

April 29. At 8 o'clock in the morning I visited Ivan Iakovlev, an ailing old man, at his home, and gave him last rites. In the meantime, Nikolai Munin read the requisite morning prayer preceding holy communion. After this I performed a rite of the lesser blessing of water and then the Divine Liturgy of St. John Chrysostom, at the end of which I gave communion. All faithful who came for confession received communion. I delivered a sermon on the topic of what kind of feelings Christians should have when they touch a holy chalice. Nikolai Munin was in charge of the church choir.

After dinner, carrying the cross and holy water, I visited private houses. At 6 o'clock in the evening sang funeral services for the deceased (three persons), then two marriages. In the evening I was occupied with writing my journal.

June 14. Today, on the ship *Reporter,* which belongs to a fishing company, I departed [from Kenai] to the northern villages of the Kenai parish, Tyonek, Susitna, and Knik, to perform various ministrations. Ivan Soloviev, my travel companion last year, again goes with me. Unfortunately, we did not sail far enough on this ship. In so-called Nikishka, we had to get off the *Reporter* and wait for *Tyoonake*, a ship that belongs to another fishing company and that goes to Tyonek. We spent a night and then Saturday in this Nikishka, killing time by chatting with local fishermen and in a futile struggle against annoying mosquitoes.

June 16. Today, at 8 o'clock in the morning we finally boarded *Tyoonake* and set out for Tyonek. Arrived at this village at 11 o'clock in the evening. The Kenaitze had just finished praying and were coming out of the chapel. There are no sick people in the village. The first fish run recently ended, so now the Kenaitze have nothing to do. This summer Tyonek looks like a very busy place. One can see on the shore a large amount of various cargoes. Besides, a whole herd of horses grazes in a neighboring field, and crowds of Americans hurry back and forth. The reason for all these activities is the official decision to bring back to this area the project of building a railroad to Yukon. The railroad route is planned to start at the seacoast, at Resurrection Bay, which is an excellent harbor accessible in any season. From Resurrection Bay the railroad, bypassing Sanraik [Sunrise] will go through Knik and Susitna up to Yukon. This summer is devoted to survey work and calculation of estimates. The whole survey expedition is divided into five large parties. Each one selected a specific area for careful exploration. As far as Tyonek is concerned, this village has been designated as a storage base. If the survey brings positive results, construction work will start next summer.

Last summer the same kinds of work was conducted on Iliamna Bay, but this area tends to freeze and turned out to be inaccessible in winter. Therefore, surveyors had to leave the Iliamna area and look for a more hospitable place, which turned out to be Resurrection Bay. Be that as it may, the project of building the railroad to Yukon, or to be more specific, to Cape and Nome, is actively debated. Sooner or later the question will find a positive solution. This is what I wanted to add about the plans of enterprising Americans who are ready for any kind of ventures.

At 6 o'clock in the evening I served the matins. There were many praying faithful in the chapel. At the end of the service I delivered a sermon on the theme "Who follows Christ and who does not," which is based on our Gospel readings for today: "Come, follow me" [Math. 4:19]. Ivan Soloviev, my travel companion, interpreted the sermon. The Kenaitze listened attentively. After the service I audited the chapel finances and found everything in proper order. The chapel itself is clean and well maintained.

June 17. At 9 o'clock in the morning the Hours followed by the liturgy without consecration. Using a reading from the Gospel I spoke about the proper preparation for holy communion. After the service I gave last rites to an ailing Kenaitze girl. Then I devoted some time to resolving a few family disagreements among the Kenaitze. At 6 o'clock in the evening vespers and matins.

June 18. At 9 o'clock in the morning the Hours followed by the liturgy without consecration, which ended with requisite service before confession. I spoke about requirements for the people who are preparing themselves for holy confession. After the service was finished, I baptized a child who received the name Leontii. Afterwards, I anointed four infants with myrrh. At 1 o'clock in the afternoon I started confession. At 6 o'clock in the evening vespers and matins. The chapel service ended with an evening prayer before holy communion. After the service I continued hearing confessions. On the whole, seventy-three people came for confession. By evening a postal ship, *Tonquine*, put in. The railroad survey expedition set out for Knik.

June 19. At 8 o'clock in the morning a requisite prayer, the lesser blessing of water and then the Divine Liturgy of St. John Chrysostom, which ended with a requisite prayer before communion. Seventy-two people and more than thirty infants received communion. After the prayer "Blessed be the name of the Lord henceforth and forever more" I delivered a requisite address. After the service, there was a meeting of Tyonek's St. Innocent Brotherhood. At present the society numbers twenty registered members. The brotherhood' finances look as follows. By June 1, 1901, there was $22.90 in the mutual fund of the brotherhood. By June of 1902 members had contributed $20.60 in dues, and a new member contributed $1 as an introductory fee. In total, the mutual fund had $44.50. Then, during the past year $17.65 was spent for help to the sick and needy. Therefore, by June 1, 1902, $26.85 remains in the mutual fund of the Tyonek brotherhood.

June 20. At 8 o'clock in the morning, on a sloop that belongs to a local Kenaitze native, I set out for the first Knik (summer) nomadic camp, and safely arrived there about 2 o'clock in the afternoon. At this camp I found mostly women and children along with a few lame and feeble men. All the other men are scattered around. They were either hired to perform some jobs or are away on hunting trips. In addition, I received information that at this time it would be hard for me to find any other natives inside of the Knik Arm. As for the natives who live in this summer camp, they do not have any boats to be able to sail to the main village, where the chapel is located.

It might be interesting to note that the Knik Kenaitze have long been accustomed to the nomadic way of life. They change their places of residency almost each season, and reside separately from each other. Families sometimes live ten and more miles from each other. Only two families winter in the vicinity of the chapel. The rest of the Knik natives stay wherever the winter catches them. Generally speaking, Knik is the most unfavorable village for the priest's activities in the Kenai mission.

Taking into account the specific conditions of this region and having no desire to waste my time, I decided to perform all requisite ministrations right here at this summer camp. I instructed the Kenaitze that in future they should come together at one place at any time, and only after this invite the priest from Kenai, who will always visit them.

At 4 o'clock in the afternoon I baptized four infants. After this, I served vespers and matins. For my service the Kenaitze constructed a decent cabin from their tents. I finished the service, ended with requisite prayers before confession along with a sermon, in which I stressed that our ailments are the sources of our sins. Twenty-eight people received confession.

June 21. At 8 o'clock in the morning a morning prayer and the Divine Liturgy of St. John Chrysostom. Twenty-six adults and fifteen infants received holy communion. The Divine Liturgy ended with requisite prayers after holy communion. At 3 o'clock in the afternoon we left this summer camp and returned on the same sloop to so-called Point Possession. Only a few people live here on a permanent basis along with four families, who stay temporarily. They asked me to stay with them through Sunday. Of course, I had to honor their request.

June 22. The whole morning I devoted to preparing a decent place for performing my services. At 4 o'clock in the afternoon I anointed with myrrh three infants. All-night vigil at 6 o'clock in the evening, which ended with requisite prayers and a sermon before confession. After this I heard confessions of eighteen natives.

June 23. At 9 o'clock in the morning a requisite prayer, and then the Divine Liturgy of St. John Chrysostom. Through the interpreter I delivered a sermon based on the following Gospel words: "But seek first His kingdom and His righteousness, and these things will be given to you as well" [Math. 6:33]. There were eighteen adult and ten infant communicants. After "Blessed be the name of the Lord henceforth and forever more" I sang thanksgiving prayers. After completing the service, at a private request I performed a customary prayer service in honor of the Mother of God, and then sang funeral services for those who passed away in Knik last winter (four people). At 6 o'clock in the evening we left this nomadic camp and came to Tyonek on the same sloop. From Tyonek I plan to proceed to Susitna.

June 24. At 10 o'clock in the morning I performed a rite of holy matrimony for one couple at the Tyonek chapel. A native woman, who had illicitly lived with Arrii Giks [Harry Hicks], now married a local Kenaitze man. Later on, I sang a funeral service for Peter, a Kenaitze native who died this morning.

June 25. At 1 o'clock in the morning on the sloop, using a high water tide, we left for Susitna. We reached the mouth of the river with the same name about 6 o'clock in the evening and spent a night in the first summer nomadic camp that we ran across. We spent the whole next day (June 26) waiting for a Susitna *baidarka* that was expected to fetch us.

June 27. The expected *baidarka* arrived. Today we had to take a difficult route: sailing upriver. So that we decided not to waste time. Early in the morning, after giving confession and communion to six people who were not able to visit the chapel (not because of their health, but for various reasons), we immediately departed. The day was very hot and calm, and the air was infested with mosquitoes, which are notorious in the Susitna area. By 8 o'clock in the evening, with great difficulty we crawled up to the village. Again, a host of mosquitoes all over the place. Susitna is also famous for its wonderful gardens, which grow fast here and do not require any fertilizers.

June 28. Today we started our services at the recently built chapel. At 9 o'clock in the morning I performed a water blessing prayer service and sprinkled the new chapel with holy water. After this, I served the Hours followed by the liturgy without consecration. Later on, in a sermon appropriate to the moment, I stressed that in order to reach spiritual beauty we should renew, and how to reach this renewal. I also spoke about the advantage of the collective church prayer over the private and home-oriented one. Ivan Soloviev interpreted my talk.

The new chapel produced a pleasant impression, especially if you compare the new structure with the old one, which looked like a cattle barn rather than a prayer house. It was Arthur McConahay, a local trade agent, who contributed a great deal to the successful completion of the new chapel. McConahay helped this holy project both with his advice and with building materials, and even provided free food to the natives who were occupied with building the chapel. I wish we had more such nice people, especially in such remote corners of Alaska as Susitna, where people's needs are still frequently restricted to only eating and sleeping, and where only recently did the light of civilization start to penetrate.

Moreover, the same American wants to send his son to the Russian Orthodox school, and is ready to cover all tuition expenses. McConahay asked me to arrange this for him by the beginning of the next school year.

After the service I audited the local churchwarden. Everything was in proper order. The Susitna chapel now has $53 in cash. At 4 o'clock in the afternoon I baptized one child and anointed with myrrh eight others. At 6 o'clock in the evening the all-night vigil service with the prayer service from the matins [*Polieley*]. The service was devoted to saint apostles Paul and Peter. Having finished the service I confessed ten adolescent children. Confession was preceded by a talk where, in a simple accessible form, I instructed natives about the basics of the Christian faith. Twenty-seven people came for confession.

June 29. At 8 o'clock in the morning while Ivan Soloviev was reading the requisite prayer, I was performing last rites for Olga, a very ill Kenaitze woman, in her tent. Then I performed the Divine Liturgy of St. John Chrysostom. Using appropriate Gospel readings, I talked about saint apostles Paul and Peter, their lives before they accepted their apostolic duties, their missionary work, and finished my sermon with relevant instructions. There were twenty-seven adolescent children who came for confession along with fifty infants. The service ended with the requisite prayers before confession for the adult faithful who were preparing themselves for communion. At 6 o'clock in the evening the all-night vigil and the evening prayer.

June 30. The morning prayer in the beginning of the day, after this there was the Divine Liturgy of St. John Chrysostom, which ended with thanksgiving prayers after the faithful received holy communion. Using the Gospel readings, I talked about the power of deep, genuine, strong faith, and also explained who we should appeal to in all our needs and sorrows. All natives who came for confession received communion. After celebrating the Divine Liturgy, at a private request I performed two customary prayer services in honor of the Mother of God. After this, I married two couples, and sang a funeral service for seven natives who died during the past year.

At 6 o'clock in the evening, having said good-bye to the Susitna inhabitants, we left their village and descended to the mouth of the river. Here we rested a little, and at midnight with a low tide we set out again for Tyonek, where we would have to wait for a boat, which would bring us back to Kenai.

July 4. Finally, after long wanderings, I returned safely to Kenai, and found everybody in good health except our songleader, whose health deteriorated during our absence. On July 8 Hieromonk, Father Sebastian Dabovich, the Dean of Clergy, arrived in Kenai to inspect our parish. From July 22 to July 28 Father Dabovich and I visited Seldovia and Aleksandrovsk, where I performed various ministrations, while the Dean of Clergy talked with the inhabitants concerning their daily life.

June 2, 1904. Today, at 3 o' clock in the morning (at this time we do not have dark nights here) Kenai parishioners were happy to meet and welcome their archpastor, the Most Reverend Innocent, Bishop of Alaska, who along with Peter I. Chubarov, his traveling companion, safely arrived at Kenai on the ship *Tyonok* [the original spelling]. His Grace did not want to disturb the villagers, who were still peacefully sleeping. And besides, he wished to rest himself after his trip. For this reason, the Bishop suggested that we postpone the ceremony of welcoming him until tomorrow.

The ceremony took place next day at 8 o'clock in the morning. Under accompaniment of solemn bell ringing all Kenai parishioners who were present at this time in the village gathered in the church. Since the coming of the Most Reverend Father happened so unexpectedly for us, in his address to the faithful he spoke about the unexpected second coming of Christ. In his sermon Father instructed his spiritual flock to take more care of their souls, and not to burden themselves with sins, or else they would be subjected to eternal death and be denied entrance to the Heavenly Kingdom. All faithful listened with great attention to these simple, accessible, and highly instructive words of the archpastor. His instructions definitely forced many of them to think about their future.

After Father's speech, in his presence I performed a customary prayer service in honor of the Assumption of the Mother of God, the feast after which our Kenai church was consecrated. Then Father examined the church both within and without, and was pleased to find everything in good order.

June 3. The whole day Father was occupied with looking into various parish-related matters.

June 4. Today his Grace examined the [Kenaitze] village, cemetery, and church lands. He did not forget to visit the modest tomb of the elder Hegumen Nikolai. Many parishioners came to see Father and to converse with him about parish life.

June 5. At 6 o'clock in the evening the all-night vigil was celebrated. While the priest [Bortnovskii] performed the service, his Grace prayed in the sanctuary. About eighty faithful visited the service. During the summer time the majority of men leave Kenai and scatter around various places in the Cook Inlet area in search of jobs. That is why so few people showed up for the service. His Grace liked how the children of school sang psalms and read prayers.

June 6. At 9 o'clock in the morning I celebrated the Divine Liturgy of St. John Chrysostom, which ended with a customary prayer service in honor of the Mother of God. Before prayer service our archpastor delivered a sermon based on a Gospel reading [Math. 21:6, 22–23]. After the sermon his Grace handed over books as gifts to the students who showed the best results in school. Also, his Grace publicly praised Aleksandr Daryin, the Kenai churchwarden, and A. A. Demidov, a local parishioner, for their zealous care of the Kenai church. Then our archpastor wished many years of life to the All-Russia Imperial Family, the President of the United States and the Holy Synod. His Grace also wished many years of life to the priest of the Kenai church of Assumption and to all parishioners. During the Divine Liturgy about thirty infants received communion. This time about 100 faithful came for the service. After dinner Father examined the vestry, archive, library, and bell tower, and he seems to have been satisfied with everything.

At 7 o'clock in the evening having provided his archpastoral blessing to everyone who gathered to see him off, his Grace, accompanied by the priest [Bortnovskii] and by his traveling companion P. I. Chubarov, left Kenai on the same ship for Seldovia in order to board *Bertha* in this village and continue the route. Pleasant bell ringing and loud gun shooting accompanied the departure of our merciful and loving archpastor. A large crowd of parishioners along with their wives and children went out to see him off. Our Lord, grant him a happy trip and a safe return!

June 7. At 7 o'clock in the morning Father and his traveling companions safely arrived at Seldovia. En route we were caught in a fresh, strong, and contrary wind, which rolled the ship. Father felt dizzy, and spent most of the time on the deck trying to breathe fresh air. It was hard for us to watch the sufferings of our archpastor, but the stormy nature of the sea knows no mercy. In this regard our archpastor instructed us, "Human life goes on in the same manner. At first, it is stormy and restless, but then the time comes that one nears a quiet harbor. May blessed be those who hold tightly the helm of their own life and who with a strong hand navigate themselves to the Divine Harbor." At 8 o'clock in the morning his Grace entered the Seldovia chapel, where, after the church bells started to ring, all the inhabitants immediately gathered and waited for him. Holding the Holy Cross and holy water the priest [Bortnovskii] met his Grace at the entrance. After this a short prayer service was celebrated. During his spare time Father inspected the local cemetery.

At 6 o'clock in the evening the all-night vigil with the prayer and service sequence from the matins [*Polieley*]. From the moment when prayers glorifying our Savior and Mother of God were read, Father himself took charge and completed the rest of the vigil service. The service was devoted to St. Nicholas, the Heavenly protector of the Seldovia chapel. The songleader, Nikolai Fomin, was in charge of the church choir.

June 8. At 9 o'clock in the morning the priest [Bortnovskii], who was holding the holy cross, met his Grace at the entrance of the chapel. Then after celebrating the Hours, they together started performing the requisite Divine Liturgy of St. John Chrysostom. After the Divine Liturgy, the Father taught the Seldovians using examples from the life of St. Nicholas. Specifically, he instructed parents to raise their children in the Christian manner, and for this purpose to send them to school. Father reminded the Seldovians to take better care of their chapel, and by next year to build a portico with a bell tower. Creole Ivan S. Aleksandrov, a former songleader in the Nuchek chapel, interpreted Father's words into the local tongue. There were four adult and thirty infant communicants during the liturgy. At 8 o'clock in the evening accompanied by bell ringing and loud gun shooting, his Grace departed from the village on the *Bertha*, and left in the minds of Seldovians the most pleasant recollections about his archpastoral visit to us unworthy people. Cordial filial gratitude to our dear archpastor from all of us. We pray for him and wish him many years of life for the sake of the prosperity of Orthodoxy in wild and severe Alaska!

Ioann Bortnovskii to Hegumen Sebastian, the Dean of Clergy of the Sitka District. June 2, 1904[55]

Nikolaevsk and Kalifornskoe [the spelling in the original], villages of the Kenai parish, which had before been small and insignificant in population, are now growing in size, mostly due to the resettlement of people from other villages. As a result, people in these settlements feel the need to build chapels, which they eagerly promised to construct at their own expense, if the ecclesiastical authorities would give them permission. I humbly request Your Right Reverence to approach his Grace about this case. I have the honor to be your most humble servant, Priest Ioann Bortnovskii.

St. Nicholas Temperance Society, Records of Minutes, 1907[56]

The new members of the society from Seldovia village who joined the society for three years: Andrei Tolchek, Nikolai Tolchek and Ivan Kanitak.

On January 15 of 1907 there was a weekly meeting of the Temperance Society. As usual in the beginning there was the singing of a troparion to St. Nicholas. Then V. A. Demidov read aloud an article "On Greediness." At the end everybody sang "Praise the Name of the Lord" and "Holy God." Then there was again reading, in translation into the Kenai language, of an article "I Have No Time." After one more song, people listened to Father Ioann [Bortnovskii] who read from an article, "Getting Sober." The first part of the meeting ended with a prayer. In the same evening during the second part of the meeting members drank tea and amused themselves with various games.

On January 21 of 1907 the following person joined the Temperance Society by taking an oath not to drink for the rest of her life: Ekaterina Mishakoff. Paros Danilova and Anna Shangai joined the society by taking an oath not to drink for a year.

On January 22 of 1907 there was a weekly meeting of the Temperance Society. The meeting was opened with a prayer to St. Nicholas. Then V. A. Demidov read a small article "Do Inhabitants of Heaven Manifest Themselves to Us at the Present Time." After this reading members sang "We Sing to You." Then A. Pamfilov read and translated into the Kenaitze language the article "Getting Sober." After this singing, of the hymn: "By the Waters of Babylon." Father Ioann read the article "Laughing and Sinning." A second part of the meeting during the same evening was devoted to tea drinking and amusements.

On January 29, 1907 there was a regular meeting of the Temperance Society. The meeting was opened with a regular prayer. Then V. A. Demidov read an article entitled "The Cross Is Our Protection." Then, reciting of "We Sing to You." After this reading, in translation into the Kenai language, "Wonder of Faith." Again singing a hymn. Then a reading by Father Ioann of "For Other People's Sins." The second part of the evening: tea drinking and games.

February 5, 1907. A monthly meeting of the Temperance Society was opened in the building of the Kenai school with singing of the *troparion* to St. Nicholas. Then V. A. Demidov, the society's secretary, read the minutes of the previous meeting and made a financial report. After this members discussed the activities of the society. There was a discussion of membership fees. Should some members contribute their regular fees or not? It was decided that those who had money should pay monthly fees (ten cents a month), while those who do not may be a member without contributing any fee. Then the chairman of the meeting addressed the audience with a speech, in which he eloquently described the ugliness of alcohol abuse and, on the contrary, the healthful influence of the Temperance Society. In response, Vasilii Kliakvae, one of the members, honestly stated (here are his actual words), "From the beginning I have seen only good things in this Society. Some time ago I myself was a miserable drunkard and wasted all my belongings on drink, to the point that I could not even buy bread for Christmas. The only thing left was vodka that I brewed myself. I thank the Savior that now I do not drink and wish everybody would quit doing this because alcohol is poison."

February 19, 1907. There was a weekly meeting of the Society's members. After a regular prayer, V. A. Demidov read a small story, "Change." Then, singing "Blagoobraznii Joseph." Then translating "Do We Wish to Get to Heaven?" into the Kenai language by A. Pamfilov.

February 19, 1907. Iosif Z. Oskolkoff quit his membership because his oath expired.

February 26, 1907. There was a weekly meeting of the members of the Temperance Society. After a regular prayer, V. A. Demidov read a story, "Strange Man," from the book "Leisure for a Christian." Upon finishing reading, members sang "It is truly meet and right." Then Aleksandr Pamfilov read and simultaneously translated into the Kenaitze "Punished Sacrilege." The chairman did not read this time. Instead, he addressed those members of the Society whose terms had expired and asked them not to return to their ugly behavior, but to renew their oaths. For the second part of the evening one of the members, Afanasii Almanakh, arranged a supper for all members.

March 4, 1907. Iakov [Jacob] Oskolkoff joined the Society by taking an oath not to drink for one year. On the same day, a few members renewed their oaths: Agripina Bakhov for her entire life, Petr Bakhov and Vasilii A. Demidov for one year.

March 11, 1907. Joined the Society: Matrena Ltultish, her entire life, Aleksandr Abakhchi (renewed his oath), and Maria Abakhchi, for her entire life (renewed her oaths). For three years: Tatiana Knukhuutil, Nikolai Mishakoff and Lukia Mamalia (renewed her oath). For two years: Tatiana Viadro, Nikolai Soloviev, Evgenii Man (renewed his oath), Anastasiia Baktuit. For one year: Anna Sorokovikov, Akilina Kiiu, Feodor Chulgin (renewed his oath).

January 29, 1907. Vlasii Anakhupak, a member of the St. Nicholas Temperance Society, died in Aleksandrovsk village.

March 12, 1907. There was a monthly meeting of members of the St. Nicholas Temperance Society. Traditionally, the meeting was opened with a singing of [the *troparion*] to St. Nicholas. Then Father chairman addressed the members of the Society with a speech. After this the society's secretary read the minutes of the previous meeting and provided a financial report. Then there was a discussion about amusements and tea drinking. Resolved: avoid any amusements during Lent. There was also a discussion about a supper meal for the coming Holy Easter. All members unanimously decided to cooperate and contributed to arrange such a supper. In addition, some female members promised to provide bread, potatoes, and other things, while some male members promised to bring meat. Simeon Chickalusion was elected as the chief cook. He also selected four members to help him.

April 2, 1907. There was a monthly meeting of the Kenai St. Nicholas Temperance Society. All members who live in Kenai participated in this meeting. As always, the meeting was opened with a prayer to St. Nicholas. Then the chairman read the by-laws of the society for the new members, and A. Pamfilov translated them into the Kenaitze language. Also, the chairman reminded all members that those who pay dues are expected to pay them in time, which is especially important in connection with the coming dinner they want to organize.

Joseph Tugubik, Afanasii Almanakh, and Aleksei Mednovsky quit their membership because of the expiration of their terms.

April 8, 1907. Akakii Kanitak, a member of the Kenai St. Nicholas Temperance Society, died in Seldovia village.

April 8, 1907. Joined the Temperance Society: For one year: Nikolai Tishdilusion. For two years: Peter Vedro, Aleksei Knikov, Alexandra Knikov and Nadezhda Mednovsky. For three years: Simeon Chickalusion. For whole life: Anna Bakhov.

April 18, 1907. Joined the Temperance Society with an oath not to drink for one year: Anna Ivanov.

April 19, 1907. Joined the Temperance Society with an oath not to drink for two years: Aleksandr D. Daryin and Stepan Knushdul (renewed his oath).

April 21, 1907. Joined the Temperance Society: Iosif Z. Oskolkoff for ten years (renewed his oath), Afanasii Almanakh for one year, Maxim Knukhuutil for three years. Grigorii P. Oskolkoff for five years, Feodor Kvasnikov for one year.

April 22, 1907. Joined the Temperance Society for one year: Aleksei Mednovsky (renewed his oath).

April 23, 1907. Joined the Temperance Society for one year: Phil[lip] Wilson.

April 24, 1907. The Society's members held a dinner arranged at their mutual expense. Upon the end of the dinner, members amused themselves with various games and stereoscopes.

April 30, 1907. Joined the Temperance Society: Pavel Kalifornskii for three years, Nikonor Ltultish for three years.

May 6, 1907. Joined the Temperance Society from the Seldovia village: Aleksandr Kvasnikov for two years. Ivan Kvasnikov for one year, Flor Fomin for one year.

May 10, 1907. For five years: Mikhail Balashov, Anisiia Balashov (his wife), Timofei Balashov, and Aleksei Berestov.

May 13, 1907. Joined for the rest of their lives: Evgeniia Agina, Irina Mamchak, Grigorii Anakhukak, Evgeniia Mamchak, Marfa Mamchak, Ljubov Ababak, Sofia Anakhupak, Elisaveta Mamchak, Andrei Agikjia, Timofei Maltsev.

May 14, 1907. For the rest of his life: Peter Nosskii, a Japanese. For one year: Paraskoviia Nosskaia, Illarion Ljuku.

June 10, 1907. Expelled from the Society for violation of their oaths: Flor Fomin and Alex Ryan.

September 17, 1907. Joined the Temperance Society: Sofia Wilson (renewed) with an oath for one year. Vasilii Petrov and Simeon Yunisin for two years.

October 8, 1907. There was a monthly meeting of the members of the Temperance Society. Participated: all members of the society who live in Kenai. The meeting was opened with a prayer to St. Nicholas. Then there was an election of the new chairman of the Society to replace Father Ioann Bortnovskii, who recently quit. Everybody voted for the newly arrived Priest Pavel A. Shadura. After this all documentation of the society was inspected. As it turned out there were twelve persons who had violated their oaths: Feodor Malia, his wife Lukiia, Evgeniia Mann, Maxim Knukhutil, his wife Tatiana, Pavel Morfei, Mikhail Kasilofsky, Aleksei Kaviak, Victor Inchidishin, Vasilii Inchidishin, Stepan Kustatanovsky and Daria Oskolkoff. Father Chairman advised all these people who broke their oaths to prepare for Communion by worshipping and fasting. He also pointed that those who want may join the society again. Then Father Pavel Shadura made a speech addressed to all members and reminded everybody that those who violate their oaths for a second time would be strongly punished.

CHAPTER SIX

Priest Pavel Shadura

Andrei Kashevarov to Pavel Shadura, June 16–29, 1909[57]

Browsing the church rosters from the Kenai parish I found the entries that require your explanations. You are to provide these explanations to the North American Ecclesiastical Consistory and attach all relevant documents from the Kenai church. In short, I ask you to send your explanations to our office as soon as possible.

In a book of birth registrations for 1908, in a marriage section under number [blank space] there is a name, Ekaterina Mishakoff, fourteen and a half years old. I assume that you are familiar with the church rule that forbids priests to marry girls before they reach sixteen. At the same time, in view of special conditions of the Alaskan life, the Most Reverend Nikolai permitted Alaskan priests to marry girls of fifteen and a half years old. Also, in the same section under number nine there is another name, Olga Vaiudulchik, fifteen years old. I ask you to explain why you married these two children. Did you receive permission from the Archbishop, who is the only one who may bypass church regulations? Ecclesiastical authorities subject those priests who marry people under their legal age to penalties. The American laws also clearly forbid this practice.

A. Kashevarov, Dean of Clergy.

Pavel Shadura's Response to Aleksandr Kashevarov, July 8, 1909[58]

The girl I mentioned was an orphan and lived with her married sister. The first couple you referred to was married by my predecessor. In fact, I can report many other similar incidents if you ask me to do so. Yes, I had to marry these two girls without permission of my church superiors. If I had not agreed, they could have simply concluded civil marriages without going to church, which might have created a bad precedent for other parishioners. In these areas men start raising brides for themselves from the time when these girls are still babies. When girls reach thirteen or fourteen, the men begin living with them in a natural way. American scoundrels also frequently abduct these young native girls and make them their concubines.

With regard to what I just mentioned, I ask you and the Ecclesiastical Consistory to provide further instructions, for I recognize that it was my fault to marry them. I want to add that when I married Ekaterina Mishakoff, fourteen years old, and Olga Vaiudulchik, fifteen years old, they were already mothers. The first one gave birth to one child, the second one had already given birth to two children. According to Orthodox and American law, both of them are indeed still under legal age.

I became familiar with similar facts during my nine-year missionary practice in Alaska. It frequently works as follows. Say, somebody brings his bride to a missionary. During his visits to native villages a priest certainly does not carry with him records of birth registrations. If a missionary sees that the girl looks physically developed and ready to be married, but is too young to fit the church and civil laws, he usually adds one, two, or three years and marries her.

I married the girl named Ekaterina Mishakoff only after persistent requests from her parents who wanted to cover the sin she had already committed. Under an oath the parents signed a statement that said that they would share all consequences of such a marriage. You will find this statement, signed by witnesses, attached to this letter.

To clarify this and other confusing problems of church practice, I approached his Grace Innocent, Bishop of Alaska, who gave me detailed guidelines how to act in such situations, and I hope that there will be no similar deviations from church practice in future.

Pavel Shadura.

Agenda for the Coming Meeting of the Kenai Brotherhood Scheduled for November 7, 1910[59]

(1) Prayer; (2) roll call; (3) financial matters; (4) to check mutual debts of members; (5) to check membership dues; (6) concerning the dues, to remind the members of the significance of the Society. Some members still do not understand or do not want to understand the usefulness of the Society; (7) to name those who did not pay the dues and indicate how much; (8) to extend special thanks to old men and women for the meticulous payments of their dues; (9) to suggest that those who do not pay their dues shall be fined; (10) in order to discipline those who do not pay to propose establishment of the brotherhood's pawnshop that will hold specific articles from belonging to nonpaying members as a guarantee that they would fulfill their obligations by a deadline; (11) to point to Stepan Mishakoff that when he was ill he had already received allowances from the mutual fund at the amount of more than $20; (12) to note in public Nikolai A. Kalifornskii's model behavior; (13) to assign one of the members (to help the brotherhood's marshal)

to supervise those members who are still prone to drinking; (14) to remind members of the fines, which are usually imposed on those who are absent from the brotherhood meetings without an excuse. Also, to remind members of the fines imposed on those members who by drinking drive themselves to the ugliest state; especially it concerns those who brew "mukola" and offer it to the others. Such evil things do not correspond to the status of a brotherhood member; (15) to check how regularly members wear brotherhood badges and to remind them to show up for the meetings with their badges; (16) to inquire if the brotherhood will provide some allowances to the poor (Peter Kiiu); (17) to talk about my cows, maybe some poor brotherhood member will take care of them?

Report to Aleksandr, Bishop of Alaska, October 10, 1911[60]

It is my duty to present to Your Grace: (1) a petition from Aleksandr Demidov, a songleader from the Kenai Assumption Church, (2) a letter from an American citizen, Matt Hute, and (3) minutes of meetings of my parishioners concerning embezzlement of church materials and money by the late churchwarden. This is also to ask Your permission to confirm in their positions newly elected churchwardens Petr Bakhov and his assistant Petr Mishakoff, who were elected on October 1, 1911.

With regard to the petition from Aleksandr Demidov, my co-worker, I would like to add that some time ago I reported his behavior to his Grace, Innocent and then to his Grace Archbishop of North America and the Aleutians. Both of them instructed me what to do about this songleader.

For two years Demidov behaved and fulfilled his duties, but this year, under the influence of American scoundrels who live here, he again slipped into card playing and drinking, which does not correspond to the position he occupies. He ruins the results of my work and corrupts local uncivilized natives. Demidov is greedy, and all my persuasions to convince him to change his behavior have failed. Recently he directly asked me to fire him beginning of the next year (1912). Your Grace, would You, please, allow him to try to rebuild his life out of the church? Would You, also, permit me to find an assistant who might replace him and to allocate money to pay to such person in 1912?

Now, concerning the letter of Matt Hute, an American citizen. In my view, it will be better for this groom to wait until the bride comes of age, which will happen on May 21, 1912. Moreover, although she is already a mature girl, the bride herself is not in a hurry. Otherwise it might create a bad precedent for the local natives and for untamed American scoundrels. Mr. Matt Hute is a good man, but many others are dishonest. I am familiar with the latter type from my own missionary practice. Some time ago I had to marry two young mothers who were under the legal age, which later dragged me into an extensive correspondence with the Dean of Clergy about the whole incident. One has to live here in order to see all these disgraceful things, which untamed American drunkards do to this people.

Asking for your archpastoral blessings, I have an honor to be your humble servant, Priest Pavel Shadura.

Report to the Dean of Clergy Mikhail [Andreevich] on Conditions in the Kenai Parish, April 25, 1913[61]

In this year, 1912, with God's help I visited all the villages of my parishioners. All residents of the village usually expect the priest and welcome him with love and fulfill their Christian duties, with the exception of those who have to be away performing their paid jobs. Yet, I noticed that last year with the opening of saloons in many villages the morality of parishioners began to decline. Almost all members of the temperance society broke their temperance oaths. Many natives drank away all their summer salaries and starved in winter, subsisting on handouts from their kind neighbors. Also, the church and chapel donations continually decreased, almost by half. Given the high food prices, the summer salaries of the natives are far from enough for living. But instead of saving an extra cent for the future, they waste their last pennies for a drink. Such a temptation do they have for drunkenness. Five or six years ago natives lived here as in a paradise. Then evil people came and built saloons, which completely corrupted these children of nature. In the villages, which are located further from the mission, starvation made some natives turn back to their shamanistic songs and dances in order to extract the last cents from their working neighbors. Headmen took away all valuable things and money from chapels and brotherhoods and wasted them on their give-away feasts [*igrushki*].[62] No threats or punishments affect them. The only thing they are afraid of is dying without receiving last rites. The natives believe that the priest exists in order to marry them (although some of them are already married by judges), baptize them, provide last rites, perform funeral services, and pray for them after they die. The question of how to live in order to deserve access to the Heavenly Kingdom does not interest them. Miserable people [*ljudishki*]. Drunkenness brings moral looseness, hypocrisy, lies, sanctimoniousness and other vices. These facts can be observed not only in the Kenai village populated by the uncivilized Kenaitze, but in the center of the mission itself, where educated Creoles live. The latter sometimes behave even worse than natives and offend the priest and God's temple by coming drunk to a collective prayer. In many other respects there are practically no differences in lifestyles between the Creoles and the Kenaitze.

With minor exceptions, everybody treats the priest with respect. Strange as it may sound, it is the poor people who usually buy candles. As for the Creoles and people who live a well-to-do life, they tend to buy candles on credit. In all villages people care about maintenance of the chapels, which are clean and are kept in proper order. Yet it is only in the Kenai village that church services are conducted on a regular basis because Kenai is the place where the priest lives. Almost each service is accompanied by a sermon. In addition, there are Sunday evening readings. Sometimes we organize solemn dinners in order to enhance the religious life of parishioners. In three villages, services are conducted by local songleaders. In the other four settlements, for lack of resources and qualified people, services are held only when the priest comes. People do believe in God and pray to Him, although they do not always know the prayers, and are able to make the sign of the cross (we should be satisfied that at least they did not forget this habit). Our parochial schools in the villages have not functioned for the past few years. Now they have only American schools. In the Kenai village there is a parochial school, where the priest himself teaches all the classes. About twenty-five children studied at the school. In such villages as Kenai, Ninilchik, Seldovia, and Aleksandrovsk almost all parishioners know how to read at least a little. They speak Russian and know prayers. As far as the northern villages are concerned, complete wilderness and darkness reign there. Yet all parishioners love their chapels and in winter, especially during great feasts, almost everybody comes to their temples. In contrast, in summer all the men leave their villages to perform various jobs or wander around with their families hunting and fishing. Therefore, during summer chapels usually stay closed. If the church or chapels need some repairing, residents readily donate from their meager salaries as much as they can. Many parishioners have a hard time making ends meet. And besides, saloons do not give them too much of a chance to save their money. If the natives had been more concerned about saving, they could have lived a decent life. Instead, in winter they usually starve, especially by the springtime, when there are no jobs available, the hunting is poor, and the skins are not so valuable. The priest does not get anything for performing ministrations except receiving from twenty-five cents to one dollar for conducting a customary prayer service. Creoles regularly send their children to school except a few stubborn Americans. As for the Kenaitze, they are very much attached to their children and still are not aware of the benefits of education. They do not like to send their children to school and I have to force them to do it. Fortunately, they listen to me and, although not regularly, the Kenaitze do send their offspring to classes. Kenaitze children are not familiar with discipline and are raised in the lap of nature. This is all I can say about the religious and moral life of my parishioners.

With the opening of saloons in some villages the temperance society in the Kenai mission is now almost gone, although some people still join the society for a short while. Almost all the people who took oaths not to drink for the rest of their lives have now broken those vows, if not openly, then secretly. The priest leads a sober life and always lectures on the harmful effects of drunkenness. Parishioners are very well aware of these effects of alcohol, but cannot resist the temptation of it and continue drinking. If natives have a chance to get hold of a drink, they would rather starve, but have the drink. I am petitioning the authorities to close all these hideous dens [*bogomerzkie zavedenia*] in my parish. In the Kenai village there is a brotherhood consecrated after Protection of the Most Holy Mother of God. On the whole, the brotherhood is doing not bad at all with a fund of about $88. Yet, many members are expelled from the society for irregular payment of dues. They have money for drinking, but do not pay membership dues for several years. If everything turns out all right, we will be able to bring many parishioners back to the brotherhood. For a long time we have wanted to invest this money [$88] in something, but still cannot decide, because we fear to lose everything. That is all.

Pavel Shadura.

Report on Conditions in the Parish for 1913[63]

For the past year, 1913, nothing special happened in the Kenai parish. When the priest visited villages to perform various ministrations, all residents welcomed him with love, and they completely fulfilled their Christian duties except those who were away for hired jobs. With the opening of saloons in many villages, I noticed that the morality and sober life of my parishioners started to decline. Almost all the people who took an oath not to drink violated it, if not openly, then secretly. Those whose oaths ended do not have a desire to renew them. My parishioners in northern villages are so uncivilized that they cannot live a sober life when saloons are around. Yet with the help of God and good people we were able to shut down a saloon in the Kenai village. After this all residents immediately turned to a sober and godly life without taking any special oaths. I do not believe the possibility of any sober life in Alaska in the areas where saloons exist.

Petition to Evdokim, Archbishop of the Aleutians and North America, December 18, 1915[64]

Your Grace, our Father, I ask you to help me resolve a few problems. After an American public school for whites was opened here in the Kenai village my congregation split into two groups: the Creole ("white") and the Kenaitze ("black") factions. Earlier, for five years in our village we had another school, which had been built for the Indians, and which was subordinated to some other department. This school for the Indians admitted everybody, and I experienced no troubles at all. Our parochial school and the Indian school worked together. Now, a school board requires that all children go only to the new American school, even during the days of Orthodox feasts. I spoke against this and explained to people the proper rules of raising their children. As a result, some of my parishioners turned against me. Many local whites, Russian Finns and Swedish Baptists, the enemies of the Russian Church and the Orthodox school, are married to Creole women, who under influence of their husbands have stopped sending their children both to the Russian school and to the church during Orthodox feasts. With regard to the latter, I warned them that those whose children would not learn prayers will be denied a confession. Was I too strict with them? I know with certainty that their children do not pray at all and know nothing, although they have a good opportunity to learn something because I teach at our parochial school each day.

Now I am switching to another question. An American teacher from the Tyonek village plans to establish a "reservation station" for all Indians, excluding whites. According to church regulations, sixteen years of age is the time when a girl is allowed to get married. This teacher has asked me to raise this minimum age to eighteen years in order to provide local native people with a more efficient education. I promised him to approach Your Grace to make an inquiry if we can help him in this matter. In my view, such a measure may be very helpful to local Indians, for their children are still immature when they are sixteen.

I congratulate you with this new year of 1916 and wish you many happy years. Priest Pavel Shadura.

A Sketch of the Kenai Parish [c. 1916][65]

Part I

(1) The Kenai village (St. Nicholas Redoubt) is located on a small hill at the very mouth of the Kenai River that flows into the Cook Inlet. To the northeast and southeast of Kenai wild forests stretch out, and the village itself looks as though it were located on the edge of the forest, in which one can find such wild animals as the moose, hare, lynx, mink, otter (along small rivers), ermine, a few types of foxes and others.

In summer red and king salmon and many other different species of fish run through the waters of the inlet. Although the Kenai soil is mainly composed of clay and sand, it appears to be fertile because local people collect good crops of potato, cabbage, carrots, and rutabaga. One can also find many other vegetables in the gardens of local residents.

(2) The Kenai parish includes eight villages populated by the Creoles, Kenaitze, Aleuts and few Russians. The overall number of adult male and female parishioners is 1070. It may be said that in terms of material well-being local residents are fairly secure. In summer time canneries often provide the inhabitants of Kenai and other neighboring villages with jobs. Local residents also do fishing for the same canneries. On average, in summer people earn from $350 to $400 per

person. In winter some of them go hunting, while others cut wood for the fish canneries.

(3) The history of the parish goes back to 1841, when the Russian-American Company operated in this area. The development and gradual advance of Orthodoxy started with Hegumen Nikolai, who baptized local heathen Kenaitze. According to stories told by older natives, the Kenaitze revered this missionary and Orthodoxy in general. These old people say that during the time of Hegumen Nikolai local residents approached church services and the temple in a sincere and openly naive manner. Hardly having any experience in and understanding of the faith, the Kenaitze expressed their religious aspirations as they could, which sometimes did not correspond with the teaching of the Orthodox Church. Aleksei Pamfilov, a Kenai old-timer who is still alive, relates such a characteristic episode. A Kenaitze parishioner, who was poor but very well disposed to the church, decided to make a donation to the temple. For this purpose, he stole a fur of black fox from his sister and brought it to Father Nikolai, saying that this was his donation to the church. Next day Father Nikolai found out about everything and to the disappointment of the poor Kenaitze imposed on him an appropriate church punishment

Part II

(1) The church occupies the best site in the village and stands on an even surface. The present church building is the second one. The first church was built in 1849 or, to be exact, was rebuilt from the local chapel erected by the Russian-American Company in 1841. In 1896 the new church was built partially at local expense and partially on the donation of $400 from the diocese authorities. The church is built of wooden logs and covered with wooden boards on the outside.

Part III

The catalogue of books from the church library and the list of various papers stored in the church archive are attached to this document.

Part IV

(1) Since the establishment of the parish no special misfortunes or calamities have visited the church with the exception of various dangerous adventures, which missionaries had to go through during their regular trips around their parish. Stories of Aleksei Pamfilov, who is one of the oldest Creole residents of the Kenai village and who also served as an interpreter for Father Nikolai (the position he occupies to the present day), shed more light on this part of missionary life. For example, he remembers that at that time more than once and frequently in win-

ter the missionary had to go on snow shoes to Skilak Lake, where in those years there was a native village, which was located sixty miles from Kenai. During one of these trips, while crossing a small river, both Father Nikolai and Pamfilov fell through the ice. The only thing that saved them was a backpack with all necessary items for church services. Father Nikolai's backpack got stuck at the edge of the ice, which eventually saved their lives.

(3) Not much information can be provided about the attitudes of American citizens toward Orthodox church services from the establishment of the mission to 1882. During these years few American citizens lived in Kenai. One Aleksandr Ryan, who has been living in Kenai since 1888, says that at that time the attitude of the American citizens to the Orthodox services was more respectful. Later, when many new people arrived in the area, the respectful attitude toward Orthodox services and to the teaching of the Orthodox Church in general decreased. For example, the missionary Aleksandr Iaroshevich reprimanded a certain Palmer, who resided in the Knik village, for an illicit cohabitation with a local Kenaitze woman. In response, Palmer attacked the missionary and severely beat him. At that time there were no judicial authorities in this region. Many other witnesses also confirm this information. As for the present-day American citizens, there are few real Americans among them. They are mostly representatives of various nationalities such as Swedes, Norwegians, Finns and others. By their background, the majority of them are sailors or fishermen, people with a very narrow worldview and indifferent, if I can say so, to any spiritual and religious life, and of course they do not care about Orthodox services. Moreover, they treat the latter in an obscene manner. They not only ignore the Orthodox services themselves, but also, if they are married to local Creole women, try to kill any desire to visit the church in their own children. Therefore, to conduct missionary work here is hard labor. The priest frequently becomes an object of various complaints and accusations and has to be dragged into disputes over the celebration of Orthodox feasts.

Part V

The Kenai church has one priest and one songleader. Neither of them is supported by the parishioners, but receive their salaries from the church mission fund: the priest receives $900 a year, and the songleader receives $360. The priests and songleaders who served in the church from the moment of its establishment are listed below.

Priests:

From 1845 to 1868 Hegumen Nikolai
From 1881 to 1886 Hieromonk Nikita
From 1888 to 1892 Priest Nikolai Mitropol'skii
From 1893 to 1897 Priest Aleksandr Iaroshevich

From 1897 to 1907 Ioann Bortnovskii
From 1907 to the present day Priest Paul Shadura

Songleaders:
From 1845 to 1853 Stefan Sorokovikov
From 1853 to 1870 Makarii Ivanov
From 1870 to 1875 Fedor Demidov
From 1875 to 1887 Nikolai Sorokovikov
From 1887 to 1902 Aleksei Ivanov
From 1902 to 1905 Aleksandr Deikar
From 1905 to 1912 A. Demidov
From 1912 to the present day Nikolai [Konstantin?] Sorokovikov

Part VII

The development of the local parochial school starts with the arrival of the first Kenai missionaries. Under Hegumen Nikolai and some later missionaries, the school (the church building) existed only as a place where children learned prayers and church singing. With the growth of the mission the school expanded its program, and finally in 1887 A. Ivanov was assigned from San Francisco as a special teacher for the Kenai school. Ivanov later became a songleader. During his work the school adopted an appropriate curriculum that corresponded to then accepted standards. In 1893 the missionary Aleksandr Iaroshevich completed the transformation of the school into a regular parochial educational institution with such subjects as Russian, Church Slavonic, and English and the four basic rules of mathematics, Bible history, Old and New Testament, and church singing. Since then this school has begun to provide a good general education, which is now very noticeable in the progress made by its graduates, who completed a required course of education.

The curriculum introduced by Father Iaroshevich existed until the establishment of the American public school in 1908. Since the introduction of the regular American education, the curriculum of the Kenai parochial school has been narrowed to teaching only Russian, Church Slavonic, God's Law and church singing. The American school is now responsible for teaching general educational disciplines. The Kenai village now numbers thirty-six boys and thirty-two girls of school age. In reality, only twenty-five boys and thirteen girls go to our parochial school. In other words, these are children of only those parents (primarily the Kenaitze natives), who show a zealous attitude towards the church. Creole parents or natives who are married to Creoles do not send their children to the parochial school. The latter demonstrate a clearly hostile attitude to our school despite the fact that their children formally belong to the Orthodox faith.

Report to the Most Reverend Phillip, Alaska, August 25, 1917[66]

Your Grace, Our Most Reverend archpastor and Father, I send you my filial appeal. Would you, please, pay the most serious attention to the miserable conditions of the Kenai missionary and save him from hunger? Would you, please, pressure the North American Ecclesiastical Consistory and convince them to send immediately the Kenai missionary's salary for 1917? Here nobody wants to give him goods on credit anymore. Moreover, the summer season, when one can find a job, has also passed. Now we are in a desperate situation because the North American Ecclesiastical Consistory does not respond to our appeals at all. On July 23, 1916, I wrote to the Consistory asking them to provide an explanation. Instead, the Consistory sent me the salary in checks, which I used to cover my debt in the local store and to extend my credit. Yet, to my deep frustration the checks turned out to be false and were returned, which undermined my credit in Kenai even more. I did not take these checks back, but forced the store manager to find out by himself why they could not be cashed and who was responsible.

On May 1, 1917, I again wrote to the North American Ecclesiastical Consistory providing a detailed description of our miserable existence. I simultaneously forwarded another letter to his Grace Evdokim, Archbishop of Alaska inquiring if the salary would be paid to the Kenai missionary for 1917. Yet to the present day I have not received any response. In the meantime, the summer season, when people can find jobs, has ended. Besides, the summer fishing was poor both for local canneries and for my parishioners. They were not able to catch even half of what they had last year. For this reason, I cannot rely on support from my parishioners either. I simply do not know how I will survive this coming winter. Everybody has now refused me credit, and everything is so terribly expensive here. The other day the store manager finally informed me that he had received his money from the North American Ecclesiastical Consistory for the past year (1916), but refused to extend my credit.

As I said, this summer did not bring us a good fishing season. There were rains with thunderstorms all the time. The companies could not harvest the amount of fish they had planned to process. For this reason my parishioners could not get jobs to earn any money to support themselves during the winter. Everything is so expensive. One sack of flour that weighs 100 pounds costs $10, and one sack of sugar costs $13. Thus, this winter I will be living the life of a beggar. To our luck, Pavel [one of Shadura's sons] was able to find work and earned $1,800 this summer, of which we were able to save only $150. For his money we bought flour, sugar, lard and other small things. As for me, last summer I was able to make only $50 by selling fish. I also salted two barrels of fish and smoked some for winter. I am sending You some red salmon. This is a fulfillment of my promise I had given to You earlier. If it did not come out right, please, forgive me. If it tastes good, please, let me know and next summer, if we are still alive, I will try to send You more.

We also own a cow and now live off it. Pavel and I are going moose-hunting to salt some meat for winter. In addition, in order to save my family from cold and hunger I had to agree to a "slave" contract with local companies to cut wood for them. I will have to cut 500 logs for $150. This work as well as collecting firewood for myself will take the whole winter. If my salary still does not come, I will think about going on a hunting trip this winter with my parishioners. Under these circumstances, I cannot guarantee that I will be able to teach the Russian parochial school this winter. To rely on the parishioners' support is impossible. These poor people themselves do not know how they will survive this winter. I wish to Your Grace a fruitful trip to Russia and success in securing help for the [Alaska] mission and for its priests. I am only afraid that You might be late for the Supreme church council meeting [Sobor] and they will reject all Your requests, and, besides, You might not be able to return to us at all.[67] I doubt that Father Vladimir Aleksandrovich is knowledgeable about the Alaska mission, because he does not know anything about its life. I remember very well how seventeen years ago en route to Alaska to the place of my appointment I was unpleasantly struck by one of his comments. Pointing to a few Kolosh, whom we noticed on the wharf and who carried fish heads for their meals, he said with scorn, "Here they are, your future parishioners." If You do not come back, I ask You to inform me by a special letter about the status of the Alaska mission and its priests. In this case I will be able to start looking for a job in spring either here in Kenai or in Anchorage. Given the present situation, I cannot rely on the Ecclesiastical Consistory anymore.

Entrusting myself and my flock to Your prayers and asking for Your archpastoral blessing, Your humble novice, Priest P. Shadura.

P.S. Your Grace,

Although I deeply and sincerely wished to fulfill Your requirement to visit three last villages such as Knik, Susitna and Tyonek, last summer I was not able to make this trip because of my beggarly conditions. As you know very well, there was only $100 left in the church, which I spent this summer for the maintenance of the church building and for my personal needs.

Untitled [On the Fate of the Kenai Natives, c. 1917][68]

About 150 years ago, when Alaska was under the rule of the Russian Emperor, its native people were respected and natural resources were not wasted. After the Americans came, various commercial companies got Alaskan natives dead drunk and also robbed all of Alaska in a predatory manner. Only recently did the American government start paying serious attention to Alaskan life and adopted the most severe laws and regulations, which stopped this robbery a little. However, the native population is difficult to save and teach something useful. During my long-time service in Alaska I had to interact with various official persons and converse with them about the improvement of the Alaskan natives' life. These officials shared the same opinion that they articulated during our talks: the sooner these dirty and ungrateful nationalities are wiped out from the face of the earth, the better for the nation. They also stressed that the natives would be replaced by the new vital population, which would ennoble all of Alaska with culture. At the present time the Swedes, Norwegians, and other civilized people come to populate Alaska and so-called progress advances. In some localities the United States government now preserves Alaskan natives for demonstrative purposes as rare specimens. Moreover, a young generation, the offspring of local native women and new arrivals, who were already raised in American schools, share new ideas. These young mixed-bloods say that they do not want like some Chinese to follow the traditions of older generations and cannot stay at the same stage of development for thousands of years. The young people argue that, according to the laws of nature, they have only two alternatives: to move forward or backwards.

In terms of material well-being it appears that the natives have advanced themselves by a span. Yet in moral respects they are now thrown a few feet back. The latter brought great misfortune to our Orthodox mission, and there is no way to return to the good old days, when the mission prospered. Therefore, we should adjust ourselves to the new state of things. Various alien denominations have also brought a great harm to the cause of our mission. These alien proselytizers have resources and manpower. Being materially crippled we cannot oppose them with anything except our strong religious spirit. [Mixed-bloods] tell us that you, Orthodox, with your Chinese-like relic of the past church are out of step with modern times. The Creoles [mixed-bloods] claim that they intend to become white Americans, while they originate from the same Mongolian roots. This is how various alien missionaries have corrupted Alaskan natives.

Short Report About Conditions in the Kenai Mission in 1920, February 7, 1921[69]

For the past year nothing special happened in the Kenai Mission. This year I visited only one village. Because of the lack of money to cover my transportation expenses, I was not able to go to four other settlements and to check their registers for three years. In these four villages almost all the people died, while the remaining residents moved to neighboring towns. As far as two more villages are concerned, I have postponed my trip there until this fall.

Although the population of the Kenai village, the residence of the missionary, is increasing, the total number of people in my parish dropped almost by half. Because of the introduction of new American laws and schools, the morality of the parishioners has also declined, especially among young people. Heavy drinking on a mass scale is now widespread. Although formally Alaska is now a "dry" territory, practically each white and native house turned, so to speak, into a home saloon. That is why people become alcoholics and reduce themselves to a state of poverty. They could have lived fairly well and could have had a pretty decent church life. Instead, natives downgrade themselves to the poverty level. They are also prone to various infectious diseases and in case of a minor epidemic die out like flies. Thus, measles and influenza wiped out five villages. The parish population declined by half. Parishioners do not fulfill their own promises to support the priest and maintain the church, although during general meetings everybody always promises to do this. More than half the natives did not pay their dues ($5 a year) to support the priest. Instead, people wasted their money on buying alcohol during the Fourth of July and other holidays. I do not mention card playing that flourishes in my parish. Some people lose up to $100 and more. If it goes like this, in two or three years I will have to leave the parish. My constant appeals to natives to live in a Christian manner and in fear of God do not help. I tried to subject some of them to church punishments, but they only persisted in their sins.

In all fairness, the majority of the natives still visit the church regularly, fulfill their Christian duties and believe in God. But in their daily life they are far from being Christians. Parochial schools in my parish also disintegrate because children who go to American schools are too tired at the end of the day to be able to devote extra time to religious education. Those few who do come, do not take it seriously. Mixed-blood children, who are the only ones capable of learning, do not visit the Orthodox school at all. My experience for the past fourteen years convinced me that all this school business is a waste of time, kerosene, and firewood. The temperance society (I wish I had not even mentioned it at all) has been closed. The brotherhood, that formally still exists, is also dead. There is no way to regenerate it simply because those poor natives who join the brotherhood are ready to invest $3, but expect to get back $36 and more in the form of allowances to the poor. Nothing good can be done with these people. I feel only mental and physical torments. I might suffer for a while as that Bible gardener, who tried to nourish the fig tree, and water this "withered tree" with my tears. If it does not bring any fruit, it will be better to cut myself from these natives. This is all I wanted to report to You about the life in my parish.

With all my due respect, I have an honor to be Your humble servant, Priest Pavel Shadura.

Extracts from Church Service Journal, 1933–1936[70]

1933. June 16. At 4 o'clock in the afternoon on the company's gasoline [motorboat] I left for the Tyonek village. Arrived at the village at 7 o'clock in the evening. We let people, who are scattered around, know to come back home and gather for church services.

June 17. Because this village is in the process of moving to a new site, and the new church has not yet been built, I had to use the building of an American school for my services. Until dinnertime we cleaned the interior of the school. After dinner we set up the altar, table of oblation and icons and performed the rite of water blessing. We blessed the altar, table of oblation and icons because all these items were damaged and fell apart from the earthquake. Using a reading from the Gospels, before the dismissal prayer, I delivered a word of address (through an interpreter) on the significance of water blessing, and explained to them the importance of the holy water, and also how it should be used. Eighty faithful participated in the service. At 7 o'clock in the evening I performed the all-night vigil. The sermon was devoted to the life of St. Nicholas, the patron saint of this village. Eighty people participated in the service. Later, I heard confession from a woman.

June 18. At 7:30 in the morning I gave last rites to an ailing person. At 8 o'clock in the morning the Divine Liturgy of St. John Chrysostom. There were twenty-five infants and [blank spot] women who came to join in holy mysteries. At the end of the liturgy service I read requisite prayers given before confession and added some words about the meaning of confession. From 1 to 4 o'clock I heard confessions from fifty-two persons.

August 5. At 2 o'clock in the afternoon I departed for Anchorage on a gasoline that carries mail. Spent all night en route.

August 6. The feast day of the Transfiguration of Christ. At 10 o'clock in the morning I gave last rights to an ailing woman at her home, where I also served at a customary prayer service devoted to the Most Holy Mother of God. I spent the whole day making various inquiries and also let people know to gather in Anchorage.

August 7. At 9 o'clock in the morning I gave last rites to an ailing woman and also served at a customary prayer service devoted to the Savior and the Mother of God. There was no service because the building of the local Episcopal Church, where I performed various ministrations for my parishioners, was busy today. I spent the day talking with my parishioners and preparing for tomorrow.

August 8. At 9 o'clock in the morning I served the Hours and the liturgy without consecration. Before the dismissal prayer, I said a word of address (through an interpreter) "On Fasting." I noticed that it was only women and children who came to church, whereas all the men were absent. As it turned out all the men had received temporary jobs on the road construction. The Anchorage area is the most inconvenient locality for missionary work. When the priest is not around, everybody wants to perform rites of fast, confession, and communion. However, when the missionary shows up, the men usually scatter being around busy with various jobs. Yet I think in reality the majority of them spend their time playing cards at gambling parlors and do not pay anything for ministrations. There were forty-five faithful at this service. At 7 o'clock in the evening I served at the all-night vigil. I delivered a sermon on the Gospel theme about the coming of the Heavenly Kingdom. There were eighty faithful at this service.

August 9. At 8 o'clock in the morning I served the Hours and the liturgy without consecration. At the end of the service I read requisite prayers before confession and spoke through an interpreter about the meaning of a confession for Orthodox true believers. There were eighty faithful including children. After the service I anointed fourteen children with myrrh and also checked birth registers. From 1 to 4:30 o'clock in the afternoon I heard confession from forty-five faithful. At 7 o'clock in the evening I served at the all-night vigil and read the evening prayer. There were about 100 praying faithful including some males who did finally come to pray. Yet, all healthy males are still busy at their jobs and their bosses do not allow them to take time off to go to church.

August 10. At 8 o'clock in the morning requisite prayers before confession, then the Divine Liturgy of St. John Chrysostom. Before confession, I delivered through an interpreter a word of address "What is confession, who introduced it and why do we need it?"

1934. August 22. [Kenai] At 9 o'clock in the morning I served the Hours and the liturgy without consecration. Before the dismissal prayer I delivered through an interpreter a short word of address about preparation for holy confession. There were fifty praying people. People are gradually gathering. At 5 o'clock in the evening I observed vespers and matins. I also spoke about negligence of the rite of fasting by some males. Also, younger people spend much of their time in gambling parlors. There were about sixty praying people.

August 24. I packed all my travel belongings and at 4 o'clock in the evening departed for Tyonek on a small gasoline. Arrived at this village at 10 o'clock in the evening.

August 25. Before dinnertime we were occupied with cleaning the American school and preparing it for the church services, because local people are still in the process of settling down at this new village site and do not have a chapel. Yet, they are preparing building materials for this new chapel. After dinner we set up the altar, table of oblation, and holy icons. Then through an interpreter I recited *stikhera* and blessing of water. The church was full of the praying faithful. In Tyonek nobody disturbs local natives, and therefore everybody showed up for the service. At 7 o'clock I held vespers and matins. Before the dismissal prayer, through an interpreter I gave an instructive talk on a Gospel verse. There were about 100 praying faithful.

August 26. At 8 o'clock I served the Hours and the liturgy without consecration. Through an interpreter I delivered a sermon on a Gospel theme, and read requisite prayers before confession. I also talked with school children and then heard their confessions. After dinner, from 1 to 5 o'clock in the afternoon I heard confessions from adults. The total number of people who came for confession was sixty-three. At 7 o'clock in the evening I served at the all-night vigil and spoke on the evil of drunkenness. Read the evening prayer. There were about 100 praying faithful.

August 27. At 7 o'clock in the morning I held confession for and gave last rites to an ailing woman at her house.

1935. August 17. I performed the Liturgy of St. John Chrysostom. There were twenty-two infants whom I joined in holy mysteries. At the end of the service I served at a customary prayer service devoted to the Most Holy Mother of God and delivered a welcoming word of address, where I made a special note of the work of local native sisters, who made holy banners [*khorugv*] and cloth for the table of oblation for the feast. At the same time, I reprimanded the male half of the congregation for neglecting the temple and the priest, although all of them in the presence of the Most Reverend Aleksii and local judge signed a pledge to contribute fifty cents each month. All the men drink like fish and do not fulfill their promises. There were eighty-seven praying faithful.

August 18. At 5 o'clock in the evening I departed for Anchorage by airplane and arrived there at 6 o'clock in the evening.

August 19. In the morning I sent a word to the local people that I had arrived and would perform ministrations. This year the Kenaitze want me to conduct church services in the chapel of the Eklutna village, and now all of them are going there. Tomorrow at 9 o'clock in the morning I myself will be going there by train. This summer his Grace, the Most Reverend Aleksii, the Bishop of Alaska, performed services, when he was passing through the town of Anchorage, and some natives were able to fast except a few lackadaisical people.

August 20. At 9 o'clock in the morning I and my interpreter departed by train for the Eklutna village, where we arrived by noon. From after dinner until 5 o'clock in the evening we were busy cleaning the chapel, where church services have not been performed since 1912. The chapel has fallen into decay, and some items have rotted, while others are already gone because there was nobody to watch them. Yet now the Kenaitze have started coming back to Eklutna and building permanent houses at the old site. Moreover, in 1933 they made some repairs on the chapel such as putting on a new roof and raising the ceiling, which earlier was very low. Still, the work on the chapel has not been finished. Therefore, we had to work hard to put this building in proper order and make it appropriate for performing church services. At 6 o'clock in the evening I performed a rite of lesser water blessing, then blessed the table of oblation, the altar and the entire interior of the chapel. Then we went by a religious procession around the chapel and sprinkled its building with holy water. Before the dismissal through an interpreter I explained the meaning of the stanza sung during water blessing. There were about fifty faithful present at this service. The others have not come. The men are mostly employed with the building of the railroad.

August 21. At 9 o'clock in the morning I observed the Hours and the liturgy without consecration. Before the dismissal prayer I delivered a sermon on a Gospel theme. After all faithful kissed the cross, I spoke about the meaning of the cross and how to make the sign of the cross correctly. I noticed that the children do not know at all how to make the sign of cross, whereas others make the sign of the cross in a Catholic manner. This locality [Eklutna-Anchorage] is the most difficult in terms of missionary work. What can the missionary accomplish when he comes here for only three or four days once a year? Thank God the natives still remember the Lord and baptize their children. Today only women and children came for the service, while the men returned to their jobs. I cannot guarantee that I will come here again to perform ministrations, although one may find a sufficient number of people who belong to our church, but only if you collect them together at one spot. Not far from here, about half a mile, there is an American Industrial School for Alaskan orphan children, many of whom are Orthodox. The school principal is a very good man and does not interfere with religious life, unlike his predecessors. On the contrary, he tries to help his wards, for children come here from various areas of Alaska and belong to different religions. Other missionaries, who have settled in the vicinity, also visit the school and conduct their talks, and they have resources. We should think about this too instead of taking the last crumbs from our Orthodox family. Our Orthodox Christians think little about their own missionary, they are more interested in drinking. That is how they were raised since childhood. At 2 o'clock in the afternoon I performed two baptism rites and anointed ten infants with myrrh. At 6 o'clock in the evening I served at the all-night vigil. Before the dismissal prayer through an interpreter I spoke on a Gospel theme. There were about sixty faithful at the service.

August 22. The local people are all scattered around in various places, in harbors and on lakes. It is very difficult for the missionary to gather them at one place and at the same time as we usually did before the town of Anchorage was built. I cannot afford going to all distant localities of this area. The male half of the local population thinks little about their Christian duties and the priest. Horrible drunkenness ruins everything.

August 23. At 8 o'clock in the morning requisite prayers before a confession, then I heard confession of the school children, who came from the local industrial orphanage school. Its principal allowed Orthodox children to partake in the rites of fasting and joining in holy mysteries. Then I performed the Liturgy of St. John Chrysostom. There were seventy adult communicants and thirty-five infants. At the end of the service I read thanksgiving prayers and delivered a welcoming word of address, reminding natives of the necessity of supporting the priest. There were about 100 faithful at the service. Local inhabitants of the male gender want the missionary to baptize their children and perform some ministrations for their wives. When the priest visits them, the men promise to help, but never keep their word. Instead, the majority of the people of male gender hang around in the town of Anchorage in gambling parlors and saloons. So I guess we will have to close our missionary "shop" here because the natives have not learned anything and will hardly learn something from us in future. That is the nature of this miserable people with the exception of very few of them. Twenty years they fool me and most probably laugh at me behind my back. It is only for the sake of innocent native children and some women that I sacrifice myself here. Local inhabitants can see the work of missionaries from alien denominations, which enjoy various benefits from their consistories and fulfill all ministrations free of charge. It is hard for us, who are destitute, to compete with them and to maintain the whole mission at our own expense as I do (I do not know how it is in other areas). After dinner I performed the general requiem service for all deceased in Knik-Eklutna for the past year. Then I delivered a farewell word and also spoke about the chapel and pointed to the drunkenness of some parishioners who cannot restrain themselves from alcohol. I especially meant those who live in Anchorage or in its vicinity. I also suggested that the residents establish a local Orthodox brotherhood and sisterhood, and they promised that they would. Although there is nobody here to be in charge of this project, we will try to do something. Then I served at five customary prayer services in private houses and also blessed some new houses. After supper we packed all my travel belongings and went to the American orphanage, where I stayed talking with some Orthodox students while awaiting the return train.

August 24. Between 8 and 11 o'clock in the morning I again spent time with the students. At 11 o'clock departed back to Anchorage by train. The rest of the day I spent at a doctor's. I also visited ailing people in the hospital.

August 25. In the evening a motorboat came from Tyonek to fetch me.

August 26. All stores and businesses [in Anchorage] are closed. I visited my old acquaintances. At 10 o'clock in the morning I served at a customary prayer service devoted to the Most Holy Mother of God for an ailing woman at her house. Since this woman did not abstain from food, I could not join her in holy mysteries. She confessed recently to our archpastor Father Aleksii that she performed the rite of fasting with a Catholic priest. Good Lord, it looks like she tries to act to satisfy both sides ["*i nashim i vashim*"].

August 27. Before dinnertime, I was at the dentist's, after dinnertime I did some small shopping and at 4 o'clock in the evening departed to Tyonek on its gasoline. At 9 o'clock in the evening I arrived at the village.

August 28. At 10 o'clock in the morning I performed a rite of the lesser blessing of water, blessed the table of oblation, the altar, and the building of the new church which is still under construction. At 2 o'clock in the afternoon I anointed four infants with myrrh. After this, I was occupied with baking communion bread. At 7 o'clock in the evening I served at the all-night vigil. Eighty faithful were present at this service.

1936. August 7. The whole day we had to spend in Kasilof and returned to Kenai about 6 o'clock in the evening.

August 8. I was occupied with my personal chores and sent some mail.

August 9. The whole day I was busy with writing my church papers. Some men in Kenai are occupied with loading boxes onto a ship, while the others continue drinking. Last summer the Kenai parishioners earned good money, yet by now they have drunk it all away, and, of course, with the exception of very few people, most of them did not fulfill their oath of donating to the church and to the local brotherhood. I can only say that this is a miserable people, and nobody will be able to reform them except Our Lord God and the grave.

August 10. At 9:30 o'clock in the morning I observed the Hours and then the liturgy without consecration. Before the dismissal prayer, using a Gospel text, I delivered a sermon on the topic "Christian and socialist teachings and the differences between them." There were thirty faithful at this service.

August 14. At 7 o'clock in the evening I read a cleansing prayer for a woman and churched an infant. Then in a solemn manner I served at the all-night vigil with the litany, blessing of bread, and censing the church and all faithful. About seventy faithful were present at this service.

CHAPTER SEVEN

Orthodox Missionaries Among Inland Dena'ina and Ahtna

Vasilii Shishkin: Report to Paul Kirolivansky, Dean of Clergy, June 31, 1878[71]

July 12, 1877. After I served a customary prayer service to our Lord God in order to secure a safe trip, we set out in two *baidarkas* for Iliamna Lake to visit the Kenaitze as well as the Kiatintsi[72] village Koshkinak on Kvichgak River. On July 27 I arrived at the Iliamna *odinochka* [Iliamna trading post].

July 30. I anointed two infants with myrrh and confessed twenty-one people. In the evening I served the all-night vigil and, as required, there was kneeling down before the Life-Giving Cross. And on August 1 I gave communion to the local Creole and Kenaitze people: seventeen men, twelve women, five children of both genders. The overall number is thirty-four people. After this I served a customary prayer service in honor of St. Nicholas the Wonderworker. Then I sang a requiem service for the deceased, and also blessed the site for a prayer house consecrated after St. Nicholas the Wonderworker.

August 20 [should be August 2, a mistake in the original]. I continued on by Iliamna Lake going to the Chikak village,[73] which takes eight hours to reach from the Iliamna *odinochka*. Having arrived at this village, I began instructing people who were preparing for baptism and continued this work the next day and on August 5. The total number of Kenaitze who were enlightened with the light of Christ's faith are seven men and seven women. Also, I anointed with myrrh five boys and six girls, who had been earlier baptized by the Creole [Savva] Riktorov. Then I started hearing confessions, and today at 6 o'clock in the evening on the feast day of the Transfiguration of our Lord during the liturgy I gave communion to the Kenaitze. The number of communicants, including the newly enlightened and the young, is seventeen men and nineteen women, or thirty-six people together, which represents the entire population of the village. During the liturgy, I delivered a sermon on the same topic I discussed earlier with the Kiatintsi, with a special emphasis on the dangers of syphilis, which God sent them [Chikak people] as a punishment for their intemperance for violating God's seventh commandment. Now the inhabitants of Chikak stand apart from their fellow Kenaitze like those lepers from the Old Testament. Of thirty-six Chikak people only nine persons are healthy. All others suffer from that disease. The children, who are all covered with festering growths, produce a pitiful impression. I do not say anything about the adults, some of whom are so ill that they have not been able to move for several years. Nobody knows where this infectious disease came from. As in the Iliamna *odinochka* and in the rest of the Nushagak parish, the Chikak people have neither medicine nor physician. Having finished all ministrations in this village and blessed the residents, on August 7 I set out for Lake Kichek [Kijik][74] to visit the village of the same name. On August 10 in the morning I arrived at Kichek [Kijik],[75] which is populated by the Kenaitze. On the same day I started teaching and instructing them about the Christian faith and continued this work from August 11 to August 14. Twenty-three men and thirteen women volunteered to accept holy baptism. I also baptized children born in Christian families: two boys and two girls, and anointed five men and nine women with myrrh. The total number of those enlightened with the Christian faith and anointed with myrrh are thirty men and twenty-four women. On the same day I confessed people, and the next day, on August 15, I gave communion to twenty men and seventeen women along with the above-mentioned fifty-four newly enlightened and anointed natives. The total number of people who joined in holy mysteries is ninety-one. In addition, I sacramentally blessed seven marriages. After this I delivered a sermon about the holiness of these mysteries. Then, I celebrated a requiem service for the deceased and a customary prayer service in honor of the Most Holy Mother of God. On the same day, at my request, the Kenaitze erected a wooden cross on the place where I performed the service. From now on the villagers will pray in front of this cross on Sundays and during feast days. It is a pity that it is hard to build a chapel in Kichik, because a greater part of a year the Kenaitze usually live scattered over the mountains, busy with hunting. They come together to the Kichik village only on August 1 for fishing. Therefore, I found that there was no need to set up a prayer house in this village.

My next plan was to continue on through the mountains and along a river to the Kenaitze village named Mulchatna, but the Mulchatna Kenaitze's *toion*, who was visiting Kichik, talked me out of this by saying that at this time the route would be difficult because of shallow rivers. The *toion* promised to come by Christmas time to Nushagak and bring his people too, or he might come again to Iliamna Lake next year to meet me. Therefore, I decided to return to my station.

Vasilii Shishkin: Report to Nestor, Bishop of Alaska and the Aleutians, April 24, 1882[76]

[From Kalignak, a Yupik village] on February 14 I set out for Mulchatna village, populated by the Kenaitze. My route lay through a portage and mountains to the

Mulchatna river. En route I met one Kiatintsi family and baptized a sick infant. With great difficulty I arrived at Mulchatna village on February 21. Because I completed the baptism of all heathen natives in this village during my last visit here in 1880, there was only one infant to be baptized, and this rite I performed on August 22. The Kenaitze were in hurry and wanted to go hunting as soon as possible. For this reason, on the same day, I had to start hearing confessions, then performed the all-night vigil and in the morning on February 22, during the liturgy without consecration, I gave communion to twenty-seven persons of both genders. Then, I served a water blessing prayer service, a requiem and visited all native houses with the cross and holy water. From last fall to the present in this village nine people have died from an epidemic that appears to be scarlet fever. During my visit Jacob [Iakov] Kakilishtukta, the Mulchatna toion, also died, and I performed a funeral service for him. Until recently, our confessional registers showed 144 natives listed as residents of Mulchatna, but then a large part of them died or moved away somewhere, I do not know where. So according to the new registers, it turns out that the village now has only twenty-seven residents of both genders (to be exact, our old registers show the number of the Mulchatna people for the time when missionary Hieromonk Theophilus worked here).[77]

Vasilii Shishkin: Report to Vladimir, Bishop of Alaska and the Aleutians, June 29, 1888[78]

In 1887 on February 12, having served a customary prayer service to secure a safe trip, I left for Iliamna Lake. En route I passed such villages as Kvichagak, Kaguian, Kashkinak, and Kakhunak (of these villages Kaguian and Kakhunak are settlements recently founded by natives from various villages). I planned to stop at these villages to perform necessary ministrations during on the way back to Nushagak. I arrived at Iliamna village at noon on February 28, and on the same day I started to perform services and teach people. On March 2 I anointed two infants with myrrh. On the same day I also started hearing confessions. In the evening after celebrating the all-night vigil, I sang a requiem service for the deceased. On March 3 I performed the liturgy during which I gave communion to twenty-four Creoles and thirty-one Kenaitze or a total of fifty-five people. After the liturgy, I served a customary prayer service in honor of St. Nicholas the Wonderworker, after whom the local chapel had been consecrated. Later on I visited the houses of the villagers with the cross. On the same day I planned to set out for Kichik village, but bad weather kept me in Iliamna until March 6. Two Kenaitze, whom I hired earlier and who accompanied me from Nushagak to Iliamna, fell ill and I had to leave them in Iliamna. Instead, I hired three new Kenaitze guides and arrived at Kichik village, populated by the Kenaitze, on March 8. Besides the residents of the village, another group of the Kenaitze has been waiting for me since the middle of February. They had come to Kichik from the Mulchatna River, and now they were in hurry to return to their village. To satisfy their spiritual needs as soon as possible I tried to work rapidly. On March 9 I anointed infants with myrrh and confessed eleven people of both genders, who had been earlier baptized here by the Creole Zinovii Daryin. Confession continued through midnight. On March 1 I served the Hours, during which I gave communion, using presanctified gifts, to 176 Kenaitze of both genders, including children (because of the lack of an oven I could not bake the communion bread and the liturgy was not served). Afterwards, I served a thanksgiving prayer service, sang a requiem for the deceased and visited the Kenaitze houses with the cross.

While in Kichik I tried to convince the Mulchatna Kenaitze to move from the Mulchatna River to the Kichik area, where hunting and fishing are more abundant, unlike the place where they live now. The Mulchatna people agreed with my suggestion and said they might settle here in Kichik or somewhere else in the vicinity of Iliamna Lake. I also tried to convince the Kichik residents to build a prayer house, and they promised to build such a house by the summer of 1888. On the same day, using favorable weather I set out through the mountains back to Iliamna, where I arrived on March 12. On the same evening I started to perform services. On March 14 I confessed four Kenaitze who had just returned from their hunting trip, and next day I gave them communion during the liturgy.

Vasilii Shishkin: Report to Vladimir, Bishop of Alaska and the Aleutians, June 5, 1889[79]

Departed at noon from Kahkunak and proceeded by Iliamna Lake to the village of the same name, where I arrived at noon on February 7. After arrival in Iliamna I gave last rites to two ailing people. I performed a rite of extreme unction with an anointment for one of them, and also sang a funeral service for a deceased Kenaitze girl. In the evening I served vespers and matins. On March 8 I served the Hours, then anointed eight infants with myrrh, and in the evening again served vespers and matins. On March 9 I served the Hours and then performed a water blessing prayer service, and sang a requiem service for the deceased people. On March 10 I started hearing confessions. In the evening, on the occasion of their chapel feast day, I celebrated the all-night vigil in honor of St. Nicholas the Wonderworker. On March 11 I performed the liturgy, where fifty-three Creoles and Kenaitze of both genders including infants received communion. Upon finishing the liturgy, I served a customary prayer service in honor of St. Nicholas the Wonderworker, and visited the houses of Iliamna residents with the cross. From Iliamna I was about to depart to [Nukilian?—the name is illegible], which is populated by the Kenaitze who had lived on the Mulchatna river and by some Kichik people. Yet because of heavy rain I had to stay in Iliamna for three more days.[80]

Vasilii Shishkin: 1881–1890 Report to the Alaska Ecclesiastical Office, August 1890[81]

[On July 21, 1890] I neared the Kahkunak village, but did not stop here because all the inhabitants were away. Instead, I continued on directly to Iliamna village, where I arrived on July 24. Iliamna village, populated by Creoles and Kenaitze, is located on Iliamna Lake 140 miles from Kashkinak. On July 25 I anointed two infants with myrrh and performed full requisite funeral services for those who died here from 1888 to 1889. Then I started to confess people, and in the evening I celebrated the all-night vigil in honor of St. Nicholas the Wonderworker, who is the patron saint of their chapel. On July 26 after midnight I served the liturgy, where I gave communion to forty-eight people of both genders including infants. At the request of the residents of the village I performed a customary prayer service in honor of the Most Holy Mother of God and St. Nicholas. Having finished the prayer service we went by religious procession [*krestnii khod*] around the village carrying the cross. The religious procession with the cross was conducted in order to ward off, in future, an epidemic disease that visited them in the fall of 1888 and continued until February of 1889. During this time twenty-one people died from this disease (it was influenza). Having visited their houses with the holy cross, I continued on by Iliamna Lake. Then we crossed the portage through the rapids of the [Nukilian] river and went to Lake Kichik to the village of the same name. Kichik village is located 160 miles from Iliamna. I arrived in Kichik on July 31. At noon of the same day I baptized four infants and then performed full requisite funeral services for those who died during 1888 and 1889 from the same epidemic that visited Iliamna village. During the above-mentioned time in Kichik sixteen people died. Later on I served a water blessing prayer service and consecrated a new prayer house the residents of the village recently built. The chapel was consecrated after the Life-Giving Cross of the Lord. In the evening we performed a requisite ceremony of veneration [*poklonenie*] of the Holy Cross. During the all-night vigil I confessed forty-one people. On August 1 after midnight I performed the liturgy, where I gave communion to fifty-six people of both genders including children. In the evening, when I had finished a customary prayer service in honor of the Life-Giving Cross of the Lord, I set out, using the same route on my return, passed by Iliamna, and arrived at Kahkunik village.

Vladimir Modestov: An Excerpt from Church Service Journal No. 180, 1895, July 17, 1894, to June 30, 1895[82]

February 9, 1895. At 8 o'clock in the morning we departed. The sky is clear and the weather is frosty. Our route again went across Iliamna Lake. By 6 o'clock in the evening we came to Iliamna village, which is located on the river that carries the same name and flows into Iliamna Lake. This village had been founded by the Creole Savva Riktorov, who worked here as a trade agent for the Russian company [RAC] and who was responsible for delivering supplies and goods from Kenai to Nushagak. At the present time, his children, the Riktorov brothers, live here. Seven brothers are alive and two others have died. Their father, Savva Riktorov, had two wives simultaneously: one was legal and the other was illicit. Four brothers were born to the legal wife and four others to the illicit one [this is the number given in the original]. The older brother, Mikhail Riktorov, works as an agent for the Alaska Company [Alaska Commercial Company]. Each brother lives in a nicely built house. At a distance of about a quarter of a mile from their houses, the Kenaitze live in ten *baraboras*. The Kenaitze speak a special dialect, distinct from the Kiatintsi tongue, and the surrounding inhabitants cannot understand them. In Iliamna there is a chapel consecrated after St. Nicholas, the Wonderworker, which Savva Riktorov had built. After my arrival, in response to the call of the bell ringing, all residents of the village gathered in the chapel, where I served a customary prayer service in honor of St. Nicholas, the Wonderworker. To accommodate us, Riktorovs placed us in a separate house and hosted us in a Russian manner. All the brothers speak Russian and still remember Russian customs.

February 10. At 9 o'clock in the morning I performed a requiem for the deceased, and sang funeral services for those who died and were buried without funeral ceremonies. After dinner I was occupied with auditing chapel funds. According to the note left by deacon Orlov, which he prepared from the words of the priest Shishkin, the Iliamna chapel owes us $46. Yet, the account prepared by Father Shishkin and kept by Ivan Riktorov, the churchwarden, indicates that the chapel received different church items at a cost of $158, of which Iliamna paid only $48. Therefore, they still owe $110. However, I found out that the churchwarden does not have a single cent left in his chapel. To my question as to where all the money has gone, the churchwarden admitted that he spent it and now cannot return it. Moreover, Ivan Riktorov does not want to accept the amount of the above-mentioned debt and insists that during the last visit of Father Shishkin to Iliamna he supposedly paid to this missionary $40. The churchwarden argues that the reason this sum of money was not written down in the accounts was because Father Shishkin supposedly promised Ivan to mark it down in his missionary book. At the same time, Ivan Riktorov, when he came down to Nushagak to fetch me, assured me that there were about 600 rubles or $120 in the chapel fund.

I gathered all the brothers and suggested they pay their brother's debt. They were able to collect only $10. They promised to pay the rest of the sum when they earn more money. To my question as to why they allowed such embezzlement of the church money, the brothers responded that the churchwarden deceived them too by saying that all the money was safe. Besides, the brothers argued that they regularly bought candles in the chapel, but now this money is also gone. With the general agreement of the residents of the whole village another churchwarden, Ignatii Riktorov, was elected, and two assistants from the Kenaitze. I explained to these assistants in detail all their responsibilities, and the goal of their appointment. I also instructed the Riktorov brothers to check the chapel money at least once a month and work to increase the amount of church items in the chapel. Their chapel now has only two crosses, the Bible and two clothes for the liturgy [*pokrova*]. At the same time, they do not look like poor people and can afford to improve their chapel. The major occupation of the Iliamna people is hunting sea otters [*morskie bobri*], black and brown bears, and sables.

February 11. At 8 o'clock in the morning I baptized two people and anointed with myrrh fourteen other people. Then I heard confession. At 6 o'clock in the evening there was the all-night vigil and the evening prayer.

February 12. At 8 o'clock in the morning I performed the liturgy, where 120 persons of adults and sixty children of different ages joined in the holy mysteries. After the liturgy I performed a rite of water blessing at the river bank and then there was a religious procession with the cross around the village, and all houses were sprinkled with holy water. At 4 o'clock in the afternoon vespers with an *akathist* to the Savior.

February 13. At 8 o'clock in the morning we intended to set out for Kichek village, which is populated only by Kenaitze. Mikhail Riktorov agreed to go with us as an interpreter. But in the morning it started to snow heavily and we had to postpone my trip. At 9 o'clock in the morning I served matins and the Hours. The Great Vespers at 4 o'clock in the afternoon. In the evening people came to me for a talk.

February 14. At 9 o'clock in the morning, in four sleds, we left the village accompanied by gun shooting and bell ringing.[83]

Vladimir Modestov: An Excerpt from Church Service Journal No. 181 for 1895, from July 1894 to June 1895[84]

January 18, 1895. We departed on two sleds pulled by twenty dogs. Three persons accompanied me including deacon Orlov, whom I took as an interpreter and who knows very well the local routes, villages and all conditions of winter traveling. Yet, on the same day, at 8 o'clock in the evening, the weather forced us to come back home. No sooner had we passed by Kanulik village (three miles from Nushagak) than a severe snowstorm started, and by 2 or 3 o'clock in the morning this snowstorm turned into rain with snow. We all got wet, the dogs were tired, and to move further became impossible. For the whole day we were able to cover no more than seven miles. So we made the decision to come back and wait for better weather.

January 19. Actually, it was a good idea to return because all day it has been either raining or snowing.

January 21. Again, the wet weather will not allow us to depart. At 4 o'clock in the afternoon I performed the all-night vigil.[85]

February 9. Quiet and clear weather. At 7 o'clock in the morning we proceeded further [going on the Iliamna Lake ice]. The dogs ran fast, the people who were in front were running on skates, and at 2 o'clock in the afternoon we came to Iliamna village, whose residents began welcoming us with gun shooting when we were still half a mile from the village. Iliamna village was founded by the Creole Savva Riktorov. At the present time his children and grandchildren live here. All Iliamna Creoles, including their wives and children, number thirty-six persons. Mikhail Riktorov, the elder brother, is considered the *toion* here and he also works as a trade agent for the Alaska Commercial Company. Each brother has a separate clean, neat house. They gave us accommodation in a house that belongs to the company and that was completely empty. The village chapel was build by Savva Riktorov in 1871, and now all the Riktorov brothers maintain it. The chapel was consecrated in honor of St. Nicholas the Wonderworker. Upon my arrival, I served a customary prayer service in honor of St. Nicholas and delivered a sermon about repentance.

February 10. At 9 o'clock in the morning I performed a requiem ceremony at the village cemetery and talked about what awaits sinners, who do not repent, in the afterlife. At noon I began auditing the churchwarden's books. According to the note I received from deacon Orlov, who had prepared it from the words of the priest Shishkin, the Iliamna chapel owes us $46. In the meantime, I found in the chapel an account prepared by the priest Shishkin, which indicates that the Iliamna chapel paid $48 for the church items estimated at $158. This means that the chapel owes us $110. The account was written in 1891. Ivan Riktorov, the churchwarden, insists that in March of 1892 he gave to the priest Shishkin $60, the sum which the priest supposedly had not included in this account, promising to mark it down in his book upon his return to Nushagak and then to send the receipt to the churchwarden. Yet during his visit to my place in Nushagak the churchwarden mentioned that there was money in the chapel and to my question: "How much?" he responded: 550 rubles, that is, $110. In reality, I found not single cent in the chapel.

I gathered all the Riktorov brothers and told them about this problem. They were able to collect only $10 and said that they would pay the rest of the money later. The churchwarden admitted that he had spent the money to support himself during 1893 when hunting and fishing was very poor. To my question how they allowed this embezzlement of chapel money to happen, the brothers said that only yesterday Ivan had assured them that the money was in place and safe, but he refused to show them this money. Ivan even pretended that he was very upset by saying that while the priest trusted him, his own relatives did not. Mikhail Riktorov, the agent of the Alaska Commercial Company, promised to withhold part of Ivan's salary as well as his hunting and fishing catch in lieu of the debt. After a long talk, we finally elected Ignatii, another Riktorov brother, as churchwarden and also two assistants for him: Aleksei Riktorov, who temporarily lives in Iliamna, and Zakhar Ivanov [Evanoff], a Kenaitze native. I explained to the new churchwarden and his assistants what they should do and what they should not. The *toion* Mikhail Riktorov was instructed to check the status of the chapel money once or twice a month, and keep it in the company's trade house. Instead of cash, from now on the churchwarden was to receive a check for the amount of this money.

I also asked the Riktorov brothers to buy more icons and other items for the chapel, because the prayer house looks too poor. They have only five or six icons, one Bible, and two crosses; the walls do not have any wallpaper, and the roof leaks in places. All this does not look good, especially when they have such plentiful hunting and fishing: sea otters [*morskie bobri*], brown and black bears, sables, wolves, polar foxes, lynx, and wolverines. The Riktorov brothers explained that they were generous to their chapel and always donated, but they saw neither improvements in the chapel nor the money itself. I want to mention that although the churchwarden admitted that he embezzled the money, he insists that the other brothers helped him in this, because they drank together. In his words, there is hardly a day, especially in summer, when they do not brew beer. The brothers said that they did drink a lot, and promised to stop drinking, or at least to reduce their drunkenness.

February 11. At 8 o'clock in the morning I baptized two people and anointed fourteen other people with myrrh. Then I heard confessions. The total number of people who came for confession was twenty-six Creoles and forty Kenaitze, including those who came from the neighboring village of Chikak. At 4 o'clock in the afternoon the all-night vigil and evening prayer for those who were preparing themselves to join in the holy mysteries.

February 12. The liturgy at 6 o'clock in the morning, during which 120 people of both genders, including children, received communion. After the liturgy we went by religious procession carrying the cross and proceeded to the bank of the river, where I blessed the water, and then our religious procession went around the village. We visited all the houses with the cross and holy water. At 4 o'clock in the afternoon I celebrated vespers and sang an *akathist* in honor of the Savior and St. Nicholas the Wonderworker.

February 13. At 8 o'clock in the morning we intended to go to Kichek village, located on Lake Clark, which is three or four days' travel from Iliamna village. Mikhail Riktorov was going to come with me as an interpreter since he knows well the residents of the village and their Kenaitze language, which is absolutely different from the Kuskokwim tongue. However, by 8 o'clock in the morning it started to snow heavily, and then came a snowstorm. As a result we had to stay. At 9 o'clock in the morning I served matins and the Hours and at 4 o'clock in the afternoon the Great Vespers. In the evening residents of Iliamna gathered in the house where I was staying for a religious and moral talk. I enlightened them about some things from the Holy History and also told them about some church rules. I also checked how well adults and children knew their prayers. It turned out that all the adults and the adolescent boys and girls know all the basic prayers. The chapel reader, Aleksei Riktorov, reads quite well, and he also teaches the local children. I showed him the sequence and order of the church service and explained how to baptize children.

February 14. At 9 o'clock in the morning, after I performed a customary prayer service in honor of St. Nicholas, we left Iliamna village in four sleds accompanied by gun shooting and bell ringing. It was still snowing and it was hard to go forward. The sleds moved slowly, the dogs repeatedly got stuck in snow and could hardly pull the heavy sleds. We covered no more than ten or twelve miles during the whole day. Earlier, when we were approaching Iliamna, it took us only one or maybe one and a half hours to cover the same distance. We stopped for the night in a wood on the bank of Iliamna Lake. The route to the Kichek village lay across Iliamna Lake.

February 15. From 7 o'clock in the morning we continued the same route across Iliamna Lake and reached the place where the road from the lake went into the mountains. When I use the word "road" it means the most convenient route from one place to another place rather than what we know in Russia as a regular road, which is normally a strip of land used by everybody to get from one place to another place. There is no such thing in Nushagak. People use those routes which appear close and convenient. For this reason, there are no regular roads here. And besides, there are few people around to travel. From two to three hundred people inhabit this huge tundra and mountain area. Of these local residents one-third might own dogs and sleds, which allows them to travel. At night a strong wind began blowing and later turned into rain.

February 16. The whole day we spent inside the tent, as it was raining heavily.

February 17. The same bad weather as yesterday. For this reason we again have to sit idly in the tent. It is dangerous to travel in rain during winter, as one can freeze to death. By evening all the snow on the lake turned into water, and above the ice there was a noticeable water current.[86]

Vladimir Modestov: An Excerpt from a Report to Aleksandr Kedrovsky, July 29, 1895[87]

Kenaitze

There remain alive only 138 Kenaitze of both genders at the present time, whereas ten or twelve years ago their number ranged from 600 to 800 people. By now almost all of them have died from epidemic diseases such as cholera and smallpox. The Kenaitze reside in the area surrounding Clark Lake, which is abundant in fur-bearing animals, but lacks good fishing. Fish run to this lake from the sea only in the fall. It is hard for the fish to move from the sea to the lake water, which affects them very much. The fish became covered with deep wounds and turn red and then disappear in the lake. It is this poor-quality fish that the local Kenaitze use as their food. As a result, the natives are constantly sick, and their bodies are covered with sore spots. I still did not have the opportunity to visit all the Kenaitze for reasons beyond my control. During my winter trip rainy weather washed away all the snow from the tundra and made traveling impossible. I wanted to reach the place from which the convenient route goes to Kichek [Kijik], but the lack of snow in the tundra forced me to come back. Although I was not able yet to see all the Kenaitze people, from what I heard and from my personal meetings with a few of them, I concluded that in terms of religion they have many positive qualities. Morally, they are also little corrupted, for they live far from all civilizers. In their village the Kichek people have a chapel.

Vladimir Modestov: Rosters of Residents of Iliamna Village[88]

	Iliamna Village: Creoles	males' age	females' age
1	Kosma [Kuzma] Riktorov	57	
2	his wife Dariia		28
3	their daughter Varvara [Barbara]		4
4	Vasilii Riktorov	51	
5	his wife Mariia [Mary]		41
	their children:		
6	Mikhail	26	
7	Stefan [Stephen]	21	
8	Paraskeva	15	
9	their adopted son Gavriil Riktorov	5	
10	Evfim [Efim] Riktorov	53	
11	his wife Agafiia		37
	their children:		
12	Ioann	23	
13	Varvara [Barbara]		11
14	Widow Dariia Tuknikhliushen		100
15	Widow Vassilissa Riktorov		38
	her children:		
16	Mikhail Riktorov, II	19	
17	Mikhail Riktorov, I	17	
18	Sofiia		16
19	Lukeriia		2

continued on next page

Continued from previous page

	Iliamna Village: Kenaitze	males' age	females' age
20	Simeon Tagnakhtukhta [his last name is illegible]	35	
21	Evdokiia [his wife?]		28
	their children:		
22	Ekaterina [Catherine]		5
23	Nikita		6
24	Agafiia		2
25	Kirill Kiltkide	32	
26	his wife Mariia [Mary]		23
27	their daughter Anna		4
28	Mikhail [Michael] Buitokha, widower	75	
29	Kirill Buitokha	35	
30	Stefanida L'kudkhugtut		22
31	her daughter Varvara [Barbara]		6
32	Aleksei L'kagliaga	43	
33	his wife Akilina		28
34	their daughter Sofia		5
35	Zakharii [Zakhar] Ivanov [Evanoff]	38	
36	his wife Anastasiia		28
	their children:		
37	Marfa		6
38	Evfimii [Efim]	5	
39	Paraskeva		2
40	Nikolai Grigoriev	43	
41	his wife Marfa		20
42	their daughter Marfa		4
43	their son Grigorii	2	
44	Ioann [Ivan] Tugnukadilen	26	
45	his wife Ekaterina [Catherine]		21
46	Ioann [Ivan] Tkil'kide	44	
47	his wife Mariia [Mary]		38
	their children:		
48	Ignatii	7	
49	Zakharii [Zakhar]	1	
50	Feodor [Fedor] Konal'tukta	36	
51	his wife Dariia		35
	their children:		
52	Stefan [Stephen]	16	
53	Zinovii	1	
54	Evdokiia Konal'tukta		18
55	her daughter Paraskeva		1

	Iliamna Village: Kenaitze	males' age	females' age
56	Widow Stefanida Bakun'		50
57	Panteleimon [her son?]	29	
58	Grigorii Zakharov	24	
59	Savva Kibul'kahk	23	
60	Nikolai L'kagliaga	21	
61	Andrei Koidul'kil [Koidul'kin, his last name is illegible]	40	
62	his wife Anna		38
	their children:		
63	Gerasim	18	
64	Mikhail [Michael]	10	
65	Nikolai	7	
66	Ekaterina [Catherine]		4
67	Paraskeva		2
68	Mariia [Mary], wife of Fred Roehl		32
	their children:		
69	Sergei	n/a	
70	Mariia [Mary]		n/a
71	Sofia		n/a
72	Feodor [Fedor]	8	
73	Vladimir	6	
74	Vasilii	2	
75	Mariia [Mary], wife of Christian Nelson		38

Vasilii Kashevarov: A Trip to the Iliamna Dena'ina, Extracts from Travel Journal, July 12, 1903, to March 7, 1904[89]

July 12. Departed from Nushagak on [...] steamer together with Father A. Kedrovski, the Dean of Clergy.

July 13. At 4 o'clock in the morning continued our route.

July 14. We approach the Bay of Ugashek. In the evening again continued our route and reached Ugashek, where we arrived on July 17.

1904. January 17. In the morning departed again. The route turned out to be very bad. In some places we had to walk in deep snow up to our waists.

January 18. Today proceeded further with great difficulty. At 8 o'clock in the evening, having noticed a grove, decided to stay here for the night.

[...] January 30. [...] Today we proceeded further on the [Iliamna] lake. At 8 o'clock in the evening came to Iliamna village.

January 31. In the morning we performed a requiem service and then anointed with myrrh four infants. In the evening we performed the all-night vigil.

February 1. The liturgy without consecration and lesser blessing of water since the morning, and I also delivered a Sunday sermon using the Gospel text. After the service there was a meeting, during which we established a brotherhood named after the feast day of the Meeting of the Lord [*sretenie*]. We also elected a chairman of the brotherhood. The *toion* of the village, Kozma Riktorov, became the chairman of the brotherhood. Evfimii Riktorov became the treasurer, and Vasilii Riktorov was elected record-keeper. Afterwards, I heard confessions from eighteen men, twenty-one women, ten boys and seven girls of school age. In the evening I performed the all-night vigil.

February 2. A morning prayer and the liturgy [without consecration?], and then taught people about the Christian life. Upon request of the village residents, I visited their homes carrying the cross and holy water. In the afternoon I checked the registers and wrote down again the names of all inhabitants. Because the chapel is falling into decay, I suggested that they prepare wooden logs to build a new one. All residents wholeheartedly decided to stock the logs and after this to start construction.

February 3. In the morning I baptized a newborn, and then departed, going to Kijik village. Continued our route until 6 o'clock in the evening. In a portage area, we stopped for the night.

February 4. In the morning continued our route, and stayed the night en route.

February 5. At dawn we set out and came to Kijik in the afternoon. I performed the rite of lesser blessing of water. Then heard confessions from eighteen men, eighteen women, four boys and two girls of school age. Anointed with myrrh two infants and then taught the people.

February 6. The morning prayer and the liturgy without consecration. Then I gave communion to those who confessed. Had a talk with the residents of the village and advised them to move closer to Iliamna Lake because Kijik is located far away from any convenient routes. The residents completely agreed with me. Performed four marriage ceremonies. Yesterday and today it is freezing. We are on the way back [to Nushagak].

Konstantin Pavlov, from the Church Service Journal for 1904[90]

January 26. Because I am planning to travel up Kuskokwim to the Stony or Kenaitze River, I performed a customary church service for those who wish to embark on a journey. At noon we departed and stopped a miner's cabin for a night.

January 27. We continued our route and stopped at Kolmakovskoe [former Kolmakovskii Redoubt] for two hours. In the evening we reached the Nakamiiut settlement, where we stopped for a night.

January 28. I read a morning prayer, heard confessions from an ailing woman and an old man, and performed a customary prayer service and a baptism rite. After this I made rounds of local dwellings blessing them with holy water. In Nakamiiut I found Kenaitze natives, who came down to this village on two sleds specially to accompany me to the Stony River. I and my travel companions departed on three fully loaded sleds. The Kenaitze carried not only part of my large baggage, but also many other items they had bought in a local store. Since I remembered very well how I had to starve for the whole month traveling the same route in 1902, I decided to take extra food for this trip. Moreover, as early as this summer I had sent with a few natives an extra supply of flour to be delivered up the Kuskokwim River and stored there exclusively for this trip. However, I had little hope this flour would be kept for me. As it turned out, I was right: Kuskokwim natives did not wait for my arrival and already used it. By the evening we reached the Ingigagimut village, where I read an evening prayer.

January 29. After a morning prayer, I heard a confession from a sick native, who also received last rites.

February 1. We stopped in another settlement, where we met a merchant named Ivan Andreanov. He told us that the route leading upriver was very bad. The entire path was covered with deep snow that became soft and hard to travel on because of the warm weather. Despite such grim prospects, Andreanov added that it was possible to reach the next *odinochka*. Incidentally, we ran across an owner of this *odinochka*, and he even agreed to accompany us by going in front of our party in his snowshoes and firming the route for our sleds. Soon we were caught in a blizzard, which made it hard for us to follow a narrow path. Instead of 5 o'clock, as we planned, we reached his *odinochka* only at 11 o'clock in the evening. Since the owner of the *odinochka* was traveling with us, there was nobody to keep a fire. So it took us a long time to start the fire in a stove and warm the whole structure. As a result, we went to bed far after 2 o'clock in the morning.

February 2. At 9 o'clock I performed a morning prayer, then a customary prayer service at noon and after this a requiem service. At 12:30 o'clock in the afternoon continued our journey. We left one of our sleds in the *odinochka* for Vasilii, whom I took as a guide. When I set out he was not ready for the trip and was to join us later. Soon we were again caught in a strong wind and a blizzard. As a matter of fact, it was helpful. The strong wind firmed the snow and it was only in a few spots that it was soft. However, when it grew darker we felt that we were losing our route. We were able to reach a village only at 8 o'clock in the evening and went to bed at 11 o'clock.

February 3. After a morning prayer at 8 o'clock, we had breakfast, repaired the sleds and then prepared fodder for our dogs. About noon the rest of our party joined us on two sleds. At 4 o'clock I served a requiem service, then a customary prayer service devoted to the Savior. After supper I read an evening prayer.

February 4. At 7 o'clock I read a morning prayer, and after having breakfast we continued our route. Our party stopped for one and a half-hour in another village, where I performed a customary prayer service, after which we departed. Today we planned to reach one more *odinochka*, yet a strong blizzard disrupted our plans, and we had to spend a night in a tent.

February 5. Today the strong blizzard did not let us move too far and again we had to spend a night in the tent.

February 6. The route was so bad that our guide refused to accompany us. Although we had enough people to move on, we did want him to go with us. To have more people in front of the dogs to firm the path with snowshoes would have made our route easier. Yet we had to accept his decision. Despite our fears, the route turned out to be not so bad. A strong wind made the snow very firm, and it did not stick to our sleds. So we moved forward very fast. The only inconvenience we had to cope with was snowdrifts. Now the dogs ran so fast that coming over snowdrifts they frequently turned the sleds over. Yet it was much easier to put the sleds back than to pull them out from deep snow, which usually gets you all wet. At noon we reached three abandoned miners' cabins. We spent a night here. I intended to take to the Kenaitze [Stony] River only people I might need there. The rest of our party was instructed to stay in the cabins and wait for my return to be prepared to accompany me in a trip up the Kuskokwim River.

February 7. At 8 o'clock in the morning we departed and traveled the whole day and stopped only for one and a half hours to make some tea. Although there is no visible path anywhere, heavily loaded sleds moved smoothly without leaving any tracks. The right bank of the [Stony] River, where our path lay, was firmed by the wind so well that a surface looked as though somebody polished it. For the first time during the whole journey we did nothing except simply sitting on sleds. To be exact, there were some spots, especially around islands, where the snow remained soft. Still, compared with the earlier route, this one was God's blessing.

February 8. We departed and remained en route the whole day by making only a short stop for one and a half hours. The route was getting better. Stopped for a night at a portage place.

February 9. Crossed the portage and met Nikita, who was busy trapping fur animals. He moved around with his family. Nikita's *odinochka* is located on another river. Our dogs that pulled three sleds consumed plenty of fodder and we hardly had any left. Fortunately, we found out that Nikita has a large supply of frozen fish. So we bought some from and paid him with tea, sugar, flour and tobacco. On two sleds three of us were to proceed further, while Pavel was to accompany Nikita to his place to bring frozen fish. Pavel was expected to catch up with us later, when we stopped for a night. To make traveling easier for him we took part of his baggage and loaded it on our sleds. Although the route was good, quite soon we decided to stop to have a meal because we did not eat anything since the morning. After the meal we spent the rest of the day waiting for Pavel. Yet he did not return, and we went to sleep.

February 10. We were about to have breakfast when Pavel finally came back. It snowed last night and Pavel lost our tracks. As it turned out, he spent the night very close to us. The whole day we were en route and made only a short stop for one and a half hours.

February 11. We departed and about noon reached the summer Kenaitze camp. Then we went a little farther upriver and found there a well-trodden path. Local people usually use this route to go fishing and hunting. As early as the last fall the Kenaitze procured in this area forty moose. The weather now grew warmer, and the snow was not so firm as earlier. Besides, at this point the river became more narrow and the mountains higher. All this complicated our travel. Moreover, our path went on a ridge, which in appearance resembled a railroad earth-bank, and our sleds constantly slipped down. After a while, we reached a tent that belonged to Mr. Hobson, a Russian Orthodox American, who was trapping in this area. Yet, since Mr. Hobson was somewhere in the woods, we did not see him personally. We stayed by the tent for a little while debating whether to stop or proceed straight to the Kenaitze settlement. This was my first trip [to Kangallen (Queghnilen)],[91] and I asked my guides how far the village was. They said that it remained about twenty miles. Then I suggested that we better spend a night at the tent because we were already en route for ten days and the dogs were tired. After we drank a tea, my travel companions started complaining that it was a mistake to stay here: the weather was so nice, the crescent lightens the path and it would have been easier to go farther. On top of everything, they added that the Kenaitze, who usually hunted in this area, were within reach. "Well, if you want so, let's move on," I said. We baked more bread [*lepeshki*] to have something to eat with tea en route when we were tired and decided again to stop. At the moment that we were ready to depart nobody thought about what was going on outside the tent. The clear sky suddenly became covered with clouds and the crescent was gone. However, this did not stop my travel companions and we proceeded. At first, indeed when we went along the bank of the river the route was very good. But then we started stumbling on small frozen river islands and soon lost the path. One of the guides said, "Here is the route." Another disagreed. Thus, we wandered around and ended up on blocks of ice heaped one upon another. At that point nobody except our Lord God knew where we were going. No matter where we turned we drowned in deep snow. By chance I stepped on a correct path, which still went along the bank. Having exhausted ourselves in this manner, we made a stop, when it was already 2 o'clock in the morning. Since we had no power to prepare our sleeping place, we only made a fire and simply dropped around it on the ground and fell asleep.

February 12. All of a sudden I woke up feeling that I was freezing. The fire was almost gone. I looked at my watch that showed 5 o'clock in the morning. I started waking up my travel companions telling them that it was time to make tea. After having tea, we departed. En route we again had to put back the sleds that kept on sliding down. Before our party reached the village, we made another short stop to have some tea. Finally, at 3:30 o'clock in the afternoon we came to the village that welcomed with guns' salute and American flags, which natives had raised on their roofs. With us we also had an American flag, which was put in use as soon as we neared the village. We stopped by a high mountain that separated us from Kangallen. My guides attached the flag to the sled where I was sitting and then told me to move on at the head of our party. After this the guides made three shots from a pistol. People of the village responded with numerous gunshots. Thus, accompanied by the guns' salute, we entered the settlement. All residents crowded outside waiting for my blessings. Among the villagers I recognized only three Kenaitze who I had met earlier. As for the rest of the inhabitants, it was the first time when I saw them. Formally, Kangallen belongs to the Nushagak mission. Yet Nushagak priests did not visit this settlement not only because it was located very far from the mission, but also because high mountains prevented their trips. Six years ago, when Father Vladimir Modestov visited the Kichek [Kijik] village, the [Stony River] Kenaitze came there to partake of Orthodox rites. It was Father Modestov who advised them at that time to turn to the Kuskokwim Mission. Although our mission is as far from the Stony River as Nushagak, travel conditions are more convenient. In 1902 Kangallen Kenaitze went down to our mission in hope to meet me, but at that time I was away on a trip to the upper Kuskokwim River area. Now when they came to our mission again, I decided to visit them.

After my arrival at Kangallen, at 6 o'clock in the evening I served a customary prayer service devoted to the Savior. There were twenty-seven people who came to pray.

February 13. At 7:30 o'clock I read a morning prayer, then I performed the liturgy without consecration and read a prayer addressed to the Mother of God. In the afternoon the Kenaitze were busy cleaning their houses and buying icons, small body crosses and candles I brought with me. In the meantime, I was preparing new registers of parishioners. At 6 o'clock in he evening I served a customary prayer service devoted to St. Nicholas and Venerable St. Sergius. After this I read an evening prayer. Then I reprimanded a Kenaitze named Big Ivan for cursing in the presence of women. I reminded him that, as an old man, he should himself serve as a model of behavior for other people. To prevent him from cursing in future I ordered Big Ivan to kneel down and to bow a few times in front of an icon depicting the image of the Savior and ask Lord to forgive him for his sins and to help him in future. I also instructed Big Ivan to approach those two women who had complained to me about him and apologize for his behavior. Big Ivan admitted that he did say bad words in the presence of those women and he also readily agreed to accept a church punishment I assigned to him. He appeared to be a religious man and kept many icons in his house. Moreover, to add to this, today Ivan bought an icon-lamp with all necessary items such as oil and wicks and two more good-looking icons famed in glass. Although his children were already grown up people, according to his fellow-villagers, Big Ivan tended to act as a fool [*s dur'iu*]. They said that his judgments sometimes betrayed infantilism and were more characteristic of an adolescent than of an adult.

February 14. At 8 o'clock in the morning I read a morning prayer, then the Hours, and anointed with myrrh four children, who had been earlier baptized by a layman. After this I served the liturgy without consecration along with a rite of a lesser blessing of water. I also instructed people how to be prepared for confession. Then, carrying holy water, I visited villagers' homes. At 2 o'clock in the afternoon people gathered to confess. After reading a prayer I taught the Kenaitze how to perform a rite of penance in a ten psalm monastic manner [*desiatislovie*]. Then I heard confession of eighteen people. At 6 o'clock in the evening I served an all-night vigil and read an evening prayer.

February 15. At 7 o'clock I read a morning prayer, then the Hours, and after this performed a requiem service. After this I served the Holy Liturgy of St. Basil the Great, during which I gave communion to twenty-five people including children. After the liturgy I reminded the people that they should thank our Lord God, who honored them with the opportunity to accept in themselves the Savior's body and blood, which finally made them participants of eternal and holy life. In my talk I praised the Kenaitze for maintaining their zeal for Lord's church after so many years of abstaining from sacraments. Only three residents of the village received sacraments two years ago, three others made it four years ago, and the rest of the villagers did not partake of the Holy Mysteries for six years. I also instructed them to stay always firm in their Orthodox faith and strive to receive God's mercy. Finally, I said that they should try to build a chapel in their village. In this case the priest most probably would visit them more regularly, and, besides, people themselves would receive more chances to gather for a communal prayer. Yet people of the village told me that they already did gather for a communal prayer anyway. To these words I responded that if they had had a chapel, even those who might be lazy would have been more involved into praying. After dinner, considering the extreme conditions under which the Kenaitze had to live, I performed four marriage ceremonies out of season in violation of the rule that our church for such ceremonies. At 6 o'clock I served a thanksgiving prayer service and read an evening prayer.

February 16. I read a morning prayer, then we had breakfast, and after this during a general meeting we elected a *toion*, his assistant and a churchwarden. We also conversed about building a village church or a chapel. Villagers decided to work together and elected people who would be responsible for supervising the construction works. We decided to build a small church with a cupola in the middle of the roof. To the other side of the building the Kenaitze decided to attach a small room to accommodate a priest. It was also decided to build a threshold with a door instead of a portico. People of the village noted that with the building of the chapel fifteen more Kenaitze, who resided fifty miles up the [Stony] River and between twelve and fifteen other people from the Kichek village, who were also their kins, would move to live here in Kangallen. As a matter of fact, local inhabitants already counted these two groups as their fellow villagers. I believe that even more Kichek people might move to the Stony River because hunting and fishing in the area surrounding Kangallen are more productive. Fish and game here are very abundant. Difficulty in transporting food supplies to the Stony River represents the only disadvantage of this place. Thus, to deliver supplies from the Kuskokwim area to the Kolmakovskii settlement is very far, hard, expensive, and usually any expenses are never worth efforts one spends. To deliver the supplies from Iliamna or Kichek will be closer, but mountain barriers again make it very difficult.

Ivan Konstantinov[92] was reelected for the position of the *toion*, while I'akov Ivanov was elected his assistant [*zakazchik?*]. An American citizen, Grigorii Mikhailovich Hobson was elected a churchwarden and Pavel Konstantinov became his assistant. G. Hobson was to keep a record of church finances and donations for the building of the chapel. He was also to supervise the construction work, for he is a white man and knows how to do it. Besides, he was familiar with carpentry work and knew how to use a saw. The Kenaitze assured me that as soon as the guides, who had been assigned to accompany me come on the way back, would return, the residents of the village together would go to the woods to cut logs and store them on a bank of the river. When the river becomes free of ice, they would bring the logs down to the village and then would place them up to the designated spot where the chapel would be built. In the fall, as they added, after the fishing season was over, they would start building the chapel. The villagers asked me to order a cross and a copy of the Gospel to be placed in the new chapel. As for the icons, the villagers might acquire the framed ones from our church storage that were usually used on a pulpit. The site that the Kenaitze selected for the chapel was even and located close to the village. They said that this site could be seen from any nearby mountain. Indeed, at some distance from the village one sees everywhere mountains and their peaks are not covered with woods. I would like to confirm that the spot selected for the future chapel was treeless and indeed could be seen from all sides. It appears that those who live in Kangallen are good people and zealous in religious life. I wish them luck and hope Lord will assist them in their plans.

At 11 o'clock in the morning the newly elected headmen were sworn in their offices. Then I served a customary prayer service devoted to the Savior. After this I instructed the newly elected to care about the well-being of their fellow villagers and to teach the people how to live in peace. Other Kenaitze were instructed to listen to their headmen and to observe their orders, especially during the construction of the chapel. I also addressed the women asking them contribute their labor to the building of the structure. It should be mentioned that in spring in this village all women usually go to the mountains to hunt *evrazhki*. Moreover, those who are younger usually trap the sable in winter. I asked Konstantin and Ivan, two old men, not to be offended that they had not been elected to the headmen positions. Konstantin was not too outspoken and for this reason would hardly reprimand those who do not listen to him or do not act as good Christians. The other old man was, on the contrary, so talkative that one hardly heard from him any useful suggestions. I doubted that the Kenaitze would observe his orders either. Still, since they were the oldest people in Kangallen, I instructed all other people to seek their advice during village meetings and generally to show them their respect, for Our Lord God rewards those who respect old people.

After dinner, accompanied by their owners, I went to bless summer *odinochkas* and caches where natives stored their fish and fishing gear. Village people supplied me with a necessary quantity (which was more than enough) of good dried fish to feed my dogs. Since the Kenaitze refused to accept money in return, I gave them tea, sugar, flour and tobacco. Furthermore, those who showed particular Christian zeal received three icons and [illegible word]. To my surprise, in the evening in the presence of the entire village including women and children the Kenaitze showered me with numerous gifts: a black sable pelt, five fox pelts, twenty deer skins, furs from deer legs to make fur boots [*tarbasy*] and [illegible word]. Many villagers approached me and stressed that they felt happy that the priest not only visited their settlement, but also stayed with them for so long, which gave him a chance to meet and to talk with everybody individually. I thanked them for inviting me and added that each priest would be happy anyway to visit and address religious needs of his parishioners without any presents. He would do it more eagerly for the people who were so attentive to his instructions and wanted to fulfill them. Never before in my life did I see a gratitude toward me expressed in such unusual manner. At first, I was stunned. Then, after giving it a second thought, I became even scared that I had accepted all those gifts. I was afraid that my advice to contribute part of their labor to the church and the presents that I had accepted could be interpreted in a wrong way. I pictured what people of Kuskokwim, where nothing like this had ever happened, would say when they learned about the gifts. They might spread a rumor that I had extracted these presents or they might say that I took the items donated to the church for myself. So I immediately informed Mr. Hobson, who acted as my interpreter, about my concerns and asked him to explain it to the villagers. At my suggestion Mr. Hobson made a list of all the presents with a written confirmation that I had received them as a gratitude. After such list was prepared people signed it by putting down crosses in front of their names. On top of everything, I gave the Kenaitze more tea and tobacco so favored by natives (*dikarskii tabak*). I shared them equally among those native who were present.

Today I also served a customary prayer service devoted to St. Nicholas and Venerable St. Sergius of Radonezh, the Wonderworker. I instructed the Kenaitze to gather regularly for a communal prayer, to work to establish a chapel in their village and credited them for the donations they had made to the construction of a new church in Chugakhpalik, the center of their new parish.[93] Regarding this, it should be stressed that the villagers donated six sable and four fox pelts, a deer skin and furs from deer legs as their contribution to the construction of the new mission church in Chugakhpalik. The total amount of the contributions after the sale of all these items is equal to $42. God will certainly reward them for this generous gesture. I added that in the same manner, little by little, they might raise money for their own chapel. This would let them not only to build the structure but also to decorate it with requisite church items.

At 9 o'clock I read an evening prayer.

February 17. At 6:30 I read a morning prayer, then drank tea and prepared myself for the return trip. At 8 o'clock in the morning all inhabitants gathered for a farewell prayer, after which I instructed them to live in peace with each other and to work to speed up the construction of the chapel without waiting for people from other villages to move to Kangallen. Although there were only eight men in the village who were able to perform the work, God would help them if they did this work together. As for the settlement located fifty miles up the river, I did not go there because it snowed very heavily. Besides, people of Kangallen and that village did not visit each other recently and no one knew exactly if somebody wintered up there or all inhabitants left for hunting trips.

During the days of my stay in Kangallen its residents not only gladly visited religious services, but never left them. Nor did they allow themselves to sit down, which is a common practice in the Kuskokwim area. I also noticed that the Kangallen people made the sign of the cross in a correct manner. They also knew and regularly sang [*prednachertatel'nie*] prayers and *troparions* devoted to St. Nicholas. They recited the prayers not only during the services, but also at home. During the services they sang "God, Have Mercy on Us." Each day of my stay in the afternoon and in the evening after services I taught them to sing the Symbol of Faith and other psalms from all-night vigil and Liturgy services. I was very grateful to Grigorii Hobson, who acted as my interpreter. He knows Russian quite well and also speaks fluently the native language. Mr. Hobson provided me with information about the inhabitants of the village and their life-ways. Because of his help, I was also able to conduct individual talks with residents of the village and to issue them various instructions.

About 9 o'clock in the morning accompanied by two guides I left the village for the Nikifor's settlement on the Kuskokwim River. The Kenaitze parted with me in the same manner as they met me by saluting with guns' shooting and raising flags over their dwellings. Being concerned about my food supplies, they instructed me to stop in an *odinochka* located en route and to help myself with frozen fish. Soon after we left the village a blizzard started and we could not reach the *odinochka*. Instead we stopped at Hobson's tent and spent a night there.

February 18. We departed and reached the route that led to the *odinochka*. While I was waiting behind, I'akov and Kirill went to the *odinochka*. In three hours they came back carrying large supply of fish. After having tea, we continued our route and stopped at the old site that we had used while going to the village.

February 19. Traveled the whole day and stopped for a night at the old spot we had used earlier.

February 20. Continued our route. Reached Nikita's *odinochka*, where we supplied ourselves with fish for the dogs because I heard that on Kuskokwim we would be able to find neither fish nor people. After I bought from him some fish for us, we drank tea. Nikita and his wife lived in the Kuskokwim area in summer and he partook of the rite of during my summer visit. We continued our route. At the portage place we met eight people who were moving from Kuskokwim to live in the vicinity of Nikita's *odinochka*. These people said that they did not eat for two days. I gave to each of them a large pike fish. Having crossed a short mountain portage, we stopped for a night.

February 21. We were en route the whole day.

February 22. About noon we came to a cabin, where I had an extra supply of food for this trip stored. We took part of that food for themselves and for our dogs. I left the rest of the provisions to be used during my next trip.

February 23. We departed and reached Nikifor's cabin where we met old Andreanov, who arrived at Nikifor's place earlier. Andreanov was on his home from Kolmakovskii. At 8 o'clock I read an evening prayer.

February 24. At 7 o'clock I read a morning prayer. I decided to stay at Nikifor's place for a day because my whole trip up the Kuskokwim River depended on Andreanov's son [Sergei], who speaks fluently both Russian and Kolchan and who I wanted to ask him to accompany me in this trip as an interpreter. Old Andreanov was ill and I doubted if his son would agree to go with me. In summer I and my songleader Kukichuk had already visited and performed services for Nikifor's family and the settlements that were scattered in the area stretched over 160 miles from our mission to Nikifor's place.

About noon Sergei Ivanovich Andreanov arrived. After numerous excuses such as the illness of his father and lack of fish supplies in the villages that I wanted to visit, he did secure permission from his father to accompany me. In return we promised to the old man that on the way back we would stay with him two or three days because Sergei Ivanovich was to finish some work for him. I had enough fish for my dogs to make a trip upriver and back. Moreover, Nikifor and his family promise to feed me when I would be staying with them. They had a large supply of frozen fish. However, they did not have any dried fish. They said that the flour that I had left with them as early as summer they had to use. Fortunately, I carried a supply of flour that might be enough to travel to up the Kuskokwim River. I also heard that there was a store up there. Although it was very expensive, I hoped I would be able to buy some extra flour there. Up there they charged $12 for a sack of flour that weighed fifty pounds.

February 25. At 6:30 I read a morning prayer and confessed an old woman named Nadezhda and also gave her communion. Then I served a customary prayer service devoted to St. Tarasii. There were sixteen persons who came for a prayer. After breakfast we departed, and about 5 o'clock in the evening we reached a residency [*zhilo*] of Ivan Andreanov. The winds that kept on blowing in this area all the time did not leave much snow on the ground. For this reason, banks and the ice surface of the Kuskokwim River, especially around islands, were covered with sand, which made it very difficult for our dogs to move forward.

February 26. I read a morning prayer. At 11 o'clock in the morning I performed a great requiem service for God's servant Paraskov'ia, the wife of Andreanov, who died on October 25 of 1903. The service was followed by the *litiia* that I served at her grave. Then I read an evening prayer.

February 27. I read a morning prayer at 7 o'clock. Then I sang a funeral service for God's servant Paraskov'ia and continued the *litiia* service at her grave. Then I performed a rite of lesser water blessing. I read an evening prayer and talked about differences among religions.

February 28. I read a morning prayer, drank tea and set out for the Venisari village. We were en route the whole day and stopped for a night not far from a large reach. After we woke up and continued our route, we met at this reach a Kolchan man with his family. In summer this man descended to our mission, then delayed his return home on upper Kuskokwim. Now he had to winter here unsuccessfully trying to catch some fish. At the same time, this Kolchan could not hunt animals because he was afraid to wander off far from his camp and to leave his wife and children without food. As a result, the whole family had to starve and subside only on [illegible word]. I gave them some flour, fish and sugar. It was the same Kolchan man with whom in summer I had sent candles, icons, small crosses and icon-lamps to the Venisari village. Since he did not reach his village, we took all these items with us. We spent this night in a spot beyond the second portage.

March 1. The whole day we spent en route, which was hard. Beginning from Andreanov's place there were no traces of any tracks or footprints. At least we rarely drowned in snow because a strong wind firmed the snow a little on one of the river banks. When it remained about eight miles to Venisari we decided to stop for a night.

March 2. After having breakfast, we continued our route, and about 11 o'clock in the morning we met a miner. He told us that he had visited the above-mentioned store and found out that it had absolutely no food for sale. He also added that people on upper Kuskokwim starved. They had neither fish nor meat and had to subsist only on the meat of sables and other small animals. The miner also added that all transport dogs up there died off [*okoleli*].[94]

Nikifor Amkan, from the Church Service Journal for 1905[95]

May 13. Three days ago a [Kenaitze] *toion* Ivan Konstantinovich [Konstantinov] specially sailed down to our mission to accompany me to his people. I got into his *baidarka* that can carry three persons and set out to visit the Kenaitze. At first we enjoyed the route because the weather was nice. Then we heard bursts of thunder and soon it already rained very heavily. So our plans to reach the Ingichagliut village at this day failed. After we made a stop for a night, I read an evening prayer, the practice I and my travel companions strictly followed thereafter during the entire trip.

May 15. At 6 o'clock in the evening, when we came to the Iugnilnuk village, I baptized two infants of a female gender.

May 18. At the mouth of the Stony River I baptized another infant of a female gender. At this point two more boats joined our party: a *baidarka*, which like ours could carry three persons, and a small boat made of birch bark. Having said goodbuy to the Kuskokwim River, we proceeded up the Stony River against the rapid current. To keep our boats steady we had to balance them all the time with long poles. On these waters paddles were of no use. The country we entered is very rich in many different kinds of animals, especially black bears. Once at night one of them even woke us up with its loud roaring. With loaded rifles my two travel companions went in the woods to check it out, but did not find anything.

May 22. At 9 o'clock we continued our route and already did not make any long stop all the way up to Kangallen. As we were moving toward the village, I noticed that the current was getting faster. Huge rocks were sticking from the river everywhere. It was these rocks that gave the name to the river. In some spots streams of water beating off these rocks got in our *baidarkas*.

May 23. Yesterday in the evening the *toion* sent his brother Pavel to inform the inhabitants of Kangallen that I was coming and to tell them to prepare accommodations for me. After we prayed to our Lord God and had breakfast, at 7 o'clock in the morning we were again en route. Yesterday's rain rose the level of water in the river, which made the current even faster. Yet we knew that our trip against the rapid current would soon be over, and therefore worked harder with our poles. The sun already hid at the horizon when the *toion* told me that we were nearing the village and shot his rifle signaling about our arrival. Suddenly, we heard sounds of dozens of gunshots coming from beyond a small cape. It was only when we reached the village that the sounds died. When we rounded the cape, a beautiful view unfolded before my eyes. At some distance from the Kenaitze dwellings at a visible spot stood a neat chapel that was under construction. A large national American flag joyfully fluttered over the village. We also had a small flag, which the *toion* attached to our *baidarka*. People, who already knew about my visit, crowded at the spot where our *baidarka* was expected to land. Finally gunshots fell silent and our boat landed to a special dock, which the Kenaitze made of boards. All inhabitants approached me for blessings. I told them to gather in one of their large houses for a service. After our baggage was unloaded, I performed an evening service during which all people together sang hymns in Slavonic language. After the service, through an interpreter, I delivered my welcoming address, in which I praised the Kenaitze for taking a trouble of going a few hundred miles to bring the priest despite all the difficulties of such journey. Having received my blessing, people went back home.

May 24. At 8 o'clock I read a morning prayer after which I performed a funeral service for an infant. At noon I baptized four infants and anointed with myrrh two others, who had been baptized by Aleksei Riktorov, a Nushagak Creole. At 2:30 o'clock in the afternoon I read requisite prayers, which are sung before confession. Also, through the interpreter, I explained to the people the meaning of the Ten Commandments. Then I confessed thirty-three souls of both genders. At 7 o'clock I performed vespers and matins that included an *akathist* devoted to the Most Holy Mother of God.

May 25. At 8 o'clock in the morning I served the Divine Liturgy. Before giving the Kenaitze communion I explained to them what Orthodox true believers were expected to feel when they approached the Holy Cup [*Sviataia Chasha*] in order to accept body and blood of Christ. Forty-four people of both genders including children received communion. Then I performed the rite of lesser water blessing, after which I went around blessing dwellings of the villagers with holy water. Then I performed the rite of holy matrimony for two couples and devoted the rest of the day to chapel-related matters. I gave instructions how to build a roof and recommended to finish the whole work as soon as possible. In this case, during my next visit I would be able to consecrate the structure. In the evening I served vespers and talked with people about the Orthodox faith through the interpreter.

May 26. At 10 o'clock in the morning I served the liturgy without consecration and delivered a farewell address, where I instructed the Kenaitze to live according to God's commandments and not listen to any shamans and miners, who here [on the Stony River] and everywhere in Kuskokwim and Kvikhpakh [Yukon] morally corrupt natives and distract them from fulfilling their Christian duties. Earlier miners were hardly seen in this area [Stony River]. Now they started to wander in here more often.

At noon having prayed to our Lord God along with everybody and having blessed all Kenaitze, I and my interpreter Ivan got in the small *baidarka* and left the village. Our departure was accompanied by the salute from rifles. Fortunately for us, at night the water rose and the rapid current quickly carried us downriver. With a sinking heart I watched how we maneuvered through sharp rocks sticking from under water and every minute expected to be smashed off them. However, my travel companion turned out to be a seasoned paddler who went over this river back and forth many times. He knew perfectly well all dangerous spots and handled the *baidarka* in a confident manner.

May 27. At 6 o'clock in the evening we reached the mouth of the [Stony] River, where I served vespers and confessed nine souls of both genders.

May 28. At 7 o'clock I read a morning prayer for whose who performed rites of penance and fast. Then I served the rite of lesser water blessing and providing sacraments to local people using presanctified gifts. After this I served great requiem at a local cemetery. At 11 o'clock we were again en route. At the Chlitmiut settlement I left Ivan, my travel companion, and at 5 o'clock in the evening I was on my way home traveling alone.

May 29. In the village of Iugnilnuk at 6 o'clock in the evening I baptized an infant of a female gender.

May 30. Today I decided to stay in this village because of a strong wind. At 4 o'clock in the evening I sang a funeral service for an infant.

May 31. At 8 o'clock in the morning I sang a funeral service at the Aniagaiak village, and at 6 o'clock in the evening using presanctified gifts I gave last rites to a woman named Akilina [Akulina?], who is seriously ill.

June 1. At 8 o'clock in the morning in the village of Napamiut I sang a funeral service for an infant, and then at 10 o'clock I continued my route without making any stops. At 7 o'clock in the evening I was already at home. Thank God, I was glad to find everybody in a good health.

My journey to the Kenaitze produced on me the most favorable impression. Earlier, when I was still a songleader attached to the Kvikhpakh Mission, I accompanied two missionaries to many other villages, but never did I see such religious people who were so committed to their Orthodox faith. I wish that in future all other people become so zealous in their faith like these Kenaitze.

Priest Nikifor Amkan.

Nikifor Amkan, from the Church Service Journal for 1906[96]

A Trip to the Kangallen Village.

A day ago the *toion* of the Kangallen village came specially to accompany me his village. On May 13, having prayed to God, I and my travel companion departed on a *baidarka*. Hardly had we started our trip than we met a steamship that belonged to Mr. Lind, who was going down the [Kuskokwim] River to the Moravian mission to take there some goods. At first, the weather was excellent, but a little later we heard bursts of a thunderstorm, and soon were caught in a heavy rain with hail. At 5 o'clock in the evening we came to the Napamiut village. Here Grigorii, an infant son of Vasilii Ashipiak, died yesterday. Yet I decided to perform a funeral ceremony for him on my way back. We stopped for a night at a next village called Ingichoagmiut and ate what God sent to us [*chto Bog poslal*]. Having prayed to God we went to sleep.

May 14. After reading a morning prayer and heaving tea, we continued our route stopping in each settlement we met on our way at least for a few minutes to provide blessings to their inhabitants, who accepted them with reverence. At 8 o'clock in the evening we stopped for a night in the vicinity of the winter portage. After having a meal of fish and having prayed to God, we went to sleep.

May 15. At 7 o'clock in the morning, after having breakfast, we continued our route. A few times our travel was interrupted by a nasty wind that blew right in our faces.

For the past few days I performed the following baptisms: (1) a daughter of a native named Makarii Chiliklanak and his lawful wife Anna. The daughter, who was born on April 3 of this year, received a name of Anisiia Tagian. Natalia, a native from the Napamiut village, who is a wife of Vasilii Tagnigakh was her godparent; (2) a daughter of Feodosia Iaganin. Was born in April of this year and received a name Irina. Mariia Chimigak, a native woman from the Napamiut village, was her godparent.

May 16. In the morning using presanctified gifts I gave last rites to an ailing woman in the Iugnil'nuk village. Having taken food supplies, we went on. Stopped for a night in the village of Chimtmiut. In the evening after supper we sang prayers in a native tongue together with the inhabitants of this settlement, who gathered in a house.

May 17. After praying to God and having breakfast we continued our route. In Chimtmiut we took an interpreter named Ivan Anikhtivkal'gea. When we passed the mouth of the Khulitnak River, we immediately noticed that the current became faster than downriver. At 8 o'clock we stopped for a night.

May 18. After praying to God and having breakfast we continued our route. At noon we stopped at the mouth of the Stony River, where we met Ivan Ignatievich Andreanov. After dinner I baptized an infant, an infant daughter of a native named Epifanii and his lawful wife Marfa Ivanov. She received a name of Mavra. Mariia, the wife of Sergei Andreanov, was her godparent. Then we were en route again and after making ten more miles we decided to stop for a night on a bank of the Stony River.

May 19. After the requisite prayer and breakfast we proceeded farther. At noon I met Mr. Hobson, who belongs to the Orthodox Church, and another

American named Rhods, who is an independent trader from the Kangallen village. At 8 o'clock in the evening we stopped for a night and after having prayed to God went to sleep. However, roaring bears kept waking us up throughout the whole night. My two travel companions went to the woods but did not see anything.

May 20. At 7 o'clock in the morning we continued the route. While ascending the river, we clearly saw how the current increased its speed. At 7 o'clock in the evening we came to the village of Kaukhtdligmiut. Its inhabitants talked me into staying with them for a day in order to have a chance to partake of sacraments. I served vespers and matins in the evening. After this I confessed four souls of both genders and instructed them through an interpreter how they should prepare themselves for communion.May 21. At 6 o'clock in the morning I served the liturgy without consecration. Then after appropriate instructions using presanctified gifts I gave communion to those who had performed the rites of fast and penance. After having tea, we continued our route. Three more people with their own *baidarka* joined our party. At 8 o'clock in the evening we stopped for a night in a desolate place. We sang evening prayers in Russian [Slavonic] and then went to sleep. In this area [Stony River] prayers are mostly sung in the Slavonic language and almost everybody knows them by heart, and all local people often sing them in unison.

May 22. At 7 o'clock in the morning after a requisite prayer, we went on and at 9 o'clock in the evening stopped for a night. The current grew faster, and in some spots we were hardly able to keep up with its speed. The Kenaitze *toion* sent his younger brother ahead of us to prepare the inhabitants of Kangallen for my visit and to arrange my accommodations. After supper and an evening prayer we went to sleep.

May 23. The village was already close. We were glad that this was the last day when we had to sail against the rapid current. At 6 o'clock in the evening the *toion* signaled to the Kangallen people about our arrival with a gunshot. Then he shot a few more times. From afar we heard how the Kenaitze responded to us with numerous gunshots, which accompanied us all the way until we entered the village. The first thing we noticed was a large American flag that fluttered over Kangallen. The *toion* had the same flag only of a small size. Before we reached the village, he attached it to our baidarka. After we stepped ashore, all people including children approached me to receive blessings. Having blessed them, I instructed the Kenaitze to gather for a prayer in a large house. In the evening I served vespers after which I delivered a sermon through the interpreter.

May 24. I and all inhabitants of the village sang morning prayers together. Then I sang funeral service for an infant and performed the following baptisms: (1) a daughter of an American citizen Grigorii Mikhailovich Hobson and his lawful wife Tatiana Konstantinovna. The daughter received a name of Ekaterina [Catherine]. Her godmother was Mariia Vladimirovna, a wife of a Kenaitze native Ivan Konst[*antinov*]; (2) Feodor, a son of Kiril Tokhteion and his wife

Agafiia; the godfather was Kirill I'akovlevich; (3) Elizaveta [Elizabeth], a daughter of Pavel Konstantin[ov] and his wife Anna; her godmother was a Kenaitze maiden named Agafiia Ivanovna; (4) Maria, a daughter of Vasilii Ivanovich and Evlalia; the godmother was a maiden named Alexandra Ivanovna Kal'tita.

At 6 o'clock in the evening I performed vespers and matins and delivered a sermon, where I explained the meaning of God's ten commandments. Thirty-three souls of both genders visited the service. Then I read prayers for those who performed rites of fast and penance and were preparing to partake of sacraments.

May 25. Instead of readings the Hours, at 8 o'clock in the morning I read the requisite prayer for those who were preparing to partake of sacraments. Then I served the Divine Liturgy during which I gave communion to those who partook of the rites of fast and penance and delivered a sermon through the interpreter. Then I served a water blessing prayer service and blessed the houses of the villagers with the holy water. After this I married two couples, and in the evening I and residents of the village sang together an evening prayer.

May 26. I read a requisite morning prayer. After dinner I prayed with everybody to God and delivered a sermon. Having finished my business in Kangallen, I set out back to the mission. When I and my interpreter got in the baidarka, people again started to salute to us with gunshots. Soon the rapid current carried us far away from Kangallen. Still, from afar for a long time we heard gunshots. Finally silence descended over the surrounding woods and mountains. The weather was good, but we again had to maneuver through the sharp rocks sticking from water. Each time when we approached one of these rocks my heart sunk. I was afraid that our *baidarka* would be smashed. However, my travel companion who was a seasoned paddler traveled this river so often that he developed an excellent knowledge of all dangerous spots. After we made about eighty miles we decided to stop. It was already midnight.

May 27. At 6 o'clock in the morning having said a prayer to God and having breakfast, we were en route again. At 7 o'clock in the evening we reached the mouth of the Stony River. Here I served vespers and confessed nine souls of both genders.

May 28. I read a requisite prayer for those who were performing the rites of fast and penance and then I performed a water blessing prayer service, during which I gave communion using presanctified gifts. Then I served a requiem at the cemetery. After having a cup of tea I continued my route. Stopped in the settlement of Chlitmiit, where I left Ivan, my travel companion. I traveled alone the rest of the route down to the village of Nukachoagmiiut, where I stopped and I met a Creole named Sergei Ivanovich and his wife.

May 29. At 8 o'clock I was en route again. At this point Sergei Ivanovich and his wife became my travel companions. All three of us used my *baidarka*. Having reached the Iugnilnuk settlement I baptized here an infant, who is a daughter of a native named Lazar Klimentov Achimati and his wife Evgeniia. The daughter was named Agnia. She was born in the month of April and her godparent was Pelageia Ivanov, who is the wife of a native named Kiril Klimentov.

On June 1 I came back home. Thank God, I found everybody in a good health and well-being. The only fact that disturbed me was a rumor about diphtheria that was spreading downriver and allegedly already killed seven people.

Nikifor Amkan: A Trip to the Stony River Dena'ina, Excerpts from the Church Service Journal for 1907[97]

January 1. Having drunk a cup of tea each, we started to prepare ourselves for another trip. We have to go by a long and deserted route all way to the Kangallen village. We anticipated that the route surface would be solid and firm, but in vain. Instead, we had to make our way through deep snow and suffer for all four days. And besides, we ran out of all our supplies. For two days our dogs did not see anything edible, which made them so tired that they had to stop practically each minute. As for ourselves, we were very tired too.

January 4. At 7 o'clock in the morning we departed and decided to reach Kangallen at all costs in order to save all our sixteen dogs. At 11 o'clock we ran across some *odinochka*, where we found a good supply of fish, but there was nobody inside. Having no other choice, we took as much fish as we needed for ourselves and for the dogs, and decided when the first opportunity arrived, to pay whoever all this belonged to. Then we made tea, had a meal. Afterwards, having fed the dogs, we continued the route. The sun already hid behind the mountains, and instead a crescent moon shone merrily in the sky, occasionally hiding behind clouds. There remained about half a mile to the village when I had my travel companion give the Kenaitze a signal by gun shooting. After we made a second shot, dozens of shots responded to us from the village. While we were entering Kangallen, the shooting still continued. A local *toion* was the first to welcome us. All other people followed their headman to accept my blessings. At midnight sharp, after having prayed to God, we finally retreated for a rest.

January 5. From 10 o'clock in the morning the Hours and vespers with the rite of the larger blessing of water. I also blessed and consecrated the village chapel and delivered a sermon through an interpreter. In this sermon I talked about what the church means for an Orthodox Christian. After dinner I baptized three infants: a son of the Kenaitze native called Nikolai Konstantinovich [Constantine?] and his wife Aleksandra. The son, who was born on December 27, 1907, was named Evfimii; a son of the Kenaitze native Pavel Konstantinovich and his wife Anna. The son, who was born on December 15, 1905, was named Feodor; a son of the Kenaitze native Vasilii Ivanovich and his wife Ivlaliia. The son, who was born at he end of October of 1907, was named Konstantin. At 6 o'clock in the evening the Great Vespers and matins.

January 6. At 7 o' clock in the morning I celebrated the Hours, then vespers along with the Liturgy of St. Basil the Great. Outdoors and even indoors there was such severe cold, which I have never yet witnessed in Alaska. Although inside the chapel the iron stove was on, it did not warm us at all. The wine in the chalice became frozen so that before I could start the rite of communion we had to warm it. By the end of the liturgy I myself was freezing all over. Early in the morning, in order to perform a rite of water blessing, we made a hole in the ice on the river. Yet the freezing weather forced me to return to the chapel and I had to complete this rite inside. I felt that I would not make it in the open air. And besides, the faithful would not be able to stay for so long outdoors. After I warmed myself a little, I visited the local houses with holy water. At 5 o'clock in the evening I conversed with the people about the Christian life, especially about chastity [*devstvo*]. As an example of chastity I told them the life story of the Most Holy Mother of God. After the talk I served vespers.

January 7. At 9 o'clock in the morning I performed a customary prayer service devoted to John the Baptist and also delivered a sermon, in which I expanded on the glorious life of Orthodox saints and on a necessity for us to pray to them, and to address them more frequently, especially those saints whose names we carry. At 6 o'clock in the evening a collective prayer.

January 8. At 7 o'clock the morning prayer. After breakfast I went, as Kangallen residents usually put it, to "cross," or in other words, to sprinkle with holy water a place where they do their fishing in summer and which is located about two miles upriver. In addition, the day after my arrival at Kangallen I sent two young men to the next village, Vonzai,[98] where two families reside, to ask them to come to partake of the sacraments along with the others. Today, Trifon [Trefon] Broder has already arrived with his family, but Simeon has not come yet. He might arrive by this evening or tomorrow. At 6 o'clock there was a general collective prayer and then I explained to the natives the meaning of prayers. Then we all together read an evening prayer. When I was about to dismiss them Simeon arrived with his family. I gave them my blessings and, after wishing everyone good night, went to sleep. Tomorrow, since everybody is here I am planning to begin confessions.

January 9. At 7 o'clock a general collective prayer. Then after breakfast I baked the communion bread for tomorrow, and after dinner I baptized an infant of a female gender. This was a daughter of Trifon Vasiliev Broder and his wife Maria, the Kenaitze natives from the Vonzai village. The infant, who was born on December 26, 1907, was baptized as Agafiia. Her godmother was Mariia Simeonovna from Vonzai. At 2 o'clock in the afternoon after requisite instructions and a prayer I started to hear confessions. There were thirty-five people of both genders who came for confession. At 6 o'clock I served matins and then read an evening prayer before giving holy communion.

January 10. A morning prayer at 8 o'clock in the morning, and the Divine Liturgy at 9 o'clock. During the liturgy I delivered a sermon about the meaning of the most holy and life-giving Christian mysteries. There were forty-six communicants including the children. After dinner there was a village meeting devoted to the election of a churchwarden for the local chapel. Of three candidates, people unanimously voted for Pavel Konstantinovich, and also elected Vasilii Ivanovich as his assistant. I instructed the newly elected how to maintain the chapel in a proper order. Then after a general evening prayer everybody went to sleep.

January 11. Today I read a cleansing prayer for a women who delivered a baby forty days ago. Then I swore Pavel Konstantinovich into his new position in the presence of all the people of the village. At 5 o'clock in the evening I gathered everyone, both men and women, at the *toion*'s house, and shared with them my long-time dream of establishing a brotherhood. I tried to show all useful things, which might come from such a brotherhood. Then I asked what they thought about the whole idea. I was so much pleased when all the natives without exception expressed their consent to establish a brotherhood in the village. Right there during the meeting we collected $4.15 as the first donations. Then I suggested they elect a treasurer, who would keep the brotherhood money. After long deliberations, they unanimously elected Trifon Broder, an honest Kenaitze, who is respected by everybody and who was entrusted to receive and keep the donated money. Twenty-six people of both genders joined the brotherhood. The newly created brotherhood selected St. Nicholas the Wonderworker as its heavenly shepherd. From now on each year the brotherhood will celebrate the feast day of this saint on December 6. It was resolved that the major goals of the newly created brotherhood would be education of children in the spirit of Orthodoxy, maintaining the local chapel, and helping the poorest people in the village. Since it was already late we sang only evening prayers.

January 12. At 7 o'clock in the morning I performed a first brotherhood customary prayer service devoted to St. Nicholas the Wonderworker, wishing many happy years to the faithful. After having breakfast we began preparations for the return trip. As soon as we packed the sleds and harnessed the dogs, I gathered people in a house to pray together before our departure. When everybody had gathered, we sang the prayer for those who are ready to commence something ["Rejoice, O Mother of God Full of Grace, the Lord Is with Thee"] and a *troparion* to St. Sergius of Radonezh the Wonderworker. Having blessed them, I delivered a short farewell address and then departed exactly at 11 o'clock in the morning. Loud gun shooting accompanied our departure. The dogs, after a week's rest, ran faster over the smooth and well-used route. We still heard behind us the gunshots and, in turn, we responded with about twenty shots. Yet the well-used route ended quite soon. Now our hardships started again, for we had to move through the deep snow. Fortunately, now we had had a good rest. Three more sleds accompanied us, and the total number of people in our group was eight. After 5 o'clock in the evening we stayed for the night on the right bank of the river (Stony).

January 13. At the first sign of dawn we continued our route, which was awful. In some spots we nearly drowned in the snow up to our waists. Until late at night two people had to move in front in snow shoes and prepare the route for the dogs. Fortunately, now we did not have to suffer so much as earlier, because now we had enough people to pack down the snow and we relieved each other from time to time. Because of an approaching snowstorm we had to make a stop a little earlier than was planned before. As a place to stop we selected a wood on the left bank of the river.

January 14. At 7 o'clock in the morning, having drunk tea, we harnessed our dogs and moved on. Same hardships as yesterday. En route we stopped for an hour to make tea. When it was already dark we reached Kaukhtulik village. Here we had dry fish for supper, and after a collective evening prayer retreated for sleep to a tiny cabin where we lay on the floor, which was extremely dirty. We had to lie very close to each other. There was no other place available for us. Some of us even had to sleep in a sitting position. Besides, a strong, overpenetrating, and disgusting smell of rotten fish troubled us from some distant corner of the house.

January 15. After collective prayer and breakfast, at 8:30 we left Kaukhtulik and proceeded further. One more travel companion joined us and accompanied us until the end of the portage. At 12 noon we passed the place we had stayed before reaching Kaukhtulik. At 6 o'clock in the evening we stopped for the night on the right bank of the river.

January 16. Early in the morning we went on. The route is the same as yesterday. At 12 noon we stopped to make tea, and after this we moved without stopping until late at night. Finally we came to a village, where only a blind old man along with his old wife resides on a permanent basis. As it turned out these good old people live here absolutely alone and have done so for a long time. The old man does not see anything, and therefore his old wife is constantly busy doing something. She weaves fish traps or places loops around to catch rabbits. This is what they do for a living. They told us that there were times when they had nothing to eat at all for several days. Yet, as they said, they firmly put their faith in God and steadfastly believed that He would not forget them. And, the Lord did grant them His all-powerful help. Each time in the most critical moments these old people were able to catch something, or some compassionate native, who happened to travel by, helped them. From church money I gave them $2 to buy the things they needed most.

Matvei Berezkin, from the Church Service Journal for 1909[99]

A Trip to the Kenaitze.

May 19. At 8 o'clock in the morning I served a customary prayer service. Three days ago Kenaitze people came on two *baidarkas* to accompany me up to their village. Having said good-bye to everybody I set out without a songleader. By noon we stopped at the Kolmakosvskii Redoubt and stayed there for a night.

May 20. At 4 o'clock in the afternoon I served a requiem for an infant named Nikita. Then we sang an evening prayer, which I and my travel companions did regularly during all this journey.

May 21. At 8 o'clock in the morning I performed a customary prayer service devoted to Equal to Apostles Sts. Constantine and Helen and also served a requiem service.

May 22. In the village of An'agogmiut I baptized a baptism an infant of a female gender.

May 23. At 8 o'clock in the morning in the settlement named Iugnil'nuk I baptized another infant. Then I confessed two Ingalik natives from the Venisari village. About 1 o'clock in the morning I read an evening prayer.

May 24. At 8 o'clock in the morning I read a requisite prayer for those who perform the rites of fast and penance, then I served the liturgy without consecration and gave communion to five souls including infants and delivered a sermon. About 10 o'clock in the morning we left Iugnil'nuk.

May 27. At 7 o'clock in the evening we reached the mouth of the Stony River. Here I read an evening prayer and I confessed six souls of both genders.

May 28. Having said good-bye to the Kuskokwim River, at 10 o'clock in the morning we set out up the Stony River and moved against the rapid current. A *baidarka* that carried two people and another small boat made of birch bark joined our party. We had to use long poles because one could not rely on paddles that can be of use only when one moved to another bank.

May 30. At 3 o'clock in the afternoon we came to Kakhtuligliut, where only two families resided on a permanent basis. These people wanted to partake of the rites of penance and fast to prepare themselves for communion. For this reason, I decided to make a stop earlier than we planned. I served vespers and matins, read a requisite prayer for those who were preparing themselves for communion. After this I confessed five souls of both genders and then read another requisite prayer and after this an evening prayer.

May 31. At 8 o'clock I read a morning prayer and then served the liturgy without consecration and taught those whom later I gave communion (eight souls of both genders). Then I performed a funeral service. This day we stayed the whole day in this small village. Because Kangallen people lived not far from this place, a Kangallen churchwarden, who accompanied me, had his brother sent ahead to warn the Kangallen people that I was coming. In the evening I read prayers and conversed with local people through an interpreter named Vasilii Uksukhpak.

June 1. At 9 o'clock in the morning we continued our route intending to reach an *odinochka*, where some Kangallen people were expected to wait for us. The fast current completely wore out my travel companions. So today our plans to get to that *odinochka* failed, and we stopped for a night at an open spot on the left bank of the river.

June 2. About 6 o'clock in the evening we finally reached the *odinochka*, but did not find anybody there. We proceeded farther for another mile before at some distance from us I noticed a canvas tent spread on the ground. I said to the churchwarden that it might be the people who had been sent to move ahead of us. He said that it was impossible. I responded that we should go there and see for ourselves if they were our people or not. When we stepped on the bank of the river we saw that it was indeed our people's tent. We found out that the people who had been sent ahead of us pitched the tent yesterday's evening and ascended to the lake and saw some Kenaitze people, who were busy with fishing. We stayed by the canvas tent about half an hour. Suddenly we heard gunshots that came from someplace that was very close to us. We looked around and noticed a *baidarka* with my travel companion [a churchwarden brother]. When my travel companion stepped on the bank, he accepted my blessing and gave me a paper. I unfolded the paper and started to read it. It was a note addressed by an American named Mr. Hobson to my name. He apologized that he could not meet us and added that it was only yesterday that he had returned from the Khulitnak River. Mr. Hobson wrote that he had to hire some Kangallen residents to carry his stuff through the portage and promised to come to the *odinochka* early next morning. I asked my travel companion about the whereabouts of the *toion*. He said that the toion was on his way to Kangallen and people expected him this day, but he had not come yet. In the evening we sang prayers in Slavonic language.

June 3. At 6 o'clock we sang a morning prayer and then waited for the Kenaitze, who were expected to descend from the lake. Finally, by 1 o'clock in the afternoon we noticed a small boat. After one of my travel companions noticed the boat, he raised his rifle and signaled by shooting a few times. Those on the boat welcomed us in the same manner by shooting their guns. After they stepped ashore, they came to receive my blessings. That American who had written the note also approached me for a blessing and greeted me. After this he, on behalf of everybody, he thanked me for taking a trouble to visit them to fulfill their religious needs. All together we sang evening prayers. Before going to sleep I conversed with the Kenaitze about religion. Mr. Hobson, who spoke Russian and Kenaitze very fluently, interpreted this talk.

June 5. Yesterday in the evening the *toion* [who evidently arrived along with Mr. Hobson] had sent two men on a *baidarka* ahead of us to notify Kangallen residents about my arrival and to instruct people to prepare the chapel for services and arrange accommodations for me. At 2 o'clock in the afternoon the *toion* told me that Kangallen was within reach and signaled by shooting his rifle. Suddenly, in response we heard dozens of gunshots, which fell silent only when we entered the village. When we rounded the cape, which separated Kangallen from us, we saw a beautiful view. On a visible spot at some distance from Kenaitze dwellings there stood a chapel in all its splendor. A large American national flag joyfully fluttered over the village and inhabitants already crowded on the bank waiting for me. Finally gunshots died out, and we stepped on a dock that they built specially for my arrival. The people approached me for a blessing. I immediately instructed them to gather in the chapel. I quickly washed my face and went to the chapel, where I performed a thanksgiving prayer service. Then through the interpreter I delivered a welcoming address. In my talk I praised the Kenaitze for making an effort to travel a few hundred miles down to the mission, despite all the difficulties of the journey, in order to bring the priest to their village. Having blessed all them again, I ended the service. Then we sang evening prayers.

June 6. At 8 o'clock we sang a morning prayer and then I baptized three infants and anointed with myrrh another one, who had been baptized by a Nushagak Creole Vasilii Riktorov. At 6 o'clock in the evening I served vespers and then confessed twenty-five souls of both genders. Read an evening prayer.

June 7. At 8 o'clock I served the liturgy without consecration, then explained to the people what Orthodox Christians were expected to feel approaching the Holy Cup to accept the body and blood of Christ. Thirty-four souls of both genders including infants received communion. I performed the rite of lesser water blessing and then held a religious procession with a cross around the chapel and the village. Then I visited Kenaizte dwellings and blessed them with holy water. At 6 o'clock in the evening I served vespers.

June 8. I performed the liturgy without consecration and then a prayer service devoted to St. Nicholas, whom a local brotherhood considers a protector saint. After the service there members of the brotherhood held a meeting. The members elected a new guardian, Ioann Konstantinovich, and also a new *zakazchik*, Pavel Konstantinovich. In the evening we sang evening prayers.

June 9. At 8 o'clock we sang a morning prayer. Then I inspected the chapel building and instructed the churchwarden and the *toion* to fix the roof a little better to prevent any leaks. At noon I performed a customary prayer service for those who wish to sail. After this I delivered my farewell address, where I told them to live according to God's commandments and to listen to their Orthodox priest rather than to proponents of alien beliefs. I also instructed them to live in peace and to take care of each other. After a collective prayer to God, I blessed the Kenaitze, then got in a *baidarka* and left Kangallen for home traveling with my interpreter, Vasilii Uksukh… [?]. While the fast current was quickly carrying us away, for a long time we heard how people shot their guns saluting to us. From behind we again heard the gun salute. Soon the rapid current carried us far away.

June 14. At 4 o'clock in the afternoon I came home. Thank God, I found everybody in a good health.

This trip to the Kenaitze produced the most favorable impression on me. Nowhere did I see such religious people committed to their Orthodox faith. I wish in future that all other people become so zealous in their beliefs like these Kenaitze.

June 20. At 5 o'clock I served the all-night vigil.

June 21. At 8 o'clock I had to perform the liturgy without consecration because of lack of wine ["Oh, really!"—a remark made by the Dean of the Alaska Clergy Petr Orlov on the margins of the Berezkin journal].

Ioann Bortnovskii: Travel Report to Hieromonk Anatolii, Dean of Clergy of the Sitka District, September 17–29, 1896[100]

This summer, during my visit to Knik village, I happened to hear from local natives that last winter fifty people of the Mednovtsy tribe came to Knik. Some of them wanted to fulfill their holy duty of confession and communion. The others, who are still heathens, came to accept holy baptism. Yet neither the former nor the latter were able to satisfy their needs, for the priest was not there that time. I also heard, which might be very true, that for a long time residents of Mednovtsy villages that are located closer to Knik have been eager to see among themselves a spiritual shepherd, who would help them to revive their spirits and bodies, and to enter a new holy and graceful life, which is full of joy. In Mednovtsy country there are hundreds of people who still remain literally in the darkness of paganism. Not only the heathen, but also those who have adopted holy baptism have to exist in the grip of indolence and crudeness, which can be seen everywhere. The pressure of shamanism towers over everybody. These are the conditions in which the Mednovtsy live. Before we make sure that the words of the holy Gospel resound in all their power among these savage children of nature, before the light of Christian teaching shines in the darkness of paganism, it is and will be hard to expect any spiritual changes in this tribe.

Realizing the importance of my priestly service doubled by my title of missionary, I gave a promise to the Knik Kenaitze that in 1897 I would winter in their village, and then, when a good opportunity arrives, visit the Mednovtsy in their own habitats. The communication with Mednovtsy country usually begins in January. Under the most favorable conditions, it takes six days to reach the first closest Mednovtsy village. During the present winter [Knik residents] have promised to build a small house for the priest. I also dare to add that the route to the Mednovtsy habitats is usually full of hardships and might be costly. Yet I console myself with the hope that the ecclesiastical authorities, considering the importance of the propagation of the Lord's word, will provide me with material support.

Presenting all above-mentioned information for the kind consideration of Your Right Reverence I have the honor to be Your humble servant, Priest Ioann Bortnovskii.

Report of Hieromonk Antonii, Dean of Clergy of the Sitka District to Tikhon, Bishop of Alaska, August 13, 1901[101]

Today with the ship *St. Paul* I have sent you a petition from the Mednovtsy tribe, who live on the Copper River. Four hundred of them expressed a desire to accept baptism and the Orthodox faith. These Mednovtsy ask that a chapel and a school be built for them. I believe that this noble goal of the Mednovtsy should be encouraged, otherwise these needs will be readily met by the Protestants, who recently have rushed to the gold mining areas of Alaska. I suggest resolving the question about the school and the chapel in the following way: to inquire if natives are ready to help partially to cover expenses. We can also send a teacher from Unalaska. Regarding a person who may supervise this project, we may solicit the assistance of those priests who work in nearby areas. For example, Pavlov might come here from Valdez, where soldiers are building a road to the Copper River, and Bortnovskii, whose parish is located close to the Mednovtsy.

Your zealous novice, Hieromonk Antonii.

Prokopii Povarnitsyn About Missionary Work Among the Ahtna Indians (from an Essay "Three Years of Missionary Work in Alaska [1937–1940]")[102]

Copper Center

1937. Chitina and Copper Center are populated by the descendants of an Indian tribe. I want to mention that Russian culture has not reached them at all. They have their own habits, inclinations, and customs. Residents of these villages accepted the Christian Orthodox faith not long ago. It is also obvious that they embraced this faith gladly without connecting their decision to any material considerations. However, various alien missionaries are trying to kill these good beginnings. It seems that for the past eight years the small Orthodox community in Copper Center, surrounded by various alien denominations, was close to disappearing. Yet, as it turned out, the opposite happened. The light of Christ dawns upon the hearts of these children and God's grace strengthens them so much that the community itself keeps growing.

In place of the old chapel that fell into disrepair, the Indians erected a new one and bought a bell for it, and each Sunday in response to the call of this bell, they all come together to their church-chapel [thus in original] and sing prayers in the Church-Slavonic language, prayers which they had once learned by heart. Among them are the Lord's Prayer, "Rejoice, O Mother of God Full of Grace, the Lord Is with Thee," "To the Heavenly King" and other simple prayers. The Indians repeat these prayers several times during a service and then peacefully return home. Indeed, it looks like guardian angels themselves converse with these native children, inhabitants of these Alaskan villages located far from any centers of Orthodoxy.

By the time I arrived at Copper Center, which happened during the last days of September, it was already quite cold. Yet not only the inhabitants of this village were ready to interrupt for a while their mundane concerns and work to devote themselves to prayer, but also residents of neighboring Copper Valley, located eighty miles from the Center. A few days before my arrival, the Indians came to Copper Center in entire families. They set up their tents around the church and lived at this camp the entire time I was completing all my church services and ministrations. Helped by an interpreter, Nikolai, I explained to them the meaning of the words "God, Have Mercy on Me," and then I taught them how to sing the words of this prayer. And then, each day during services, all the natives sang together litanies, which endowed these new Christians of this area with happiness and enthusiasm. The total number of people who confessed and received communion was 300! The number of newly baptized, in age ranging from infants to natives of sixty-four years old, was eighty-four people! I delivered to Andrei, the leader of these Indians, a man of extreme religious zeal, the church vestment that he had been awarded for his work. During my last service, standing at the pulpit by my side, Andrei delivered quite a long sermon in his native language. From time to time while speaking he pointed to the Holy Cross, which I kept in my hands in front of the people. The silence during the sermon was striking, and in the eyes of many people one could see tears. Indeed, the Christian light touches everybody!

Chitina

Coming cold and snowstorms forced me to finish my missionary trip. Yet I decided to make a trip to Chitina, the last village populated by Orthodox Indians. Chitina is located fifty miles from Copper Center. A good highway connects both villages with each other. It was very interesting to drive through the most beautiful locality in Alaska in a good automobile and without any trouble. It was nice to watch how our automobile either climbed a high mountain, which unfolded for us beautiful scenery, or descended to a welcoming valley full of various berry bushes and small trees. Unfortunately, our 1926 Ford, which our interpreter Nikolai secured in order to bring me to Chitina, this time turned out to be unreliable. No sooner had we moved about twenty miles than its engine died. It took no less than an hour before Nikolai fixed the automobile. Then we went about five miles and had a flat tire. We crept on for about twenty-five miles before we reached Chitina. In Chitina, in terms of missionary work, we observed the same attitudes as in Copper Center only on a smaller scale. During my return travel from Chitina, I used a train that took me to Cordoba, which connected me to the rest of Alaska and the States.

A chapel in the Iliamna village, c. 1910. Courtesy of the Kodiak Historical Society.

A cemetery in the Iliamna village, c. 1910. Courtesy of the Kodiak Historical Society.

Old and new church buildings in Nondalton village, 1998. Photograph by the author.

Michael "Jimmy" Balluta, a lay Orthodox leader in Nondalton's St. Nicholas Church. Mr. Balluta holds an old copy of the Russian-Slavonic Bible, which had been brought from the Kijik chapel. Photo by the author, August 1998.

Was Trefon (1898–1958), a Dena'ina from Old Nondalton village, with a Russian Orthodox cross. Courtesy of Helena Seversen Moses.

Chief Zakhar Ivanov [Zackar Evanoff] (1860?–1935), 1921. At first Chief Ivanov served as an assistant to a lay chapel reader in the Iliamna village and then as a chapel reader and lay Orthodox leader in the Old Nondalton village. Courtesy of Sandra Orris.

A Russian Orthodox prayer book and a bag it was carried in. These items (from the collections of the Copper River Historical Society) were used by the Ahtna Indians, members of the Russian Orthodox Church, in the 1920s and 1930s. Photograph by the author, June 2000.

An old grave "spirit house" of an Orthodox Ahtna Indian in the Copper River village cemetery. Photograph by the author, June 2000.

"Old" William [Vasilii?] Rickteroff, a lay Dena'ina-Suqpiaq chapel reader in the Iliamna St. Nicholas chapel. Courtesy of Mr. and Mrs. Gus Jensen.

Chief Alexie Balluta, right, at Old Nondalton in the late 1930s. Alexie Balluta wears a badge that indicates his belonging either to a mutual aid Russian Orthodox society or a temperance society. While in the Cook Inlet area mutual aid and temperance societies declined, in Iliamna and Queghnilen they continued their activities. Courtesy of John Lee.

Dena'ina of the Kijik village in front of St. Nicholas chapel, c. 1901. Left to right: Evdakia Karshekoff, Mary Ann Trefon, Trefon Balluta, Wassillie [Vasilii] Trefon (front), Gabriel Trefon (front), unidentified female, Evan [Ivan] Koktelash, four unidentified individuals, Chief Zakhar Ivanov. The rest of the people are not identified. Courtesy of Cook Inlet Region, Inc.

A Dena'ina family from the Queghnilen village on the Stony River. Left to right: Gustingen Constantine [Kostantin], Katherine Constantine [Konstantin] and Anisha Constantine [Konstantin], 1930. Courtesy of Sophie Balluta Austin.

Anton Balluta (1905–1937) fixing the cross atop St. Nicholas Russian Orthodox chapel at Old Nondalton village in 1930. In the early 1900s many Dena'ina abandoned the Kijik village and moved to the Old Nondalton site. Courtesy of Sophie Hobson Austin.

A family of the Ahtna Indians in a summer camp. Courtesy of the U.S. Geological Survey Photographic Library, Denver (Schrader, 116).

Priest Vasilii Shishkin with his deacons. Father Shishkin visited the Dena'ina of the Iliamna and Kijik villages in the 1870s and 1880s. Courtesy of the Weinland Collection, Henry E. Huntigton Library and Art Gallery, San Marino, California.

Notes

1. Michael Z. Vinokouroff Papers, Alaska State Historical Library, Juneau, AK., box 22, folder 46.

2. I was not able to locate the original manuscripts of Nikolai's travel reports for these and earlier years. For this translation I use the excerpts from his travel journals published in an Orthodox periodical *Tvoreniia sviatikh ottsov v russkom perevode* 19, no. 1 (1860), 117–133.

3. This Russian publication was prepared by the priest Afanasii Vinogradov, an inspector of the New Archangel (Sitka) Theological Seminary, who provided a short introduction to Nikolai's notes.

4. Most probably Nikolai refers to Efim Borisov, the manager of the St. Nicholas Redoubt at this time.

5. This village, which was also referred to in missionary writings as Titukilskoe or Titukilek, was apparently an old Dena'ina settlement *Tiduqilts'ett* ("abandoned place") located between the Swanson River and Bishop Creek. James Kari and Priscilla Kari, *Dena'ina Elnena/Tanaina Country* (Fairbanks: Alaska Native Language Center University of Alaska, 1982), 32.

6. A three-stringed Russian traditional musical instrument.

7. Hegumen Nikolai [Militov], *Vipiska iz zhurnala Kenaiskago missionera igumena Nikolaia s 1858 po 1862 God* (Moskva: n. p., 1863), 1–9.

8. Russian name for the Eyak Indians culturally close to the Tlingit.

9. Russian name for the Tlingit Indians.

10. Russian name for the Ahtna Indians.

11. From Dena'ina *Susitnu* "sand river." Kari and Kari, *Dena'ina Elnena/Tanaina Country*, 34.

12. Evidently, a Dena'ina village called *Kechan Dalkizt*, which was located near the mouth of the Kasilof River.

13. The Kenai River (from Dena'ina *Kahtnu* "river-mouth river"). Hegumen Nikolai also called it "Kakna."

14. An old Dena'ina village on the Skilak Lake.

15. Hegumen Nikolai [Militov], "Iz zhurnala Kenaiskago missionera, Nikolaevskii redut, 1862," *Pravoslavnoe obozrienie* 24 (1867), 1–10.

16. Ninilchik was originally populated by retired RAC workers who received a status of free settlers. For more about the history of this village, see Katherine L. Arndt, "'Released to Reside Forever in the Colonies:' Founding of a Russian-American Company Retirement Settlement at Ninilchik, Alaska," in *Adventures Through Time: Readings in the Anthropology of Cook Inlet, Alaska*, eds. Nancy Yaw Davis and William E. Davis (Anchorage, AK: Cook Inlet Historical Society, 1996), 235–249.

17. By this word Russians defined both the Upper Mednovtsy (Ahtna), who spoke a dialect different from Lower Ahtna dialect, and the Tanana, who were occasionally defined as "second" or "distant Kolchane." Andrei V. Grinev, "On the Banks of the Copper River: The Ahtna Indians and the Russians, 1783–1867," *Arctic Anthropology* 30, no. 1 (1993): 56.

18. "Zhurnal Kenaiskago missionera za 1863-ii god" and "Zhurnal Kenaiskago missionera igumena Nikolaiia za 1864-ii god," ARCA, roll 201, box D300.
19. An old Dena'ina village in the vicinity of the present-day Anchor Point.
20. Most probably, this is a reference to Nikolai's requests to relieve him from missionary duties and send him back to Russia. Ecclesiastical authorities did not want to satisfy his requests at this time.
21. A lower level Russian-American Company manager, a head of a work crew [*artel*].
22. About P. Zazubovich, a Pole, Stafeev noted that he "liked to curse and was always angry." After beating a Kenaitze native, Zazubovich narrowly escaped his death and a native revolt. After this incident, one night the Dena'ina put on warrior garb and singing war songs were approaching the RAC headquarters. Zazubovich was saved by the Dena'ina wife of his assistant. The woman, who heard the song and understood what it meant, woke up her husband. After this all the Russians woke up and went outside and eventually convinced the Kenaitze to retreat. Vladimir V. Stafeev, "Ubienie russkikh v Tuinake," Vladimir Vasiliev Stafeev Papers, l. 3–4.
23. Michael Z. Vinokouroff Papers, box 28, folder 36. Most probably Hegumen Nikolai wrote this description of the Kenai area at the request of the Imperial Geographical Society. The document carries no date, but it appears that it was written during the 1860s. The style of the document suggests that Nikolai received a questionnaire from the society and provided his responses about the climate, vegetation, people, and industry of the region.
24. ARCA, roll 201, box D300.
25. Ibid., roll 201, box D300.
26. Ibid.
27. Or *Susni Kaq'*, which in Dena'ina means "sand-island mouth," mouth of the Susitna River. According to Kari, this locality "was an important spring camping area on the Inlet at the mouth of the Susitna River. Dena'ina from all the Upper Inlet villages gathered here to obtain beluga, ducks, and geese, to fish for hooligan and salmon, and to trade." Kari and Kari, *Dena'ina Elnena/Tanaina Country*, 85.
28. ARCA, roll 201, box D299.
29. In the end of the nineteenth century in their letters and reports missionaries often indicated dates simultaneously in the old and new style calendars.
30. Ibid., roll 201, box D300.
31. Ibid., roll 201, box D299.
32. Ibid.
33. Ibid., roll 20, box B20.
34. Ibid., roll 201, box D299.
35. Ibid., roll 201, box D300.
36. Ibid., roll 201, box D299.
37. Ibid., roll 181, box D262.
38. Ibid.
39. Aleksandr Iaroshevich, "Putevoi zhurnal Kenaiskago missionera sviashchennika Alexandra Iaroshevicha," *Pravoslavnyi blagoviestnik* 18 (1894): 87–91; 19 (1894): 119–125; 20 (1894): 180–188; 8 (1896): 373–381; 11 (1896): 142–146; 4 (1896): 276–279; 13 (1896): 231–236.
40. Evidently, Iaroshevich refers to the debates within the Orthodox Church about permitting native people to conclude early marriages.
41. A Dena'ina village in the vicinity of present-day Nikiski. In the nineteenth century there were several Dena'ina village or camp sites in the Nikishka area. Kari and Kari, *Dena'ina Elnena/Tanaina Country*, 27.

42. A garment of the skins of sea mammals usually worn by the Aleut, Sugpiaq and coastal Yupik.

43. In Russian these proverbs are: "*kto v more ne bival, tot strakha ne vidal,*" "*kto v more ne bival, tot Bogu ne malivalsia.*"

44. ARCA, roll 202, box D301.

45. Ibid., roll 193, box D287.

46. Also spelled as Chubutna in missionary records; a small Dena'ina village that was apparently located at the mouth of the Chuitna River. In Dena'ina *Ch'u'itnu*, *Ch'ubetnu* means "river." Kari and Kari, *Dena'ina Elnena/Tanaina Country*, 35, 84.

47. ARCA, roll 201, box D299.

48. This is not exactly true; there was a trade store in Tyonek, where the Ahtna also came to trade on a regular basis.

49. *Russian-American Orthodox Messenger* 2, no. 18 (1898): 529–533; 2, no. 19 (1898): 558–559.

50. Ibid. 3, no. 19 (1899): 513–517; 3, no. 22 (1899): 595–599.

51. It appears that Bortnovskii refers here to Chubutna/Chuvitna village, which he placed earlier seven miles from Tyonek.

52. Bortnovskii refers both to Old Knik (Knik town) and New Knik (Eklutna).

53. A part of the all-night vigil where the priest comes out of the altar and censes the whole church and the faithful.

54. Ecclesiastical authorities had already sent $60 for purchase of the bell (a note of *Russian-American Orthodox Messenger*'s editor).

55. ARCA, roll 181, box D263.

56. Ibid.

57. Ibid., roll 182, box D266.

58. Ibid.

59. Ibid.

60. Ibid., roll 201, box D299.

61. Ibid.

62. Most certainly these *igrushki* is a reference to Dena'ina traditional potlatch (give-away) ceremonies.

63. ARCA, roll 201, box D299.

64. Ibid.

65. Lydia Taradonova, Personal Collection, Kenai, AK. It appears that this sketch of the history of the Kenai parish was written at a request from ecclesiastical authorities.

66. Lydia Taradonova, Personal Collection, Kenai, AK.

67. Bishop Phillip went to Russia and unsuccessfully sought financial help for the mission. See his pamphlet published in Russia where he appealed to the country's population to save the Alaska mission: Bishop of Alaska Filipp, *Pogibaiushchaia missiia* (Moskva: tip. Russkaia pechatnaia, 1918).

68. Lydia Taradonova, Personal Collection, Kenai, AK.

69. ARCA, roll 201, box D299.

70. Ibid., roll 196, box D291.

71. Ibid., roll 149, box D216.

72. A Russian name for one of the Yupik groups.

73. A small Dena'ina village (*Chix Kaq'*) that was located not far from Iliamna.

74. Lake Clark.

75. *Qizhieh*, a Dena'ina village, which was later abandoned. The village was located on a bank of the Lake Clark.

76. ARCA, roll 149, box D216.

77. Shishkin planned to go from Mulchatna to Kijik, but on his way to this village he met a Kenaitze family who informed him that all the residents had left the village for a hunting trip, and Shishkin had to come back to Nushagak.

78. ARCA, roll 149, box D217.

79. Ibid.

80. On March 14 Shishkin again wanted to start, but because of warm eastern winds the snow melted and he had to cancel his entire trip to the Kijik and Mulchatna Kenaitze.

81. ARCA, roll 149, box D217.

82. Modestov's travel journal for 1894–1895 exists in two versions. This is variant 1. Ibid., roll 144, box D207.

83. Yet Modestov and Riktorov again were not able to reach Kijik because of the weather and had to turn back.

84. This is variant 2 of the previous journal. ARCA, roll 144, box D207.

85. Because of the bad weather, the visit to Iliamna was postponed and they could not depart for this village until February 4.

86. The following day again the weather did not allow Modestov to move to Lake Clark. Finally, on February 18, Mikhail Riktorov refused to go further because they had almost run out of food and the dogs were tired. Therefore, they had to move to a neighboring Yupik village, which was located on the other side of Iliamna Lake. Modestov decided to postpone his trip to the Kichek [Kijik] people until August. From the available documents it is clear that the trip did not materialize.

87. ARCA, roll 149, box D216. This is an excerpt from the Modestov report with a general description of various localities in his parish. In this specific excerpt Modestov informs his superior Kedrovsky about the conditions of Dena'ina who lived in the Lake Clark area, whom the priest did not have a chance to visit. He was familiar only with Dena'ina from Iliamna village.

88. Undated. The handwriting indicates that the notes were prepared by Modestov in 1894 or 1895. Vital Statistics. Nushagak, 1876–1918. ARCA, roll 150, box D217.

89. Ibid., roll 149, box D216.

90. Konstantin Pavlov, "Bogosluzhebnii zhurnal za 1904–ii god," St. Herman's Theological Seminary Archive, Kuskokwim Mission, box 5, 1898–1907, Journal of Worship Service, folder 5, l. 7–31.

91. *Qeghnilen* in Dena'ina means "flows through canyon." This village located on the Stony River was later abandoned. Last residents of *Qeghnilen* later moved to Lime Village, Nondalton and to other Stony River localities. Kari and Kari, *Dena'ina Elnena/Tanaina Country*, 16–17 and James Kari, personal communication, February 12, 1999.

92. Other missionary journals (see below) call the same person Ivan Konstantinovich. In American usage the name Konstantinov (Konstantinovich) was rendered as Constantine.

93. The Chugakhpalik (Chuathbaluk) or so-called Little Russian Mission was the center of the Yukon-Kuskokwim Mission.

94. Pavlov had to return home and his trip to the Upper Kuskokwim Indians did not materialize that year.

95. Nikifor Amkan, "Bogosluzhebnii zhurnal za 1905-ii god," St. Herman's Theological Seminary Archive, Kuskokwim Mission, box 5, 1898–1907, Journal of Worship Service, folder 6, l. 29–38.

96. Nikifor Amkan, "[Bogosluzhebnii zhurnal za] 1906-ii god," St. Herman's Theological Seminary Archive, Kwikhpak Mission, Parish Records, Priest Nikifor Amkan Journal, 1906, l. 23–34.

97. The Alaska Church Collection (the Library of Congress) has another more condensed copy of this journal. Antoinette Shalkop, who prepared a microfilm publication of the collection, ascribed the authorship of this record to Matvei Berezkin (ARCA, roll 171, box D247). In reality, the latter took over the position of the Kuskokwim priest only in 1908. Since both versions have slight differences, in translating this journal I used both variants incorporating missing parts from the full version of the Amkan journal. Nikifor Amkan, "Bogosluzhebnii zhurnal," Journal of Priest Nikifor Amkan, 1907–1908, Parish Records, Kvikhpakh Mission, St. Herman Theological Seminary Archive, Kodiak, AK.

98. Also described in missionary records under the names of Venisalli or Vynzali. One of the villages along the Stony River with a mixed and fluctuating Creole, Kolchan and Dena'ina population.

99. Matvei Berezkin, "Bogosluzhebnii zhurnal za 1909 god Kuskokvimskoi missii," St. Herman's Theological Seminary Archive, Kuskokwim Mission, box 6, 1909–1944, Journal of Worship Service, folder 1, l. 7–15. Careful comparison of this report with the journal of Amkan, who served in this mission before Berezkin, exposes numerous textual borrowings made by Berezkin. In some sentences he exactly repeats Amkan's report word for word. Although the reader will hardly feel it in the translated text, the Berezkin report also betrays him as a person of a poor command of written Russian. Numerous grammar and stylistic mistakes, lack of punctuation marks, and unfinished sentences made rendering of his notes into English hard work. The fact that he experienced difficulties with expressing himself on paper might partially explain why he copied Amkan's notes. After making a trip to Kangallen by the same route as earlier missionaries, he might have found it easier to combine what he was able to put on paper himself with sentences and paragraphs he borrowed from his predecessors.

100. Ibid., roll 202, box D301.

101. Ibid., roll 203, box D303.

102. *Iubileinyi sbornik v pamiat' 150-lietiia Russkoi oravoslavnoi tserki v Sievernoi Amerikie* (New York: Izd. izdatelskoi iubileinoi komissii, 1944), 59–61.

Glossary

Akathist. Hymns praising the Savior, Mother of God, St. Nicholas and other saints. During the reciting of such hymns sitting down was not allowed. *Akathists* could be sung both in church and in private houses.

Antimins. A silken cloth, which depicts the laying of Christ in the tomb and the Four Evangelists. The *antimins* is placed on the altar during the Divine Liturgy and is folded up as soon as the service is finished.

Archbishop. The chief bishop, a church rank that preceded the rank of metropolitan.

Archimandrite. The supervisor of a few monasteries, the highest title among monks. In Alaska, this term was also applied to clerics responsible for the administrative life of the mission.

Archpriest. In the Orthodox church the chief priest in a parish.

Baidarshchik. A lower-level manager in the Russian-American Company (RAC), usually head of a hunting party [*artel*].

Baidarka. A small skin boat for a few individuals, with open hatches; a very light and highly maneuverable craft used by some natives of the northern Pacific Rim for open sea hunting. The Aleut *baidarka*, for example, was twenty-five feet long and had two or three cockpits and sharp sterns. Russians frequently applied the word *baidarka* to all native boats, although they differed from one another.

Chapel. A small prayer house that has all the attributes of a church except an altar. All religious services can be performed in a chapel except a liturgy. However, if a movable *antimins* is attached to the chapel, it may be used to serve a liturgy.

Chugach. A Russian name for the *Sugpiaq*, a Pacific Eskimo group, neighbors to the Dena'ina.

Consistory. The administrative center of a diocese.

Epitimia. A church punishment.

Slavoslovie (*Doxology*). Literally "word of praise," a hymn that praises the Savior. There are "Great" [*velikoe*] and "Little" [*maloe*] *slavoslovie* depending on whether sung or chanted during church services.

Hegumen (*Igumen*). A head of a monastery. As applied to the missionary enterprise, also a title of respect.

Hieromonk. A monk ordained as a priest; a monk who may perform religious services as a priest.

Holy Synod. The council of bishops, the chief administrative department of the Russian Orthodox church. After Peter the Great subordinated Orthodoxy to imperial control in 1721, the Holy Synod was transformed into a branch of the government headed by the ober-procurator, a secular official who supervised the Orthodox church.

Hours. A short set of standard prayers recited every day.

Ingalik. A subarctic Athabaskan-speaking group who resided in the Yukon River basin, central Alaska, whose major occupation was hunting moose and caribou. They numbered around 500 people in the nineteenth century. Neighboring Yupik heavily influenced Ingalik's ceremonial life. At the same time, a strong emphasis on the potlatch giveaway ceremonies pointed to intensive contacts with the cultures of the Northwest. Russians established trade relations with the Ingalik during the early nineteenth century.

Inorodtsy. Officially adopted term in the Russian empire for the designation of nomadic and seminomadic native groups of the Siberian and Alaskan borderlands, peoples of the Caucasus and Central Asia and also the Jews. By the turn of the twentieth century this term acquired a broad meaning to classify all non-Russians within the empire. There is no exact equivalent for this word in English. The closest variants would be "of a different kin," "of other origin," or "aliens."

Kontakion. In content and designation this short musical composition is very similar to *troparion*.

Litany [*Litiya* in Russian]. A litany is served in the porch of a church, on the steps, or in the back of the church itself. It is a collective praying of the faithful and the clerics conducting the services. A characteristic feature of the litany is the repeating by the faithful of "Lord, have mercy" in response to prayers read by a priest. During feast days and on Sundays litanies are celebrated as part of the all-night vigil at the end of the vespers. There is a special kind of litany, which is known as a religious procession [*krestnii khod*], when in case of a social calamity or somebody's illness the faithful and a priest go by religious procession with holy banners, the cross, and icons, and pray.

Potlatch. A ritual redistribution of goods practiced by Athabaskans and especially by Northwest coast tribes of North America (such as the Tlingit and Haida). Individuals who organized such giveaways sought to raise their prestige and power in the eyes of fellow tribesmen. Scholars still vigorously debate the meaning of this ceremony.

Presanctified gifts. Holy gifts that are consecrated on a previous Sunday and used in the Liturgy without consecration, which means the liturgy where consecration of the holy gifts is omitted.

Promishlenniki. Independent groups of Russian and Creole fur hunters/fur traders in the northern Pacific in the eighteenth century. They were frequently united in rival groups (called *artels* in Russian). In the nineteenth century in Russian America this term referred to RAC employees of various occupations, such as farmers, hunters, and carpenters.

Prokeimenon. These are Psalter verses sung before Scripture lessons.

Protection by the Most Holy Mother of God. An Orthodox feast (called *Pokrov* in Russian) that is celebrated in October. According to an Orthodox legend, in 910, when Constantinople, the Byzantine capital, was besieged by enemies, people prayed in the city church asking God to help them. During the church service Holy Andrei saw a vision of Holy Lady Theotokes (Virgin Mary), who was floating in the air spreading her protection [*pokrov*] over the praying people. Soon the siege of Constantinople was lifted. To commemorate the protection provided by Lady Theotokes the Orthodox church established a special feast. The Orthodox brotherhood organized in Kenai, Alaska, was named after this feast.

Ruble. Russian paper and coin money. In the nineteenth century one ruble roughly corresponded to fifty cents.

Spirit House. A style of tomb accepted by Orthodox Dena'ina in the Lower Cook Inlet area, Alaska. In appearance it is reminiscent of a miniature four-corner house with a Russian Orthodox cross in front. Such tombs are one of the most vivid examples of the blending of Christian and native elements. It is interesting that Upper Inlet Dena'ina do not have "spirit houses."

St. Nicholas. One of the most revered saints in Russian Orthodoxy. Russian and later native popular beliefs treated this saint as a people's protector and placed him close to Jesus Christ.

Stikherion (pl. *Stikhera*). A liturgical stanza sung between verses taken from the Book of Psalms.

Sugpiaq. Indigenous people, southern neighbors of the Dena'ina, in old Russian sources known as the Chugach and Koniag. The Alutiiq are members of the Eskimo-Aleut language family and occupy the Alaska Peninsula, Kodiak Island, the southeastern part of the Kenai Peninsula, and the coastal areas of Prince William Sound.

Tlingit. A native group in southeastern Alaska. Despite persistent attempts of the Russian-American Company (RAC) to subjugate them, they maintained their political and economic sovereignty until the end of Russian America in 1867.

Toion. A Sakha word that means "leader." Russians applied this term to define indigenous chiefs and headmen in Alaska and Siberia.

Troparion. The word *troparion* could define any short musical composition which can be performed during various church services in general. Narrowly, this is a song composed to honor an Orthodox feast or a saint. In this case, such a song describes in a short form the meaning of a feast or details of a saint's biography.

Yupik. A group of native peoples in Alaska and the easternmost part of northeastern Siberia. The Yupik are members of the Eskimo-Aleut language family and consist of two major groups: the central Alaskan Yupik and the Siberian Yupik.

Zakazchik. In Alaska, native headmen who were responsible for the economic well-being of communities and the maintenance of chapel buildings. By his administrative status, the *zakazchik* was second to the *toion*.

Bibliography

Abbreviations

ARCA	The Alaskan Russian Church Archives Records. Washington, DC: Library of Congress.
DRHA	Documents Relative to the History of Alaska. Fairbanks, Alaska.
RRAC	Records of the Russian-American Company. Washington, DC: National Archives.
RGIA	Rossisskii gosudarstvennii istoricheskii arkhiv (Russian State Historical Archive). St. Petersburg, Russia.

Unpublished Primary Sources

Alaska State Historical Library, Juneau, AK. Michael Z. Vinokouroff Papers, 1764–1984.

Alaska State Historical Library, Juneau, AK. Vladimir Vasiliev Stafeev Papers, 1869–1895.

Library of Congress, Washington, DC. The Alaskan Russian Church Archives Records, 1733–1938. Washington, DC: Library of Congress Photoduplication Service, 1984. Microfilm. 376 reels.

National Archives, Washington, D.C. Records of the Russian-American Company, 1802–1867. Washington, DC: National Archives, 1942. Microfilm. 77 reels.

Russian State Historical Archive, St. Petersburg, Russia. Fond Sviashchennogo Sinoda. Fond 796.

St. Herman's Theological Seminary Archive, Kodiak, AK. Papers of Kvikhpakh and Kuskokwim Missions.

Taradonova, Lydia, Kenai, AK. Pavel Shadura Papers.

University of Alaska, Fairbanks, AK. Alaska History Research Project. Documents Relative to the History of Alaska. Fairbanks, AK: Alaska History Project, 1936–1938. Microfilm. 6 reels.

Published Primary Sources

Allen, Henry T. *Report of an Expedition to the Copper, Tanana, and Koyukuk Rivers in the Territory of Alaska, in the Year 1885*. Washington: GPO, 1887.

Barsukov, Ivan, ed. *Pisma Innokentiia, mitropolita Moskovskago i Kolomenskago*. 1828-1878. St. Petersburg: Sinodalnaia tipografiia, 1897. Vol. 1–2.

Black, Lydia, ed. and transl. *The Journals of Iakov Netsvetov: The Yukon Years, 1845–1863*. Kingston, Ontario: The Limestone Press, 1984.

Bortnovskii, Ioann. "Kenaiskaia missiia (istoriko-statisticheskoe opisanie)." *Russian-American Orthodox Messenger* 2, no. 18 (1898): 529–533; 2, no. 19 (1898): 558–559.

________. "Zimovka pravoslavnago missionera v Kenaiskom selenii Knik." *Russian-American Orthodox Messenger* 2, no. 20 (1898): 583–587.

________. "Iz putevogo zhurnala sviashchennika Kenaiskoi missii I. Bortnovskago." *Russian-American Orthodox Messenger* 3, no. 19 (1899), 513–517; 3, no. 22 (1899): 595–599; 3, no. 23 (1899): 624–628; 3, no. 24 (1899): 639–641; 4, no. 9 (1900): 181–183; 4, no. 10 (1900): 204–208; 5, no. 13 (1901): 275–277; 5, no. 14 (1901): 301–304; 5, no. 15 (1901): 320–323; 5, no. 16 (1901): 337–340; 5, no. 17 (1901): 365–367; 6, no. 10 (1902): 223 225; 6, no. 11 (1902): 243–245; 6, no. 12 (1902): 263–269; 7, no. 11 (1903): 180–182; 7, no. 12 (1903): 200–203; 7, no. 13 (1903): 223–225; 8, no. 17 (1904): 332–334.

Branson, John, ed. *Lake Clark-Iliamna, Alaska, 1921: The Travel Diary of Colonel A. J. Macnab*. Anchorage: Alaska Natural History Association, 1996.

Breece, Hannah. *A School Teacher in Old Alaska*. New York: Random House, 1995.

Compilation of Narratives of Explorations in Alaska, 56th Congress, 1st Session, Senate, Report no. 1023. Washington, DC: Government Printing Office, 1900.

Doroshin, P. P. "Iz zapisok, vedennikh v Russkoi Amerike." *Gornii zhurnal* 1, no. 3 (1866): 365–400.

Dzeniskevich Galina I., comp. "Pravoslavnie missioneri na Aliaske." In *Russkaia Amerika: po lichnym vpechatleniiam missionerov, zemleprokhodtsev, moriakov, issledovatelei I drugikh ochevidtsev*, ed. A. D. Dridzo and R. V. Kinzhalov, 191–253. Moskva: Mysl, 1994.

Filipp, Bishop of Alaska. *Pogibaiushchaia missiia*. Moskva: tip. Russkaia pechatnaia, 1918.

Aleksandr Iaroshevich. "Putevoi zhurnal Kenaiskago missionera sviashchennika Alexandra Iaroshevicha." *Pravoslavnyi blagoviestnik* 18 (1894): 87–91; 19 (1894): 119–125; 20 (1894): 180–188; 8 (1896): 373–381; 11 (1896): 142–146; 4 (1896): 276–279; 13 (1896): 231–236.

Hapgood, Isabel F. *Service Book of the Holy Orthodox-Catholic Apostolic Church*. Englewood, NJ: Antiochian Orthodox Christian Archdiocese of North America, 1996.

Iubileinyi sbornik v pamiat' 150-lietiia Russkoi oravoslavnoi tserki v Sievernoi Amerikie. New York: Izd. izdatelskoi iubileinoi komissii, 1944.

Kari, James, comp. *Dena'ina Noun Dictionary*. Fairbanks, AK: Alaska Native Language Center, University of Alaska, 1977.

McClanahan, A. J., ed. *Our Stories, Our Lives: A Collection of Twenty-Three Transcribed Interviews with Elders of the Cook Inlet Region*. Anchorage, AK: CIRI Foundation, 1986.

Hegumen Nikolai [Militov]. "Zapiska o nekotorikh deistviakh kenaiskago missionera igumena Nikolaia (s 1853-go do polovini 1857 goda) i sluchaiakh s nim byvshikh." *Tvorenii sviatikh ottsov v russkom perevode* 19, no. 1 (1860), 117–133.

________. *Vipiska iz zhurnala Kenaiskago missionera igumena Nikolaia s 1858 po 1862 god*. Moskva: n. p., 1863 (reprint from *Pribavlenie k tvoreniiam sviatikh ottsov* 22, no. 4 (1863): 463–492; also reproduced in *Pribavleniia k Khersonskim eparkhial'nim viedomostiam* 10 (1863): 341–352).

________. "Iz zhurnala Kenaiskago missionera, Nikolaevskii redut, 1862." *Pravoslavnoe obozrienie* 24 (1867): 1–10.

Nikolai, Archbishop of Warsaw. *Iz moego dnevnika: putevyia zamietki i vpechatlieniia po Aliaski i Aleutskim ostrovam*. St. Petersburg: Synodalnaia tip., 1893.

Shalkop, Antoinette. "The Travel Journal of Vasilii Orlov." *Pacific Northwest Quarterly* 68, no. 3 (1977): 131–140.

Townsend, Joan. "Journals of Nineteenth Century Russian Priests to the Tanaina: Cook Inlet, Alaska." *Arctic Anthropology* 11, no. 1 (1974): 1–30.

Znamenski, Andrei A. "Native Culture Through Orthodox Eyes: Russian Missionary Ioann Bortnovskii on the Dena'ina and Ahtna, 1896-1907." *Alaska History* 13, no. 1–2 (1998): 1–26.

Published Secondary Sources

Ackerman, Robert E. *The Kenaitze People*. Phoenix, AZ: Indian Tribal Series, 1975.

Arndt, Katherine L. " 'Released to Reside Forever in the Colonies': Founding of a Russian-American Company Retirement Settlement at Ninilchik, Alaska." In *Adventures Through Time: Readings in the Anthropology of Cook Inlet, Alaska*, eds. Nancy Yaw Davis and William E. Davis, 235–249. Anchorage, AK: Cook Inlet Historical Society, 1996.

Balluta, Andrew. "The Dena'ina of Kijik and Lake Clark National Park and Preserve." In *Russia in North America*, ed. Richard P. Pierce, 40–45. Kingston, Ontario: The Limestone Press, 1990.

Barrett, Thomas M. "Lines of Uncertainty: The Frontiers of the Northern Caucasus." In *Imperial Russia: New Histories for the Empire*, ed. Jane Burbank and David L. Ransel, 148–173. Bloomington and Indianapolis: Indiana University Press, 1998.

Black, Lydia. "The Daily Journal of Reverend Father Juvenal." *Ethnohistory* 28, no. 1 (1981): 33–58.

________. "Creoles in Russian America." *Pacifica* 2, no. 2 (1990): 142–155.

________. *Orthodoxy in Alaska*. Berkeley, CA: Patriarch Athenagoras Orthodox Institute, 1999.

Bergelson, Mira. "V kraiu pravoslavnikh indeitsev." *http//www.prof.msu.ru/ book/articles2.htm*.

De Laguna, Frederica. *The Archaeology of Cook Inlet, Alaska*. Philadelphia: University of Pennsylvania Press, 1934.

Dzeniskevich, Galina I. *Atapaski Aliaski: ocherki materialnoi i dukhovnoi kultury: konets XVIII–nachalo XX v.* Leningrad: Nauka, 1987.

Ellanna, Linda J. and Andrew Balluta. *Nuvendaltin Quhtana: The People of Nondalton*. Washington, DC: Smithsonian Institution Press, 1992.

Grinev, Andrei V. *Indeitsy Tlinkity v period Russkoi Ameriki (1741–1867)*. Novosibirsk: Nauka, 1991.

________. "On the Banks of the Copper River: The Ahtna Indians and the Russians, 1783–1867." *Arctic Anthropology* 30, no. 1 (1993): 54–66.

________. "The Forgotten Expedition of Dmitrii Tarkhanov on the Copper River." *Alaska History* 12, no. 1 (1997): 1–17.

________. "Torgovo-promyslovaia deiatelnost Rossiisko-Amerikanskoi kompanii v 1825–1849 g.g." In *Istoriia Russkoi Ameriki*, 1732-1867*: Russkaia Amerika: ot zenita k zakatu, 1825–1867*, 15–56. Moskva: Mezhdunarodnie otnosheniia, 1999. Vol. 3.

Herlihy, Patricia. *Strategies of Sobriety: Temperance Movement in Russia, 1880–1914*, Kennan Institute for Advanced Russian Studies, Occasional Paper no. 238. Washington, DC: Woodrow Wilson International Center for Scholars, 1990.

Hultkrantz, Ake. *The Religions of the American Indians*. Berkeley: University of California Press, 1979.

Kan, Sergei. *Memory Eternal: Tlingit Culture and Russian Orthodox Christianity Through Two Centuries*. Seattle and London: University of Washington Press, 1999.

Kari, James and Priscilla Russel Kari, *Dena'ina Elnena/Tanaina Country*. Fairbanks, AK: Alaska Native Language Center University of Alaska, 1982.

Lynch, Alice J. *Qizhjeh: The Historic Tanaina Village of Kijik and the Archeological District*. Fairbanks: Anthropology and Historic Preservation Cooperative Park Studies Unit, University of Alaska, 1982.

Oleksa, Michael. "The Death of Hieromonk Juvenal." *St. Vladimir's Theological Quarterly 30*, no. 3 (1986): 231–268.

Osgood, Cornelius. *Ethnography of the Tanaina*. New Haven, CT: Human Relations Area Files Press, 1976.

Pierce, Richard. "Tyonek in the 1880s: from the Diary of V.V. Stafeev." In *Adventures Through Time: Readings in the Anthropology of Cook Inlet, Alaska*, ed. Nancy Yaw Davis and William E. Davis, 175–179. Anchorage, AK: Cook Inlet Historical Society, 1996.

Potter, Louise. *A Study of a Frontier Town in Alaska, Wasilla to 1959*. VT: Thetford Center, 1963.

Shevzov, Vera. "Chapels and the Ecclesial World of Prerevolutionary Russian Peasants." *Slavic Review* 55, no. 3 (1996): 585–613.

Solovjova, Katerina and Aleksandra Vovnyanko. "The Rise and Decline of the Lebedev Lastochkin Company: Russian Colonization of South Central Alaska, 1787–1798." *Pacific Northwest Quarterly* 90, no. 4 (1999): 191–205.

Springer, Susan Woodward. *Seldovia, Alaska. An Historical Portrait of Life in Zaliv Seldevoe/Herring Bay*. Littleton, CO: Blue Willow, 1997.

Tarasar, Constantance J. and John H. Erickson, eds. *Orthodox America, 1794–1976: Development of the Orthodox Church in America*. Syosset, NY: Department of History and Archives, Orthodox Church in America, 1975.

Tikhmenev, Petr A. *A History of the Russian-American Company*. Seattle: University of Washington Press, 1978.

Townsend, Joan B. "The Tanaina of Southwestern Alaska: A Historical Synopsis." *Western Canadian Journal of Anthropology*, no. 2 (1970): 2–16.

VanStone, James W. *Athapaskan Adaptations: Hunters and Fishermen of the Subarctic Forests*. Chicago: Aldine Publishing Company, 1974.

Zernov, Nicholas. *The Russians and Their Church*. Crestwood, NY: St. Vladimir's Seminary Press, 1994.

Dissertations

Fall, James Arthur. "Patterns of Upper Tanaina Leadership, 1741–1918." Ph.D. diss., University of Wisconsin,1991.

Townsend, Joan Broom. "Ethnohistory and Culture Change of the Iliamna Tanaina." Ph.D. diss., University of California, Los Angeles, 1965.

Index